IN THE OLDEN TIME

VICTORIANS AND THE BRITISH PAST

IN THE OLDEN TIME

VICTORIANS AND THE BRITISH PAST

ANDREW SANDERS

Published for

THE PAUL MELLON CENTRE FOR STUDIES IN BRITISH ART

by YALE UNIVERSITY PRESS, NEW HAVEN AND LONDON

Designed and edited by Guilland Sutherland
Printed in China

Library of Congress Cataloging-in-Publication Data
Sanders, Andrew, 1946-
In the olden time : the Victorians and the British past / Andrew Sanders.
    pages cm
  ISBN 978-0-300-19042-7
  1. Arts and history—Great Britain. 2. Arts, Victorian—Themes,
motives. 3. History in art. 4. Great Britain—History. I. Title.
  NX180.H57S26 2013
  700'.45841—dc23
                                2012037478

A catalogue record for this book is available from the British Library

CONTENTS

LIST OF ILLUSTRATIONS

PREFACE

The seed of this book was first germinated some twenty years ago when I was asked to contribute a chapter on the Victorians and the English Renaissance to a proposed anthology on nineteenth-century responses to the Renaissance. The anthology never appeared in print but I was able to draw on my essay as the basis of my Inaugural Lecture at the University of Durham which took as its subject Victorian perceptions of the reign and character of the first Queen Elizabeth. This too was never published. Over the subsequent years I toyed with developing the subject but various other projects and commissions intervened. In my final years at Durham I did, however, manage to formulate a detailed outline for a study of Victorian responses to the British past but the project was again shelved. It was only with the liberating opportunities presented by early retirement that new research perspectives opened up. Again, other projects intervened until certain friends pressed me to return to the subject of the present book. They offered both intellectual support and enthusiastic encouragement (though they were not always aware of the degree to which they had stimulated me). In this context I would particularly like to thank Martin Postle, Robin Simon, Alison Shell, Daniel Anlezark, Corinne Saunders, David Fuller and Richard and Leonee Ormond. My profound thanks are also due Guilland Sutherland for her sympathetic and wonderfully informed work on the manuscript and its illustrations.

IN THE OLDEN TIME

VICTORIANS AND THE BRITISH PAST

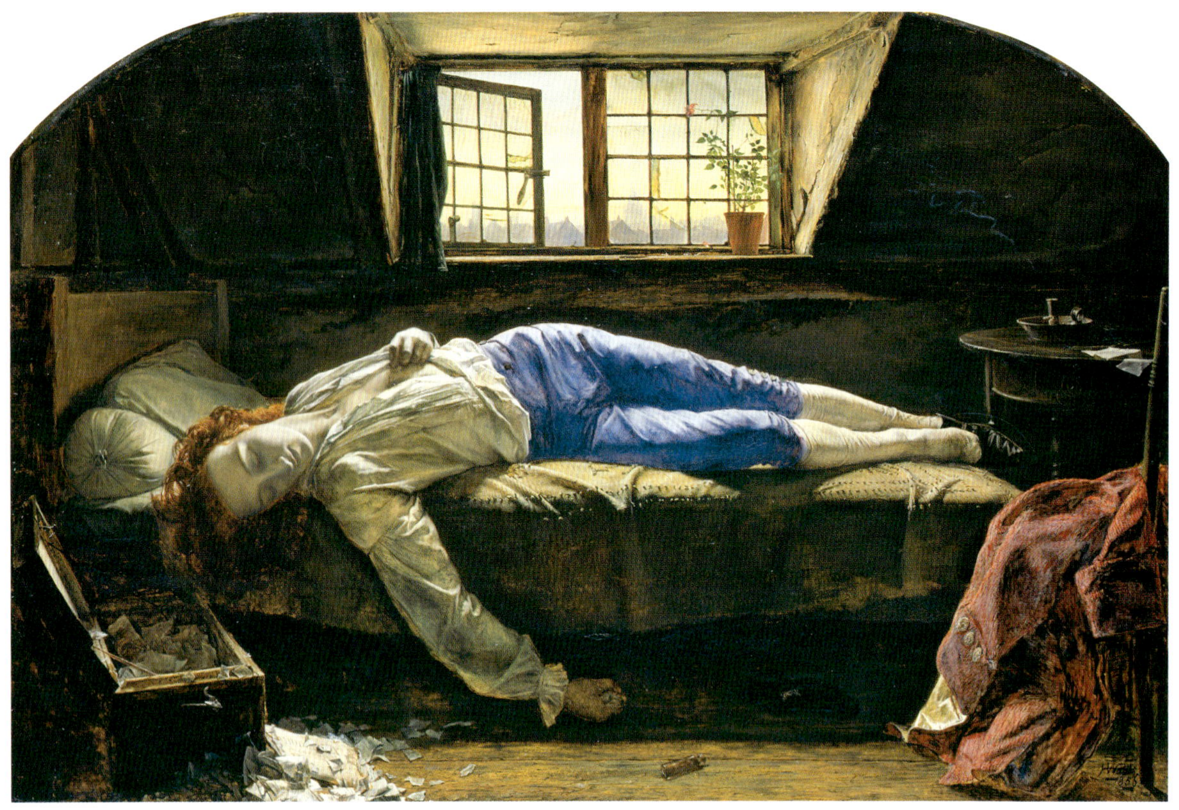

1 Henry Wallis, *The Death of Chatterton*, 1856, Oil on canvas, 62.2 x 93.3 cm. Tate, London

INTRODUCTION

When the painter Henry Wallis first exhibited his *Chatterton* (fig.1) at the Royal Academy in 1856 the painting was acclaimed by the public and critics alike. When he showed it again in the 'Modern Masters' section of the great Manchester Art Treasures Exhibition in the following year it caused a sensation. Two policemen were required to keep the admiring crowds at a safe distance from the canvas. John Ruskin proclaimed Wallis's canvas 'faultless and wonderful' and 'a most noble example of the great school.' By the time it was displayed in Manchester, the painting had been sold by Wallis to a fellow-artist, Augustus Egg, for a reported 100 guineas, and Egg, keenly alert to the picture's rapport with the public, went on to sell the copyright and the right to have it engraved to a Newcastle publisher for princely sum of £150.

Wallis's *Chatterton*, or *The Death of Chatterton* as it is sometimes known, is the most familiar representation of a suicide in English art. It shows the lifeless but fashionably dressed poet Thomas Chatterton stretched out on a bed in a London garret. Through an open window we see dawn breaking over London, with the dome of St. Paul's looming through the haze. The hues of the rising sun serve to accentuate both the pallor of the dead poet's face, his red hair and his bluish purple silk breeches. Wallis's choice of colours helps to give the picture an unsettling, even slightly nauseous quality, and suggests that the living poet had a somewhat garish taste in dress (the discarded red coat in the foreground can scarcely be said to complement either Chatterton's red hair or the colour of his breeches). Wallis wanted his picture to be disconcerting, of course, and his public admired him for it. Chatterton was a deeply ambiguous figure to Victorian audiences. He had died by his own hand in 1770 and his most celebrated work, the 'Rowley' poems, had appeared posthumously seven years later. However, by 1856 he was celebrated more for the nature of his untimely death than for any innate quality in his literary achievement. Wallis had underlined this ambiguity by quoting moral lines from the concluding chorus of Christopher Marlowe's *Doctor Faustus* both on the frame and in the accompanying catalogue to the Royal Academy Exhibition: 'Cut is the branch that might have grown full straight / And burned is Apollo's laurel bough.'[1] Chatterton, like Faustus, is summed up as an over-reacher, a man cut off in his prime because he demanded too much of life. Faustus had thirsted for intellectual fulfilment and his unsatisfied thirst had driven him into a diabolic pact; Chatterton, by contrast, had proved a too-quick despairer and had died unfulfilled. The critic of the *Saturday Review* in May 1856 spoke of the 'sad history of Chatterton's misdirected genius and boyish vanity,' a history which had culminated in the 'mad deed' of his self-murder. When the twenty-six-year-old Wallis painted his *Chatterton*, suicide remained an offence against both Divine and Civil law and was regarded as a challenge both to God's providence and to the good order of society. Chatterton, whom William Wordsworth had famously described as 'the marvellous boy,' might well have been canonised as some kind of exemplary martyr by the Romantic poets, but to many amongst the respectable Victorian public he was little more than a *pasticheur* with a singularly unsteady literary reputation. The figure of the dead Chatterton is less exemplary than it is monitory. By the 1850s his place in the literary tradition was unsteady, his poetry largely unread, and his suicide in his seventeenth year likely to have been viewed as damnable.

Henry Wallis was no stranger to representations of figures from literary history. He had shown pictures of Shakespeare's birthplace and of Dr Johnson in 1854, and in 1857 he exhibited his *A Sculptor's Workshop: Stratford-upon-Avon, 1617* at the Royal Academy (the painting, which will be discussed later in this study, shows the embellishment of Shakespeare's monument for Stratford church). None of his other 'literary' paintings has, however, quite the *frisson* of the *Chatterton*. Here Wallis had found a subject which provoked immediate moral responses and which had ramifications for his own time. As with his pictures of Shakespeare's birthplace, the painter had sought out an exact location (some believed it to be the actual room in which Chatterton had died), but on this occasion he went beyond mere topography by including a figure, that of the newly dead poet.[2] As a model Wallis used a living poet, the ambitious, but as yet unestablished, twenty-four-year-old George Meredith. As so often in Victorian historical painting, past and present are fused together by the presence of a modern figure who physically stands in for an historic personage. Wallis may be representing a tragic event of 1770, but his technique, as well as his fashionably red-headed model, are unmistakeably of the mid-1850s, and the young George Meredith, like Chatterton, was a poet ambitious for fame. This is history seen through, and enhanced by, Pre-Raphaelite principles. For admirers of Wallis's painting, however, there was always something of a 'double take.' This was not only a picture of a dead poet whose poetry was not much admired: here too was a man who could be seen as the representative poet who had died before he came to maturity. This was not only a painting of a writer who had despaired of success: here was the man of letters, ignored by his contemporaries, who ironically enough is seen as triumphing in death over those who had set him at nought.

Though representations of suicide and of suicides were rare, Victorian connoisseurs of historical painting were very familiar with scenes of death and dying. Indeed, a great deal of British history before the eighteenth century seems to have been popularly characterised as being little more than a series of judicial executions and violent or untimely deaths. The sad stories of the death of kings were retold with relish, and the sword, the axe, the assassin's dagger and the poisoned cup became a stock in trade of history painting. Mary, Queen of Scots, her grandson, Charles I, the Marquis of Montrose and Duke of Monmouth, and Archbishop Laud were all to be depicted as they approached their judicial ends on the scaffold. But Chatterton was no king. He was not even a courtier, let alone a statesman or an eminent churchman. In terms of the society, and even the literature of his own times, Chatterton was something of a footnote.

Nevertheless, in painting this minor poet's suicide Henry Wallis was exploring the sad fortunes of the kind of man whom Thomas Carlyle had described in the 1840s as a new breed of hero: the man of letters. Chatterton is shown as a victim, but not of a jealous monarch, of a civil war, or of a contentious political faction. He has died by his own hand, supposedly rejected by a society that has failed to appreciate his talent. Rather than paint the heroic dignity of a dying monarch or the stoic resolve of a condemned nobleman, Wallis shows us instead an unacknowledged artist cut off in his prime. Whether or not we are called upon to morally condemn the rash deed that has brought about Chatterton's demise, Wallis bids us contemplate the solitary artist rendered memorable in death. He is heroic despite himself.

Wallis's *Chatterton* is a new kind of history painting. It was not single-handedly to transform the nature of Victorian history painting – representations of the captains and the kings remained popular enough to the end of the century – but it nonetheless suggests a new interpretation of the past in which the prime movers of history have been supplanted, in this instance, by the heroically lonely artist. This is not exactly history 'from below,' but it is decidedly no longer a historical landscape which is inhabited exclusively by monarchs and statesmen. *Chatterton* does not attempt to show us a community in action, or the uneventful lives of unconsidered men and women, but it does attempt to endow an ordinary man with an iconic dignity which had formerly been reserved for religious or courtly figures. This is a *pietà* without supporting saints and a ceremonial lying-in-state without the ceremony and the state. Here is the ordinary man posthumously elevated to fame by the respect of his peers. The poet Chatterton's failure to achieve celebrity and honour in his lifetime is transfigured by a posterity that belatedly condescends to recognise his cultural significance. Monitory it may well be, but it also offers an *amende honorable* to an historical figure overlooked by history.

It is significant, however, that Wallis chose to represent an historical figure in this iconic painting. In the 1850s Wallis's *Chatterton* presented Victorian admirers with both a retrospect on the eighteenth century's neglect of the man of letters, and a modern assertion of the new social status of the artist. It thus tells us a good deal about a thoughtful Victorian's response to national history and about the ways in which that national history was being rewritten. From the opening decades of the nineteenth century the study of history had begun to offer both an imaginative release from the present and the possibility of learning pertinent lessons which could be readily applied to the present. Writing in the essay 'Looking Backward' in her *Impressions of Theophrastus Such* of 1879 George Eliot contemplated the strange freedom granted by meditating on the 'might have beens' presented by past ages:

> I have often had the fool's hectic of wishing about the unalterable, but with
> me that useless exercise has turned chiefly on the conception of a different
> self, and not, as it usually does in literature, on the advantage of having been
> born in a different age, and more especially in one where one's life is imagined

to have been altogether majestic and graceful. With my present abilities, external proportions, and generally small provision for ecstatic enjoyment, where is the ground for confidence that I should have had a preferable career in such an epoch of society? An age which in every department has its awkward-squad seems in my mind's eye to suit me better.[3]

Eliot's Theophrastus Such does not seek out an heroic or an elegant age in which to indulge his fancy, but one marked by the influence of an 'awkward squad.' This meditation leads him to conclude that the very nature of the 'awkward squads' of the past render the awkwardness of the present more generally acceptable:

Except on the ground of a primitive golden age and continuous degeneracy, I see no rational footing for scorning the whole present population of the globe, unless I scorn every previous generation from whom they have inherited their diseases of mind and body, and by consequence scorn my own scorn, which is equally an inheritance of mixed feelings concocted for me in the boiling cauldron of this universally contemptible life, and so on – scorning to infinity … Reflections of this sort have gradually determined me not to grumble at the age in which I happen to have been born …[4]

A pragmatic faith in the mixed virtues of the present therefore precludes a wilful escape into a 'golden age' located somewhere (or anywhere) in the past. As Eliot was well aware, 'awkward squads' had helped to mould the Victorian age. It was they who had pressed for the abolition of the slave trade and later of slavery itself; it was they who had obliged Parliament to remove the restrictions on the civil liberties of non-Anglicans and to pass the Reform Act in 1832; it was they who continued to argue for the benefits of rolling constitutional reform; and they who shaped the very nature of a 'plural' society which allowed for active expressions of dissent from the status quo. Victorians generally believed that progress was the key to life in the nineteenth century, but it was the 'awkward squads' who both formulated and articulated the intellectual arguments that made progress seem to be not only inevitable but beneficial.

To Thomas Babington Macaulay, a steady proponent of Parliamentary reform, the history of England was 'emphatically the history of progress … the history of a constant movement of the public mind, of a constant change in the institutions of a great society.'[5] This principle was not only central to Macaulay's arguments in support of the Reform Bill; it was to become the central pillar of his highly influential *History of England* (1848–61). For Macaulay the very act of writing history in the nineteenth century was an art which required reference to the skills perfected by painting and literature. He was, for example, insistent in his essay 'On History' of May 1828 that 'History has its foreground and its background' and that 'it is principally in the management of its perspective that one artist differs from another.' Later in the essay he goes on to describe the ideal modern historian as a cultural chronicler who can use both the carefully observed detail and the sweeping gesture. The parallel now is with the art of the novelist rather than with that of the painter:

> The perfect historian is he in whose work the character and spirit of an age is exhibited in miniature. He relates no fact, he attributes no expression to his characters, which is not authenticated by sufficient testimony. But, by judicious selection, rejection, and arrangement, he gives to truth those attractions which have been usurped by fiction. In his narrative a due subordination is observed: some transactions are prominent; others retire. But the scale on which he represents them is increased or diminished, not according to the dignity of the persons concerned in them, but according to the degree in which they elucidate the condition of society and the nature of man. He shows us the court, the camp, and the senate. But he shows us also the nation. He considers no anecdote, no peculiarity of manner, no familiar saying, as too insignificant for his notice which is not too insignificant to illustrate the operation of laws, of religion, and of education, and to mark the progress of the human mind. Men will not merely be described, but will be made intimately known to us.[6]

The ideal historian is thus acutely sensitive to, and expressive of, a *Zeitgeist*. He is a man of his own times, but he is also one who responds to the culture of a given historical period. He responds, moreover, as a man observant of the multifarious details that serve to elucidate 'the condition of society' and thus moves his focus down from an exclusive concentration on those at the top of society to the broad mass beneath them. If not quite a 'democratisation' of history, Macaulay's 'ideal' implies that the new historian should be as alert to the daily life of the cottage as to that of the mansion, to the duties of the curate as much as to the commands of the bishop, and to the failure of the suicidal poet in his garret as much as to the crowned laureate striding through the corridors of power.

When it came to the composition of his own *History* Macaulay told his readers that he had purposed 'to write the history of England from the accession of King James the Second down to a time which is within the memory of men still living.' He was, therefore, determined to explore a constitutional crisis (for Macaulay it was *the* constitutional crisis) that marked the modern history of England (and, by extension, the modern histories of Scotland, Ireland and to a lesser degree the United States of America). This was to be the quintessential 'Whig' history of the English-speaking nations, one which explored the late-seventeenth-century pivot on which he believed all subsequent national history turned. It was also to demonstrate how a modern nation was made and it was to be a history that offered an analysis of a grand and complex social movement. Macaulay was intent on describing James II as the last representative of a dynasty of would-be tyrants. But James was also to be exposed as an inept tyrant, one who had wilfully sacrificed the good will of his people and whose ambitions were thwarted by a high-minded generation of Whig aristocrats. These noblemen were to emerge as the foster-fathers of the progressive nature of the British constitution, men who secured the personal liberties and the constitutional obligations of all classes of freedom- loving English (and by extension Scots, Irish and Americans). If he did not ultimately manage to extend his *History* into the time of 'the memory of men still living' (death cut him short in 1859), he nevertheless articulated the Whig belief that England changed irrevocably, and beneficently, thanks to the 'Glorious Revolution.' If, as he had originally intended, he had drawn out his narrative into the middle years of the eighteenth century, he would have attempted to demonstrate that it was the settlement of 1688–89 that had saved Britain from a Revolution akin to that which had ravaged France a hundred years later. It was also the settlement of 1688–89 that, he believed, had established the principles of the 'Age of Reform' in the 1830s, the Whig reforms that had essentially shaped the liberal Victorian cast of mind.

The very popularity of Macaulay's *History of England* with Victorian readers helped to mould progressive prejudices about national history. But it was not just susceptible liberals who were fascinated by the past and who communicated their enthusiasm to their fellow citizens. Macaulay's contemporaries were singularly alert to the importance of the study of history in all its aspects and they did not always require professional historians to tutor them. Their Romantic sensibilities had been stimulated from boyhood (and girlhood) up by the novels of Sir Walter Scott, and those sensibilities were further fostered by a new, and pervasive, delight in antiquarianism. On one level, that antiquarianism could be as eccentric and ephemeral as that pursued by Dickens's Pickwick Club. On another and more profound level it helped cultivate a new and scholarly appreciation of historic buildings in general and of mediaeval architecture in particular. It was not just the great gothic minsters that benefitted from this new antiquarian empathy: virtually every parish church in the land attracted the attention of amateur scholars and professional 'restorers' alike. Attitudes to great secular buildings were equally transformed. Both the Tower of London and Edinburgh Castle attracted multitudes of curious Victorian visitors, as intent on exploring the murky reputations of the two fortresses as in delighting in their royal associations and their claims to antiquity. The opening of the State Rooms at Hampton Court Palace in the late 1830s proved to be a highly successful venture, attracting impressive numbers of curious tourists and day-trippers from the metropolis (though it must be admitted that many of these visitors were drawn more by ghostly memories of Cardinal Wolsey and Henry VIII than they were by the stately rooms built to house Macaulay's hero, William III). This new generation of visitors was often as historically informed and aesthetically discriminating as their Grand Tourist forebears had been, but their attentions now were as likely to be directed to relics of national history as by the decaying palaces of Venice and by the ruins of Rome. The long drawn-out European wars with which the nineteenth century opened had closed the Continent to all but the most adventurous tourists. After the defeat of Napoleon, and the return of Europe to a semblance of the old political order, early Victorian tourists proved to be as fascinated by British history and landscape as their predecessors were by that of Italy. They had not ceased to be thrilled by the Alps but by the 1830s the Scottish Highlands and Islands possessed an unequalled Romantic charm, haunted as they were the shades of Ossian and Bonny Prince Charlie. The English Lakes, too, drew visitors whose eyes had been opened by Turner's watercolours and whose ears were alert to the cadences of Wordsworth. Prosperous Victorians had not abandoned the architectural pleasures of Italy, but they supplemented them with a relish for native ruins and native palaces and they keenly sought out associations from their own rather than classical history.

My survey of Victorian responses to national history begins not in the ancient, the mythical or the mediaeval world, but in the mid-sixteenth century. It describes a Victorian fascination not with monuments and ruins, but with inhabited and functioning buildings; not with remote figures, but with historical men and women whose lives, tastes and predilections directly informed those of the nineteenth century.

My study is initially premissed on an ambiguity. The nineteenth century was fascinated with Tudor domestic architecture, but it appears to have had scant admiration for the Queen in whose reign the great Elizabethan houses were constructed. Unlike most mediaeval castles, Elizabethan mansions and manor houses struck Victorian observers as both romantic and agreeably habitable. Their high, wainscotted rooms were well ventilated, they were well lit by diamond-paned casement windows, and they were deemed to be adequately warmed by fireplaces in which log-fires blazed on winter evenings. These houses were also firmly established in the English landscape and seemed to bespeak a tradition of lordly hospitality and ancient family roots. It is hard to think of an old house in a Victorian novel or a topographical painting that is not Elizabethan (or at most Jacobean) in style. The great classical and Palladian houses of the eighteenth century had no such charm, and far fewer ancestral associations.

Queen Elizabeth, by contrast, seems to have had infinitely fewer attractions for most Victorian commentators. Her peremptory style of government vexed the liberal-minded, her irresolution distressed the resolute, and her personal vanity offended the moral. She was regularly described as a tyrant and as a monarch who had scant regard for political niceties. Her personal traits were deemed to be so unlike those of the happily married and thoroughly maternal Queen Victoria that Elizabeth's character could regularly be readily disparaged as unbecoming both in a woman and in a sovereign. This sense of *odi et amo*, of attraction to and repulsion from conflicting aspects of Elizabethan England, therefore offers a good starting point for an exploration of Victorian responses to national history. It has often been casually assumed that many sentimentally minded Victorians saw themselves reflected in Elizabethan looking glasses, but there is little evidence for this. Accounts of the enterprise of Elizabethan sea-dogs certainly had an immediate rapport for English Victorians but other aspects of the period – the bloody uncertainties of late-Tudor political life for example – struck few sympathetic chords. On the one side the adjective 'Elizabethan' conjured up happy images of blazing yule logs in hospitable hearths; on the other there was the cold and assertively virginal Queen herself.

In 1814 Sir Walter Scott had famously given his novel *Waverley* an epigraph from Shakespeare's *Henry IV, Part One*: 'Under which king, Bezonian? Speak or die.' *Waverley* gave a new and challenging context to Pistol's retort to Justice Shallow from the last scene of Shakespeare's play. Pistol is referring to the succession of a new King Henry who assumes the throne of a dead King Henry. Scott's novel explores a far more disputed succession, for in his novel choices between kings truly are a matter of life and death to the subjects and adherents of those kings. In *Waverley* characters are obliged to chose between loyalty to King George II and his heirs and fealty to the cause of the 'Pretender,' King James III and VIII. When Victorian readers encountered parallels between the personalities of Queen Elizabeth and Queen Victoria, very few would have chosen the last of the Tudors over the last of the Hanoverians. When it came to the later periods of the Civil War, the 'Glorious Revolution' and the Jacobite rebellions, questions of legitimacy continued to trouble many Victorian commentators. The period of the 'Great Rebellion' (as it was still frequently described) was highly factious, and those factions remained real enough in Victorian England. They moulded modern social and religious prejudices, and they provided novelists and painters alike with the kind of subject matter that evidently appealed to a wide range of readers and discriminating art-lovers. Comfortably situated Victorians did not necessarily aspire to change places with their ancestors, but they were acutely aware of the dilemmas and discomforts experienced by their ancestors. Like George Eliot's Theophrastus Such they were happy enough by their firesides meditating on the past rather than yearning to escape into it. Having opened with an exploration of the culture and politics of the period that Victorian academic historians styled 'the early Modern Age,' my study moves steadily forward through the Age of Revolutions to the eighteenth century and finally to the reigns of George IV and William IV, a period covering some two hundred and fifty eventful and contentious years. I have begun by looking at an age that most Victorians considered familiar, but essentially and generically unlike their own present, and have ended in the 1820s and 30s, the period in which many of the first generation of Victorian writers and artists spent their impressionable childhoods.

In this study I have not attempted a longer retrospect, for I am well aware of the rich pioneer study of nineteenth-century interest in the culture of ancient Greece represented by Richard Jenkyns's *The Victorians and Ancient Greece* (1980). I am equally alert to the many fruitful studies of Victorian responses to the Middle Ages which have stretched well beyond analyses of the 'Gothic Revival.' Alice Chandler's *A Dream of Order: The Medieval Ideal in Nineteenth-Century Literature* (1971) has been superbly supplemented by Mark Girouard's *The Return to Camelot: Chivalry and the English Gentleman*

(1981). Most recently Rosemary Hill's *God's Architect: Pugin and the Building of Romantic Britain* (2007) has introduced a wide audience to the polemics of the most articulate advocate of mediaeval cultural values over those of the Victorian period.

In much of what he wrote in the late 1830s and 40s, Pugin seems to have readily accepted the idea that he lived in decadent and depraved times and that any period of the Christian era anterior to the Reformation was morally superior to any age that succeeded it. Before Pugin, the radically-minded William Cobbett had insisted in the 1820s that 'all sensible and just Englishmen' ought to agree with him that the Reformation had 'impoverished and degraded the main body of the People' and that England, 'the happiest country, and the *greatest* country too, that Europe had ever seen,' had fallen victim to the 'master butcher', Henry VIII, and that things had been made much worse in 'the *pauper* and *ripping-up* reign' of Elizabeth (or 'Betsy' as he prefers to style her). Cobbett's *A History of the Protestant 'Reformation'* might well have been dismissed by contemporaries as wildly eccentric and a prime example of unscholarly anti-establishmentarianism. Pugin was different. He was addressing a new and more restless generation, with an eye for the Gothic style. Although his books primarily addressed architectural issues, readers might have supposed that he had taken Cobbett's antipathy to the Reformation a stage further: Pugin linked a firm, anti-Benthamite conservatism to a new and radical aesthetic. His vision is ostensibly that of a lost Catholic England peopled by benevolent gentlemen whose faith is fostered by a bountiful Church, the mother of charity and good taste. The plates in Pugin's *Contrasts* (1836, 1841) expose the cheapskate nature of modern architecture by contrasting it to the buildings of the mediaeval period. These plates also suggest that modern industrial cities have replaced chantries with toll-houses, abbeys with panopticon prisons, almshouses with workhouses, and church spires with smoke-stacks. In Pugin's eyes the world had fallen away from an ideal. For Macaulay the re-writing of history was monitory: it not only suggested why modern society was what it was, but also where the modern world had come from. For Pugin history was a prime means of suggesting that the modern age had lost it way and that its errors were ancestral. Macaulay believed that progress was the dynamic which defined the modern world. Pugin, by contrast, chose to insist that only a recall of a long-lost 'Christian' order could heal the festering wounds which defined the unhappy nature of modern life.

The ostensible conflict between the world views of Macaulay and Pugin was not as stark as it might now appear. The Victorians lived more happily with contradictions and inconsistencies than posterity often allows for. The great State monuments of the nineteenth century, those that housed Parliament and the Royal Courts of Justice, were for example both constructed in the Gothic style. The architecture of both buildings was not an exercise in nostalgia but what was seen as an expression of continuity. Internally, however, both great civic buildings were planned according to modern demands and both contained the kind of modern conveniences appropriate to the efficient functioning of Parliament and the Law. Moreover, when it came to determining the decorative schemes for the new Houses of Parliament decisions were made according to Macaulayan principles rather than in the mediaevalising mode. Again, when the city of Manchester built its magnificent Gothic-style Town Hall in 1867-77, the building's carefully planned and highly functional interiors were decorated with a plethora of heraldic display and allusive mural painting. Both the heraldry and the murals were expressive not of a retrospect on a lost golden age but offered a celebration of Manchester's radical traditions and of its mercantile present. Ford Madox Brown's murals on the walls of the Great Hall show both scenes of scientific and technological innovation and of radical, anti-Establishment religious movements (though a proposed painting of the Peterloo Massacre was never to be realised). Above the murals the wooden ceiling displays the bearings of Manchester's major trading partners, each coat of arms being bordered by a pattern of crossed weaving-shuttles. The Gothic and other historically referential styles were able happily to co-exist with what was essentially progressive.

The frontispiece to Pugin's *True Principles of Pointed or Christian Architecture* of 1841 showed a mediaeval architect at work (fig.2). He sits in a thoroughly Gothic room furnished with an elaborately spiky lectern, a shrine, a prayer-desk and a solid designer's table decorated with rich tracery. On the border of the illustration are the names of those rare mediaeval architects and designers whose names we know (or guess at). Pugin knew, and his illustration serves to emphasise the point, that most mediaeval craftsmen/master builders were anonymous. He does not name his idealised architect and, though his picture may well be self-referential, it is not a self-portrait. What is significant is that Pugin is reading history through the figure of an artist. He is also suggesting that we read history best by observing historical styles and artefacts. It is the artist who has the greatest *rapport* with his descendents because it is he who expresses his own *Zeitgeist* and most readily communicates it beyond his own time. What might, at first sight, seem to be a narrow expression of impassioned Gothicism is in fact an assertion of artistic integrity, because the artist is both an interpreter and an intermediary. If not himself (or herself) the embodiment of the common man (or woman), many Victorians were persuaded that the artist was more expressive of the spirit of any given age than were the captains and the kings, the courtiers and the queens.

This study links literature and the writing of history to the visual arts. It explores the essentially *literary* nature of Victorian history writing and explores the degree to which painters were indebted to written records, be they fictional or factual in their bias. It also looks at the figure of the historical artist as he (or she) is represented (and misrepresented) in the art of the period. Those artists are poets and painters, essayists and dramatists, architects and novelists. They range from Shakespeare to Jane Austen, from Donne to Johnson, from Wren to Soane. Henry Wallis's *Chatterton* may have struck Victorian admirers as a painting of an artist in defeat, but it also reminded them that art itself could, in a sense, re-make history and help change historical perspectives. Wallis's picture of a dead poet ought properly to be seen for what it is: history brought strikingly to life for, and in, the nineteenth century.

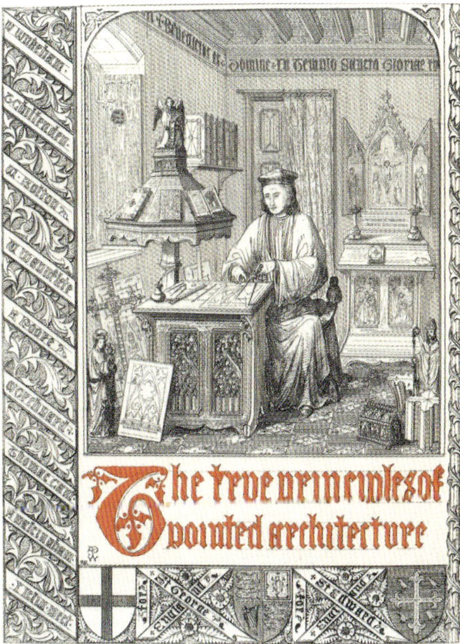

2 A.W.N. Pugin, frontispiece to *The True Principles
of Pointed or Christian Architecture* (London 1841).
The British Library

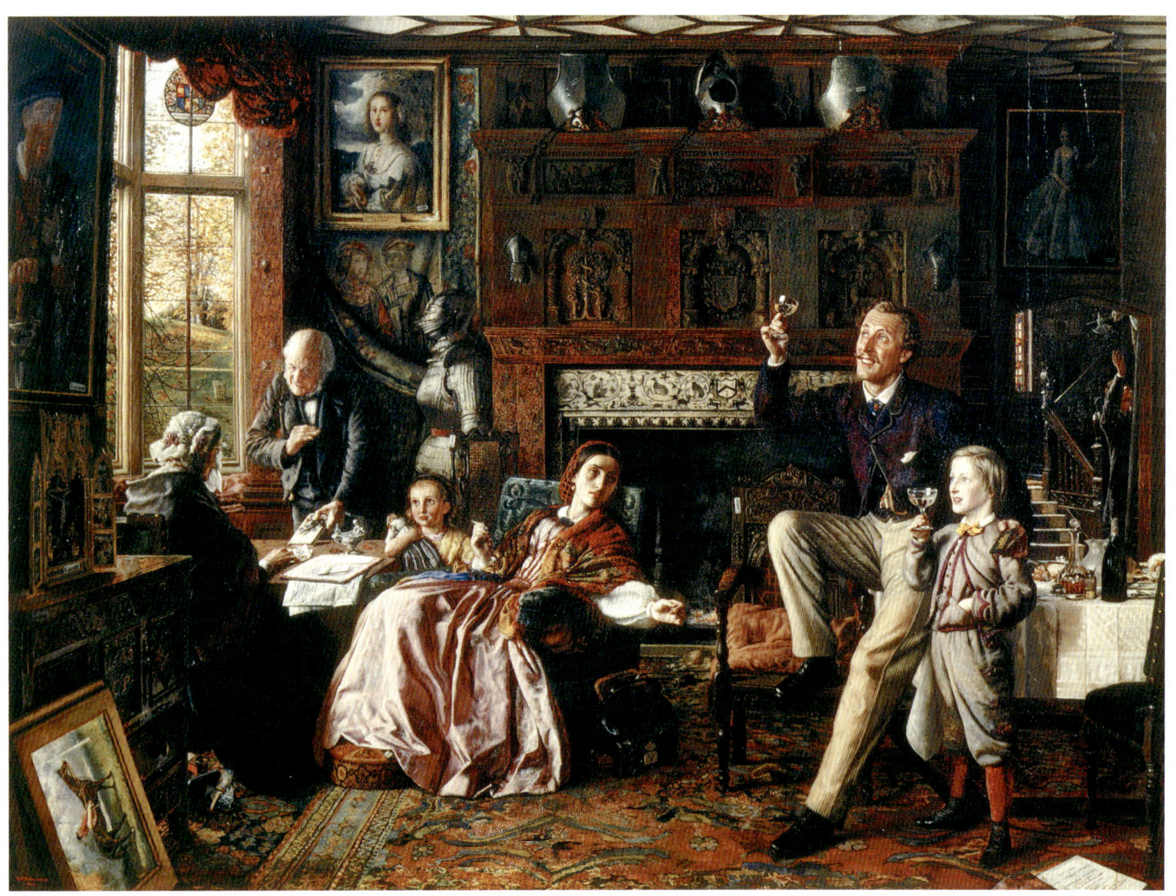

3 Robert Braithwaite Martineau, *The Last Day in the Old Home*, 1862, Oil on canvas, 107.3 x 144.8 cm. Tate, London

I

WHICH QUEEN?

Elizabethans and Jacobeans

Robert Braithwaite Martineau's painting *The Last Day in the Old Home* (fig.3) depicts the passing of an era. The picture, famous for its meticulous detailing, had taken Martineau ten years to paint. When it was finally displayed to an admiring Victorian audience at the International Exhibition of 1862 its title may well have reminded visitors of other famous 'lasts.' Last days, last things and last rites, and what succeeded them, were in the air. For most Victorians, progress was the order of the day. The word 'last' had famously been reiterated in the titles of Edward Bulwer-Lytton's popular novels *The Last Days of Pompeii* (1834), *Rienzi, The Last of the Tribunes* (1835), *The Last of the Barons* (1843) and *Harold, The Last of the Saxon Kings* (1848). Bulwer-Lytton, a devotee of the 'progressive' school of Victorian historians, firmly believed that old orders steadily and properly gave place to new. Crucial elements of the plot of *The Last Days of Pompeii* had probably been shaped by a strain of modern millenarianism, reflecting the belief of many early nineteenth-century evangelical Christians that they were living in the Latter Days and that Armageddon was imminent. Nevertheless, Bulwer's novels contemplate not destruction but essentially a painfully creative process. Pagan Pompeii is lost under the ashes of Vesuvius but at the end of the novel a new, strident Christian order is glimpsed, ready to transform the Roman Empire. The medieval tribune, Rienzi, may well fall victim to the conservative forces ranked against him in Rome, but his heroic example is prophetic of revolutionary struggles in the ages to come (this is certainly what appealed to Richard Wagner when he used to novel as the inspiration for his opera *Rienzi, der Letzte des Tribunen* of 1842). In *The Last of the*

Barons the old aristocratic hegemony of Plantagenet England is seen as tearing itself apart in the Wars of the Roses, while a new social, intellectual, and indeed technological, order of things is suggested by the appearance in the novel of the first English printer, William Caxton. In *Harold*, Saxon England is forced to yield to the superior energy of a Norman invasion, a violent invasion which will begin the transformation of both the nation and the English race. In each case the defunct is supplanted by the dynamic. The processes of change have an inevitability about them and they are, ultimately, creative.[1]

Bulwer-Lytton had probably imbibed this progressive lesson from his childhood reading of the novels of Sir Walter Scott, and it is probably to Scott that we should look in order to comprehend both the subject and the detailing of Braithwaite's painting. It is not just that the panelled drawing-room depicted in the painting could have passed for one of the antique-cluttered rooms at Abbotsford, it is the mood of nostalgia for a passing way of life. Scott was a realist, but that had never stopped him mourning the steady disappearance of old orders and old manners. His private collection of Scottish artefacts was a way of celebrating a Scotland that no longer existed. What Robert Martineau probably meant to suggest to admirers of his *The Last Day in the Old Home* was that the 'Old Home' is decorated not with 'collectables' but with private 'heritage,' and that this particular heritage is under threat. The evidently English family in the picture is obliged to dispose not of a newly assembled 'collection' but of the very history of its own ancestors.

Martineau's picture tells us that his family is both English and of ancient lineage. Their house appears to date from the early seventeenth century, but a fragment of medieval tapestry hangs by the window recess and the window contains armorial stained glass. A suit of armour stands by the fireplace and further pieces of armour are displayed on the overmantle. The family portraits show a substantial-looking Elizabethan gentleman, a half-length of a lady in Van Dyke costume and an early eighteenth-century woman in a hooped skirt. Slightly incongruously perhaps, a medieval triptych stands on a Jacobean chest (there is no other indication that the family might be Catholic and they would seem unlikely to share the taste of 'advanced' connoisseurs for collecting such things). Nevertheless, this long-established family is now about to abandon their old home and its contents. A Christie's sale catalogue lies on the floor; the dowager of the family is handing a £5 note to an agent who now holds the keys; an open newspaper advertises 'apartments' and, in the hall beyond the

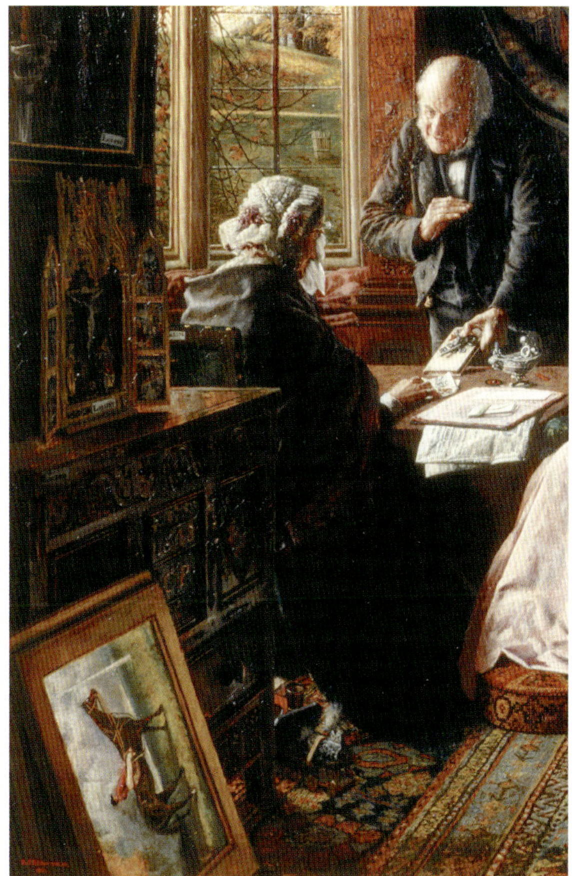

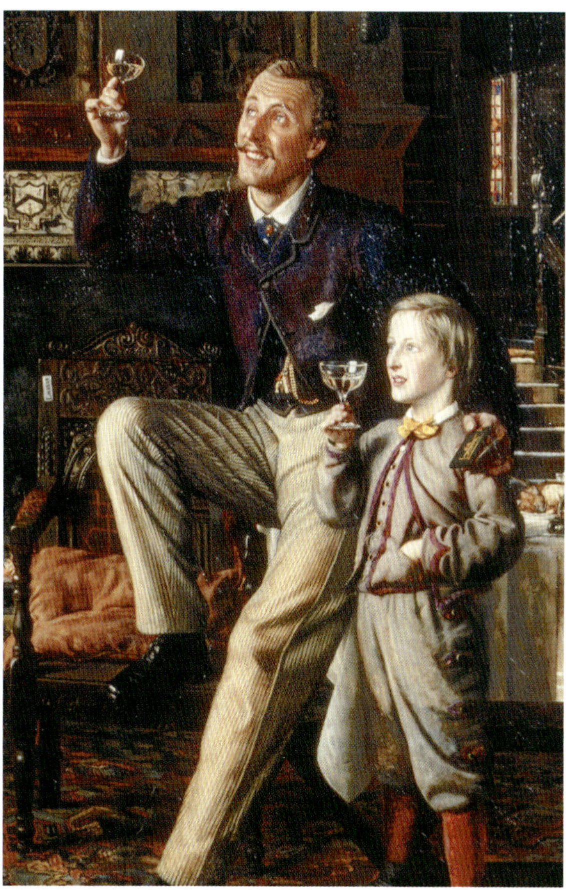

The Last Day in the Old Home
(details of fig. 3)

drawing room, a pair of broker's men seem to be dismantling yet another display of armour. The reasons for the family's abandonment of their heritage is clear from the picture. A painting of a mounted racehorse is propped against the Jacobean chest, and perhaps most significantly, the house's owner encourages his son to blithely toast the end of their occupation. They are, it seems, drinking to the end of an era, and the family's demise has been hastened by an over indulgence in wine and horse racing.

What Martineau is showing was not, it could be argued, a rare event. Gambling and extravagance had seen the end of many an old family by the time the picture was exhibited in 1862. The 'Old Home' in his picture, established it would seem since the time of the first Elizabeth, is to be unceremoniously broken up in the reign of Victoria. The question we should perhaps ask is whether or not Martineau's painting is an exercise in nostalgia or a muted celebration of progress. Should we regret the decline of an evidently profligate aristocratic family or see their end as a sign of the times with the old order yielding place to the new. Old money has been frittered away. Perhaps the house will be demolished and its memory erased? Or perhaps new money will take it over and replace it with something representative of the essentially mercantile success of modern England?

It is just possible that Martineau was thinking of the sad fate of one of the finest Elizabethan houses in all England, Kirby Hall in Northamptonshire. By 1809 Kirby Hall was described as 'unaccountably neglected, and … fast going to ruin and decay.' It was abandoned in the 1820s by its owner, the 11th Earl of Winchilsea and Nottingham, who was encumbered with vast gambling debts. Its contents were sold, its woodlands depleted, and the house was left to degenerate into a picturesque ruin. These ruins are now lovingly tended by English Heritage, but the mid-nineteenth-century condition of the Hall is described for the curious visitor by the author of Murray's *Handbook for Northamptonshire and Rutland*:

> Its situation among the remains of its avenues, and other tokens of departed magnificence, will appeal to the ordinary tourist, while the varied and unusual detail of the stonework will attract the lover of architecture … The house was in habitable condition as recently as 1820 … The house buried in deep woods, was, when Canon James wrote, 'the lair and the fuel of the common labourer.' It was falling slowly to pieces … 'A moderate and timely outlay, a few years ago, would have preserved a house that tens of thousands could not now restore.'

The Canon James referred to in Murray's *Handbook* was the Revd. Thomas James, a Canon of Peterborough and the author of a series of topographical essays on Northamptonshire which he had published serially in the *Quarterly Review* in the mid-1850s. His essays were collected and republished shortly before his death in 1864.[2]

The sad neglect of Kirby Hall in the nineteenth century is in many ways balanced by the vagaries of the history of an equally eminent, if architecturally less distinguished, seventeenth-century country house, Aston Hall. Kirby Hall was left neglected amid the wild woodlands. Aston, by contrast, first became the preserve of a rich industrialist and then, by a tortuous route, entered public ownership. When it was built in 1618 Aston Hall might once have been described as situated in the parish of Aston 'near Birmingham'. It, and its vastly truncated park, is now swamped by, and indistinguishable from, Birmingham. It is also owned, and cherished, by the Corporation of Birmingham. In the closing years of the eighteenth century, with the industrial suburbs of the burgeoning city already encroaching on its park, Aston Hall was finally abandoned by the Holte family and the Legges who had succeeded them. In April 1818 the empty mansion was offered for sale, evidently with an eye to its imminent demolition and the redevelopment of its park as suburban building land. Unexpectedly it was leased by James Watt junior, the bachelor son of the great engineer. Watt was determined to restore, refurnish and live in the rambling semi-derelict house. His achievement was hailed by the novelist, Maria Edgeworth, who visited him at 'the fine old brick palace' at Aston in 1820:

> Mr Watt has fitted up half of it as to make it superbly comfortable; fine hall, breakfast room, Flemish pictures … After breakfast … we went over all the habitable and uninhabitable parts of the house: the banqueting room, with a most costly, frightful ceiling, and a chimney piece carved up to the cornice with monsters, one with a nose covered in scales, one with a human face on a tarantula's body. … But come on to the great gallery … and at the farthest end we came to a sort of oriel, separated from the gallery only by an arch, and there the white marble bust of the great Mr Watt struck me almost breathless … as I looked down the closing lines of this superb gallery, now in a half ruined state.[3]

Watt, the quintessentially 'new' man with decidedly radical sympathies, had assumed the style and the lifestyle of the old gentry. He installed new steam kitchens, but he also furnished the house in a modern version of the Elizabethan style. Significantly too, as Maria Edgeworth noted, he asserted his presence by placing a bust of his father in the Long Gallery. It was probably the talisman of Watt's name, rather than the lost aristocratic associations of the house, that drew the young Princess Victoria here for dinner in 1830, for the Princess, accompanied by her mother, was engaged on an instructive tour of the 'manufactories' of her future kingdom.[4]

When Watt died in 1848 the house became vacant again and its contents dispersed. Its subsequent history is in many ways as extraordinary as the period of Watt's long tenancy. In 1856 the City Surveyor was instructed 'to select from Aston Park, for a place of public recreation, such as an eligible portion thereof, comprising the Hall, as might be purchased for a sum not exceeding £30,000.' Eighty-two acres surrounding the house subsequently passed into the hands of a public company while the mansion itself was separately acquired for a further £35,000. With an Elizabethan-style glass pavilion built against its west façade and the stables converted into tea-rooms it was hoped that it might begin to rival the Crystal Palace as a public attraction. It was patently no longer serviceable as a private residence and the Aston Hall and Park Company, who managed its affairs, seem to have been determined that any surviving relics of gentility should be transformed into something far more 'accessible' to the general public. Aston was effectively 'dumbed down.' Nevertheless, when Queen Victoria formally opened it in June 1858 she told the assembled guests that 'the improvement of the moral, intellectual and social conditions of my people will always command my earnest attention, and in the opening of this Hall and park today I rejoice to have another opportunity of promoting their comfort and innocent recreation.' The 'instruction' given to her during her visit in 1830 had doubtless had its effect. In 1859 she lent pictures and objects from the Royal Collection to an Art Exhibition, though one suspects she might have been less than delighted by the 'innocent recreation' provided by tableaux of Eskimo life in the former chapel and the representation of a Chinese street scene, complete with a barber's shop, in the Library. Outside the mansion the Park was given over to those who pandered to what one critic called 'the demands for the sensational and vulgar': in 1863 a woman acrobat, Selina Powell, was killed when she fell from a tightrope. The news of the accident so shocked the Queen that she wrote to the Mayor of Birmingham expressing her dismay that 'one of her subjects – a female – should have been sacrificed to the gratification of the demoralising taste unfortunately prevalent for exhibitions attended with the greatest danger to the performers.' The City Corporation's hand was forced and in February 1864 they finally took full control of the House and what was left of the park. Much of the estate had already been sold off for housing developments, however, and at the end of the century the Lower Grounds became the site of Aston Villa Football Club stadium. Despite these serial depredations, Aston Hall was the first of the great country houses of England to be opened to the public under the management of a municipal authority (though by 1864 one might have been hard pressed to describe it as a 'country house'). Birmingham therefore not only saved the greatest architectural treasure in its immediate environs, it also established the kind of principle on which the National Trust and English Heritage were one day to be based.[5]

With the contradictory examples of Kirby and Aston in mind therefore, it remains difficult to determine whether Martineau's *The Last Day in the Old Home* should be read as a lament for the loss of an old aristocratic order or as a shrewd comment on the aristocratic tendency to prodigality and profligacy, a tendency which the modern commercial world could well do without. Given his Unitarian background it is more than likely that Martineau's sympathies lay solidly in the latter area. In Victorian terms his picture is 'modern', but its representation of 'modernity' must be seen as having emerged from a painful evolutionary process. Loss had always to be balanced against gain and, as Charles Darwin had meticulously explained in 1859, in the natural world those who failed to adapt were likely to face extinction. In 1862 the moralising 'nostalgia' of Martineau's picture would have had a thoughtful poignancy about it. His prodigal old family has wasted its inheritance as we can see, but what lies in the future for the family and for their 'Old Home' remains indeterminate. When, twenty years earlier, Alfred Tennyson first published his 'Morte D'Arthur' he prefaced it with an introductory section set in a modern country house at Christmastide (this introduction was later to be abandoned when he re-used the poem as the climax of his Arthurian cycle). Tennyson concluded the original version with lines reflecting on Arthur not as a figure shrouded in the mists of historical vagueness but as 'a modern gentleman / Of stateliest port.' Thus the context of those vital Victorian sentiments, put into the mouth of the gentlemanly Arthur, originally had their own distinctive ambiguity:

> 'The old order changeth, yielding place to new
> And God fulfils Himself in many ways,
> Lest one good custom should corrupt the world,
> Comfort thyself …'

For Tennyson and his contemporaries the modern world was to be premised on change. Change may prove to be unwelcome, but it must be accepted nonetheless. That was the only real comfort to be taken. Some might have thought it cold comfort.

OLD HOMES AND THE OLDEN TIME

William Powell Frith exhibited his painting *Coming of Age in the Olden Time* (fig.4) at the Royal Academy 1849. The painting shows a richly attired young aristocrat being greeted by family retainers and by his tenants. He stands proudly on the steps of his mansion on the morning of his twenty-first birthday while his parents and an aged matriarch look on approvingly. The mansion is clearly a fine Elizabethan house and the meticulously observed costumes worn by the multitude of figures indicate a sixteenth-century setting.[6] The painting, like the young gentleman himself, exudes confidence. This is 'Merrie England' celebrating the opening of a prosperous future with roast beef and ale. There is nothing of the ambiguity of Martineau's *Last Day in the Old Home*, for here the English aristocracy is in its prime, still firmly rooted both in its ancestral home and in the affections of its tenantry. Nevertheless, both pictures would have had a very particular architectural resonance in mid-nineteenth-century England. The great houses shown in both paintings are manifestly buildings of the late sixteenth or early seventeenth centuries. Martineau's interior even shows a great oak staircase rising in the hallway beyond the panelled room where the family is bidding farewell to their inheritance. His 'Jacobethan' mansion has, up to now, represented ancestral continuity and its fittings suggest that the family has been eminent in both social and military enterprise. The exterior of Frith's great house is still new and appears to be an amalgam of architectural elements drawn, as the artist himself admitted, from Hever Castle in Kent and from Heslington Hall near York (though its porch is that of Wroxton Abbey in Oxfordshire).[7] The physical setting of both paintings clearly indicates much of the resonance associated with Elizabethan country house architecture by Victorian commentators. In Martineau's case the choice of setting for this last act in his family's drama was far from arbitrary. A medieval fortress might have appeared extravagantly improbable as the 'old home' of an established family, a medieval manor house too modest, and a Palladian mansion as both too slickly modern and too commonplace. The point was that, as most Victorian observers would have noted, the majority of wealthy, landed English families had rebuilt their country houses during the long eighteenth century. An eighteenth-century house would, however, indicate only minimal ancestral, let alone architectural, enchantment. Thirteenth-century castles (where they had survived the Civil War) were massively undomestic and draughty, while

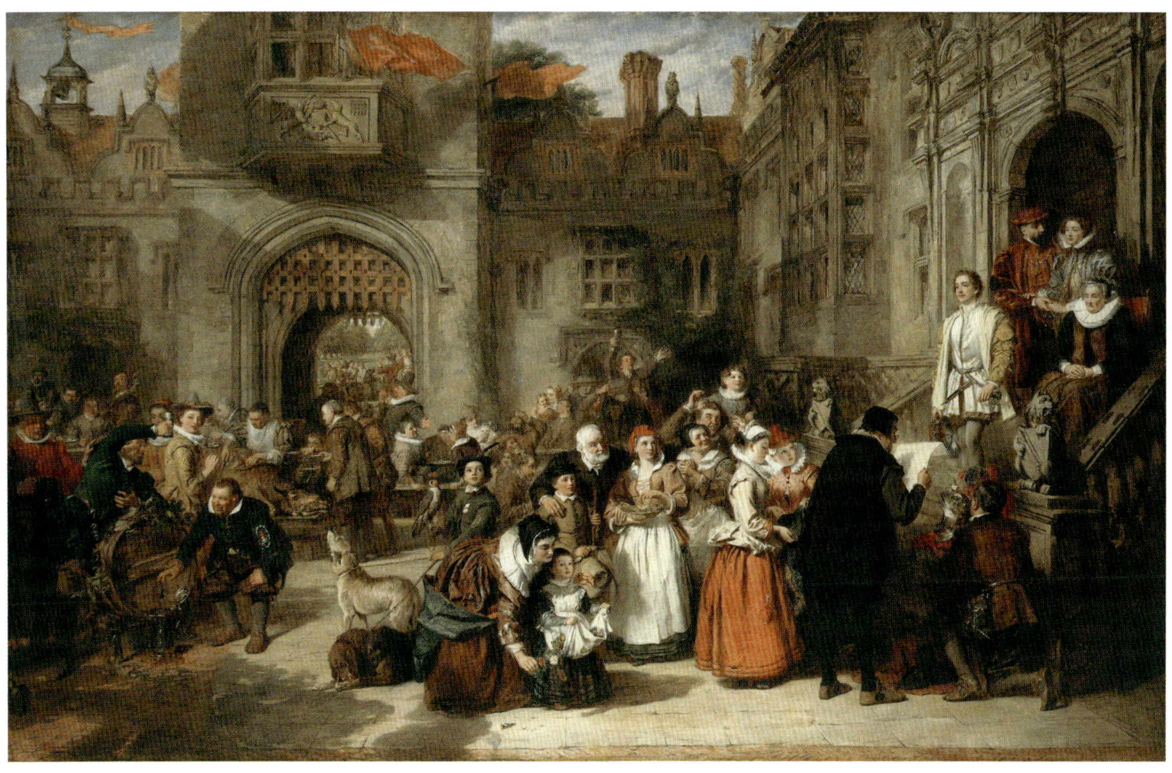

4   William Powell Frith, *Coming of Age in the Olden Time*, 1849, Oil on canvas, 127 x 200.7 cm. Private Collection

fourteenth- or fifteenth-century manor houses were regarded as quirky, ill-planned and inconvenient. Generally speaking, for Victorians the only large country houses to survive into the 1860s as relatively comfortable, habitable and impressively substantial were those constructed in the reigns of Elizabeth and the first King James. This is precisely the kind of house shown in Frith's painting. The historical atmosphere they evoked was unrivalled. They were, as Frith's picture suggests, the truest embodiment of secular English history.

Lithographic representations of that secular history were to carry a distinctive English architectural style around the world in the 1840s. The first volume of Joseph Nash's handsome folios entitled *The Mansions of England in the Olden Time* was published in London in 1839, containing twenty-six architectural plates. Its title page showed the early Tudor gatehouse of East Barsham Manor in Norfolk, in front of which a mounted gentleman, attired in what passes as early Tudor costume, appears to be about to leave on a falconing expedition. A further three sumptuous volumes, each with twenty-six lithographs of country houses, appeared between 1840 and 1849. Nash, a fine topographical watercolourist, had trained with Augustus Pugin (the father of the architect) and had contributed to Pugin's *Views Illustrative of Gothic Architecture* in 1830. His four volumes of *The Mansions of England* were an epoch-making celebration not of the Gothic but of Tudor secular architecture and, as his title readily suggests, Frith drew on them in his *Coming of Age in the Olden Time*. Crucially, Nash's lithographic plates showed domestic buildings in domestic circumstances. All the plates picture historic houses, peopled by men and women in historical costume, going about their historical business and their historical pleasures. His drawings of Great Halls, Great Chambers and Long Galleries show interiors that are occupied. Here was Nash revealing himself as the heir of Sir Walter Scott, for history is embodied in living people not in empty period rooms. Some of the characters are readily recognisable. Cardinal Wolsey, somewhat incongruously, dines in state in Henry VIII's Hall at Hampton Court; William Cecil, Lord Burghley purposefully descends the staircase at Burghley House (fig. 5); Bess of Hardwick is conducted down hers at Hardwick Hall; Shakespeare appears to be caught in the act of poaching at Charlecote; and Henry VIII courts Anne Boleyn in the Gallery at Hever Castle. Some of Nash's incidents are dramatic: a cannon ball shatters the staircase at Aston Hall (fig. 6), the damage is still shown to modern visitors!) and Bolsover Castle is plundered by Cromwellian soldiers. Generally, however, Nash's great rooms look stately, his privy chambers are warm and comfortable, his chapels are full of devout worshippers, and his formal gardens appear to delight the elegant ladies and gentlemen who take their gentle exercise in them.[8] It was small wonder that the influence of Nash's *Mansions of England* is still to be seen in nineteenth-century country houses and palaces from the Danube to the Hudson. Visitors to the interiors of the Liechtenstein palace at Lednice or to the Rohan castle at Sychrov in the Czech Republic might readily imagine that they are walking through one of Nash's more fanciful lithographs. Perhaps the most unlikely consequence of Nash's influence is Tsar Nicholas I's vast neo-Tudor Imperial Court Stables of 1847-54 at Peterhof on the Gulf of Finland. At the heart of these brick stables lies a great Riding School closely modelled on the Hall at Hampton Court, complete with a hammer-beam roof. The twists of the whirligig of time have long rendered these stables redundant.

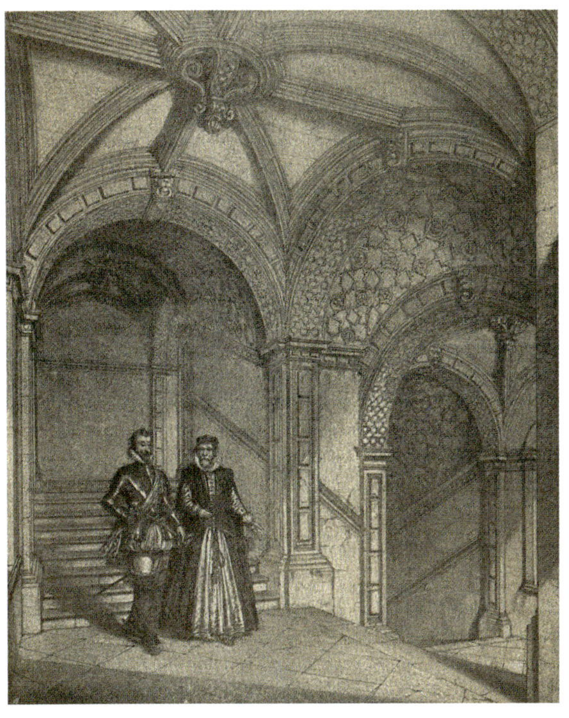

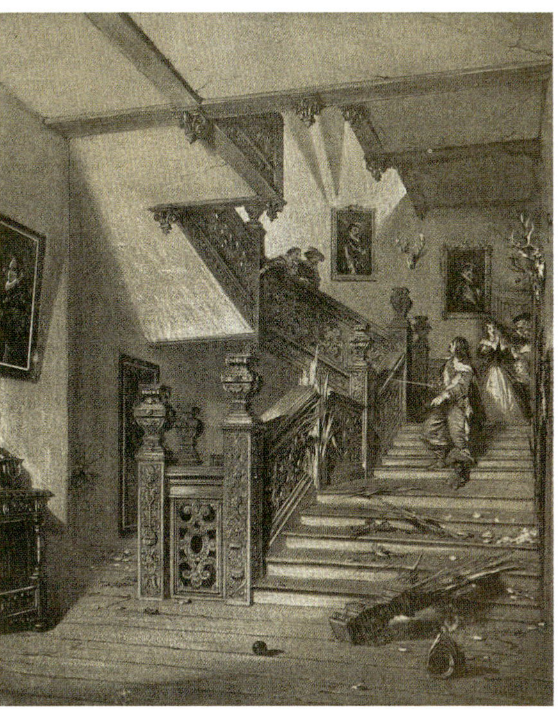

5 The Staircase at Burghley House, lithograph illustration in *The Mansions of England in the Olden Time* by Joseph Nash, 1839. Private collection

6 The Staircase at Aston Hall, lithograph illustration in *The Mansions of England in the Olden Time* by Joseph Nash, 1839. Private collection

They have served as a sanatorium since Soviet times, with the great, draughty Riding School as a refectory.

Nash's volumes had a far more limited currency in England. There had been a fashion for neo-Tudor architecture in the first thirty years of the nineteenth century, but that fashion was dying in the 1840s. At its most refined its fashion was exemplified by the 'restoration' of Charlecote in Warwickshire by George Hammond Lucy and his wife Mary in the late 1820s and early 1830s. The proximity of the house to Stratford-upon-Avon, and the legend of Shakespeare's having been caught *in flagrante* as a deer-poacher in the park, may well have provided a stimulus to this wholesale reconstruction of the sixteenth-century house, but Queen Elizabeth's two-night stay at the old house in August 1572, returning from her sojourn at Kenilworth, must also have influenced the choice of style. So too did family pride. George Hammond Lucy (who was a Lucy only through his great-grandmother) filled the windows of the reinstated Great Hall with heraldic glass by Thomas Willement in order to proclaim his distinguished, adoptive, pedigree. It was probably Willement who also designed the heavy, stencilled Tudor roses on the plaster barrel vault in the Hall and provided models for the neo-Elizabethan ceilings and fittings in the newly built Library and Dining Room. Effectively, Lucy and his architect–designers re-made Charlecote by removing Georgian accretions and by adding new wings to the house, obliterating a good deal of sixteenth-century brickwork in the process. Charlecote, with its often sumptuous interiors, managed to convince many curious, but myopic, visitors that it was the epitome of the high Elizabethan style. It seems to us to exemplify the taste for the flock wallpapers, the ebonised furniture and the padded comforts of a late Regency escape into a period fantasy.[9]

The years 1820-45 produced plethora of stuccoed suburban villas in the Tudor style. They are exemplified in P.F. Robinson's illustrated architectural handbook *Designs for Ornamental Villas* of 1827. Here 'Elizabethan' villas share floor plans with detached middle-class villas in styles variously described as Swiss, Greek, Palladian, 'Picturesque' and 'Castellated' (that is, Gothic). Robinson, who was later to publish detailed studies of two major 'Jacobethan' houses, Hatfield and Hardwick, seems to have rejoiced in the fact that Elizabethan architecture consisted of 'a jumble of heterogeneous forms' and freely admitted that his aggrandised villa designs drew, ambitiously enough, on Longford Castle, Longleat, Wollaton Hall and Audley End.[10] Far less domestically, it was in the Elizabethan style that Isambard Kingdom Brunel chose to build the new Great Western Railway offices at Temple Meads Station in Bristol (1839-41). Brunel, a man of some discrimination in matters of architectural taste, evidently saw nothing incongruous in housing his station personnel in what could pass as a Tudor college. Nevertheless, the real achievement of the Elizabethan revival in architecture lay not in the suburbs, in the new seaside resorts and spa-towns, or in railway buildings, but in the wide range of newly designed country houses constructed for aristocratic families and parvenus alike. These include Merevale Hall in Warwickshire, designed on a fine hillside site by Edward Blore for the Tory landowner, William Stratford Dugdale, between 1838 and 1844; Highclere Castle in Hampshire, a spectacular remodelling of 1839-42 of a plain Georgian mansion for the third Earl of Carnarvon by Sir Charles Barry (though its interiors, completed after Barry's death, are more Gothic than Elizabethan); and, belatedly, Bear Wood in Berkshire, a sprawling monster of a house, built at vast expense in 1865-74 for John Walter, the proprietor of *The Times*, by Robert Kerr, the author of *The Gentleman's House*. Perhaps the most impressive, and most splendidly whimsical, of all of these Elizabethan-style houses is Harlaxton Manor in Lincolnshire built for Gregory Gregory, a relatively modest local landowner, by Anthony Salvin in 1831-38. It, like the sixteenth-century houses it imitates, is a true prodigy. It rises on a hump in the flat countryside, a joyous jungle of fussy masonry. Its greatest feature, however, is its theatrical staircase hall which culminates in an ecstatic explosion of giant Baroque plaster clouds and swags. It is precisely the kind of Elizabethan fantasy that was likely to offend the high-minded Goths who were determined to return England to the 'true principles' of medieval architecture.[11]

The revival of Gothic, or as he insistently termed it 'Christian,' architecture in the middle years of the nineteenth century owed much to the energy and articulacy of Augustus Welby Pugin. Thanks to Pugin, Tudor architecture in general came to be regarded with suspicion as little more than an impure coda to the medieval, but the fleetingly popular Elizabethan style was steadily damned as some kind of aesthetic abortion. Pugin himself insisted in 1841 that the modern gentleman, if he required a new house, needed one appropriate both to his social standing and to the demands of the age. The modern age had its distinctive demands as did past ages, but those demands did not include looking back favourably on the style of the late sixteenth century:

Every person should be lodged as becomes his station and dignity … but the mansions erected by our ancestors were not the passing whim of the moment, or mere show places raised at such an extravagant cost as impoverished some generations of heirs to the estates, but solid, dignified and Christian structures, built with due regard to the general prosperity of the family … There is a great reviving taste for ancient domestic architecture, but a vast many pretended admirers of old English beauties, instead of imitating the Tudor period, when domestic architecture was carried to a high state of perfection, stop short at the reign of Elizabeth, the very worst kind of English architecture; and, strange to say, these unmeaning conglomerations of debased forms have been classed into a regular style, and called after the female tyrant during whose reign they were executed. The only reason I can assign for the fashionable rage for this architecture (if so it may be called) is, that its character is so corrupt, mixed, and bad, that the anachronisms and anomalies so frequently perpetrated by modern architects are made to pass muster under the general term Elizabethan; and certainly I cannot deny that the appellation is very appropriate when applied to corrupted design and decayed taste.[12]

As a Catholic convert, we might expect Pugin to have a particular distaste for the reign of a woman whom he dismisses as a 'female tyrant,' but the aesthetic fastidiousness evident in this paragraph stems from an awareness that, for him, Elizabethan architecture was as much a bastard as the monarch after whom it was named. Of course, he is also implying that the Reformation had served to pervert both the English and their architecture from their pure Gothic (that is, *Catholic*) perfection. For most of the Victorian period, the influence of Pugin and his disciples meant that the Elizabethan style came to be seen as synonymous with corrupt taste.

After the mid-1840s it seems to have been assumed in educated circles that there was something aberrant, even immoral, about Elizabethan architecture. Take, for example, the comments of Charles Locke Eastlake in his highly influential book, *Hints on Household Taste*, in 1869:

> Long after Venice and Verona could boast of a splendid Renaissance, English architecture continued in a degraded state of transition between the two styles. It had lost the purity of ancient Gothic. It had not yet developed the principles of Italian design. The result was a miserable compromise, by which classic details of the clumsiest description were grafted on buildings supported by the Tudor arch, and crowned with the Tudor gable. It is, perhaps, the bizarre and picturesque character of this bastard style which still renders it popular with the uneducated. To this day Elizabethan mansions are admired by sentimental young ladies (who, by the way, often call them Elizabeth*ian*) as perfections of architectural taste.[13]

This takes aesthetic fastidiousness into the realm of snobbishness. It also attempts to make a rigorous and moral distinction between good design and bad design. Pure blood, it implies, properly looks down on bastards.

What Eastlake might have had in mind when he referred to the taste of 'sentimental young ladies' was a taste for the Elizabethan style cultivated not by architectural pundits but by popular literature. It is extraordinary how many country houses in Victorian fiction appear to date from the reigns of Elizabeth and James I. Historical novels are a special case, of course, though we should not overlook the influence of Sir Walter Scott's vastly popular *Kenilworth* (1821) in forming a picture of the hospitality traditionally associated with the great house. It was to Scott that the American writer, Washington Irving, dedicated his *Sketchbook* of 1819. It was Irving, perhaps even more so than Charles Dickens, who re-invented crucial elements in the English Christmas through his loving accounts of the Yuletide festivities at Bracebridge Hall. The author describes himself as happily lodged in a wainscoted bedchamber in Bracebridge Hall's 'ancient wing':

> My chamber was in the old part of the mansion, the ponderous furniture of which might have been fabricated in the days of the giants. The room was panelled, with cornices of heavy carved work, in which flowers and grotesque faces were strangely intermingled; and a row of black-looking portraits stared mournfully at me from the walls. The bed was of rich though faded damask, with a lofty tester, and stood in a niche opposite a bow window.

Despite Irving's vagueness about dates and styles, who can doubt that we are in an Elizabethan room? Christmas at the Hall is celebrated with all the elements the Victorians clung on to with a sentimental delight: yule logs, waits, carols, groaning tables, beef, bread and ale distributed to the poor, and mince pies and wassail bowls for the house-guests. It is small wonder, given his attraction to this vision of a 'stronghold of old fashions,' that Irving should have dedicated two further volumes of essays to accounts of gentlemanly bounty and country house tradition.[14] The impact of Irving's sketches can instantly be recognised in the illustrations to *Christmas with the Poets: A Collection of Songs, Carols, and Descriptive Verses relating to the Festival of Christmas*, an anthology evidently published for the Christmas market in 1851 (fig. 7). The fifty coloured lithographs by Myles Birket Foster that accompany the verses variously show feasting, the relief of the poor, mumming, wassailing, carolling and dancing. The setting, more often than not, is a Tudorbethan house of the kind that boasts a fireplace ample enough to contain a huge yule log.[15] Not many other imagined country houses are as bountiful. The frontispiece to Dickens's *Bleak House* of 1852–53 shows a large Tudor house rising up on a low, damp ridge in marshy Lincolnshire. As Dickens's illustrator, 'Phiz', represents it, the house bears a close resemblance to Burghley (also, nowadays, in Lincolnshire). Given the placing of this illustration, original readers

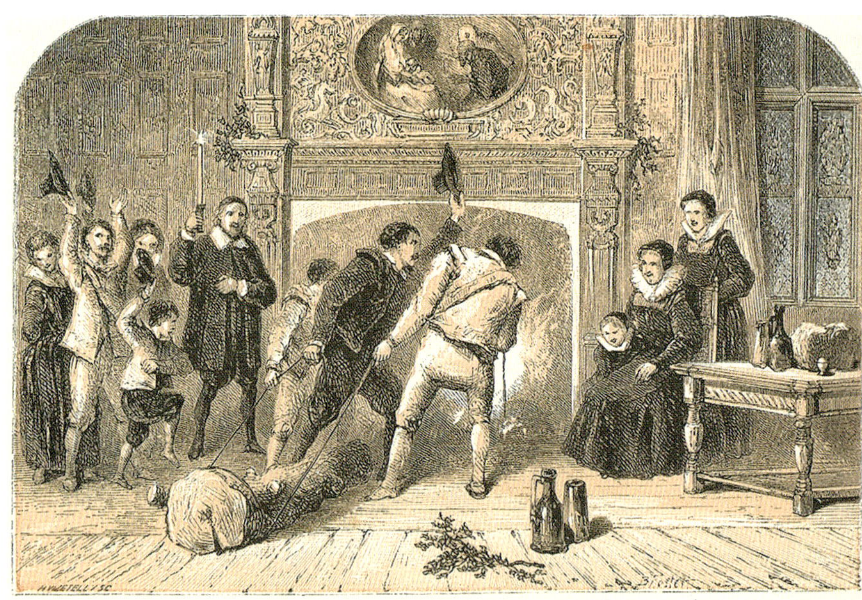

CEREMONY FOR CHRISTMAS EVE.

7 Myles Birket Foster,
lithograph illustration in
*Christmas with the Poets:
A Collection of Songs,
Carols, and Descriptive
Verses Relating to the
Festival of Christmas* by
Henry Vizetelly, 1851.
Private collection

of the novel might have assumed that Chesney Wold was indeed the 'bleak' house of the title. What we learn of the house's troubled history as the novel develops in fact does little to dispel its general atmosphere of coldness, formality and empty pomp.[16] When we first encounter the Hall in Anne Brontë's *The Tenant of Wildfell Hall* (1849) it is equally bleak and unwelcoming. The Hall is described as 'a superannuated mansion of the Elizabethan era, built of dark grey stone, – venerable and picturesque to look at but, doubtless, cold and gloomy enough to inhabit, with its thick stone mullions and little latticed panes.'

There is a direct association of another distinguished fictional baronet's residence with Queen Elizabeth in Thackeray's *Vanity Fair* (1847–48). In Chapter 7 we are given a sardonic potted history of Sir Pitt Crawley's heritage:

It is related, with regard to the borough of Queen's Crawley, that Queen Elizabeth in one of her progresses, stopping at Queen's Crawley to breakfast, was so delighted with some remarkably fine Hampshire beer which was then presented to her by the Crawley of the day (a handsome gentleman with a trim beard and a good leg), that she forthwith erected

Crawley into a borough to send two members to Parliament; and the place, from the day of that illustrious visit, took the name of Queen's Crawley, which it holds up to the present moment.

It is now a 'rotten borough' of course. Sir Pitt's mansion has little in it that appeals to Becky Sharp's uninformed architectural tastes, but it does tickle something in her literary sensibility. As she describes it to Amelia, Queen's Crawley strikes Becky as

> an odious old-fashioned red brick mansion with tall chimneys and gables of the style of Queen Bess … the great hall I am sure is as big and as glum as the great hall in the dear castle of Udolpho. It has a large fire-place … and the grate is big enough to roast an ox at the very least. Round the room and I don't know how many generations of Crawleys, some with beards and ruffs … At one end of the hall is the great staircase all in black oak, as dismal as may be … I think there are at least twenty bed-rooms on the first floor; one of them has the bed in which Queen Elizabeth slept …

A Crawley family tradition seems to have extended the Queen's breakfast to bed *and* breakfast but nineteenth-century stories of beds Elizabeth slept in seem to have been legion. It is interesting, however, that Becky finds little to admire about the architecture of Queen's Crawley. Thackeray's readers would probably have recognised that her aesthetic shallowness is telling. At this point in the novel she is impervious both to the tradition embodied in Queen's Crawley's architecture and to what it ought to tell her about the family who occupy it. There is, however, no mistaking the inconveniently venerable nature both of the Thorne family and of their house at Ullathorne in Trollope's *Barchester Towers* (1857):

> Ullathorne Court … formed two sides of a quadrangle, which was completed on the other two sides by a wall about twenty feet high … With those who are now adepts in contriving house accommodation, it will militate much against Ullathorne Court that no carriage could be brought to the hall-door … On entering the front door, which you do by no very great portal, you find yourself immediately in the dining-room. What, — no hall? Exclaims my luxurious friend, accustomed to all the comfortable appurtenances of modern life. Yes, kind sir; a noble hall, if you

will but observe it; a true old English hall of excellent dimension for a country gentleman's family; but, if you please no dining parlour.

The 'square mullions' and the 'huge fire-place' described later by Trollope indicate that this is indeed yet another late-Tudor house, one that has been left relatively unaltered, but decidedly not neglected, by post-Tudor generations of Thornes. By contrast Thornfield Hall, Mr Rochester's country seat in Charlotte Brontë's *Jane Eyre* (1847), has 'been neglected of late years,' but that is because Rochester has felt obliged to live abroad. Thornfield's housekeeper, Mrs Fairfax, tells Jane that it is 'a respectable place.' She is probably implying that Rochester's family is distinguished and that his house is appropriately old. Jane briefly gives us her impressions of it in Chapter 11 as Mrs Fairfax conducts her upstairs to her bedroom:

> First she went to see if the hall-door was fastened … she led the way up stairs. The steps and bannisters were of oak; the staircase window was high and latticed; both it, and the long gallery into which the bed-room doors opened, looked as if they belonged to a church rather than a house. A very chill and vault-like air pervaded the stairs and gallery, suggesting cheerless ideas of space and solitude; and I was glad when finally ushered into my chamber, to find it of small dimensions and furnished in ordinary modern style.

Jane, like Becky Sharpe at Queen's Crawley, may well be reading Thornfield imperceptively. She has, we assume, been accustomed to cramped, thronged and unadorned spaces during her schooldays and this historic and substantial gentleman's house daunts and disturbs her. Empty spaces seem 'cheerless' and the latticed windows suggest something ecclesiastical. She is evidently unaware of Nash's *The Mansions of England*. If anything 'the olden time' has no real resonance for Jane and the 'ordinariness' of her 'modern' bedroom offers both a refuge and an aesthetic consolation. On one level Jane seems something of a philistine. On another, she reveals a troubled Gothic sensibility. Though she doesn't actually articulate it, gentlemanly Thornfield seems to remind her, as Queen's Crawley did Becky Sharp, of Udolpho. As the novel unfolds we know that she has been uncannily right all the time.

Under Which Queen?

When in Chapter 27 of Dickens's *Dombey and Son* Mr Dombey, Major Bagstock and Mr Carker accompany Mrs. Skewton and her daughter Edith on an excursion to Kenilworth and to Warwick Castle, their trip is undoubtedly inspired by memories of Sir Walter Scott's *Kenilworth*. When they reach Warwick Castle, Mrs Skewton waxes lyrical about 'those darling byegone times … with their delicious fortresses, and their dear old dungeons, and their delightful places of torture, and their romantic vengeances, and their picturesque assaults and sieges, and everything that makes life truly charming!' 'How dreadfully,' she concludes 'we have degenerated.' This is not exactly the kind of moral that Scott would have assumed might inspire an intelligent reader of *Kenilworth*. Mrs. Skewton gushes on and seems to be particularly inspired by the portraits of Queen Elizabeth and her father, Henry VIII, which once hung at Warwick (the so-called 'Coronation' portrait of Elizabeth is now in the National Portrait Gallery, fig. 8). She finds Henry VIII 'so bluff … so burly. So truly English … with his dear little peepy eyes, and his benevolent chin.' When, however, she looks at the portrait of the 'inestimable Queen Bess' Mrs. Skewton's calculatingly shallow mind is reminded of 'golden days.' The Queen was 'a dear creature! She was all heart'. This again is scarcely an idea that she could have found either in Scott or in the popular memory of the celebratedly unmarried queen.

What Dickens is doing in this section of *Dombey and Son* is preparing us for Mr Dombey's proposal of marriage to Edith. Like Henry VIII he will not prove himself to be an ideal husband. But it is Mrs Skewton's physical connection to Elizabeth which is particularly fascinating. Ostensibly the two women seem poles apart, especially as the painted, artificially preserved Skewton contemplates a portrait of the young Elizabeth. In *A Child's History of England* (1851–54) Dickens was to reveal himself as ambiguous about the Queen's qualities and historic reputation:

> She was well-educated, but a roundabout writer, and rather a hard swearer and coarse talker. She was clever, but cunning and deceitful, and inherited much of her father's violent temper. I mention this now, because she has been overpraised by one party, and so over-abused by another, that it is hardly possible to understand the greater part of her reign without first understanding what kind of woman she really was.[17]

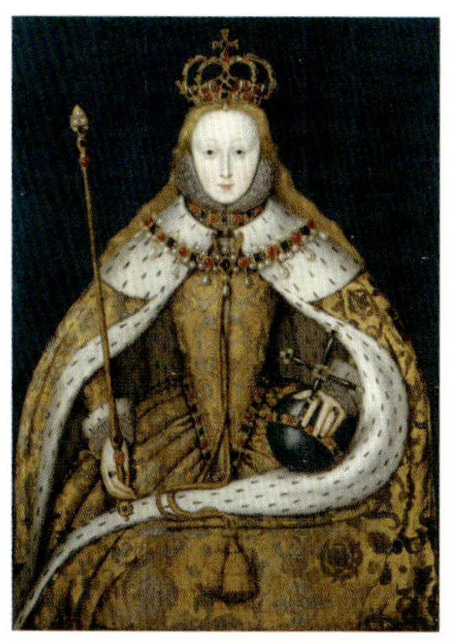

8 Unknown English artist, *The Coronation Portrait of Elizabeth I*, c1600, Oil on panel, 127.3 x 99.7 cm. National Portrait Gallery, London

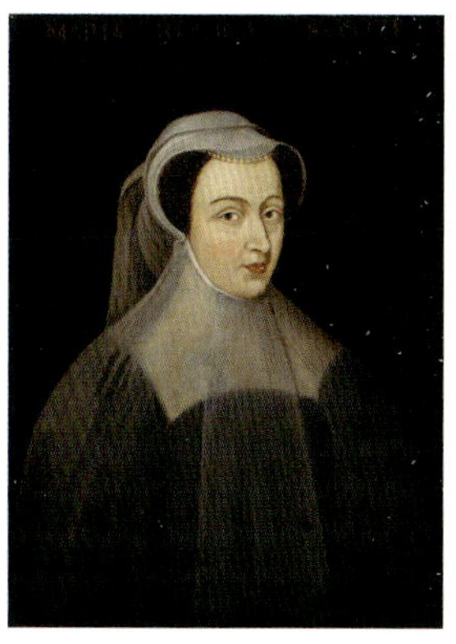

9 After François Clouet, *Mary Queen of Scots*, 1560, Oil on canvas, 71.1 x 53 cm. National Portrait Gallery, London

What Dickens is implying is that by commonly received mid-nineteenth-century standards Elizabeth possessed few admirably feminine qualities. She was 'coarse, capricious, and treacherous, and had all the faults of an excessively vain young woman long after she was an old one.'[18] She was Machiavellian and Dickens was no admirer of Machiavels, especially if they were women. His ideal women were morally better than men and they were married; they were not politically calculating harridans and professional virgins. What Dickens may also be implying is that the bewigged and ageless Elizabeth shown in later portraits may physically resemble the artificial Mrs. Skewton with her 'false curls … false eyebrows … false teeth … [and] false complexion.' One can only speculate as to whether or not he ever discussed Elizabeth with his painter friend Augustus Egg who was at this time working on his graphic representation of the Queen's personal vanity in his painting *Queen Elizabeth discovers she is no longer young* (fig. 10). Egg's painting, which was exhibited at the Royal Academy in 1848, shows a haggard, hook-nosed queen grumpily averting her eyes from a looking glass. The message seems to be not that her glory has departed, but that her attendant ladies have not yet had the opportunity to help her assume it. Both Dickens and Egg were probably aware of engravings of Paul Delaroche's dramatic, but equally unflattering, painting of the dying Elizabeth of 1828 (fig. 11).[19] In Delaroche's canvas the royally attired, but physically drained, queen lies slumped on cushions on the floor of her throne room, having according to contemporary accounts, categorically refused to go to bed. Her anxious ladies in waiting, variously fret, pray or cry as Elizabeth finally admits to the truth of her mortality and names her successor. Delaroche's queen seems to cling to the last signifiers of royalty, but the very fact that she can no longer stand seems to deprive her of princely dignity. Ultimately she, like Mrs. Skewton, is just a vain and crumpled old woman.

Neither Elizabeth's character nor her style of government were generally admired in Victorian England. She was generally assumed to have failed both as a liberal-minded ruler and as a dynastic progenetrix. On Queen Victoria's accession in 1837 commentators looked back critically to the reigns of two earlier female monarchs in particular. Lord John Russell expressed the hope in a parliamentary speech that the new Queen might prove 'an Elizabeth without her tyranny, and Anne without her weakness.'[20] In 1841, on the birth of the new Prince of Wales, *The Times* took up a similar theme, describing Victoria as 'more pure and womanly than Queen Elizabeth, more firm of mind and royal of demeanour than Queen Anne.'[21]

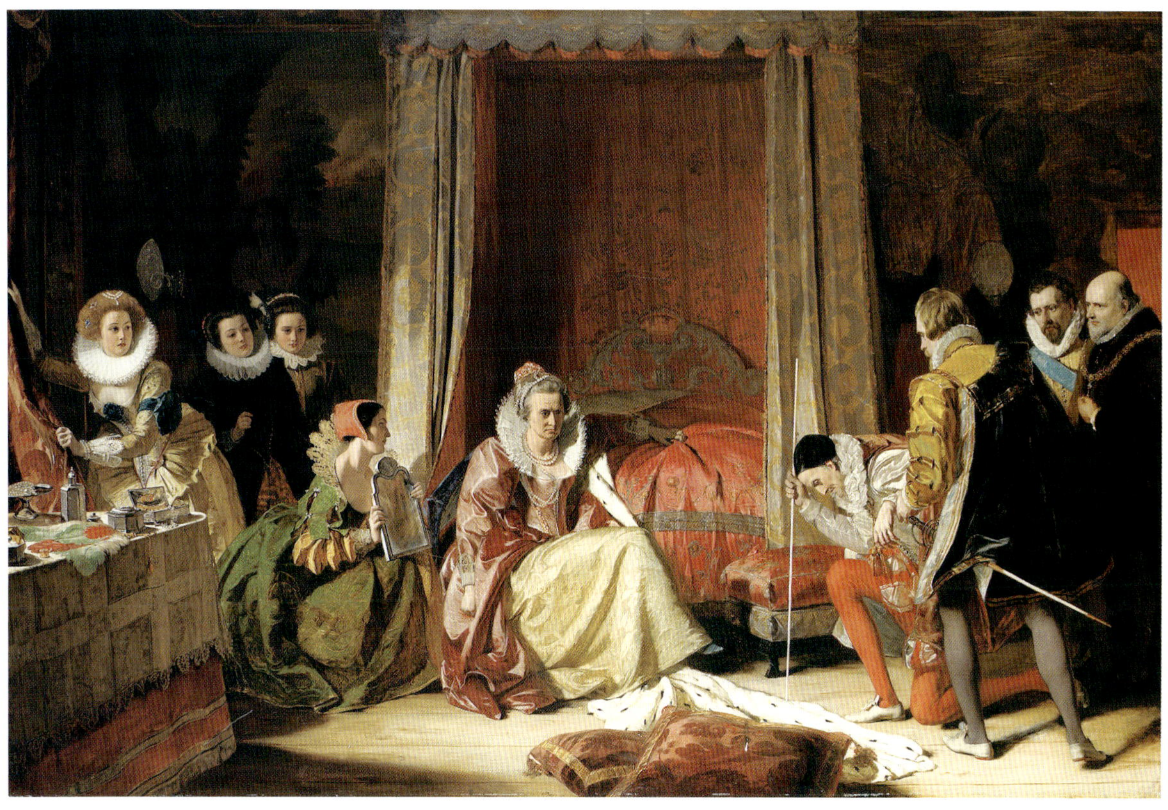

10 Augustus Egg, *Queen Elizabeth Discovers She is No Longer Young*, 1848, Oil on canvas, 122 x 183.2cm. Private collection

It is notable that when the Palace of Westminster was rebuilt in the 1840s images of the 'tyrant' Elizabeth and her reign appear only sporadically in the carefully thought-out decorative scheme. In 1863 Daniel Maclise produced designs for a fresco showing 'Elizabeth at Tilbury' to flank his huge painting of Wellington's meeting with Blücher after Waterloo, but the scheme was dropped a year later.[22] The absence of any image of the armed and militant Elizabeth as she appeared at the time of the defeat of the Armada is especially surprising given the fact that the old House of Lords had famously been hung with ten large sixteenth-century tapestries showing the manoeuvres of the English fleet in its campaign against the Spanish in 1588. These tapestries were destroyed when the Palace of Westminster was gutted in the fire of 1834, but they had been carefully recorded in a series of engravings published by John Pine in 1739.[23] Elizabeth's painted presence in the Houses of Parliament is now rather more marked, but in

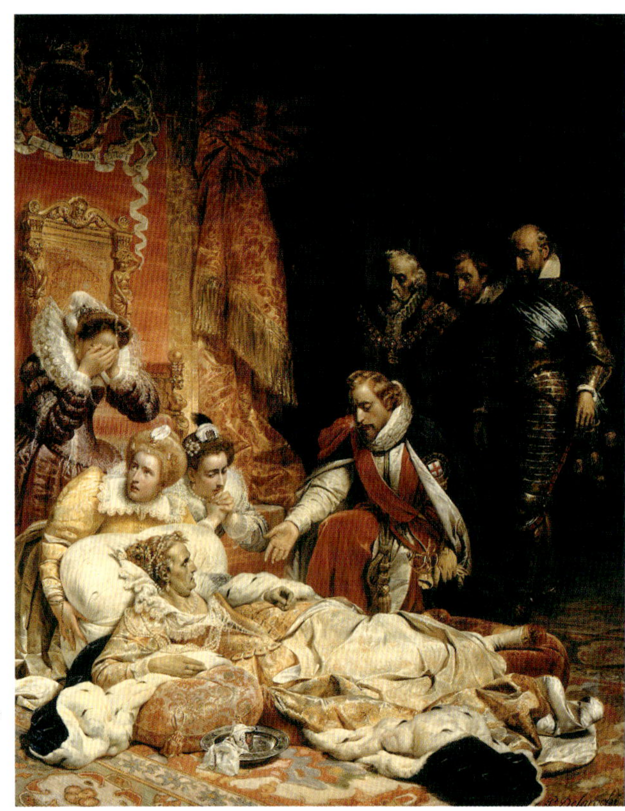

11 Paul Delaroche,
*The Death of
Queen Elizabeth*, 1828,
Oil on canvas,
422 x 343 cm.
Louvre, Paris

the mid-nineteenth century decorative scheme it was minimal. There was one statue of her amongst those of other monarchs in the Royal Gallery, and one portrait amongst representations of all of the Tudors and their connections in the Prince's Chamber. There were also two bronze reliefs by William Theed, one showing the knighting of Drake and the other *Raleigh spreading his coat as a carpet* in the same room.[24] This could scarcely be seen as a wholehearted celebration of one of most distinguished reigns in English history, especially as the Prince's Chamber also has three bronze reliefs showing scenes from the life of Mary, Queen of Scots. But then, as the Parliamentary Commissioners responsible for the decoration of the new Palace were well aware, Elizabeth was no democrat and the committees who drew up the original plans for the art work seem to have chosen to place a greater stress on those figures who had contributed to the emergence of representative government in Britain.

In general, popular opinion in the nineteenth century was wary of praising a Queen who did not conform either to modern ideas of temperate government or to contemporary perceptions of femininity. Take for example the author of *The Young Man's Companion, or Youth's Instructor* of 1824. The author opens by informing his impressionable juvenile readers that 'papists … represent her as … a monster of cruelty, avarice and lasciviousness.' Good Protestant boys might, however, consider another point of view: Elizabeth had 'a deep, penetrating and elevated mind,' her judgement was 'solid' and her courage 'invincible.' Nevertheless, her 'glorious reign' ended in 'a most dismal melancholy.' The author's final comments scarcely seem like a ringing endorsement of Elizabeth's achievement: 'This Queen makes a considerable figure among learned ladies.'[25] Elizabeth Penrose, the author of the enduring, popular and influential *Mrs Markham's History of England* (1823) describes her character as being 'very far … from faultless' and adds that, despite her 'sense and shrewdness,' Elizabeth's 'vanity and caprice' made her seem in her later years 'both vexatious and ridiculous.'[26] Even less sympathetic to the queen is William Howitt's account of Elizabeth's reign in John Cassell's *Illustrated History of England*. This history, decorated with lively woodcuts, was published for the popular market in 1857. Howitt is grudgingly positive about the tenor of the times: 'a period more remarkable than any which had gone before, and which, with all its dark and repulsive features, was the gloomy dawn of the glorious day which we now enjoy.' He is, however, infinitely less complimentary to the Queen herself. She is initially defined in a series of negatives:

> Her vanity, her irresolution, her belief in astrology, her thousand dresses which were discovered at her decease in her wardrobe, her being painted up in her old age, face, neck and arms, her numerous heads of hair, or even her cursing, swearing, and beating with her own trusty fists her maids of honour and her ministers may be passed over. But the licentiousness in which she is known to have lived, whilst calling herself a maiden queen; the licentiousness which, in consequence of her example, pervaded her whole court … on such indisputable proofs, Elizabeth can never more be held up as a model queen to this nation.[27]

This is pretty racy stuff, going well beyond the familiar enough complaints about Elizabeth's vanity and fickleness into wild accusations of sexual immorality. Clearly, impressionable readers in 1857 must have been led to assume that Elizabeth was some kind of sexual ogress. Her home life, they would readily have concluded, was singularly unlike that of the happily married and thoroughly well-mannered Queen Victoria.

Catholic Englishmen and women were particularly likely to harbour a particular animus against Elizabeth. She and her ministers had after all initiated a regime of legal suppression, punitive fines and active persecution, aspects of which had effectively lasted until the Emancipation Act of 1829. The circumstances of an Elizabethan recusant family are vividly described in Lady Georgiana Fullerton's somewhat creaky novel *Constance Sherwood*. Fullerton, who had been received into the Roman Catholic Church in 1846 'after an interval of devout Puseyism,' serialised this 'autobiography of the sixteenth century' in the pages of the Catholic periodical the *Month* and it was republished in three-volume form in 1865. Constance, the daughter of an 'ancient' family, has remained faithful to the 'old' religion but finds her intimate circle caught up in the great debates about 'loyalty' which followed the Queen's excommunication. When Elizabeth herself enters the narrative, Constance finds her 'very majestic' but somehow 'not made in the same mould as that of whom the Scriptures do say, that dust they are, and to dust they must return.'[28] Later, Constance will sharply question the Queen's ostensible popularity with her subjects: 'What is the art this queen doth possess by which she holdeth the hearts of her subjects in so great thrall, albeit so cruel to them which do offend her?' This sentiment is expanded into an emotional plea for understanding in the last volume of the novel:

> The life of a Catholic in England in these days must needs, I think, produce one of two frames of mind. Either he will harbour angry passions, which religion reproves, which change a natural indignation into an unchristian temper of hatred, and lead him into plots and treasons; or else become detached from the world, very quiet, given to prayer, ready to take at God's hand, and as from Him at men's also, sufferings of all kinds; and even those as yet removed from so great perfection learn to be still, and to bethink themselves rather of the next world than of the present one, more than even good people did in old times.[29]

This is not an apology but an appeal against the historical injustice meted out to Catholics by the state and popular opinion alike. In her definition of the Catholic 'two frames of mind' Fullerton is, however, adding a distinctive nuance to the singularly ambiguous perception of Elizabeth in the nineteenth century.

Prejudices against Elizabeth's public policies and her private life (or the lack of it) went back to the eighteenth century when a growing sentimental attachment to the fate of the Catholic Mary, Queen of Scots cast an unflattering light on the Protestant English Queen's supposed 'heartlessness.' In 1791 the sixteen-year-old Jane Austen had completed her *History of England*, a work written, Austen freely admitted, 'by a partial, prejudiced and ignorant Historian.' The prejudice is nowhere more clearly evident than in the extraordinarily slanted account of Elizabeth's reign. There is no sense here of Elizabeth as a bluestocking or a wise ruler. The Queen is introduced as 'that disgrace to humanity, that pest of society … the destroyer of all comfort, the deceitful Betrayer of trust reposed in her, and the Murderess of her Cousin.' Like many of her contemporaries and their Victorian successors, Austen cannot bring herself to forgive Elizabeth's treatment of the 'bewitching princess' Mary. Indeed, most of Austen's short chapter on Elizabeth is given over to a paean on the 'amiable' Mary. This is the account of Mary's acceptance of her death:

> Firm in her Mind; Constant in her Religion; and prepared … to meet the cruel fate to which she was doomed, with a magnanimity that could alone rise from conscious Innocence.

Having made it perfectly clear where her sympathy lies, and why she disagrees with the standard apologias for Elizabeth given by the Protestant historians, Austen allots the remainder of her chapter to praise of that 'ornament of his Country and his profession,' Sir Francis Drake, and to a disparaging commentary on Elizabeth's fickle treatment of her one-time suitor, Robert Devereux, Earl of Essex.[30] Readers of Austen's minor writings might be accustomed to her fondness for sharply individualistic opinions, but in the *History* (not of course written for public circulation) she unexpectedly reveals herself as far more Romantically inclined than we might have suspected.

The full-blooded Romantic, and residual Jacobite, Sir Walter Scott, seems to have been disinclined to paint a wholly flattering picture of Queen Elizabeth in *Kenilworth* in 1821. Mary Stuart does not appear in the novel, though Scott had already dealt sympathetically with her sad history in *The Abbot* of 1820. *The Abbot* shows Mary marginalised in her kingdom, held captive at Lochleven and finally defeated at the battle of Langside. *Kenilworth,* by contrast shows us an Elizabeth, preening herself like a peacock, triumphant, adulated and feared. As she appears in the novel, Elizabeth is indubitably royal, but she is also whimsical, ill-tempered and showy. In his second volume Scott's narrative pauses, as he offers his readers a brief historical and psychological analysis:

> Queen Elizabeth had a character strangely compounded of the strongest masculine sense with those foibles which are chiefly supposed proper to the female sex. Her subjects had the full benefit of her virtues, which far predominated over her weaknesses; but her courtiers, and those about her person, had often to sustain sudden and embarrassing turns of caprice, and the sallies of a temper which was both jealous and despotic. She was the nursing mother of her people, but she was also the true daughter of Henry VIII; and though early sufferings and an excellent education had repressed and modified, they had not altogether destroyed the hereditary temper of that 'hard-ruled king.'[31]

This picture of a temperamental, capricious, cruel Elizabeth was to prove singularly influential throughout Europe where it chimed with Johann Christoph Friedrich von Schiller's deeply uncomplimentary portrait of the calculatingly heartless queen in his *Maria Stuart* of 1800 (a play which famously includes the dramatic, but unhistorical, encounter between the two royal cousins). Schiller's play was in turn to provide the basis of the libretto for Gaetano Donizetti's opera *Maria Stuarda* of 1834, the success of which was to stimulate Donizetti to write two further operas touching on the life of Elizabeth, both of them indirectly derived from Scott: *Elisabetta al Castello di Kenilworth* and the better-known *Roberto Devereux* of 1837 (the overture of which anachronistically quotes *God Save the Queen*). *Roberto Devereux* ends with the Queen, guilt ridden and tormented by visions of her crown wet with blood, of a man running through the Tower of London with his severed head in his hands, and of a tomb gaping where her throne had once proudly stood.

In terms of nineteenth-century painted representations of Elizabeth and Mary, Queen of Scots, Mary wins hands down. In his lists of historical subjects shown by painters who exhibited at the Royal Academy in London between 1769 and 1904, Roy Strong lists 32 pictures showing Elizabeth and 73 of Mary.[32] Aspects of Mary's unhappy life were represented by Victorian painters as various in their ambitions as Joseph Severn, John Callcott Horsley, Ford

Madox Brown, William Powell Frith, James Drummond, John Lavery and Alfred Elmore. The Scottish artist, Robert Herdman (1829-1888) seems to have made a speciality of such a (for Scotland) patriotic subject. He was probably working under the influence of Henry Glassford Bell's highly persuasive and romantically sympathetic biography of the Queen first published in 1830. Herdman's *The Happier Days of Mary Queen of Scots* (location unknown) shows the young queen playing the lute to her female companions in what we assume is a French garden while the infinitely more melancholic *Mary Queen of Scots' Farewell to France* (1867, National Galleries of Scotland) depicts the royal widow's voyage back to Scotland. Her wistful glance is either back to France, the land of lost content, or forwards to fraught, gloomy Scotland. In Herdman's *The Conference between Queen Mary and John Knox at Holyrood Palace, 1561* (1875, Perth Museum and Art Gallery) the seated queen, desperately clutching her rosary, recoils from a singularly aggressive verbal harangue by Knox while in his *Mary receives the Death Warrant* the Queen stands resolute but tensely gripping her voluminous skirt as the warrant is read to her. In what is perhaps his masterpiece, *The Execution of Mary, Queen of Scots* (fig. 12), Herdman shows Mary sweeping up the steps of the scaffold with a serene dignity.[33]

The many state beds shown to curious Victorian tourists as having been occupied by Queen Elizabeth during her progresses were nothing compared to the virtual shrine dedicated to Mary in nineteenth-century Edinburgh. At the heart of the tapestried Royal Apartments displayed to visitors in the Palace of Holyrood was (and is) Mary's bedroom. Adjacent to the bedroom there was a 'secret' staircase and the small apartment where Rizzio was murdered. A wonderful account of the furnishings of the bedchamber in the 1860s is appended to a stereoscopic photograph of the room (fig. 13):

> Here stands, with fragments of the blankets, the bed of Queen Mary, the decayed hangings of which are of crimson damask, with green silk fringes and tassels; and the chairs, tables &c are of the same period. The Queen's workbox is on the table. The needlework ... worked by her own fair hands.

This was a romantic invention, for the bed once anachronistically displayed was manifestly a state bed of the late seventeenth century, and the furniture surrounding it probably dates from the same period. Apart from its ceiling nothing in the room would have been remotely familiar to a Queen who left Edinburgh for the last time in 1567. When the account turns to the 'little

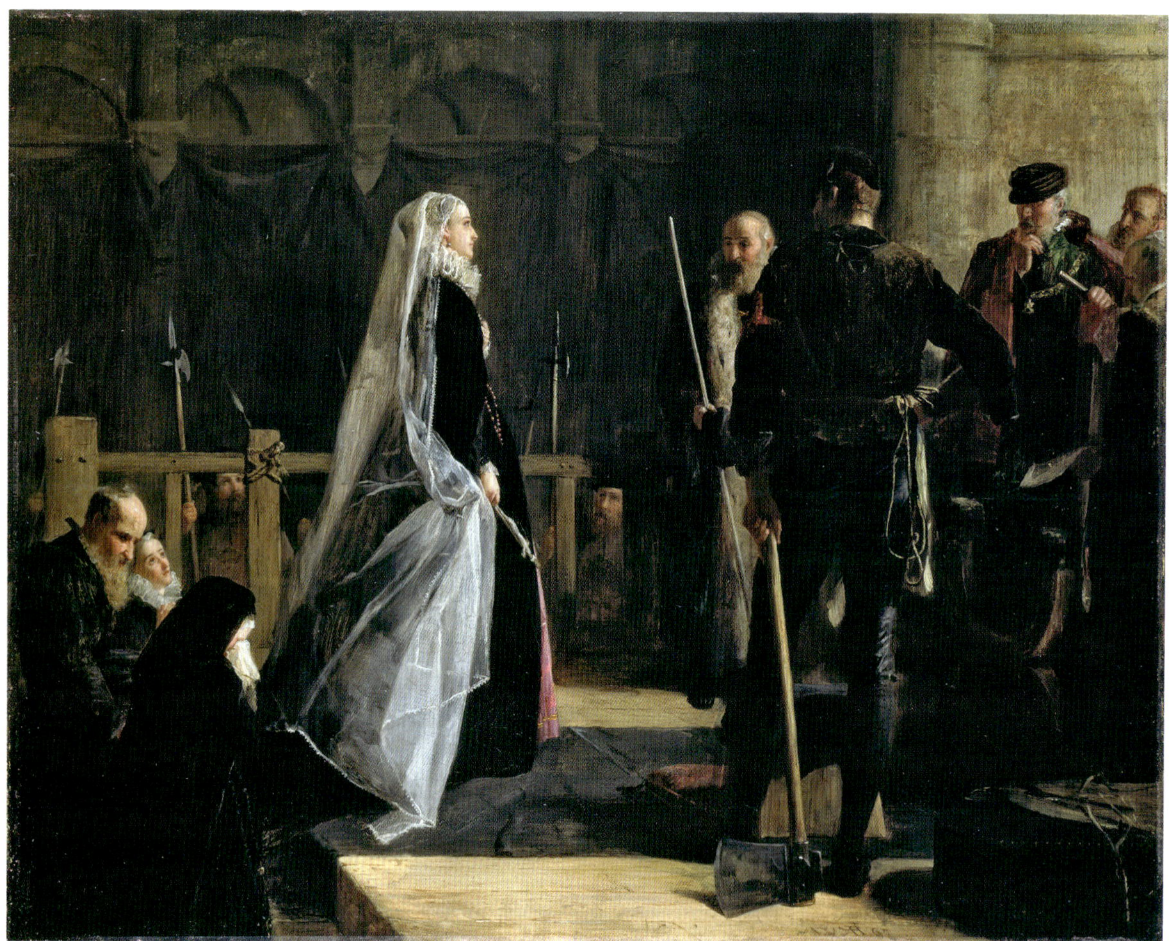

12 Robert Herdman, *The Execution of Mary, Queen of Scots*, 1867, Oil on canvas, 74.9 x 95.3 cm. Kelvingrove Art Gallery and Museum, Glasgow

apartment so famous in Scottish story as the scene of the assault upon the unfortunate Italian in the presence of the Queen', visitors are informed that 'every one whose imagination is at all vivid will here easily realise the particulars of that terrible event.' Mary's singularly eventful, and indeed tragic, life clearly had a great appeal to vivid imaginations. In nineteenth-century Edinburgh those imaginations were fed with what can best be described as cultivated visual 'fictions.' The equivalent late-Romantic response to Elizabethan England was generally fed not by narrow reference to the Queen but to the broad cultural achievement of her reign. It was not Elizabeth who fired Victorian imaginations, but Elizabethans.

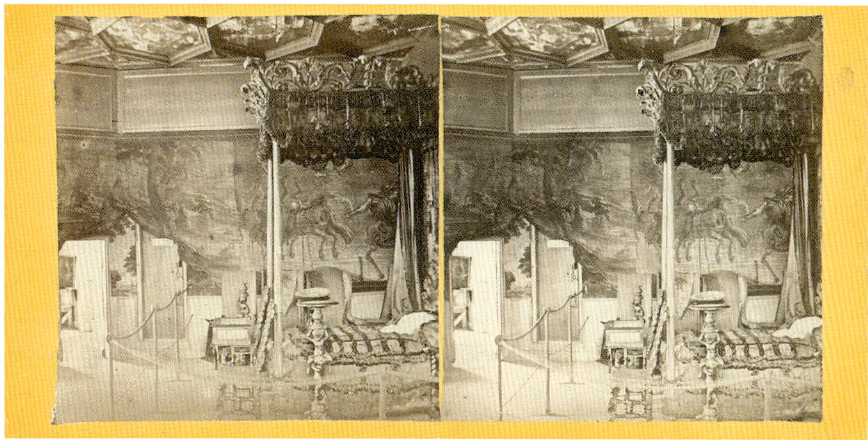

13 Late 19th-century stereoscopic photograph of Mary Stuart's Bedroom, Holyrood House. Private collection

THE SEA DOGS

John Everett Millais exhibited his picture *The Boyhood of Raleigh* (fig.14) in the newly opened galleries at the Royal Academy in Piccadilly in the summer of 1870. A contemporary critic wrote expressing the deep approbation shared by many of that summer's visitors:

> The work glows in the warm light of a Devonshire sun, and shows the sunburnt, stalwart Genoese sailor – one of those who were half pirates, half heroes, such as Kingsley has delighted countless boys by describing – seated, with his brawny, bronzed shoulders towards us, on a sea wall, while before him, and at ease upon the floor, are Raleigh and his brother, listening eagerly and with rapt ears to the narration of wonders on sea and land.[34]

Given Millais's limited intellectual prowess, it might surprise us to recognise how very *literary* his picture is.[35] The great feats of English seamanship in Elizabeth's reign had recently been celebrated in James Anthony Froude's *History of England from the Fall of Wolsey to the Defeat of the Spanish Armada* (12 volumes, 1856–1870). Froude had earlier singled out Raleigh's achievements as a navigator and explorer in his essay 'England's Forgotten Worthies' published in the *Westminster Review* in 1852, an essay which directly shaped the subject of *The Boyhood of Raleigh*. This essay had also inspired Froude's brother-in-law, Charles Kingsley, to write his swashbuckling anti-Catholic novel *Westward Ho!* in 1855. A series of narratives therefore lie both behind and parallel to Millais's painting. Significantly too, the picture itself contains an implied but unspoken narrative. This is usefully defined by an imaginative early critic of Millais:

> The sailor points to the southward, for there lies the Spanish main, the scene of all his troubles, and adventures. The young Walter sits up on the pavement, and with his hands locked about his raised knees, and with fixed, dreaming eyes, seems to see El Dorado, the islands of the east and west, the 'palms and temples of the south,' as well as the Mexican and other monarchs he had read about. Ships, gold, the hated Spaniards, and (most brilliant of all) that special object of his life's endeavours, the 'fountain of youth,' were before his fancy. The other, whose intelligence is not of the vision-seeing sort, but rather refers to the visions of others, lies almost at length on the ground leaning his chin within both hands. A toy ship stands near the boys. The scene includes a low pier or wall, as of a battery looking on to the sea, which, shimmering and barred with delicate hues of blue and green, reflects on a sunny sky. At the feet of the group lie a starfish, seaweed, a rusty anchor, and waste of the beach, with some stuffed birds of outlandish sorts and bright plumage, and dry flowers.

As ever in Millais's painting, artefacts carry considerable symbolic weight. One of the exotic 'stuffed birds' has, for instance, been identified as a toucan, a bird native to tropical South America.[36] These dead birds are not, as some commentators have seen them, emblems of Raleigh's ultimate tragic fate, but the kind of exotic trophy brought back by sixteenth-century adventurers. They are also precisely the kind of specimen preserved by nineteenth-century naturalists (one has only to think of Darwin's famous finches). Millais, who used two of his own sons as the models for Raleigh and his brother, painted his picture in south Devon, close to Raleigh's ancestral home. He was not merely expressing an historical, topographical and zoological 'truth' in his image; he was also very consciously linking himself and his own family to a resonant past. Raleigh and his brother are shown responding to an Elizabethan adventure narrative; the Millais brothers are therefore not merely reflecting historical experience, they are projecting it forward into the nineteenth century.

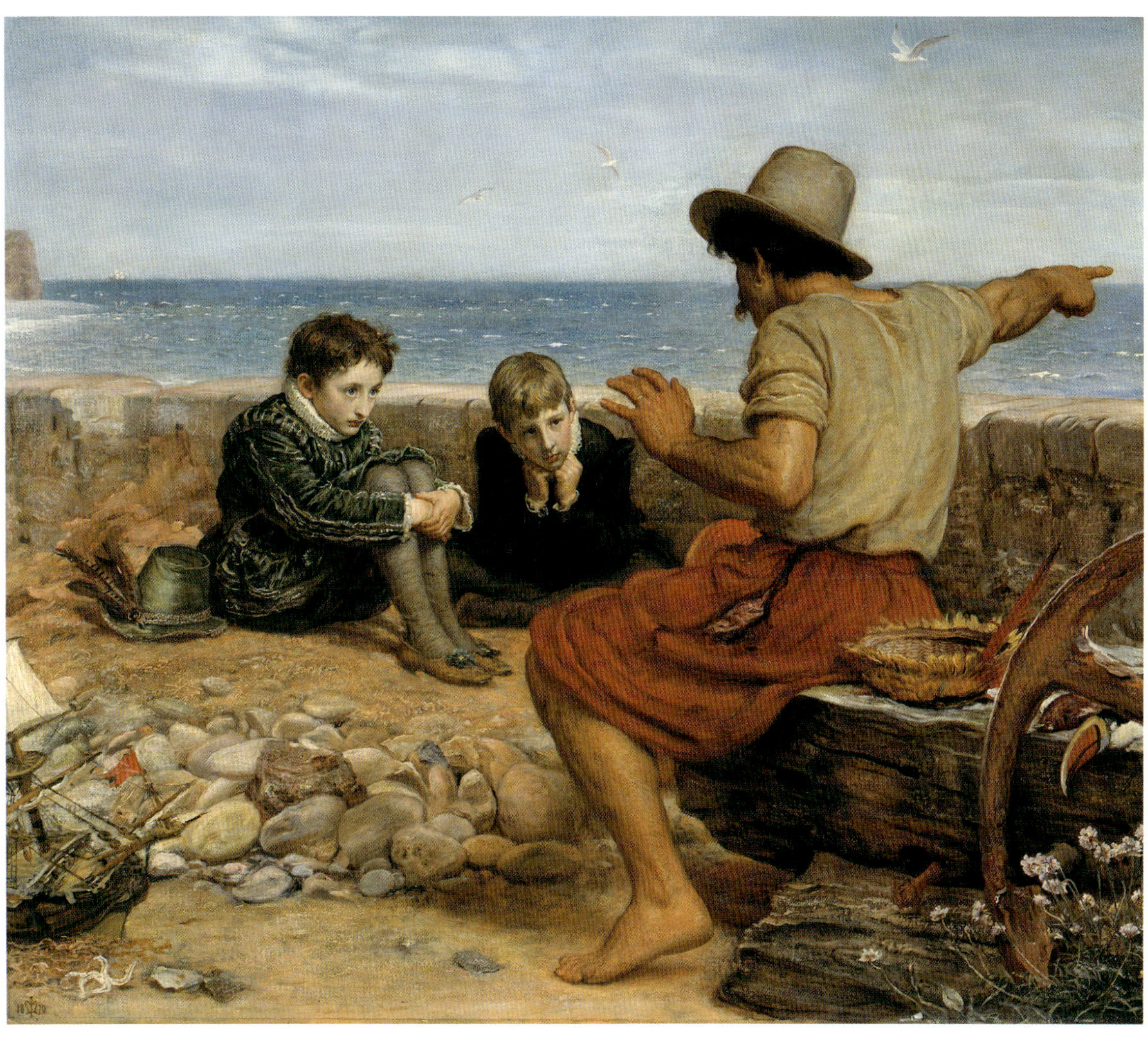

14 John Everett Millais, *The Boyhood of Raleigh*, 1870, Oil on canvas, 120.6 x 142.2 cm. Tate, London

There is no room for nostalgia here, and no sense of a *lost* adventurousness The Spanish Main, El Dorado and the threat of the Armada may by 1870 have become the stuff of history. New frontiers, new Darwinian knowledge and new empires were, however, very much modern preoccupations. As Charles Kingsley had also suggested in his novels, there were new foes a-plenty out there in the wide world, and many of them had old faces.

Froude's 'Forgotten Worthies' and his vast *History of England* were unequivocally written from the point of view of the victor. Froude was determined to substantiate the thesis that 'the greatest achievement in English history' had been the 'breaking of the bonds of Rome' and 'the establishment of spiritual independence.' His central heroes are not, however, courtiers or churchmen but the determinedly Protestant seamen, many of them Devonians, who fought to establish English supremacy in the Atlantic. Froude, who was himself Devonian by birth, was not necessarily expressing a narrow provincial pride. The wholesale transformation of sixteenth-century England had been forged by ordinary Englishmen, and by English seamen in particular. In his 'Forgotten Worthies' he had praised the Elizabethan navigator Richard Hakluyt's *Voyages* as 'the Prose Epic of the modern English nation,' and he directed his readers' attention to simple, upright epic heroes of relatively humble birth. Hakluyt's book, he believed, described something akin to 'the day of the apostles,' a vital period in which the central actors were 'men of the people – the Joneses, the Smiths, the Davises, the Drakes.'[37] Even that quintessential courtier Raleigh had been better remembered for his chivalrous act of throwing his cloak over a puddle in front of his Queen rather than for his exploits as a colonial pioneer and seeker for El Dorado. Froude's 'apostolic' Elizabethan sailors were, he believed, worthy to be remembered and they were best evoked imaginatively as living figures:

> The high name of these men [Raleigh, Drake and Hawkins], and the high objects which they pursued, will only rise out and become visible to us as we can throw ourselves back into their times and teach our hearts to feel as they felt.[38]

Here then is the key to Millais's picture: the Millais boys, like the Joneses, the Smiths and the Davises, are the living embodiment of the doughty champions of liberty who once faced down fanatic Spaniards and the wily Jesuits who encouraged their religious fanaticism. Reflecting on the old mission, they inspirit the modern one. The gesturing old sailor sitting on the seashore in *The Boyhood of Raleigh* is not merely firing the boys' imaginations; he is, in a sense, calling them just as Jesus called his first disciples by the Sea of Galilee. The divine call is meant to resonate into the nineteenth century.

In common with other commentators Froude sharply criticises the policies and motives of Elizabeth and her courtiers (the Queen's 'despotism' was, for example, 'as peremptory as that of the Plantagenets').[39] In the *History* he describes Elizabeth's whole conduct as 'saturated with artifice, and the performance was as poor as the object was paltry.' The Queen was, moreover, 'too clever to be simple and straightforward' and she 'never chose a straight road when a crooked one was open to her.'[40] Froude will, however, brook no criticism of his sea-faring heroes and he scrupulously defends the virtues of Drake and Hawkins, Grenville and Raleigh even when their enterprise might readily be dismissed as piracy, or at best officially sanctioned privateering. Froude's prejudices are clearly spelt out in the swellingly patriotic opening of his eighth volume (published in 1863):

> In the English nature there were and are two antagonistic tendencies – visible alike in our laws, in our institutions, in our religion, in our families, in the thoughts and actions of our greatest men: a disposition on the one hand to live by rule and precedent, to distrust novelties, to hold to the experience of the past as a surer guide than the keenest conclusions of logic and to maintain with long reverence the customs, the convictions, and traditions which have come down to us from other generations: on the other hand, a restless impetuous energy, inventing, expanding, pressing forward into the future, regarding what has been already achieved only as a step, a landing-place leading upwards and onwards to higher conquests – a mode of thought which in the half-educated takes the form of a rich disdain of earlier ages, which in the best and wisest creates a sense that we shall be unworthy of our ancestors if we do not eclipse them in all they touched, if we do not draw larger circles round the compass of their knowledge, and extend our power over nature, over the world, over ourselves.[41]

The English therefore have a destiny and a God-given mission. That mission, having first been defined by the sixteenth-century Reformation settlement and by the antagonism of Catholic Spain, was now to be re-defined in the nineteenth century. The essence of the mission was to promote the virtues of universal progress and to brook no opposition from those who were viscerally opposed to change.

As Charles Kingsley observed in his review of the first two volumes of Froude's *History* in 1856, the work had been written against the background of a Romanticised pro-Catholic view of the Reformation. Such sentiments, Kingsley believed, represented 'an utterly un-English tone of thought:'

> It suited the sentimental and lazy liberality of the last generation to make a show of fairness by letting the Popish historian tell his side of the story, and to sneer at the illiberal old notion that gentlemen of his class were given to be rather careless about historical truth when they had a purpose to serve thereby.[42]

Here is Kingsley, the doughty Protestant, identifying 'truth' with his own religious perspective. Opposition has to be swept aside, and infamy crushed. Throughout his career as a writer Kingsley was acutely aware that he was surrounded by what he saw as duplicitous foes, and these foes were generally to be identified with Roman Catholics abroad and with John Henry Newman and Anglo-Catholic sympathisers at home. For him sixteenth-century history was particularly vivid because it was a period when the gloves appeared to be off and religious antagonisms were raw. It was in reaction against the 'lazy liberality' of Catholic apologists that Kingsley began his novel *Westward Ho!* in 1854 (he was staying in Torquay at the time).[43] Like Froude's, Kingsley's Protestant patriotism had a distinctively Devonian accent. *Westward Ho!* is set in the south-west of England and on the Spanish Main in 'the reign of her most glorious majesty Queen Elizabeth.' The narrative veers between refined evocations of landscapes (both familiar and exotic) and what the novelist freely admitted was 'bloodthirstiness.' This was a book addressed to the youth of England fired by the Crimean War and it was written, Kingsley insisted, 'to make others fight' because it contained 'doctrine profitable for these times.' It was, in short, 'just what the times want.'[44] Kingsley's 'doctrine' consists of a fictionalised explication of the idea that the challenge to Spanish power and the defeat of the Armada were just as providential, and morally justified, as Israel's crushing of the Amalekites or the Philistines. Modern Spain, bereft of its gold and its colonies, was scarcely viewed as a threat to Victorian England, but despotic Russia, with its greedy eyes on British India, presented a palpable challenge. But enemies, as Kingsley's novel implies, are not merely ancient and external. In *Westward Ho!* Amyas Leigh and his companions in arms are represented in terms of Biblical heroism: they fight because they believe they have a severe Protestant God on their side and because they oppose themselves to a superstitious and alien enemy. The real and lasting danger to England is, as Kingsley's novel also implies, a devilishness of far greater subtlety. Amyas Leigh has a Jesuit kinsman, Eustace, and Eustace is presented as typical of those men, past and present, who are enslaved by an 'utterly un-English tone of thought.' Like Newman in the nineteenth century, the sixteenth-century Eustace has given his allegiance to an alien faith and to a foreign potentate, and espoused Catholic darkness over Protestant light and defunct traditionalism over progress. Eustace may be an old foe, but his various progeny still threaten the steady advance of liberal Britain.

Here then lies the key to Victorian responses to Elizabethan England and its historic resistance to Spanish domination. England had seen off the threat to its independence in 1588 thanks to the Drakes, the Raleighs, the Grenvilles and their nameless 'forgotten' companions. The victory of those 'heroes' was not transitory but a fundamental statement of an 'Englishness' which was insistently Protestant and progressive. Froude and Kingsley were far from lone voices in their emphasis on this redefinition of England and the English (let alone of Britain and Britishness). Take for example Tennyson's patriotic 'Ballad of the Fleet', 'The Revenge' published in the journal, the *Nineteenth Century*, in March 1878. The poem proved to be hugely popular. Tennyson's cue was Froude's historical writing, much as Froude had inspired both Millais and Kingsley. Froude had, somewhat pre-emptively, declared that Sir Richard Grenville's recklessness in pitting the unsupported *Revenge* against the might of the Spanish fleet in the Azores had 'struck a deeper terror … into the hearts of the Spanish people [and] dealt a more deadly blow upon their fame and moral strength than the Armada itself.'[45] Tennyson finds this recklessness unequivocally heroic. The rashly intrepid Grenville thus addresses the wary English Admiral, Lord Thomas Howard:

> I've ninety men and more that are lying sick ashore.
> I should count myself the coward if I left them, my Lord Howard,
> To these Inquisition dogs and the devildoms of Spain.

Grenville, deserted by Howard's ships, embarks his sick men (in order to save them from the Spanish Inquisition) and fights alone until his mortal wounds and the damage to his ship preclude further resistance:

And the stately Spanish men to their flagship bore him then,
Where they laid him by the mast, old Sir Richard caught at last,
And they praised him to his face with their courtly foreign grace;
But he rose upon their decks, and he cried:
'I have fought for Queen and Faith like a valiant man and true;
I have only done my duty as a man is bound to do:
With a joyful spirit I Sir Richard Grenville die!'
And he fell upon their decks, and he died.

Here, as Tennyson well knew, was an act of extravagant heroism as admirable as that of the Greeks at Thermopolae and as futile as that of the Light Brigade at Balaclava. When the poet read the poem to Thomas Carlyle, that definer of nineteenth-century heroics, Carlyle, with his eye to an inconvenient truth, remarked: 'I knew that Alfred would treat that episode in a masterful manner, and he'd not allude to Elizabeth's starving the poor sailors.'[46]

Some three years earlier Tennyson had risked one other foray into Tudor history. This was *Queen Mary,* the first play in what he was to style his 'historical trilogy' (the trilogy was later to include *Harold* and *Becket*). As we might expect, *Queen Mary* was written under the *aegis* of Froude though Tennyson also appears to have read widely in order to prepare himself for the composition of what he saw as a 'chronicle play'.[47] Tennyson's son remarked of his father's choice of subject: 'In few ages of the Christian era can the words "I come not to bring peace but a sword" have been more sorrowfully verified than in the life of Mary Tudor.' The play explores Mary's royal arrogance and religious narrowness and it treats her unrequited and unfulfilled love for Philip of Spain with some sympathy; but its real heroine is Princess Elizabeth who, as she is proclaimed Queen in the closing scene, promises to 'make England great.' Tennyson, whose play otherwise suggests that he is firmly in the Protestant progressive camp, nevertheless leaves us at the end with a tableau which strikes a note of deep ambiguity:

Enter PAGET, and other LORDS OF THE COUNCIL. SIR RALPH BAGENHALL etc.

LORDS
God save Elizabeth, the Queen of England!
BAGENHALL
God save the Crown: the Papacy is no more.

Paget (*aside*)

Are we so sure of that?

Acclamation

God save the Queen!

This was not necessarily an ambiguity that disturbed the many distinguished admirers who wrote to Tennyson to congratulate him on his achievement. Amongst these admirers were Robert Browning ('I see nowhere the shade of a fault'), W. E. Gladstone ('you have struck a note for the nation') and, unsurprisingly, Froude who asserted that the poet-dramatist 'had struck a more fatal blow than a thousand pamphleteers and controversialists' and had 'reclaimed one more section of English history from the wilderness and given it a form in which it will be fixed for ever.' Froude then added words which must have given Tennyson the most profound satisfaction: 'No one since Shakespeare that is.'[48]

The Bard and Victorian Bardolatry

Factual details of William Shakespeare's life are notoriously thin and, despite considerable efforts on the behalf of biographers, we certainly have no record of his meeting Queen Elizabeth. This did not prevent fond Victorian commentators from inventing a lost page of history by making the assumption that Good Queen Bess could not possibly have ignored a playwright who, in the minds of future generations, was the most eminent of her subjects. Ford Madox Brown had, after all, famously painted a picture of Chaucer reading the *Canterbury Tales* to Edward III (1856–68, Tate), cheerfully ignoring the fact that Edward was dead before Chaucer even began his *Tales*. Imaginative inventiveness has proved to be far from dead even in the late twentieth century: the romantic film *Shakespeare in Love* (1998) includes a deeply improbable scene in which the Queen arrives *incognito* at the Globe Theatre. One wonders how, of all monarchs in English history, Queen Elizabeth could ever have gone anywhere *incognito*, let alone in her lumbering state coach to a public theatre in the *louche* Bankside.

As Samuel Schoenbaum wonderfully demonstrates in his *Shakespeare's Lives* (1970) the first half of the nineteenth century had a particular fondness for imaginative constructions of Shakespeare's lost life. In C. A. Somerset's play *Shakspeare's Early Days*, first performed as *The Life of William Shakspeare* at Covent

Garden in 1829, the role of the aspiring Bard was acted by Charles Kemble. The play makes much of Shakespeare's enforced departure from Stratford after the deer-poaching episode at Charlecote (fig. 15). Penniless in London, the would-be dramatist bemoans his state in lines he will later allot to Hamlet, but is rescued from penury and neglect by the Earl of Southampton (whose life he has fortuitously saved when the Earl's horse bolts). In the last scene, Queen Elizabeth, flushed with the news that the Armada has been defeated, hangs a portrait of herself around the neck of 'England's noblest bard.' The sagacious Queen shows great prescience here for, as far as we know, in 1588 Shakespeare had not yet begun his career as a playwright.[49] Similar liberties were to be taken by novelists, all of them now probably justly forgotten. In Emma Severn's *Anne Hathaway: or, Shakspeare in Love* (1845) the young poet recognises Anne as his Muse, but finds that the course of true love does not run smooth. Complications, both legal and accidental, mar the wooing of this faithful swain, the most unlikely of which is Edmund Spenser's rival passion for Anne, briefly conceived at a Shottery sheep-shearing feast. There is yet greater invention in Robert Folkstone Williams's trilogy, *Shakespeare and his Friends; or 'The Golden Age' of Merry England* (1838), *The Youth of Shakspeare* (1839) and *The Secret Passion* (1844). At times the fiction topples over into travesty. In the first novel the Stratford schoolboy finds a patron in a discriminating landowner who rejoices in the name of Sir Marmaduke de Largesse. Sir Marmaduke not only opens his library to the boy, he also takes him to see the Queen at Kenilworth. Here, the Queen is so impressed by the boy's precocious talents that she presents him with a gold coin. Later in the story, after the debacle at Charlecote, Shakespeare leaves for London and is arrested by a constable who mistakes him for Mary, Queen of Scots (who has apparently disguised herself as a man in order to escape from her confinement). Long-awaited triumph comes when *Romeo and Juliet* is rapturously received by its first London audience ('Who wrote this play?' someone shouts. 'An' it please you, I wrote this play,' Shakespeare announces as he steps onto the stage). The wonderful preposterousness of Robert Williams's invention reaches its apogee in the *The Secret Passion*, set largely in Stratford during Shakespeare's retirement. Town gossip reports that the now aged Shakespeare was such a success in London that Queen Elizabeth 'would have had him right willingly to have been her husband, had he not already a wife of his own.' That, however, was not the Bard's 'secret passion.' *He* was Mr. W. H., William Herbert, 'the representative, image, and second self' of his mother, Mary Sidney, the Countess of Pembroke.

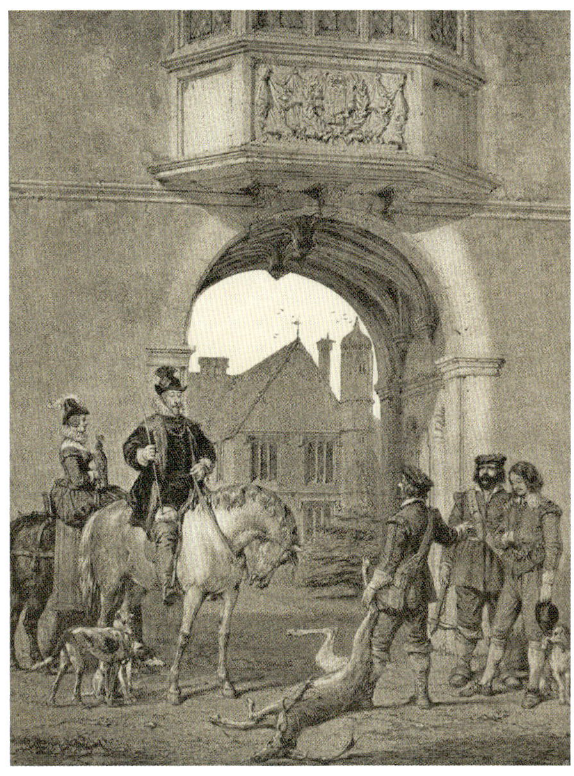

15 'Charlcote. The Young
Shakespeare Caught
Poaching A Deer', lithograph
illustration in *The Mansions
of England in the Olden Time*
by Joseph Nash, 1839.
Private collection

Shakespeare had apparently been requested by the good Countess to accompany
her son on a Grand Tour of Europe. Thus Williams neatly accounts for
Shakespeare's European sophistication (including, presumably, his working
knowledge of the sea-coast of Bohemia). Interestingly, too, he explains the
dedication of, and the passion within, the *Sonnets*.[50] We cannot tell whether or
not Oscar Wilde was aware of Williams's novels, but the charged speculations
about 'Willie Hughes' contained in Wilde's *The Portrait of Mr. W. H.* (1889) were
not completely without fictional precedent.

It was the Victorians who, with some real success, invented 'Shakespeare's
England'. They also attempted to re-invent Shakespeare but in that, as the
novels by Severn and Williams suggest, they signally failed. Unlike the Queen,
or Drake or Raleigh, Shakespeare, 'the soul of the age,' was patently, as Ben
Jonson had properly observed in 1623, 'alive still.' For Jonson, Shakespeare
lived while his 'book' lived, and each subsequent century since the publication

of the First Folio has had to rediscover that 'book,' both as a series of play-scripts and as 'literature'. Though many tried, the man Shakespeare was not easily re-made in the form and image of a Victorian man of letters. Take, for example, Thomas Carlyle in the third of his lectures on Heroes and Hero-Worship delivered in May 1840:

> Well: this is our poor Warwickshire Peasant, who rose to be Manager of a Playhouse, so that he could live without begging; whom the Earl of Southampton cast some kind glances on; whom Sir Thomas Lucy, many thanks to him, was for sending to the Treadmill: we did not account him a god like Odin, while he dwelt with us … In spite of the sad state Hero-worship now lies in, consider what this Shakspeare has actually been among us. Which Englishman we ever made, in this land of ours, which million of Englishmen, would we not give-up rather than the Stratford Peasant? … He is the grandest thing we have yet done. For our honour among foreign nations, as an ornament to our English Household, what item is there that we would not surrender rather than him? Consider now, if they asked us, Will you give up your Indian Empire or your Shakespeare? … Indian Empire will go, at any rate, some day; but this Shakspeare does not go, he lasts forever with us; we cannot give-up our Shakspeare![51]

Here then is the Victorian national treasure, a jewel in the Crown richer than India. Here too is the Bard cast romantically in the role of the impoverished rustic who rises above misfortune through the power of his genius. Shakespeare is like the peasant Robert Burns and, dare one say it, like Carlyle himself. Though he readily acknowledges that English speakers beyond the seas may soon outnumber the natives of Great Britain, Carlyle nonetheless yearns to possess the 'Hero-Poet' not only for the nation but also as a specific example for his own time.

For many Victorians the 'heroic' Shakespeare, and the texts of his plays, came most vividly to life in the popular illustrated editions published by the enterprising Charles Knight. As he had earlier done in his *Library of Entertaining Knowledge* (1829), in his *Penny Cyclopaedia* (1833-44) and in his *Pictorial History of England* (1837-44) Knight strove to disseminate useful and improving information to as wide an audience as possible. His *Pictorial Shakspere*, first published in instalments between 1838 and 1841, offered readers richly illustrated, economically priced and readily accessible texts of the accepted Shakespeare canon, together with apocryphal material. Each play was provided with a brief textual and historical introduction and each was accompanied by at least one illustration drawn from the work of an eminent modern artist. *The Pictorial Shakspere* was aptly named and wildly successful. It ran through many editions, reaching its zenith in the sumptuous two-volume folio, *The Imperial Shakspere*, which appeared shortly after Knight's death in 1873. This final edition contained handsome engraved pictures of scenes from all of the plays by artists such as Daniel Maclise, W. P. Frith, Richard Dadd, C. R. Leslie, E. M. Ward and C. W. Cope, whose reputations had been established by the mid-century, and by prominent artists of the latter half of the century including W.Q. Orchardson, W.F. Yeames, H.S. Marks and Marcus Stone.

From the initiation of the project the *Pictorial Shakspere* included Knight's *William Shakspere: A Biography*. This popular and, to some degree, influential Life of the Bard first appeared in 1843 and was given a final revision in the early 1870s. Though it redeployed the sparse materials that had long been in the public realm, it supplemented them with new archival research and with speculations based on a personal visitation of sites supposedly familiar to Shakespeare. Knight even travelled to Scotland in order to investigate the evidence of a Shakespearian visit to the North, but his discoveries there proved to be negligible. Essentially Knight was attempting to give the general public a sense of the artist in his historical context, and he illustrated his text with facsimiles of documents, with maps and with explanatory drawings of monuments. All too often his presentation of character and context is little more than an imaginative reconstruction which veers headily towards the novelistic. Take, for example, his account of Queen Elizabeth holding court at Greenwich in 1587:

Elizabeth, the Queen, is now in her fifty-fifth year … The wrinkles of her face, oblong and fair, were, perhaps, not yet very marked. Her small black eyes … were pleasant even in her age. The hooked nose, the narrow lips, and the discoloured teeth, were, perhaps, less noticeable when Shakspere looked upon her in his early days. The red hair probably not false, as it afterwards was. The small hand and the white fingers were remarkable enough of themselves; but, sparkling with rings and jewels, the eye rested upon them. The young poet, who has been lately sworn her servant, has stood in the backward ranks of the presence chamber to see his dread mistress pass to chapel. The room is thronged with councillors and courtiers. The inner doors are thrown open, and the gentlemen pensioners, bearing their gilt battle-axes, appear in long file … The procession moves …[52]

It is a fantasy worthy of Hollywood. Although his frontispiece was an engraving of the Chandos portrait, the first picture acquired by the new National Portrait Gallery in 1856 (fig. 16), there are no other pictorial representations of Shakespeare the man. Indeed, apart from the facsimile illustrations in the text, the biographical section of the *Pictorial Shakspere* conspicuously lacked the rich steel engravings of paintings that appeared elsewhere. Given his sometimes extravagantly imaginative word-painting Knight evidently felt that he did not need them.

It is significant that most Victorian paintings of Shakespeare's characters, or of scenes from his plays, do not actually relate to the theatre. This may well have been a reaction against the elaborate productions mounted by W.C. Macready in the 1840s and by Charles Kean at the Princess's Theatre in the 1850s, the latter being particularly noted for the 'scholarly' richness of their costume and set-designs. Victorian artists may simply have chosen not to enter into competition with the stage while still finding it perfectly proper to select appropriate subjects from a 'national' poet.[53] Daniel Maclise's *The Play Scene in 'Hamlet'* (c. 1842, Tate), which Knight used as an engraved illustration, certainly shows a play, but it is, of course, the play within a play. Most of the reproduced artworks in Knight's *Imperial Shakspere* show scenes that might ordinarily have passed for examples of contemporary historical or narrative painting rather than as episodes from a drama. Knight also reproduced Maclise's *Scene from 'Twelfth Night'* (c. 1840, Tate) and his *Orlando and the Wrestler* (1855) as illustrations to their respective plays. Elsewhere, the two pictures that accompany *The Merry Wives of Windsor* (by George Clint and C. R. Leslie respectively) might well have served to pad out Nash's *Mansions of England* while C.W. Cope's *Wolsey at Leicester Abbey* has very little direct relevance to the text of Shakespeare's *Henry VIII*. Extraordinarily, the illustrations selected for *Julius Caesar* and *Antony and Cleopatra* are classical set pieces by the French artist Joseph Gérôme (who was much given to such scenes). The only vaguely 'Pre-Raphaelite' painting in *The Imperial Shakspere* is Arthur Hughes's *Ophelia* (1851–52, Manchester City Art Gallery). Given the 'star-status' accorded to Shakespeare by the founding Pre-Raphaelite Brothers, and given the public acceptance of their art by the early 1860s, this omission might surprise us. It is very likely, however, that no painting by Millais or Holman Hunt would have met with the conservative Knight's approval in the 1840s and that by the time that later editions of the *Pictorial Shakspere* appeared such pictures were no longer available for popular reproduction. Nonetheless, to twenty-first-century eyes, it is the Shakespearean emphasis in early Pre- Raphaelite art which is now most enduringly memorable. Millais's *Mariana* (1850-51, Tate), *Ferdinand lured by Ariel* (1849-50, Makins Collection), and, supremely, his *Ophelia* (1851-52, Tate) are now seen as prime examples of the symbiotic relationship of Shakespeare and Victorian high culture. Given the care with which Millais represented both the overgrown river-bank and the saturated dress that Ophelia is wearing as she drowns, we readily sense that nothing could be further from a stage representation. Indeed, Shakespeare's accounts of both Ophelia's death and of the abandoned Mariana tell us of off-stage events. Three other important early Pre-Raphaelite paintings, Walter Howell Deverell's *Twelfth Night* (1849-50, ex-Forbes Collection) and Holman Hunt's *Valentine Rescuing Sylvia from Proteus* (fig. 17) and *Claudio and Isabella* (1850-53, Tate) emphasise the weight of Shakespeare's influence over these key years in British painting. It is significant, however, that not one of these pictures attempts to show characters in anything resembling the costume of Shakespeare's own time.

Henry Wallis exhibited his *A Sculptor's Workshop: Stratford-upon-Avon, 1617* at the Royal Academy in 1857 (fig. 18). The painting, which shows the finishing touches being put to Shakespeare's monument for Stratford church, is now preserved in the collection of the Royal Shakespeare Company. This is appropriate, because the subject of the painting is a complete theatrical fiction. As far as we know, Shakespeare's monument was made in Southwark and not in Stratford, and the death mask, shown being held by Ben Jonson in the painting, was a pious fraud discovered in Germany in 1849. Moreover, the stone spire of Holy Trinity, Stratford, which appears through the open frontage of the workshop, was only added to the church in 1763 (it replaced an earlier wooden spire). Wallis, most famous for his *Death of Chatterton* (1855-56), was much drawn to representations of literary associations and literary events. He painted *In Shakespeare's House, Stratford-on-Avon* for Dickens's friend, John Forster, in 1854 (V & A) and in the same year exhibited *The Room in which Shakespeare was Born* and *The Font in which Shakespeare was Christened* (both untraced).[54]

It was in Stratford that the Victorian cult of Shakespeare came to be centred, especially so in the years succeeding the tercentennial celebrations of the Bard's

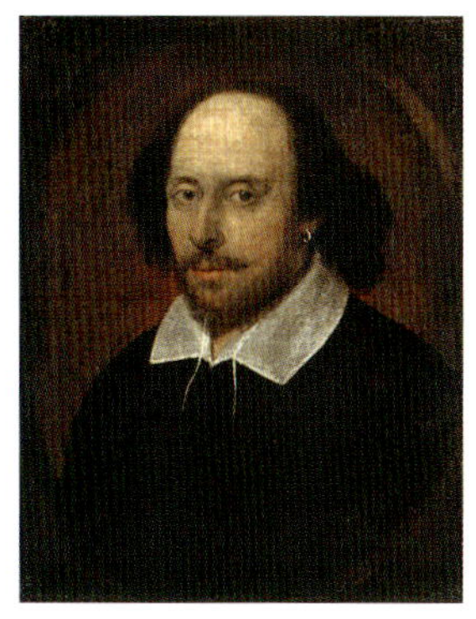

16 Attributed to John Taylor, *The Chandos William Shakespeare Portrait*, *c*1600s, Oil on canvas, 55.2 x 43.8 cm. National Portrait Gallery, London

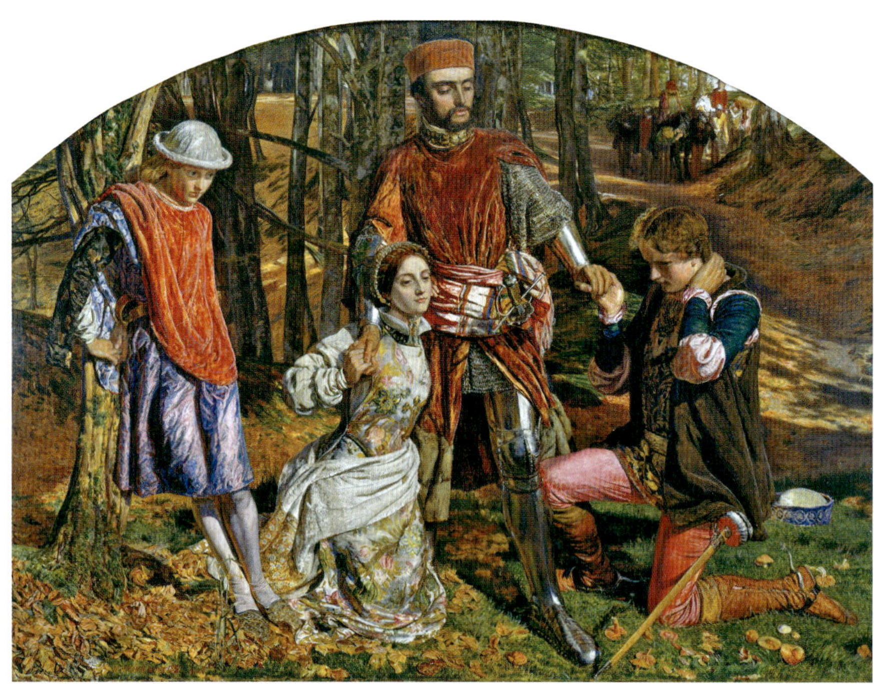

17 William Holman Hunt,
*Valentine Rescuing Sylvia
from Proteus*, 1851, Oil on
canvas, 98.5 x 133.3 cm.
Birmingham Museums
and Art Gallery

birth in 1864. The town came to be linked inseparably to the very name
'Shakespeare' in the national, and indeed the international, consciousness.[55]
David Garrick had belatedly celebrated the bi-centenary with a Jubilee held
in Stratford in a rainy September in 1769, but the town's corporation had never
given Garrick's project much support. 1864 was to be very different. A railway
had opened in 1860 and Stratford was now determined to prove that it could
host a celebration that would be as much national as it was local. As the Earl
of Warwick, who declined to offer his patronage, somewhat ineptly informed
the town's corporation, the event was likely to be 'a splendid affair' because a
recent Agricultural Show had already demonstrated 'what it could do on such
occasions.'[56] To ensure success, and to counter the likelihood of the kind of
inclement weather that had blighted Garrick's procession through the streets,
Stratford constructed a dodecagonal wooden Pavilion, capable of holding 5,000,
in a paddock on Southern Lane on the far side of the River Avon. The galleried
Pavilion contained both an orchestral space and a large stage screened by a
curtain showing an imagined statue of Shakespeare with Holy Trinity Church
in the background. There was a banquet in the Pavilion and a grand fireworks

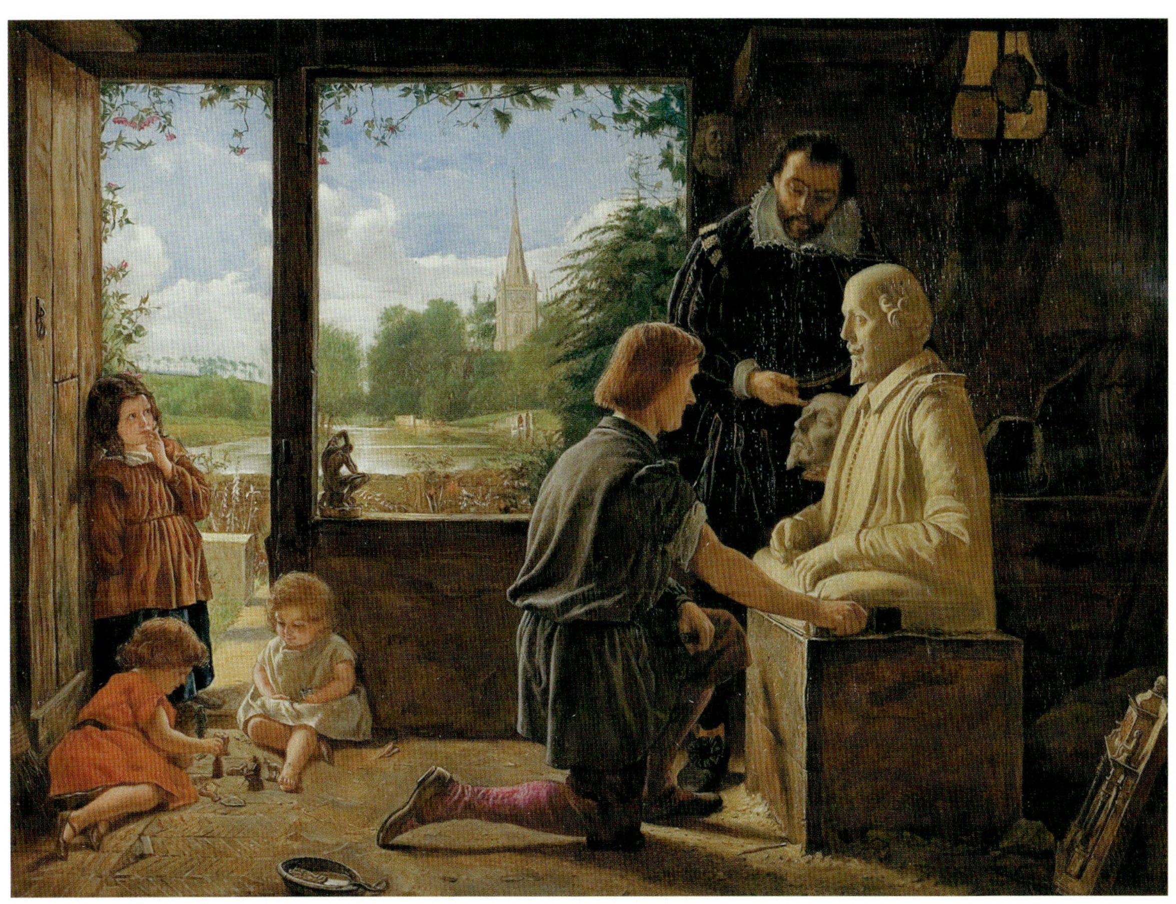

18 Henry Wallis,
*A Sculptor's Workshop:
Stratford-upon-Avon 1617*,
1857, Oil on canvas,
39 x 53cm. Royal
Shakespeare Company,
Stratford-upon-Avon

display on Shakespeare's birthday. On the following day, a Sunday, Archbishop Trench of Dublin preached what was reportedly an inaudible commemorative sermon ('Every now and then,' commented one member of the congregation, 'I heard the word Shakespeare'). In the Town Hall an extraordinary collection of paintings, including twenty-eight portraits of the Bard, was displayed, and on 25 April the Pavilion somewhat incongruously hosted a festive performance of Handel's *Messiah*, a work more naturally associated with national 'feel-good' factors than with Shakespeare. In the evening, however, a second concert featured music which either set Shakespeare's words or which had Shakespearean associations (though the concert included Beethoven's overture, *Coriolan*, which had no immediate connection with Shakespeare's play). The

Stratford celebrations ended on 29 April with a Grand Fancy Dress Ball attended by the Lord Lieutenant of Warwickshire and the town's mayor (both of whom wore their official robes rather than suffer the indignity of even fancier dress).[57]

Stratford's brave festivities were deemed a great success. Those in London, though ostensibly more various and ambitious, proved to be ill-organised and were received with far more mixed responses. Under the auspices of the National Shakespeare Committee, London theatres put on special performances of Shakespeare's plays and there were concerts and recitals at established metropolitan venues. At the Royal Agricultural Hall, for example, a colossal bust of Shakespeare, modelled by Charles Bacon, looked down on a 'Character Ball and Masque' and on a Festival Concert with 'Dramatic Readings'. As a more permanent domestic souvenir of the tercentenary, the Committee sponsored a memorial bust by F. M. Miller, which was reproduced in parian china and distributed through the Art Union of London. The main public event was, however, the planting on Primrose Hill of an oak sapling given by Queen Victoria. This ceremony came to be remembered for all the wrong reasons. On 23 April 1864 a procession left from Russell Square, led by the artist George Cruikshank dressed as Colonel of the Havelock Volunteers. When the procession arrived, late, at Primrose Hill a large crowd had already assembled, many of whom were members of the Working Men's Shakespeare Committee. Once the sapling had been placed in the ground in the name of 'the workmen of England,' and blessed with water from the River Avon, the solemn occasion was usurped by a rival popular demonstration celebrating not Shakespeare but the Italian patriot, Garibaldi (who had been obliged to leave England the day before). When a splinter group on the crest of the hill was told by a radical orator that Garibaldi's departure was the result of a conspiracy between Napoleon III and Lord Palmerston the assembly was abruptly, and unceremoniously, broken up by the police.[58] The Shakespeare Oak survived until 1958. It was replaced in 1964, without the threat of a complementary political demonstration, as part of the Shakespeare quartercentenary celebrations.

For commercial reasons Victorian Stratford-upon-Avon needed to keep Shakespeare's memory green far more than did London. It had suffered a major blow to its growing tourist potential in 1759 when New Place, the house Shakespeare had bought in 1597 and in which he died in 1616, was demolished by its disgruntled owner, the Revd. Francis Gastrell. Gastrell, who objected to paying taxes on a house in which he lived for only part of the year, ordered that it should be destroyed, much to the chagrin of his fellow Stratfordians. Although New Place had been reconstructed in the classical style in the early part of the eighteenth century it still attracted many curious sightseers. Having also insisted that 'Shakespeare's mulberry tree' in the garden should be cut down, the unloved Gastrell left the town (though the wood of the mulberry tree, bought by an enterprising watchmaker, was shaped into a multitude of souvenirs). The loss of New Place meant that Shakespeare's birthplace in Henley Street took on extra significance to pious Bardolaters. The great Jubilee procession through Stratford, organised by David Garrick in 1769, had duly marched in the rain down Henley Street. An engraving of the scene appeared on the binding and title page of Knight's *Imperial Shakspere* (fig. 19). Knight was very well aware of the significance of the Birthplace to his Victorian audience, indeed he devoted the last paragraphs of his biography to its history and included a gilt vignette of the building on the morocco-leather covers of his volumes. The house in Henley Street had remained in the hands

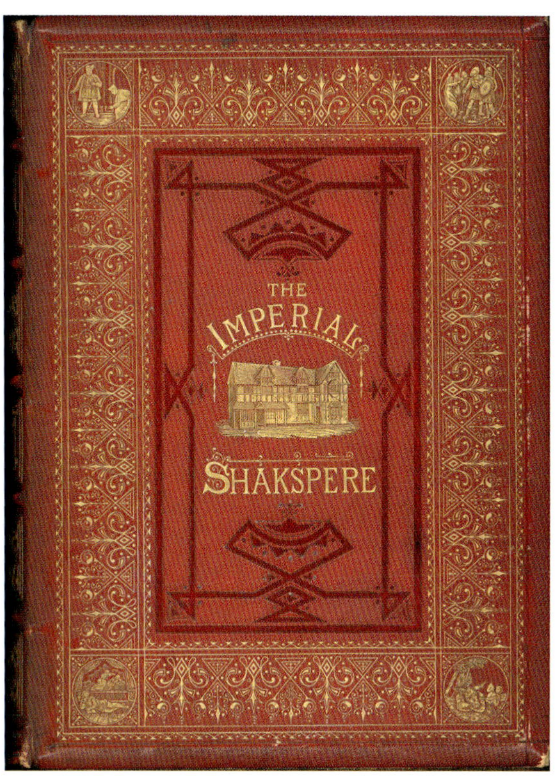

19 Binding to Volume I of *The Imperial Shakspere*, edited by Charles Knight, 1873, stamped with the Birthplace of the Bard.
Private collection

of the descendents of Shakespeare's sister Joan until the opening years of the nineteenth century, although in a state of semi-disrepair. It was visited amongst others by Keats (who signed both the visitors' book and the wall of the room where it was supposed Shakespeare had been born), by Sir Walter Scott and by Carlyle (who both scratched their names on the window-panes). Early in 1847 it was announced that the house was to be sold and, much to the horror of British patriots, the American showman, P. T. Barnum, put forward the proposal that he should buy it and ship its timbers to the United States. A public meeting was called at the Thatched House Tavern in St. James's St. in London and a 'Shakespeare Birthplace Committee' was duly formed, with Knight and John Forster as prominent members. The intention was to purchase the building but, there being a deficiency in the monies originally subscribed, various fundraising activities were launched. These included a Charity Performance at Covent Garden and public readings by the actor W. C. Macready. Charles Dickens, who was determined that the house should be established with an endowed curatorship (for his needy friend, the playwright James Sheridan Knowles), enthusiastically threw himself into organising amateur theatricals in London, Edinburgh and Glasgow in order to raise money. The Birthplace was finally purchased by the Committee in late 1847 and adjoining buildings (paid for by a separate subscription in Stratford) were added to the site. The Birthplace Committee, which would in due time become the Shakespeare Birthplace Trust, then embarked on a wholesale restoration which entailed the removal of the brick facades which had hitherto concealed much of the half-timbering. They also laid out the garden in a style which Charles Knight described as having 'pleasing associations, for its shrubs and flowers are those mentioned by Shakspere.' The Birthplace Trust was later to acquire other properties in and near Stratford which had associations with the Bard, most notably in 1892 the picturesque thatched and half-timbered Anne Hathaway's Cottage at Shottery.

The enterprise and energy of the Birthplace Trust in securing 'black-and-white' memorials to Shakespeare was perhaps typically Victorian. By their actions they not only firmly established Stratford-upon-Avon on the international tourist trail, they were also instrumental in helping to change how the English viewed their architectural heritage. Distinguished as it is Stratford is but one among many half-timbered English towns, and it could never have held its own as a centre of tourism when faced with the architectural competition of a Shrewsbury or a Tewkesbury, let alone a Strasbourg or a Nuremburg, without the *cachet* of Shakespeare's name. Possessed with that *cachet*, however, images of the Bard's Birthplace or of Anne Hathaway's thatched cottage came to represent a particular and precious vision of the English past. By the 1850s half-timbering, much of which had been concealed behind brick or stucco in the eighteenth century, was directly associated with the very notion of 'Merry England.' The public acquisition of buildings with Shakespearean associations seems to have begun the process of turning the tables on those connoisseurs and historians who had once rejected the Elizabethan style or who had denigrated the Queen after whom the period had been named. Stratford, and Stratford-style half-timbering, became a cynosure of Englishness. 'Elizabethan' was no longer just the style in which the mansions of the rich were built, it now was the birthright of everyman and his wife.

By the end of the century the actress Ellen Terry was typical of many middling men and women in seeking to retreat to a 'black-and-white' sixteenth-century house at Smallhythe in Kent, but she would probably have balked at the thought of acting in a wooden playhouse of the kind that

Shakespeare would have recognised. Indeed, when it was proposed to erect a permanent memorial to Shakespeare at Stratford in the 1870s in the form of a new theatre, no thought was given to constructing anything resembling the Globe. Thanks to the generosity of the brewer, Charles Flower, the first Shakespeare Memorial Theatre was designed by the architects William Unsworth and Edward Dodgshun in brick in the Gothic style, but with distinctly Elizabethan chimneys and half-timbered detailing. It boasted an enclosed auditorium with a chamfered proscenium arch, and the upper galleries were enclosed in pointed arches. It opened on the Bard's birthday in 1879 with a production of *Much Ado About Nothing*. The theatre burned down in 1926, but the Library and Art Gallery which were integral to its design survived, and indeed survive still.[59]

MERRY ENGLAND

The Elizabethan style had slowly begun to be rehabilitated throughout England soon after the 1847 acquisition of Shakespeare's Henley Street birthplace. This rehabilitation was in part a reaction against the severe strictures of the Gothic Revival. It was also part and parcel of a positive response to what was assumed to be English 'vernacular' architecture, the wooden-framed houses and cottages that were common in the southern, eastern and Midlands counties of England. Half-timbering, rather than the stone, brick or stucco fantasies which had been dismissed by the Goths, came to be seen by later Victorian generations as the normative rural setting for 'Merry England,' and the style became known by the shorthand term 'Old English.' The fashion for the cottage style, and for rural idylls associated with it, was further popularized by the delicate watercolours by Helen Allingham (1848-1926) and Myles Birket Foster (1825-1899). 'Old English' was an assertion of an idealised, pre-industrial England, a happy world where squire, yeoman and peasant had once collaboratively co-existed. According to this ideal, not only had all classes shared patterns of social intercourse, they had feasted communally on beef and ale thanks to the lordly bounty of the gentry. During the 1850s and 60s architects such as George Devey resurrected, and reconfigured the kind of brick and half-timbered cottage which he associated in particular with vernacular building in the counties of Kent, Surrey and Sussex. Devey used what he termed the 'Wealden' style for estate buildings at Penshurst between 1851 and 1871 and went on to employ it for grander country houses for the aspirant middle classes.[60] From Devey's example developed the far more assertive, and more sophisticated, houses designed by Richard Norman Shaw during the first phase of his varied career. Shaw's Leyswood in Sussex (1864-71), Merrist Wood in Surrey (1876-7), Cragside in Northumberland (1870-84) and Grim's Dyke at Harrow Weald near London (1870-2) are well-lit, irregular but sturdy brick or stone houses with substantial half-timbered features.[61] These houses could no longer claim a lineage with the stone or brick mansions, such as Kirby, Aston, Longleat, Wollaton, Charlecote or Burghley, which had so impressed early-Victorian connoisseurs. Shaw's houses make no pretence to emulate aristocratic mansions; they are overgrown manors, not prodigy houses, and they testify to comfort rather than to pomposity, to easy middle-class wealth rather than show.

Two years after his success with *The Yeomen of the Guard*, which ran for some four hundred and twenty-three performances in the autumn of 1888, W. S. Gilbert bought Shaw's Grim's Dyke at Harrow Weald (fig.20). The success of *The Yeoman of the Guard* seems to have given a new boost to Gilbert's collaborative partnership with Sir Arthur Sullivan, and it marked a turning away from work which, in one form or another, satirised modern whims and affectations. This was a historical comic drama which, as Gilbert explained to Sullivan, was 'a pretty story, no topsy turvydom, very human.' One cannot be certain whether or not the sixteenth-century setting of the latest Savoy Opera came to influence Gilbert's choice of architectural setting for his domestic life, though in fact nothing could in fact be further in atmosphere from the bleak fortifications of the Tower of London. Gilbert certainly made the most of his residence at Grim's Dyke for he not only lavishly entertained guests, he also added a spectacular alabaster chinneypiece to the hall. He was to die of a heart attack there following a mishap to one of his female guests in the lake in the garden in 1911. What really links the plot of *The Yeomen of the Guard* to the architecture of Grim's Dyke is that both are expressions of a new Victorian sensibility about the Elizabethan period. That new sensibility was often enhanced by the use of Tudor-rose-tinted spectacles, and it often provided cushioned escapes from the drab realities of the modern world. The threats once posed by the axe or the temperamental fickleness of a Tudor monarch now seemed utterly remote from nineteenth-century reality.

By the 1890s distance seems to have added a felicitous charm to any retrospect on the age of Elizabeth. Certainly, by the time that Edward German's two-act opera *Merrie England* opened at the Savoy Theatre in April 1902 Queen Elizabeth had forcefully emerged from her Victorian wilderness years into a new Edwardian sunlight. The opera, set in Windsor on May Day, may still characterise the Queen as peremptory and capricious, and as a woman who finds love and lovers elusive, but the contralto who plays her has one substantial aria accompanied by the chorus. That aria, 'O Peaceful England,' expresses all the imperial confidence of the first years of a new reign and a new century, but it does so by means of a retrospect to 'the olden times'.

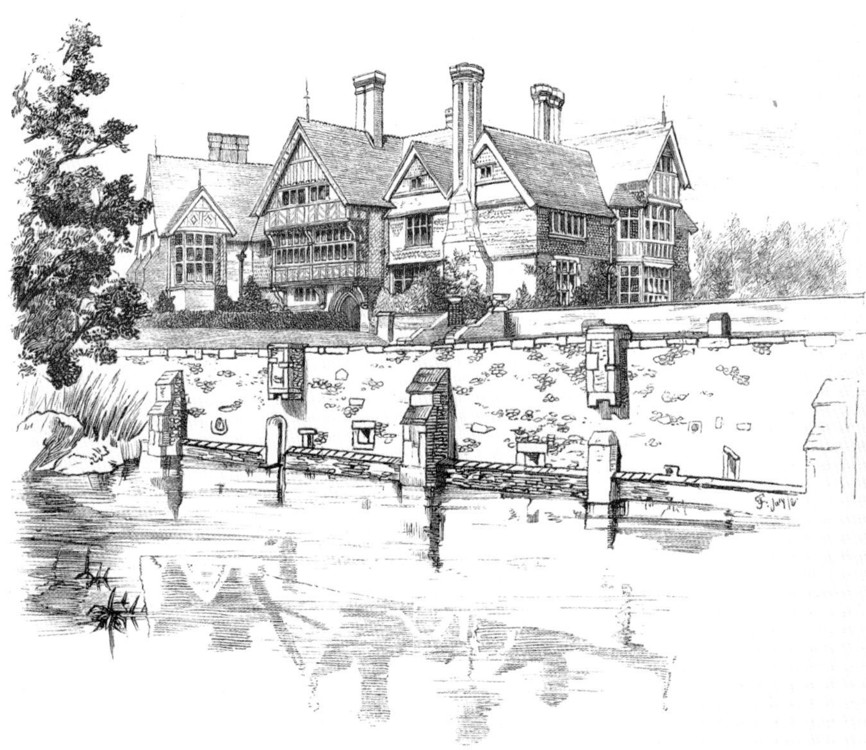

20 'Grim's Dyke', 1870-1872, illustration in *The Art Journal,* 1881

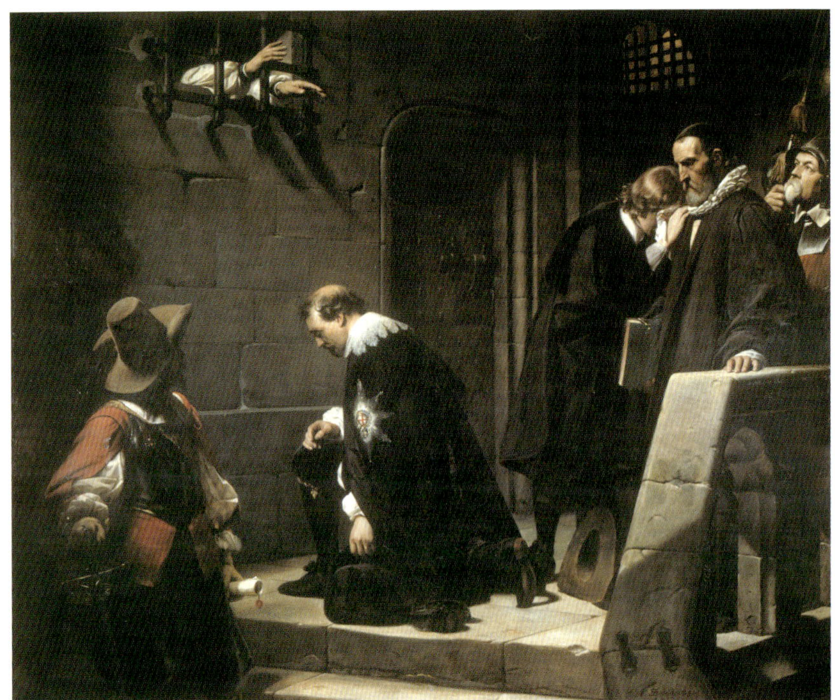

21 Paul Delaroche, *Strafford on his Way to Execution*, 1836, Oil on canvas, 249 x 310 cm. Private collection

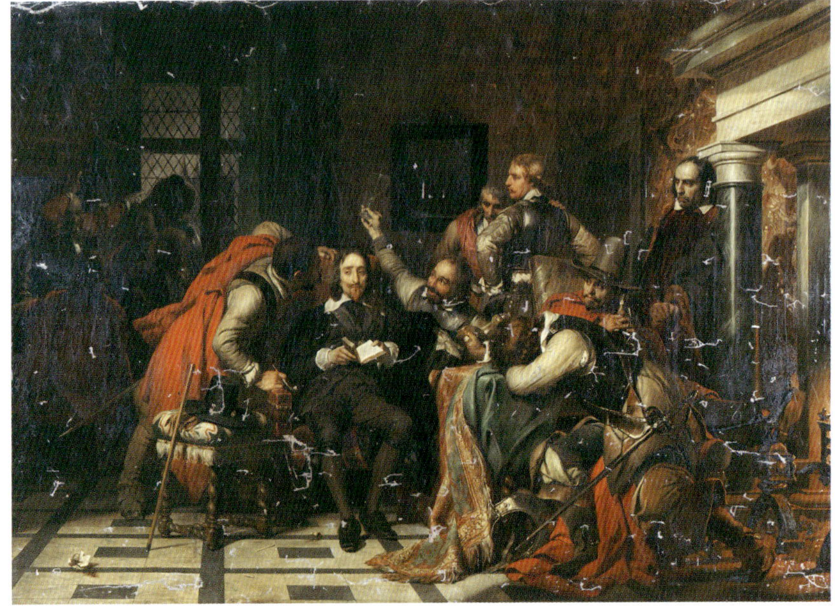

22 Paul Delaroche, *Charles I Mocked by Cromwell's Soldiers*, 1836, Oil on canvas, Oil on canvas, 284 x 392 cm. Scottish National Gallery (on loan from a Private Collection)

II

WHICH KING OR NO KING?

CHARLES I TO THE COMMONWEALTH

In 1836 the immensely rich second Duke of Sutherland purchased Paul Delaroche's monumental canvas showing *Strafford on his Way to Execution* (fig.21) from the painter's studio in Paris. In the same year Sutherland's brother, Lord Francis Egerton, commissioned a further painting from Delaroche with a tragic subject also drawn from seventeenth-century English history. Egerton's picture, *Charles I insulted by the Soldiers of Cromwell* (fig.22), was finished a year later and both pictures were exhibited together at the Paris Salon. Though the figure of the seated King Charles is clearly based on contemporary portraits by Van Dyke, the whole composition owes more to Renaissance representations of the mocking of Christ than to Van Dyke's habitual aggrandisements of the slightly built Charles as a heroic or divinely ordained monarch. The king is now slumped in his chair, distracted from devotional reading by carousing Roundhead soldiers, one of whom blows smoke in his face. An equal degree of historical research had gone into the costumes in *Strafford on his Way to Execution*. A hatless Strafford, in a black velvet cloak with a large Garter star embroidered on its shoulder, kneels before a high barred window through which the arms of Archbishop Laud stretch in a final blessing. Laud, vested in his Episcopal rochet, has evidently raised himself to the window with difficulty and his arms are strained as they hover over Strafford's head. One of the Earl's grieving supporters buries his head on the shoulder of an accompanying chaplain.[1]

Although he had earlier painted a series of sombre scenes from French history (*Joan of Arc in Prison* of 1825, *Le Cardinal Richelieu* of 1829 and *Le Cardinal Mazarin mourant* of 1830, all Wallace Collection), and he was memorably to portray *Marie-Antoinette before the Tribunal* in 1851 (Forbes Collection), Delaroche was steadily drawn to English history. He was, moreover, attracted to the darker side of that history and particularly to royal murders, royal executions, and royal confinements.[2] Delaroche possessed, as the critic Tardieu put it, an extraordinary ability to find subjects 'that attack the nervous system of the public.'[3] In the early twenty-first century his once despised and neglected *The Execution of Lady Jane Grey* (1834, National Gallery) again found itself the object of popular enthusiasm and academic esteem. When the huge, dramatic canvas was first exhibited in Paris it was not only greatly acclaimed by the public, but also earned its artist the title of Officier de la Légion d'Honneur. Its purchaser at the Salon, the young but vastly wealthy Russian Count Anatole Demidoff, paid 8,000 francs for the picture and transported it to his villa in Florence for his private delectation (though its reputation was fostered through engravings).[4] Other pictures from this fertile period of Delaroche's career also originally enjoyed vast international celebrity and commanded staggering prices. In 1843 the Marquis of Hertford had paid 4,500 francs for a version of the celebrated *Edward V and the Duke of York in the Tower* (Wallace Collection), the original of which, now in the Louvre, had been bought by the French state from the Salon of 1830 for the princely sum of 6,000 francs. In the same year the state commissioned the strikingly morose *Cromwell uncovering the Coffin of Charles I* (fig.23). Thanks to the influence of the great French historian and *homme d'affaires*, François Guizot, it was sent to Nîmes in 1834 where it was ceremonially displayed in the famous Roman temple, the Maison Carrée, which then functioned as the city's public art gallery.

The *Cromwell* uncannily caught the public mood when it was first exhibited at the Paris Salon in the summer of 1831. In the July of 1830 the last of the restored Bourbon kings, Charles X, had been toppled by a Revolution and driven into exile. The very name of 'Cromwell' carried symbolic weight. Forty years earlier, in the opening phase of the first French Revolution, both Mirabeau and Lafayette had been hailed as latter-day Cromwells (though no such comparison seems to have been drawn with Napoleon Bonaparte). Guizot, a Minister in Louis-Philippe's government, was acutely alert to parallels between English and French history and would later during his own exile write a considered study of seventeenth-century England. One French critic noted that Delaroche's painting had managed to reflect on 'a period like our own, in a century when the destinies of kings have been found to weigh little

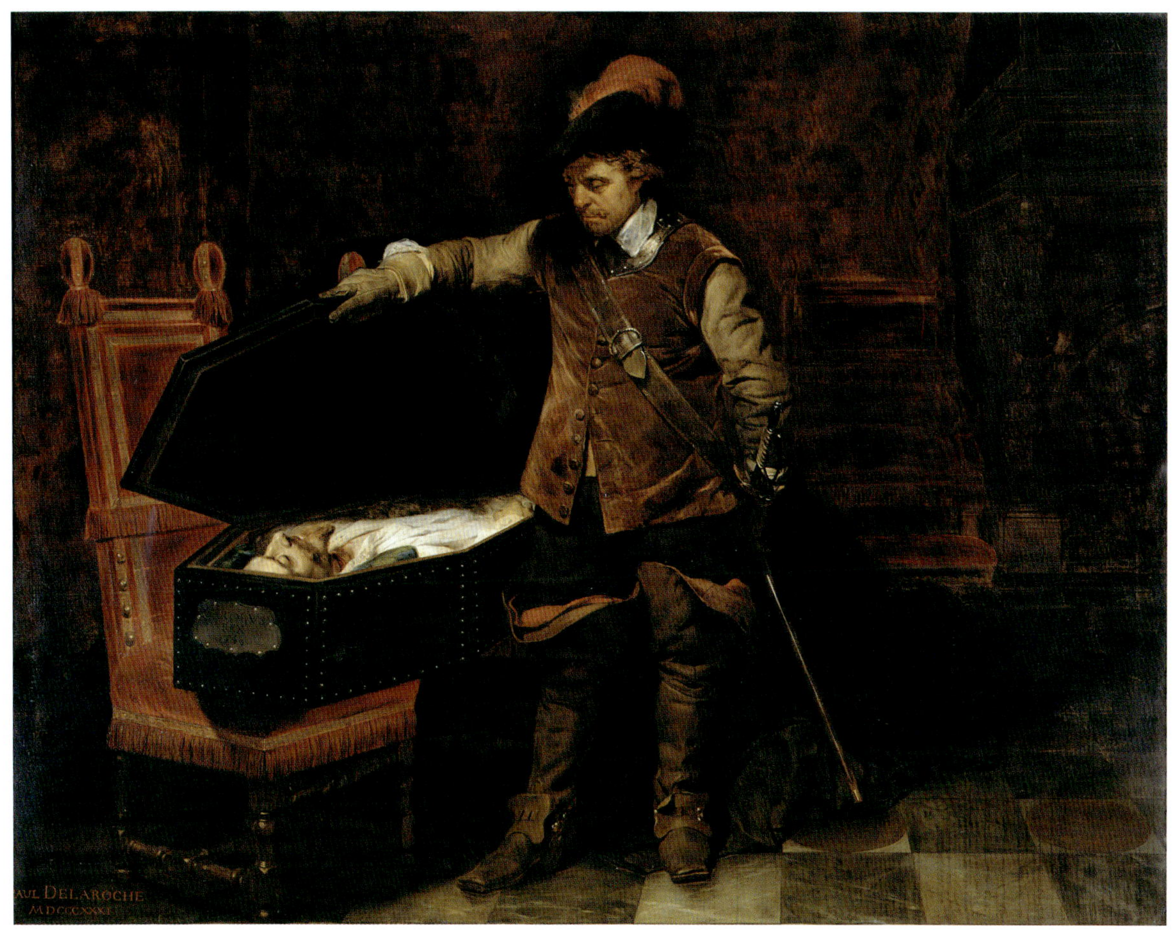

23 Paul Delaroche, *Cromwell Uncovering the Coffin of Charles I*, 1831, Oil on canvas, 230 x 300 cm. Musee des Beaux-Arts, Nimes, France

in the scales of the great interests of the people' and the German poet, Heinrich Heine, noted of the figure of Cromwell, as he stands contemplating Charles's decapitated corpse, that he was 'firm as earth, "brutal as fact", powerful without pathos, naturally supernatural, marvellously commonplace … beholding his work almost like a woodman who has just felled an oak.'[5] Nevertheless, when the Bourbon Kingdom had commissioned the *Cromwell* neither Charles X's ministers nor the painter had wind of the impending revolution. What Delaroche certainly knew, however, was that all of his paintings of English subjects had profound emotional and political ramifications in France. Having been born in Paris 1797, the painter must have been brought up surrounded by vivid and bloody memories of recent events in the first Revolution. He was also a well-read man, imbued in the reassessments of history in France that followed the Revolution and fascinated by the vastly popular fiction of Sir Walter Scott. Both Delaroche and his public would have recognized the ghosts of Louis XVI and Marie-Antoinette haunting the figures of the mocked Charles I and the submissive Lady Jane Gray on the scaffold. Were there not obvious, but subtle, parallels between the fate of the Princes in the Tower and the disappearance of the Dauphin in the Temple? Could not the executions of Strafford and Laud find echoes in the demise of so many distinguished men and women at the hands of the Revolutionary Tribunal?

The causes of the English Revolution in the seventeenth century, its bloody progress and its aftermath, carried not very complex codes by which the potentially Revolutionary nineteenth century could interpret itself. Those codes could be read on both sides of the Channel and well beyond the confines of the Paris Salon, Bridgewater House or the Villa Demidoff. Delaroche's international celebrity meant that the memorably exact images that he had created had a wide international circulation through the medium of engraving. Sorrowing royalists and triumphing republicans alike could draw both comfort and inspiration from them. The unjustly imprisoned, the politically marginalised and the victims of oppressive regimes could examine historical evidence from vastly different perspectives. Delaroche's paintings touched on raw nerves. Although, after the passage of two hundred years, the British were less starkly divided in their reading of the politics of their Civil War than the French were in their understanding of their Revolution, there were still real fissures in received opinion. The posturing of Cavaliers and Roundheads may have been reduced to the stuff of romance, but the trial and beheading of a King and his closest supporters, the old debates about the rights of Parliament and the rights of Man, the Cromwellian suppression of the Church of England, and the misery attendant on widespread civil dissention were vivid issues in the Victorian world-view. The wide, but often starkly divided, culture of the long seventeenth century had a particular currency for the Victorian century.

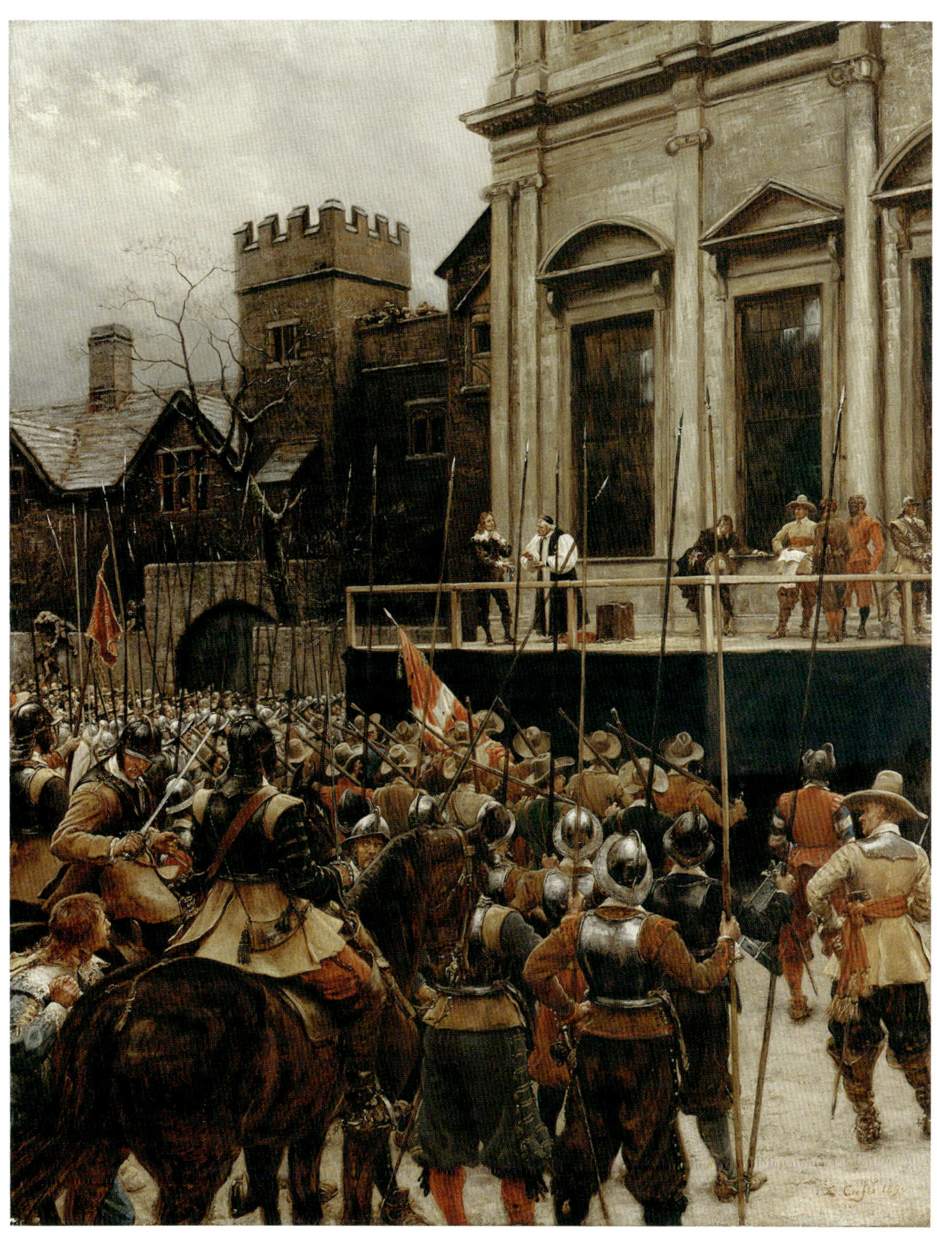

24 Ernest Croft,
*Whitehall, 30
January 1649*, 1890,
Oil on canvas,
68 x 129.5 cm.
Private collection

Inigo Jones and the Banqueting House

Ernest Croft's historical painting *Whitehall, 30 January, 1649* (fig.24) was completed in 1890. It shows a body of armed Cromwellian soldiers in a foreground that bristles with pikes. Behind them rises a largely fanciful view of the Tudor buildings of the old Whitehall Palace and the northern corner of Inigo Jones's Banqueting House, represented as having somewhat attenuated pilasters and no visible rustication. King Charles I stands on a scaffold addressing Bishop Juxon, and, between them and a group of Parliamentary commissioners, is the executioner's block. No-one has ever for certain identified the window through which Charles passed to reach the scaffold and whether or not window frames or mouldings had been removed for the solemn occasion (one contemporary account had mentioned that a passage had been 'broken through the wall'). There is also debate as to the height of the execution block. The two windows shown by Croft are firmly shut and block stands knee-high. The very drama of the memorable scene shown in the picture was evidently of greater significance to its artist than was any pursuit of painstaking historical research.

No other surviving building of the 1600s had figured more prominently in the history of the seventeenth century than the Banqueting House in Whitehall. It was as familiar a sight to Victorian Londoners as it had been to their Carolean ancestors. This substantial fragment of the sprawling Royal Palace of Whitehall had been designed by Inigo Jones in 1619 for 'festive occasions, for formal spectacles, and for the ceremonials of the British Court', and was finished in 1622. Some thirteen years later the great painted Baroque panels by Rubens were installed in the compartmentalised ceiling of the hall. In them the royal union of England and Scotland is celebrated and King James I is drawn up into a crowded heaven surrounded by figures of Justice, Zeal, Religion, Honour and Victory. James's successor, King Charles I, had paid Rubens £3,000 to paint this triumphant apotheosis. In the eastern oval of the ceiling Minerva is shown driving Rebellion into Hell. It was profoundly ironic therefore that Charles was to be led to his execution through this great room. Did he, perchance, have time to look up at the figure of Rebellion and wonder why, given the nature of the last years of his own troubled reign, Minerva (or Rubens) had got it so wrong?

Once Rubens's ceilings had been installed, the Banqueting House lost any function it might have had as the setting for the elaborately expensive Masques which had been such a feature of Stuart court life. The pollution rising from the flames of torches and candles was deemed likely to put the pictures at risk, though by the middle of Charles's reign the staging of Masques was already little more than a smoky memory. Following Charles's death, it was in the Banqueting House that Cromwell, as Lord Protector, received ambassadors from those states that acknowledged his title to rule. Here, at the Restoration, Charles II received members of the upper and lower Houses of Parliament. Charles's brother James II erected a large weathercock on the roof of the Banqueting House in order to judge whether or not the arrival of William of Orange's fleet was imminent, and – that 'Protestant Wind' having proved an ill wind for James – here in 1689 William and Mary were formally offered the crown by the estates of the realm. When the rest of Whitehall Palace was destroyed by fire in 1697, Jones's masterpiece remained intact, but bereft of any useful function either as a formal entertainment space or the setting for great state occasions. A year later it was converted into a Chapel Royal without ever being formally consecrated. Thus it languished, largely deprived of ceremony and royal favour. It was as a chapel that most Victorians would have known it, though for Augustus Hare it was 'one of the dreariest places of worship in London.'[6] For much of Queen Victoria's reign it hosted only one major state service, the distribution of the royal Maundy Money. Here, accompanied by a party of the Yeomen of the Guard, the Archbishop of York, as Lord High Almoner, distributed silver pennies and victuals to a select group of poor men and women 'as many as the queen was years old.'[7] It lost even this last royal association when the Chapel was closed in 1890 and the ceremony moved to Westminster Abbey.

In the closing decades of the nineteenth century Whitehall was gradually transformed by a series of new buildings designed to house the offices of state and a burgeoning civil service. A new War Office was constructed immediately to the north of the Banqueting House in 1886 and in 1893 the Royal United Service Institution was housed in a new building to the south. The former Chapel Royal was ignominiously degraded to serve as the Institution's museum. Under Rubens's great ceiling was displayed a ragbag of military memorabilia including Nelson's dirk, the cocked hat worn by the Duke of Wellington at Waterloo, and the sword carried by Cromwell at the siege of Drogheda. Those Victorian commentators who deigned to notice the Banqueting House bemoaned its sad condition and the evident disregard of its

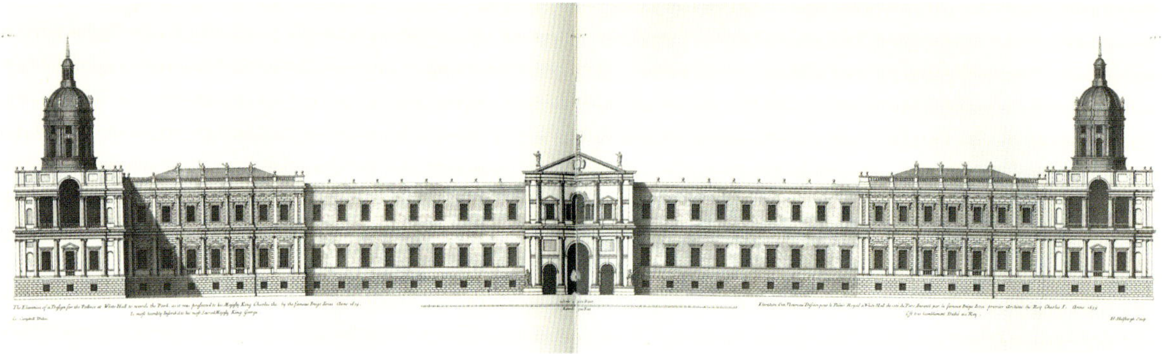

25 John Webb, Inigo Jones's
unrealised designs for
Whitehall from *Vitruvius
Britannicus* by Colen
Campbell, 1717.
Private collection

historical associations. Yet more, they rued the disappearance of the great palace that once surrounded it and the fact that Inigo Jones had never been given the opportunity to rebuild Whitehall in the 1630s, thus depriving London of a palace to rival those of royal Paris, imperial Vienna and papal Rome.

Jones's great, but impractical, scheme for the rebuilding of Whitehall was, it now appears, largely an invention of the eighteenth century when speculative drawings by Jones and his pupil, John Webb, were splendidly engraved and published in the second volume of Colen Campbell's great architectural tome, *Vitruvius Britannicus* in 1717 (fig. 25).[8] Nevertheless, the palace designs ascribed to Jones by Campbell, and later William Kent, had by the mid-nineteenth century become the touchstone for the architect's swollen reputation. The antiquarian, Augustus Hare, who was so dismayed by the degradation of the Banqueting House, went so far as to calculate the scale of the unbuilt palace: 'The plan of Inigo Jones would have covered twenty-four acres, and one may best judge of its intended size by comparison with other buildings, Hampton Court covers eight acres, St James's Palace four acres, Buckingham Palace two and half acres. It would have been as large as Versailles, and larger than the Louvre.'[9] Peter Cunningham, in his *Hand-Book of London. Past and Present* of 1850, informed visitors to Victorian London what they were missing as they passed down Whitehall:

James I intended to have rebuilt the whole Palace, and Inigo Jones designed a new Whitehall for that King, worthy of our nation and his own great name. But nothing was built beyond the Banqueting House. Charles I contemplated a similar reconstruction, but poverty at first

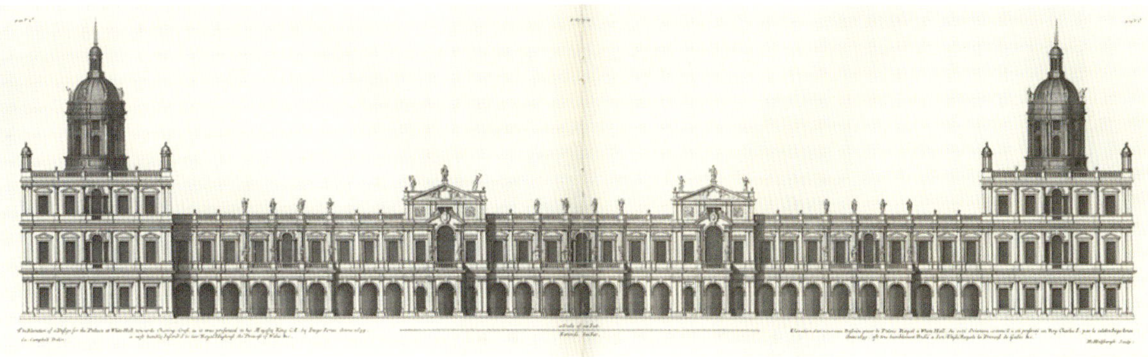

prevented him, and the Civil War soon after was a more effectual prohibition. Charles II preserved what money he could spare from his pleasure to build a palace at Winchester. James II was too busy about religion to attend to architecture and in William III's reign the whole of Whitehall … was destroyed by fire. William talked of rebuilding it after Inigo's designs … Nothing however was done.[10]

Bohn's *Pictorial Handbook of London* of 1854 waxes yet more lyrical about the unbuilt palace and even includes a ground plan of the proposed ensemble with the Banqueting House taking up a minuscule portion of it. This, we are told, was 'the first structure from which all vestiges of Gothic forms were banished by the imported Italian taste,' but it is not the style but the very scale of the palace that seems to impress the author:

> The extent of the northern and southern fronts was to be 1152 ft., and that of the eastern (on a river terrace) and western, towards St. James's Park, each 874 ft. Of the seven enclosed courts, the smallest would have equalled in grandeur anything of the kind now existing; while the largest, 740ft. by 378 ft., and the circular one (surrounded by two stories of arcades, faced by colossal Persian and caryatid figures), would have produced effects that modern architecture has never reached, hardly perhaps ever projected. The design of Whitehall is indeed the most stupendous for a secular building that has ever been actually commenced, at least since the time of the Caesars; and, by excelling, in every respect, both Versailles and the

Louvre, the Caserta and Escurial, it would have reversed the taunt that English sovereigns are the worst lodged in Europe.

When he turns to a consideration of the architectural details of Jones's unbuilt design there is no hint of disapproval either of the palace's vast size or of Jones's rejection of the last spectres of Gothicism:

> The variety, without breach of unity, that pervades the numerous fronts, external and internal, of this wonderful design, the well-studied adaptation of each to its aspect and light, together with the noble boldness, and total absence of petty breaks and divisions, are qualities that distinguish this greatest, but at the same time most un-English, of our architects, from all his successors; and it seems marvellous that a work so generally in their hands, should have had so little effect on the national taste, which is chiefly distinguished by qualities exactly the reverse of those in which he excelled.[11]

Bohn seems anxious to persuade his readers that this was a lost architectural opportunity, one which would have rendered the Stuart Kings the envy of their European rivals and their great palace the *stupor mundi*. There is no sense that such an extravagant project, even if it had gone beyond the sketch-book stage, might have served to dislodge the Stuart monarchy even sooner than did a recalcitrant Parliament in the 1640s. The only note of doubt seems to lie in the suspicion that Jones's style and his ambition were somehow 'un-English.'

Bohn was writing for the informed visitor to London in the 1850s, but his was not a lone voice in sensing that modern London was deficient in a historic royal palace worthy of the intrinsic Greatness of Great Britain. In 1862, with the new Palace of Westminster nearing completion, the perceptive architectural historian, James Fergusson, offered yet another appreciative retrospect on Jones's great project:

> Had a palace been executed, it would have been by far the most magnificent erected in Europe, either before or since. … The river façade of the new Houses of Parliament is nearly identical in extent with that proposed by Jones for the river front of his palace; except that its proportions are destroyed by being much less in height; and the smallness of the parts and details contrasts painfully with the grandeur

of Jones's design. If the new Parliament House were continued westward so as to include the Abbey towers in their western façade, their extent would be nearly the same, and thus some idea may be formed of the scale on which Whitehall was designed.[12]

In 1862, with the Gothic Revival in England in its high and palmy days, this is an extraordinarily flattering comment on the inventiveness and articulation of Jones's plans, especially so as Fergusson had included an engraving of Barry's Houses of Parliament as his own frontispiece. Nevertheless, he does manage to find fault by analysing the façade of the now isolated fragment of the palace, the Banqueting House:

> At present it looks stuck up and rather meagre in its details; but as part of a curtain between two higher and more richly-ornamented blocks of building this would have disappeared. Its real defects of detail are the pulvination of the lower frieze, which is very unpleasing, and the height of the balustrade. But, on the other hand, the windows are well-proportioned and elegant in ornament, – the voids and solids are well balanced, and the amount of ornament sufficient to give an appropriate effect without being overdone; and, what is perhaps of as much importance as anything else, the whole is designed on so large a scale as to convey an idea of grandeur, giving a palatial effect irrespective of any merits of detail it may possess.[13]

This close, detailed analysis indicates that Jones's architecture continued to be both admired and studied in mid-Victorian England. Jones remained 'the first English architect,' one to whom many anonymous early seventeenth-century buildings were automatically ascribed (though as Fergusson sagely remarked 'if he was guilty of many of these, we must place him in a lower rank that he is generally supposed to be entitled to'[14]). The high rank that *was* still accorded to him by Fergusson's contemporaries may not have been as stellar as it had been in the century before, when Colen Campbell, William Kent and Lord Burlington so adulated the man and his work, but they had by no means been eclipsed. If London had indeed possessed Jones's giant Whitehall Palace one can but speculate as to what its subsequent history might have been. Being of stone it might well have survived a conflagration more efficiently than the rambling Tudor buildings it should have replaced. Would Cromwell have taken up residence in such a proud manifestation of royal rule, or would there have ever been a Lord Protector? Perhaps, awed by the spectacle presented by such a palace, Parliament would have backed away from the struggle with the King and left Charles I to transform himself into a fully autocratic monarch as his nephew Louis XIV was to do in France. Charles certainly would have inherited appropriate surroundings in which to rejoice in his Divine and Royal right. Since it never became a practical proposition, such speculations about Whitehall are, of course, absurd. Nevertheless, as James Fergusson suggests, London was not to get a great civil building worthy of its status as a European capital until another fire destroyed the old Palace of Westminster in 1834 and it was replaced by Barry and Pugin's masterpiece. But, given the political, architectural and historicist sentiments of the late-1830s it was, by then, virtually impossible to think of a Thames-side Palace in the Jonesian manner. In the first years of Queen Victoria's reign, the late-Gothic style was deemed to be proper for the surroundings of yet another great architectural survival: the ancient Westminster Hall. That great Hall was not the setting for Charles I's transient triumphs but the scene of his State Trial. Moreover, by the 1830s the Gothic style had come to be sentimentally associated with the very history of Parliamentary government in Britain and mystically emblematic of a democracy deeply rooted in a native soil which had been enriched by Anglo-Saxon Witenagemots and by Magna Carta.

THE PEERS CORRIDOR

In 1841 a Parliamentary Fine Arts Commission was established to consider the future mural decoration of Charles Barry's Houses of Parliament, then still under construction. The Commission was chaired by the newly married Prince Albert. It was Albert who had insisted that its secretary should be Charles Eastlake, a painter and perhaps the most informed connoisseur of the arts in early Victorian England. Amongst the Commissioners were Lords Melbourne, Aberdeen and Palmerston, Lord John Russell and Sir Robert Peel, representing the parliamentary interest, the respected historian Henry Hallam, and Samuel Rogers, a much-esteemed poet and an eminent collector of old masters. In 1843 the Commission announced that a competition should be held for cartoon drawings 'not less than fifteen feet in their longest dimension' and 'executed in chalk or charcoal' illustrating subjects drawn from British history and from the works of Spenser, Shakespeare and Milton. One hundred and forty of the submissions were exhibited in Westminster Hall in July 1843. Of the subjects chosen by the artists, the highest percentage was derived from Anglo-Saxon history and, extraordinarily enough, from the works of Milton. Two further open competitions were to be held in 1845 and 1847. In a typically British way, nothing effective emerged from these grandiose open competitions. Most of the art that subsequently decorated the empty walls of the new Houses of Parliament resulted from direct commissions to artists approved by Prince Albert and Eastlake. William Dyce was given the task of frescoing the Royal Robing Room with Arthurian scenes and Daniel Maclise was allotted the two great murals of Wellington and Nelson in the Royal Gallery. In the Chamber of the House of Lords, quite the most lavishly decorated space in the entire Palace, it was determined that the great themes were to be appropriate to their Lordships' house. Here sat the Lords Spiritual and Temporal and, perched on the Woolsack, the Law Lords. High up in the south gallery, and facing the throne, appear large symbolic frescoes of *The Spirit of Religion* (1847, by J. C. Horsley), *The Spirit of Justice* (1849, by Daniel Maclise) and *The Spirit of Chivalry* (1847, also by Maclise). On the opposite wall, are complementary scenes demonstrative of Religion, the Law and Chivalry in action: *The Baptism of King Ethelbert* (1846, by William Dyce), *Prince Henry acknowledging the Authority of Chief Justice Gascoyne* (1849, by C. W. Cope) and *Edward III conferring the Order of the Garter on the Black Prince* (1848, also by Cope). Around the walls were statues of the barons, knights and prelates who had secured the signing of Magna Carta and both the stained glass in the high windows, and any remaining wall space, glows with the armorial bearings of these same mediaeval worthies.[15] The decoration of the Peers' Chamber was therefore substantially a celebration of the revived Middle Ages and the nineteenth century's constitutional inheritance from the period.

Radically different decisions were to be made by the Commissioners when it came to the decorative scheme chosen for the adjacent Corridor linking the Chamber to the Central Lobby of the Palace of Westminster. This public space contains eight frescoes by C. W. Cope showing scenes from the period of the English Revolution. It is as if we are moving away from predominantly royal and aristocratic preserves into the province of the third estate. Here, the evolution of British representative government begins to assert itself. The subjects of Cope's paintings are remarkable for the political balance it reveals and what it tells us of

Victorian perceptions of the seventeenth century. That balance directly reflects the influence of two particular Commissioners: Lord John Russell, the scion of a noble family traditionally associated with the Whig interest, and Henry Hallam, the author of the much-respected, and Whig-biased, *Constitutional History of England* (1827).[16] It is also likely that the very drama of these highly charged representative scenes reflects the concerns of that influential but still emergent historian, Thomas Babington Macaulay, a recently appointed Commissioner.[17] It is not simply that Cope has juxtaposed images equally sympathetic to the King and his contentious Parliament; he parallels Royalists and Republicans, Anglicans and Puritans with an apparently equable tolerance. Though King Charles appears as a military leader raising his standard at Nottingham, and again, posthumously, as his coffin is taken into St. George's Chapel, there is not a single representation of Oliver Cromwell. To use a twenty-first-century term, the Peer's Corridor is an exemplary exposition of social and political 'inclusiveness.' Together, the eight paintings form the most dramatic, and thoughtful, representation of fractious events of the seventeenth century produced anywhere in England in the Victorian period. Their place in Parliament is exceptionally telling.

To many latter-day observers the events Cope was asked to portray often now seem obscure, even tangential. The painter received the commission for the series in 1853 and completed them, in various media, in 1867. The earliest painting (in fresco) shows *The Embarkation of the Pilgrim Fathers for New England in 1620* (fig. 26). Here a Puritan minister and his flock kneel in exhortatory prayer on a Dutch beach as an English family is pushed away from the shore in a longboat prominently labelled 'Mayflower'. They carry a banner emblazoned with the words 'Freedom of Worship.' The picture treats the Pilgrims' evasion of 'prelatry' as a libertarian prelude to the ever-broadening conflicts of the 1640s, but it also offers a link to the English-based religious and political traditions of the New World. If the Pilgrims are a prelude, the second fresco to be completed (in 1859) shows an episode in 1683 as a kind of postlude. *Lord Russell taking leave of his Wife before going to his Execution for Complicity in the Rye House Plot* must have held a good deal of poignancy for their descendant, Lord John Russell (though this ancestral reverse had, indirectly, been the making of his family's fortunes under King William). It must also be recalled that the aristocratic victims of the suppression of the Rye House Plot, Lord William Russell and Algernon Sidney, had been accorded the status of popular martyrs in the cause of liberty by eighteenth-century Whig commentators. The plot, which had aimed to declare

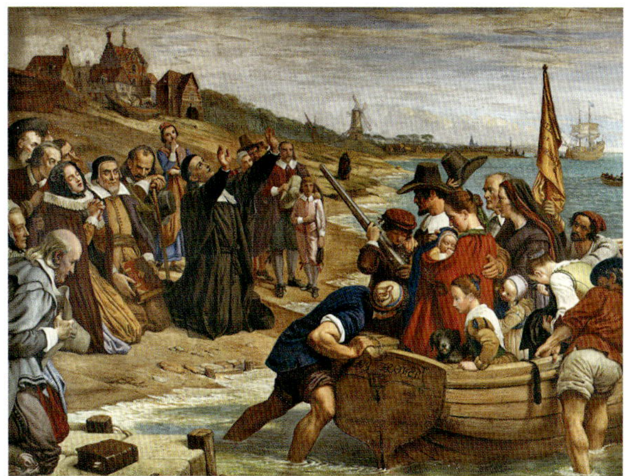

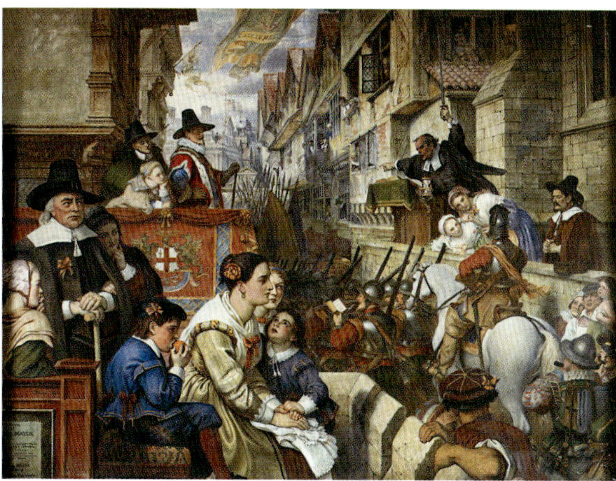

the Duke of Monmouth heir to Charles II in preference to the Catholic James, Duke of York, had been discovered in June 1683. At his trial Russell had requested to have an intimate friend take notes to assist his memory and turning to his wife had declared to the court: 'My wife is here and will do it for me.' The tenderness between the affectionate couple had become legendary, though Cope also makes a point of stressing Russell's Protestant piety. A simple Communion service has evidently taken place in the background and a distressed, and evidently Puritanical, clergyman turns towards us in the foreground with his right hand pressed firmly onto the pages of an open Bible. Two further avowedly anti-Royalist scenes, both painted in waterglass, followed in 1865 and 1866 respectively. *The Setting out of the Train Bands from London to Raise the Siege of Gloucester, 1643* (fig.27) is an exceptionally lively representation of the kind of half-timbered London street that disappeared for ever in the Great Fire. A Puritan alderman and his family sport Parliamentary favours as they and the Lord Mayor, standing on an adjacent balcony, look down on the departing volunteers (one of whom is singing Psalms). Opposite them a particularly fiery Puritan preacher harangues the assembly, brandishing a sword above his alfresco pulpit. With *Speaker Lenthall asserting the Privileges of the House of Commons when King Charles I came to arrest the Five Members, 1642* (fig.28) Cope moved to a far more familiar, and constitutionally vital, episode in national history. Here King Charles stands awkwardly in front of the Speaker's chair while Lenthall, hat in hand, kneels before him. Lenthall may appear submissive, but his left hand is raised, not to

26   Charles West Cope, *The Embarkation of the Pilgrim Fathers for New England in 1620*, 1856, Fresco, 219.7 x 285.8 cm. Palace of Westminster Collection

27   Charles West Cope, *The Setting out of the Train Bands from London to Raise the Siege of Gloucester in 1643*, 1865, Water glass painting, 219.7 x 285.5 cm. Palace of Westminster Collection

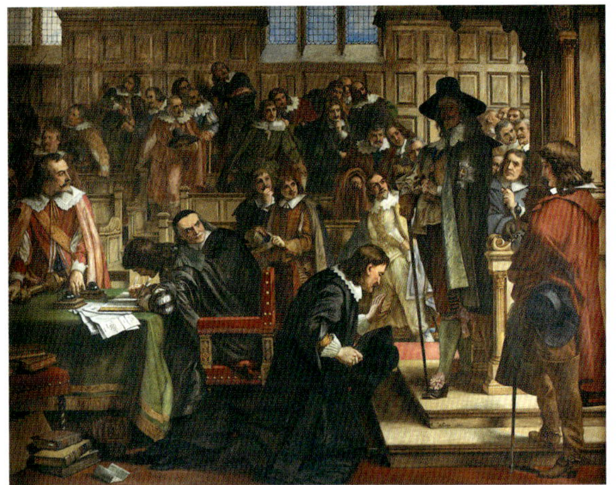

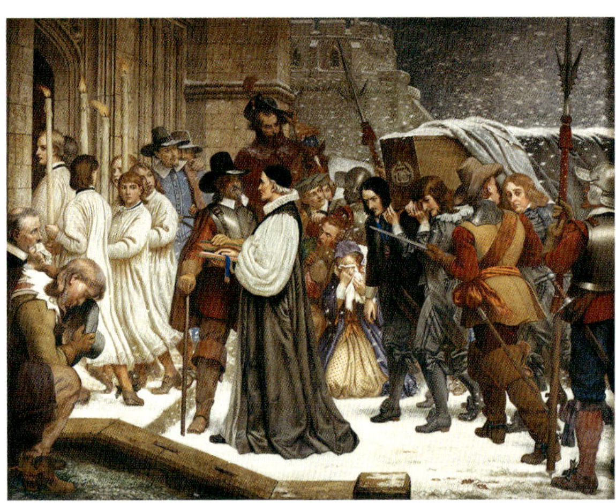

28   Charles West Cope, *Speaker Lenthall Asserting the Privileges of the House of Commons when Charles I Came to Arrest the Five Members in 1642*, 1866, Water glass painting, 219.7 x 285.5 cm. Palace of Westminster Collection

29   Charles West Cope, *The Burial of Charles I at Windsor*, 1857, Fresco, 219.7 x 285.5 cm. Palace of Westminster Collection

apologise but to assert the rights of the Commons. The King's impassive face is in shadow thanks to the wide-brimmed hat he wears. Some members are looking anxiously to the door through which the Parliamentary birds have flown, but most have their eyes fixed on the King, except for one clerk who records the dramatic exchange between Sovereign and Speaker for posterity.

King Charles and his adherents are viewed in a far more benign light in the remaining four paintings, even when they are cast as the victims of fate, unhappy circumstance, justice or persecution. Cope finished *The Burial of King Charles I at Windsor* (fig.29) in 1857. Here, in a snowstorm, Charles's coffin is borne up the steps of St. George's Chapel. Both the pall-bearers and the genteel mourners are evidently in a state of some distress. An armed trooper is harrying two young men in academic caps and a Cromwellian officer bars the way of Bishop Juxon and forcibly closes his Prayer Book. Cope's painting would have had real resonance for Victorian Anglicans of a ritualistic bent. Here the Church of England, loyal to its King, is being persecuted by an intolerant successor state. Its liturgy has been banned and there is evident suspicion of the ritualistic candles being carried before the coffin by four surpliced, but anxious, choirboys. There are no footsteps in the snow, but perhaps the martyred 'White King' has miraculously ordained it to be so. A living Charles looks rather ill at ease in Cope's fresco *King Charles I Raising his Standard at Nottingham, 1642* (fig.30) (dated by the artist 'August 4 1861'). Here is the King's military challenge to his Parliament made manifest. The King has his arm affectionately around the shoulders of his eldest son as he returns the

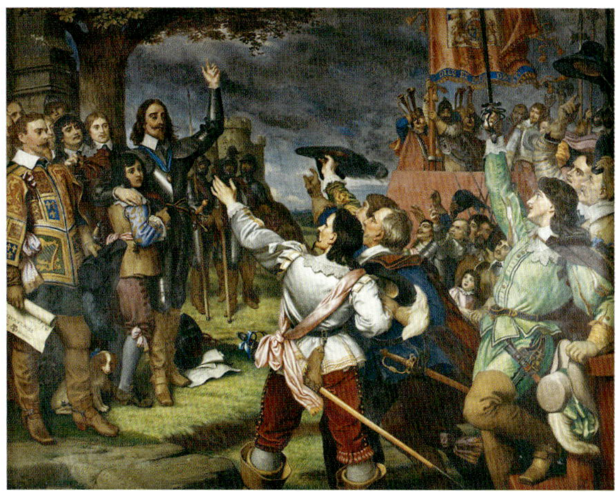

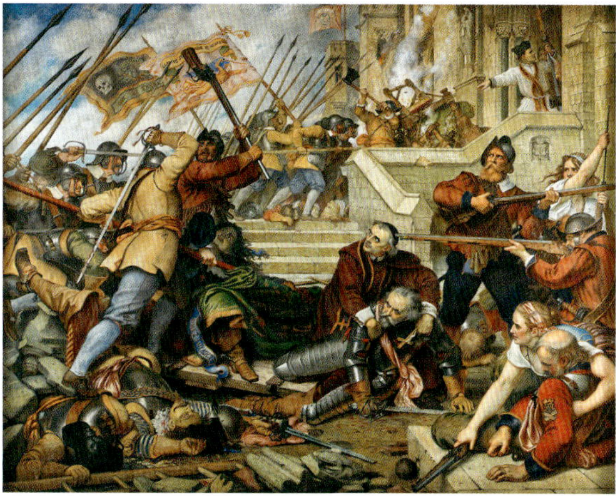

acclamations of his enthusiastic supporters, little knowing that this act of war will later give substance to those of his enemies who will accuse him making war against his own people. The last two episodes in the series, both painted by Cope in waterglass, show far less familiar historical events. *Basing House Defended by the Cavaliers against the Parliamentary Army, 1645* (fig. 31) was finished in 1862. Basing House in Hampshire, which commanded the great western road from London, had been nicknamed 'Loyalty' by Royalists. It was the seat of the Catholic Paulets, Marquises of Winchester, and the House had become an important refuge for distressed and displaced adherents of the King. In October 1645 the garrisoned Basing House was besieged by Parliamentary forces, commanded by Cromwell. It finally fell after a great assault, in the course of which around a hundred defenders were killed, including six Catholic priests. An ageing Inigo Jones was one of the prisoners taken by the victors. Cope's picture, perhaps the finest of the series, shows the wounded Marquis, surrounded by dead and dying Cavaliers, succoured by Franciscan friar carrying a crucifix. Another priest, vested in an alb, stands at the head of the staircase vainly attempting to rally the waning defence of the house. The juxtaposition of the vigorous Cromwellian soldiers to the left and the defeated Royalists in the centre and right foreground of the picture is particularly striking. Cope may well have been influenced in his central placing of the figure of the fallen Marquis by Maclise's great fresco of the *Death of Nelson* (see Fig. 111, p.298) that was nearing completion in the nearby Royal Gallery. The last of the paintings, *The Expulsion of the Fellows of a College at Oxford for refusing to sign the Covenant*

30   Charles West Cope, *King Charles I Raising his Standard at Nottingham in 1642*, 1861, Fresco, 219.7 x 285.5 cm. Palace of Westminster Collection

31   Charles West Cope, *Basing House Defended by the Cavaliers Against the Parliamentary Army in 1645*, 1862, Water glass painting, 219.7 x 285.5 cm. Palace of Westminster Collection

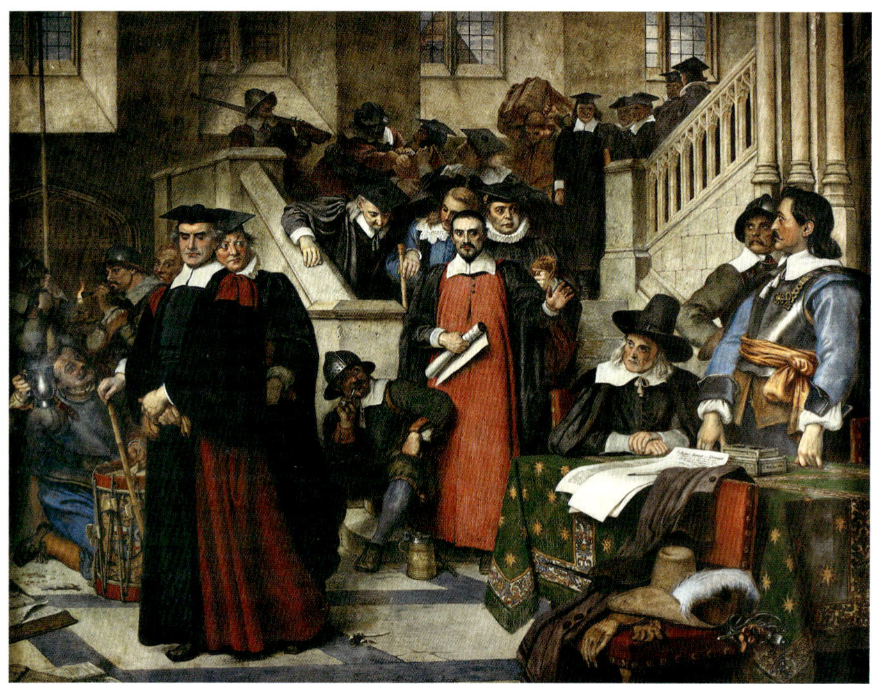

32   Charles West Cope. *The
Expulsion of the Fellows of
a College at Oxford for
Refusing to Sign the
Covenant*, 1865, Water
glass painting, 219.7 x
285.5 cm. Palace of
Westminster Collection

(fig.32), is dated 1865. Cope shows the dons, resplendent in their academic
robes, defiantly rejecting the demands of the Parliamentary commissioners,
one civil, one military. A trunk is being brought down from the College Hall
behind the motley band of Fellows while two carousing soldiers jeer at them.
Another soldier is actually attempting to throttle one of the Dons on the
staircase (which is evidently that at Christchurch). Torn and defaced books, of
a kind evidently unacceptable to Puritans, are strewn on the floor. It is an
extraordinary picture in many ways. Dons rarely enough form the subject of
art, and defiant dons in dramatic poses must be even rarer birds, even in
historical painting. Cope is showing an assault on academic independence,
with men of principle standing by their religious principles. *The Expulsion of
the Fellows of a College at Oxford* forms a poignant complement to *The
Embarkation of the Pilgrim Fathers*. In the latter painting one kind of religious
Establishment drives Puritans into exile. In the former, triumphant Puritanism
exacts its revenge. The implication of both pictures for the nineteenth century
seems to be that the modern plural state, with all its pledges of toleration, is
none the less heir to a sharply divided history.

FAITH AND WORKS

No section of the British population in the nineteenth century remained more alert to the divisions of the seventeenth century than those who claimed membership of a Christian church, chapel or sect. In the years immediately preceding Queen Victoria's accession non-Anglicans in England, Ireland and Wales had been freed from the stringent civil disabilities that had been variously enacted since the time of Queen Elizabeth. In 1828 the repeal of the Test and Corporations Acts enabled those Protestant non-conformists who had separated themselves from the Established Church of England in the reign of Charles II to sit in Parliament and to enjoy full civil rights. The same toleration was extended to Roman Catholics in England in 1829 (it was soon after granted to Irish and Scottish Catholics). Only the two ancient English universities still precluded non-Anglicans from taking degrees (and they continued to do so until 1871). Even so, dark memories and an ingrained bitterness had worked themselves deep into the psyche of many pious men and women. Catholics readily recalled the Penal Laws that had impoverished so many families and had produced a multitude of priest martyrs up to the time of Charles II (the last Catholic to be hung, drawn and quartered at Tyburn was Archbishop Oliver Plunkett in July 1681). Quakers looked back to the persecution of George Foxe, Baptists to the imprisonment of John Bunyan, Unitarians, Independents and Congregationalists to the wholesale loss of livings and civic offices at the time of the Restoration (Elizabeth Gaskell makes much of this in *North and South* of 1855 while giving Mr. Hale's ' religious difficulties' an historical context). In Scotland the outlawing of the Covenanters in the reign of Charles II had become an integral part of a national mythology, while the discrimination against Episcopalians, imposed in 1696 when William III's administration sanctioned Presbyterianism as the official form of Church government north of the border, served to marginalise an otherwise intensely loyal section of the population. It was, however, Victorian Anglicans who most scrupulously raked over the coals of their singularly mixed seventeenth-century heritage, and it is the literature and the scholarship produced by and for Anglicans that has left the most lasting legacy.

Although some senior members of the Church of England felt that its position had been compromised, even undermined, by the passage of the 1832 Reform Bill and by the concessions accorded to Catholics and Dissenters in the late 1820s, the Established Church never found itself sidelined, let alone persecuted, during Queen Victoria's reign. The intellectual assaults directed against its creeds and traditions occasioned by the publication of Darwin's *On the Origin of Species* in 1859 resulted in what has been styled 'the Victorian Crisis of Faith,' but no slight was ever sanctioned by the state. The English Church could by no means compare itself to the Catholic Church in France which, having been actively suppressed during the Revolution, found itself having to live with the aftermath of the ideas, politics and unbeliefs that had been fostered by the Revolutionary and Napoleonic regimes. Post-revolutionary French Catholicism had the advantage of being bolstered by the kind of romantic sympathy expressed in Chateaubriand's *Génie du christianisme, ou beautés de la religion chrétiennne* of 1802 and by a resurgence of religious orders. The English Church had Coleridge's liberal ramblings and the Oxford Movement. Significantly, it was those inspired by the Oxford Movement who were to feel victimised, and indeed persecuted by the very Establishment that they felt themselves called to redeem.

Any Anglo-Catholic contemplating an engraving of *Strafford on his Way to Execution* (see fig. 21) in 1888 might have recognized something familiar, but mildly chilling, in the hovering arms of Archbishop Laud. In that year Bishop Edward King of Lincoln was prosecuted by a group of extreme Anglican protestants who had formed the 'Church Association' in order to counter the advance of ritualistic practices. King, who was the first Anglican bishop since the Reformation to wear a cope and mitre during church services and who habitually used vestments when he celebrated communion, was not charged with any extraordinary breach of Church Law but with facing eastwards when he celebrated, with having lighted candles on the altar, and with using the sign of the cross at the absolution and the final blessing. There was no real risk of King's being sent to prison, but the Bishop was accused of offences against the Public Worship Regulation Act of 1874 and that act had already led to the imprisonment of five parish priests for contempt of court.[18] The case against King was heard by the Archbishop of Canterbury in the Library of Lambeth Palace and the proceedings were generally deemed to be something of an embarrassment. It ended in 1890 with a typically Anglican fudge on the part of the archbishop. Nevertheless, the history of Anglican ritualism in the nineteenth century was periodically marked by skirmishes with Church Courts, by restrictive legislation and by unruly protestant agitators. In the 1830s the founding fathers of the Oxford Movement had had to contend with an orchestrated opposition to their carefully framed intellectual propositions about church order and doctrine. Their successors, variously known as Tractarians, Puseyites and, ultimately, Anglo-Catholics, were consistently demonised by their opponents as superstitious *poseurs* or, more damningly, as crypto-Romanists inviting the Antichrist into England by the back door. Chief amongst those who mocked their pretensions were the newly founded satirical magazine *Punch*, that self-proclaimed oracular newspaper *The Times*, and pig-headed figures such as Sir Peter Laurie who declared in his Mayoral speech at the Lord Mayor's Banquet in 1850, 'Britons never would be slaves either to Puseyism or to Popery.'[19] It was no wonder that baited Puseyites should have claimed common cause with the martyred Laud. As Chancellor, Laud had reformed the statutes of the University of Oxford, and the city of Oxford had served as the sainted King Charles's capital in 1642-44. It must now have seemed that Oxford was once again fostering a beleaguered but holy cause. Few seem to have deemed it a lost one.

Seventeenth-century Puritans within the English church had generally accused Archbishop Laud and his followers of 'Arminianism,' that is, with doctrines deemed to be incompatible with the strict interpretation of Calvin's theology. Laud was blamed not only with persecuting recalcitrant protestants but also with introducing ceremonial practices and vestments which reeked of 'Popery.' Laud might, ultimately, have fallen foul of a Puritan majority in Parliament but his steady rise to the Archbishopric of Canterbury under Charles I had been marked by an uncanny talent for making powerful enemies. The rise and fall of Laud, and the systematic assaults on Laudianism, offered salutary warnings to nineteenth-century Tractarians. The consequent triumphalism of Puritan zealotry during the Civil War and the Commonwealth did not only entail the smashing of images or the breaking of stained glass in parish churches, it also meant the imposition of the Covenant on Oxford colleges (so dramatically painted by Cope), the sacking of the Laudian chapel at Peterhouse in Cambridge, and the breaking up of the 'Arminian' community at Little Gidding in Huntingdonshire. The former chaplain to the Royalist army, Jeremy Taylor, first endured a period of imprisonment, before being obliged to retreat to Wales (where he produced his influential devotional tracts, *The Rule and Exercise of Holy Living* of 1650 and its sequel *The Rule and Exercise of Holy Dying* of 1651). In Wales too, the poet Henry Vaughan maintained the passive loyalty to Church and King which echoes through his verse. Deprived of the Deanship of Peterborough, the gifted Laudian cleric, John Cosin, bided his time, serving as a royal chaplain at the court of the exiled Henrietta Maria in Paris (he was later rewarded for his loyalty by being created Bishop of Durham at the time of the Restoration). Cosin's fellow exile in Paris, the poet Richard Crashaw, having lost his fellowship at Peterhouse, succumbed to the enticements of the Church of Rome and ended his career as a canon of the Basilica at Loreto in Italy. The 'Golden Days' of the restored King Charles II may have seen the formal canonisation of 'Charles the Martyr' and may have reintroduced the hierarchy and the liturgy of the Church of England, but the last forty years of the seventeenth century remained traumatic for many High Church Anglicans. The 'Merry Monarch' flirted with Catholicism, much as he flirted with his numerous mistresses, and he was finally received into the Roman Church on his deathbed. His brother, James II, had never made a secret of his loyalty to Rome, but all his pretences of extending toleration to Dissenters and Catholics served merely to antagonise the Anglican Church of which he was the Supreme Governor. Seven of his Bishops, opposed to his policies, went to the Tower in June 1688, and when William of Orange invaded later in the same year Anglican support for the King melted away. Nevertheless, five of those Bishops, and four more of their brethren as well as some four hundred of their clergy, scrupled over taking an oath of allegiance to the new King because they believed it would entail breaking their earlier oaths to James and his successors. All were deprived of their livings and many were driven into exile. The loss of these so-called 'Nonjurors,' all of whom held a principled view of the monarchy and an equally 'high' conception of the Church as a spiritual society, meant that Anglicanism had a distinctly Latitudinarian stamp as it entered the eighteenth century. The example set by the 'Nonjurors' proved to be an inspiration to the earnest adherents of the Oxford Movement, and the work of one prominent nonjuring priest, William Law, seems to have proved a decisive milestone on the religious journey of John Henry Newman.[20]

The spiritual tone of the Oxford Movement had been first set in 1827 when John Keble's hugely influential volume of verse *The Christian Year* was published anonymously. In 1868, by which time Keble's name had become synonymous with Tractarianism, it had sold 265,000 copies.[21] Keble's work has often been seen as deriving from a Wordsworthian impulse, but *The Christian Year* is equally indebted to the devotional poetry of the first part of the seventeenth century and to the work of George Herbert in particular. The volume had laid a stress on the liturgical year, providing poetic meditations for each Sunday and for the major feast days of the Anglican calendar. It proved to be a readily accessible aid to private devotion and an essential, but domestic, companion to the public worship of the Church of England. Keble and his fellow Tractarians knew that it was the usages of the *Book of Common Prayer* that had always set Anglicans apart from all other non-Roman Catholic churches in England. And it was through the same *Book of Common Prayer*, edited into its final and most enduring form by Bishop Cosin in 1662, that they persuaded Catholic-minded Anglicans of the nineteenth century that their Church was part of a larger Christian tradition. Consequently, generations of priests and the congregations in their charge took a new delight in the beauty of their liturgical heritage. The scholarship stirred and fostered by the Oxford Movement revealed not only the complex history of the Prayer Book, but also explored much of its potential flexibility and the felicity of its expression. The Tractarian stress on the beauties of the 1662 *Book of Common Prayer* made it the focus of an essentially Catholic interpretation of the Anglican tradition.

The renewed interest in the Anglican tradition of worship, devotion, and poetry is evident in the spectrum of books issued by what has been rightly called 'the foremost name in Victorian book design': the Chiswick Press. The imprint was first used by its founder, Charles Whittingham, in 1811, but it was Whittingham's nephew, Charles the younger, and his partner William Pickering, who gradually transformed it into what became the premier press of the 1840s. It produced finely designed books tailored for a discriminating and educated market. It was Pickering who introduced the exquisite 'Diamond Classics' in the late 1820s (probably the first books to be sold in cloth covers) and it was typical of the printer's discerning tastes that one of the first books issued in this miniature series was Isaac Walton's *Lives of Donne, Wotton, Herbert and Sanderson* in 1827. It was, however, in Pickering's larger format books of the 1840s that his distinctive style became evident. Each had an innovative title-page, printed in red and black, with a woodcut border and ornament reminiscent of sixteenth- and seventeenth-century book design. He also revived the early-eighteenth-century Old Face type, perfected by William Caslon. Pickering's greatest achievements include a set of six elegant volumes of the texts of the Prayer Books of 1549, 1552, 1559, 1604, 1637 and 1662 (1844), and William Maskell's scholarly

Monumenta Ritualia Ecclesiae Anglicanae of 1846-47. The Chiswick Press was also notable for its reissues of certain key seventeenth-century books of devotion: Bishop Lancelot Andrewes's *Preces Privatae*, first issued in Latin in 1830 and translated into English as *The Private Devotions* in 1839 and again in 1848; Thomas Fuller's *The Holy State and the Profane State* appeared in 1840; Jeremy Taylor's *Holy Living and Holy Dying* in 1840 (reprinted in 1844, 1847, 1850, and 1852); Henry King's *Poems and Psalms* in 1843; and the respected nonjuror, Bishop Thomas Ken's *Exposition of the Apostle's Creed* in 1852. Perhaps most strikingly, Pickering also published John Donne's *Devotions, with Two Sermons* in 1840, Henry Vaughan's *Silex Scintillans. Sacred Poems and Private Ejaculations* in 1847 (with a memoir by the Revd. H. F. Lyte, the author of 'Abide with Me') and several handsome editions of the *Poems* of George Herbert.[22] Unlike Donne, Vaughan or King, Herbert's work had never lacked admirers in the eighteenth century. His reputation remained high in the early nineteenth century across a broad spectrum of readers (Ruskin was, for example, a consistent admirer of his work). Nevertheless, the number and the quality Pickering's editions of Herbert are remarkable. An edition of *The Temple* (with a frontispiece showing Bemerton church) appeared in 1835, followed by *The Remains* a year later. Both were reprinted several times. In 1846 a fine new edition of *The Works of George Herbert in Prose and Verse* appeared in two volumes octavo, containing *The Temple* the poems in Latin and English, an engraved portrait (fig. 33), a view of Bemerton church, Walton's and Benjamin Oley's *Lives* of the poet, Christopher Harvey's *The Synagogue* of 1640, and a selection of Herbert's surviving letters. In 1848 a more compact edition was published with the same wide range of contents but with both title pages decorated with an elaborate, engraved design suggestive of a seventeenth-century church monument. Thus early Victorian readers were presented with something approaching a model edition of a poet who had come to be regarded as the model of the Anglican parish clergyman, pious, humble and dedicated both to his parishioners and to the rhythms of the Christian year.

When the Revd. Robert Aris Willmott published his finely illustrated anthology *English Sacred Poetry of the Sixteenth, Seventeenth, Eighteenth and Nineteenth Centuries* in 1861 he evidently felt that Herbert was so familiar a figure to readers as to be able to refer to him simply by his surname. Willmott's volume is typical of the woodblock-illustrated volumes published in the 1860s. It was designed to combine poetry and good modern design and thus to enhance the middle-class home by flattering the intellectual and aesthetic pretensions of

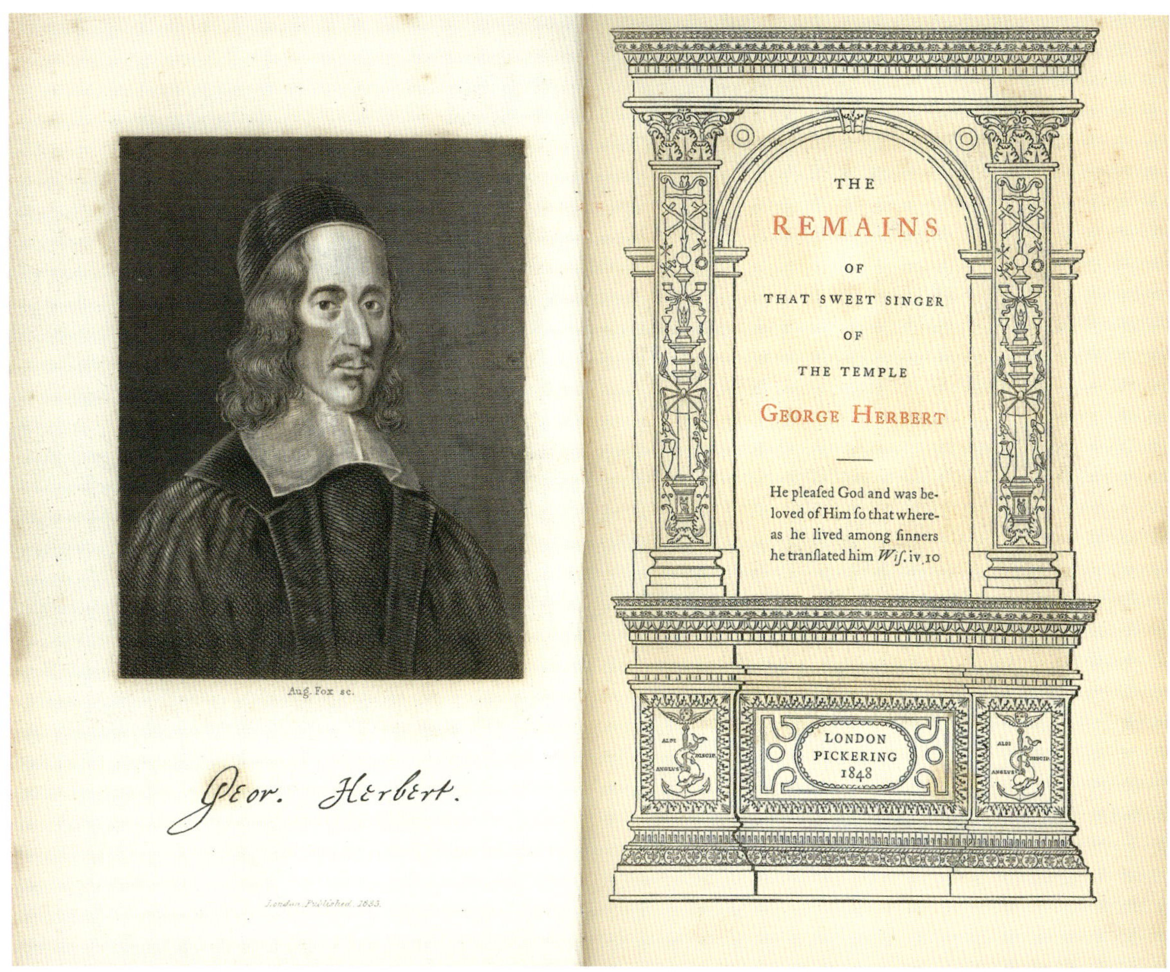

would-be readers. Volumes such as Willmott's were the precursors of the coffee-table book. His illustrators included both the Pre-Raphaelite William Holman Hunt and some up-and-coming younger artists, Frederick Sandys, Henry Stacey Marks, and Frederick Walker. Unsurprisingly, there are eight poems by Herbert in the volume, more than any other of the selected poets, but it also includes one poem each by Donne, Crashaw, Thomas Ken, Henry King and Milton, two by Sir Henry Wotton, and four by Vaughan (whom the editor describes in his introductory essay as possessing 'a soothing, plaintive softness' in his 'hard and knotty rhymes'). The volume as a whole is a singular tribute to the quality of the devotional verse of the seventeenth century, especially so as the

33 Frontispiece and title page from George Herbert's *Remains* published by William Pickering, 1848. Private collection

contemporaries represented in the volume include Tennyson, Keble, Elizabeth Barrett Browning and Adelaide Proctor and well as some five poems by Willmott himself. The poets appear in alphabetical rather than chronological order, and Herbert's pre-eminence is again suggested by the fact that he merits three woodblock pictures, two of which, uniquely in the book, show the poet himself. The first, by the prolific book illustrator John Dawson Watson, accompanies the poem 'Employment' and pictures Herbert in cassock and bands contemplating a vase of roses by an open casement window. The second, illustrating 'The Quip,' is also by Watson. Here the poet sits raptly, looking up from his book and detached from the flashy, well-dressed and mocking representatives of the 'merry world.'[23]

The fact that Herbert's face was evidently so recognisable to Willmott's readers in the 1860s is striking. The portrait illustrations in the Pickering edition of *The Works of George Herbert* was drawn from the engraving by Robert White published posthumously in 1674, and it was from White's engraving that the painter William Dyce derived the face and dress of the poet in his serene *George Herbert at Bemerton* (fig. 34) which was exhibited in 1861 at the Royal Academy. Dyce's painting serves to confirm Herbert's distinguished place not only in the then-received canon of English verse but also in the list of divines most revered by contemporary Tractarians. Dyce, who in 1849 had been commissioned to paint a reredos for All Saints, Margaret Street in London (the foundation stone of which had been laid by Dr Pusey), was a favoured artist in High Church circles. Dyce's painting of Herbert evidently had a real and immediate rapport. One anonymous clergyman wrote expressing thanks to the artist for the pleasure the painting had given him and hoping for an engraved reproduction of this 'ideal of the man' in order to 'help strengthen me when I am wearied or disappointed or our of humour with myself.'[24] Dyce had been encouraged to paint the rectory garden at Bemerton by his sometime model, Herbert's successor as incumbent of the parish the Revd Cyril Page, though it would seem probable that the painter was attracted to the character of the poet not just by his religious verse but by their shared passion for church music. A lute rests against a stone bench in Herbert's rectory garden and in the distance, across the water-meadows, we glimpse Salisbury cathedral to which, as Walton tells us, the poet was drawn by its choral services. The sense of Godly calm and inspiriting stillness that pervades the picture may also derive from the sentiments Dyce had expressed in an earlier letter:

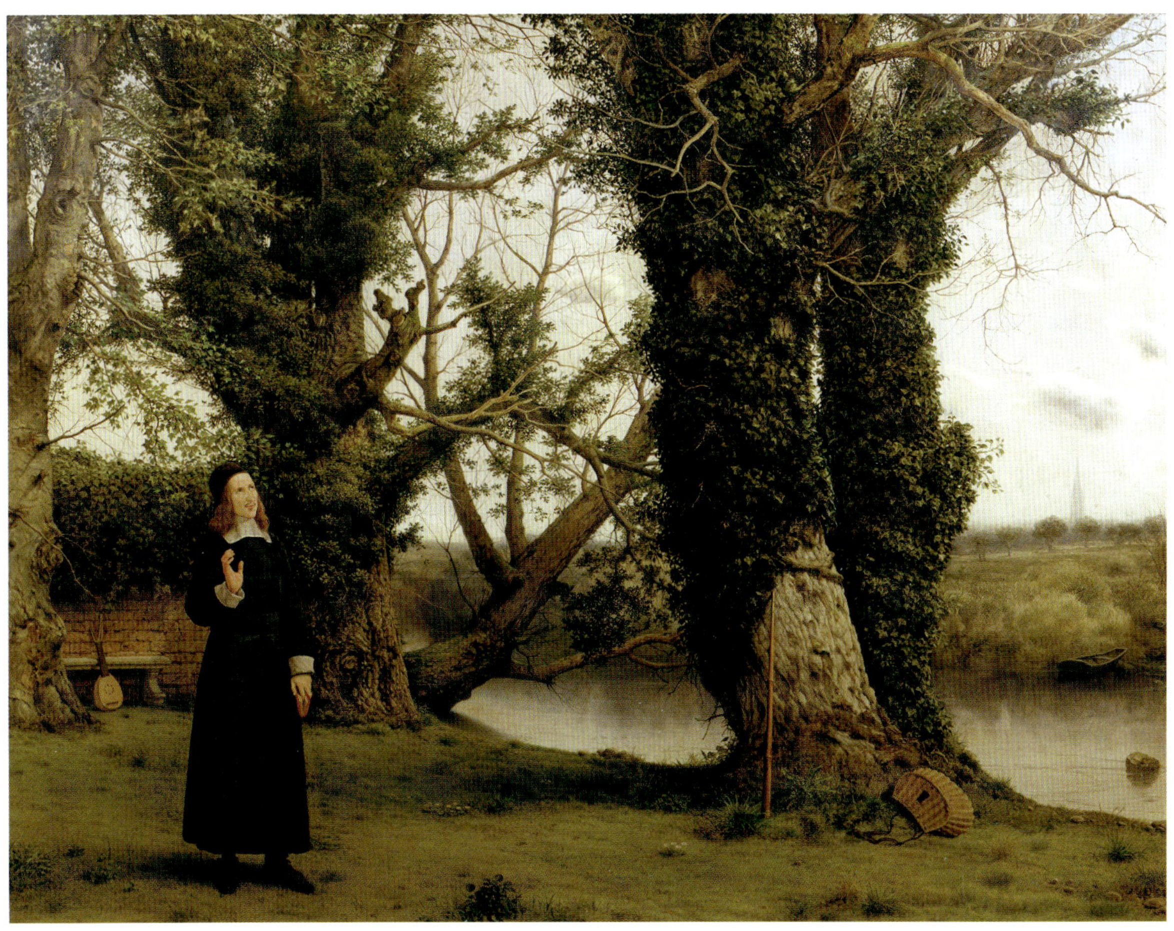

34 William Dyce,
George Herbert at Bemerton,
1861, Oil on canvas,
86.4 x 111.8 cm.
Guildhall Art Gallery,
City of London

A relish for Christian art, in its highest form, is not the offspring of taste
… but taste subdued by the power of religion; – a taste, in its origin
ethical rather than physical … that uses the realities of art only as the
figures, the sacraments, the shadows, the language, – the conventional
means, in short, by which expression is given to sentiments and
emotions, that have their birth not in nature alone, but in nature
transubstantiated (if we may be pardoned the use of the word) by the
spirit of Christianity.[25]

Dyce was speaking here about music, but he might as well have been referring his responses to pictorial art. It is interesting how very *Anglican* his expression is, especially when he warily employs the idea of transubstantiation to describe how 'sentiments and emotions' are given a new 'sacramental' form by art.

CHURCH MONUMENTS

In late 1844 the London publisher W. J. Cleaver of Baker Street advertised the appearance of a new volume by the Revd. George White entitled *Lachrymæ Ecclesiæ*. Its subtitle was *The Anglican Reformed Church and her Clergy in the days of their destitution and suffering during the Great Rebellion in the 17th century*. The very terms employed in this subtitle would have given prospective readers a good idea as to where George White stood on matters ecclesiastical and historical. 'The Great Rebellion', as Clarendon had termed it in his *History*, was still the received way of referring to the Civil War and the Commonwealth, and in 1844 the term 'The English Revolution' was far from accepted, let alone intellectually acceptable. The real 'Revolution' remained that of 1688 and, perhaps less 'gloriously,' the French Revolution of 1789. Although White calls the Anglican Church 'Reformed,' he is explicit about its 'destitution and suffering' in Cromwell's time. The publisher quotes press reviews of the book which refer variously to its being 'timely' and 'well-timed' and a critic in the *Carlisle Churchman* is cited as saying that he trusts its message 'will not be lost upon those who imagine that dissent in our day is a widely different system from that of the Puritans.' Battle lines are then clearly drawn, and the Victorian Church, the Apostolic heir to the destituted Church of the 1640s, must be alert to a continuing threat of persecution. The threat hanging over the Church is no longer that of Popery and of a tyranny imposed from without. As in 1640, so in 1840 the threat comes from within the body politic. In the seventeenth century it came from those Puritans who sought to disrupt the Anglican settlement. In the nineteenth, as White saw it, the Establishment had to hold on to its principles and traditions in the face of those who had an historic grudge against it. 'Reformed' the Church might be, but a hostage to Calvinistic narrowness it must never again be.

Some months after the warm reception accorded to White's *Lachrymæ Ecclesiæ* his publisher Cleaver also published a slim novel by John Mason Neale called *Shepperton Manor: A Tale of the Times of Bishop Andrewes*. Neale had already established himself as the most articulate of the Ecclesiologists and the most prominent figure in what has since become known as 'the Cambridge Movement.'[26] Where the leaders of the Oxford Movement had stressed the essentially 'catholic' nature of Anglican doctrine and tradition, Neale and his Cambridge colleagues looked to the visual inheritance of the Church of England: to its architecture, ceremonial and vesture. As his novel shows, Neale was addressing his work to an audience as receptive to the niceties of seventeenth-century theology as White's had been, but he also makes a determined effort to prove that Laudian Anglicans had rejoiced in properly vested altars, coped clerics and the occasional whiff of incense. Indeed, despite its relative brevity, his is not a text for the ritually uninformed or the theologically faint-hearted. When, for example, we learn from the mouth of Lancelot Andrewes that James I has insisted that preachers at Court should not 'touch on the Quinquarticular controversy' because the King holds that it 'gendereth questions, and tendeth not to edifying,' we sense that edification is emphatically the main theme of the book.[27] Neale's characters include not just Bishop Andrewes, but the antagonistic Puritan William Prynne, and briefly John Donne. There is a great deal of intense discussion of the niceties of creeds, ceremonies, traditions and definitions and the godly Anglican interpretation of each is carefully explained (with a good deal of Latin terminology and reference to the Fathers). All of the arguments are won by Anglicans, of course. Sour Puritans are discountenanced and at the end the daughter of an obstinate Roman Catholic gentleman makes a deathbed confession of the essential Catholicity of the Reformed Church of England. Despite the intricacies of many of the theological issues explored in *Shepperton Manor* the novel contains some sharp observation and informed historical evocation. The account of John Donne preaching at St. Paul's Cross is, for example, particularly striking:

> Highly ingenious, full of the most quaint turns, keeping the hearers always on the stretch of expectation, often almost enigmatically obscure, and with learning enough in it to fill twenty modern discourses, Donne's sermon was well calculated for those whom he was addressing: although, perhaps, it might seem otherwise to a reader of the nineteenth century. His powerful voice might be heard from the very bottom of Ludgate Hill: and yet the exertion which it cost to maintain that pitch, seemed, as indeed it was, too

much for the preacher. As the sand in the hour-glass beside him ran low, his manner became more excited; the veins, from the fatigue, formed a net-work on his forehead, his face flushed, and his voice occasionally failed; indeed Dr. Lenton knew not at last whether he listened with more admiration or sorrow, and was heartily glad, when after a peroration perfectly glittering with wit, the preacher pronounced the benediction, and dismissed the congregation.[28]

Here, as throughout his narrative, Neale offers us a contemporary view (Dr. Lenton's) and a zoom forward to the likely response of a nineteenth-century reader. The ritualistic and scholarly world described in *Shepperton Manor* is, we realise, over idealised but it is, as we glimpse it, a world on the brink of being fragmented and suppressed. At the end of the novel we are told that King Charles has raised his standard at Nottingham and has called 'all the good men and true of our country to join him.' None of Neale's readers could have been blind to the fact that by 1642, with Bishop Andrewes and John Donne in their graves and Archbishop Laud imprisoned in the Tower, dark shadows were closing in on the kind of Anglicanism that rejoiced the soul of Neale and his fictional characters.

When it appeared in 1880 J[oseph] H[enry] Shorthouse's novel *John Inglesant: A Romance* offered a rather more ample perspective on the religious debates of the first half of the seventeenth century. It proved to be one of the most popular and influential books of its generation, selling some ten thousand copies in its first year of publication. Shorthouse, who came from Birmingham Quaker stock, had been baptised into the Church of England in 1861 and had served as churchwarden of a famously 'High' church in his native city. He was profoundly absorbed in the history of Laudian Anglicanism but his novel, the second part of which is set in Italy, also reveals a deep and sympathetic fascination with Roman Catholicism. It was small wonder that his admirers were to include both the 'High' Gladstone, the ex-Anglican Henry, Cardinal Manning and, we might assume, somewhat belatedly, the convert Anglo-Catholic T.S. Eliot. Shorthouse's central character, John Inglesant, variously experiences a Court Masque, Jesuit intrigues amongst the nobility, mass at the Queen's catholic chapel in London, a nodding acquaintance with the poets and divines of the 1640s, the execution of Archbishop Laud, and prison under the Commonwealth, but perhaps most memorable are the accounts of the several visits he makes to Nicholas Ferrar's community at Little Gidding:

> The Church was kept in great order, the altar being placed upon a raised platform at the east end, and covered with tapestry stretching over the floor all round it, and adorned with plate and tapers. Mr. Ferrar bowed with great reverence several times on approaching the altar, and directed Inglesant to sit in a stalled seat opposite the reading pew, from which he said evening prayer. The men of the family knelt on the raised step before the altar, the ladies and servants sitting in the body of the Church. The Church was very sweet, being decked with flowers and herbs; and the soft autumn light rested over it. From the seat where Inglesant knelt, he could see the faces of the girls as they bent over their books in prayer. (Chapter 4)

The whole tone of this passage reflects High Anglican piety and the 'good order' and precision of the kind of ritual that Shorthouse would have experienced in the late-Victorian period. As with J. M. Neale's *Shepperton Manor* this is both an imagined ideal and a model for the emphatically English strain of Anglo-Catholicism that was emerging in the last years of the nineteenth century. Later in his narrative, Inglesant contrasts the staid reverence of worship at Little Gidding with what replaces it after the death of the King and the triumph of Parliament:

> A revolting coarseness marks every detail of the tragic story; the flower of England on either side was beneath the turf or beyond the sea, and the management of affairs was left in the hands of butchers and brewers. Ranting sermons, three in succession, before a brewer in Whitehall, is the medium to which the religious utterance of England is reduced. (Chapter 14)

There may be more then a hint of social snobbery here. There is certainly a deep sigh of regret at what England has lost with the 'murder' of its King and the decimation of its national Church. Inglesant is a romantic observer of a world which seems, in his eyes, to have been steadily coarsened once the 'romance' of the religion to which he is attached has been so violently extirpated.

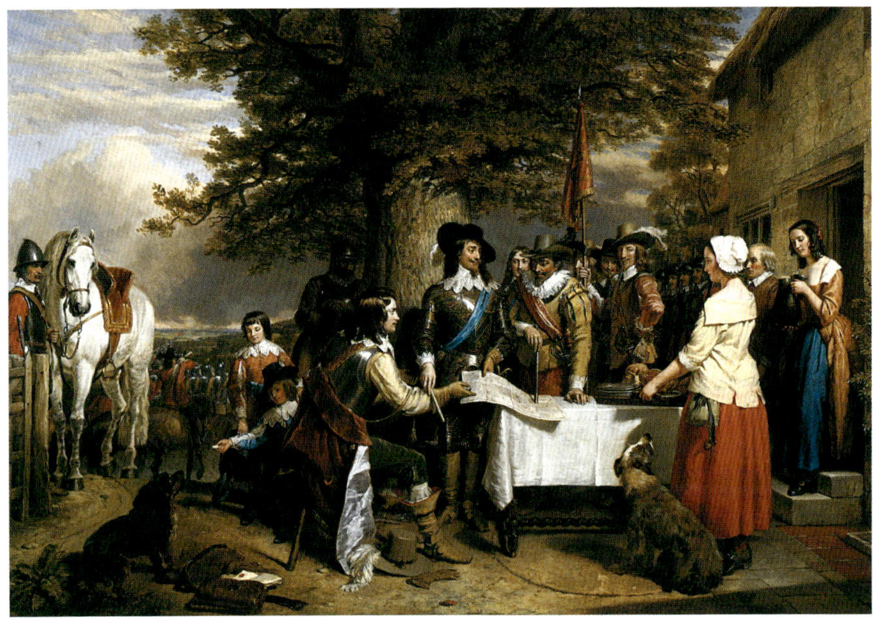

35   Charles Landseer,
*The Eve of the Battle of
Edgehill*, 1845, Oil on
canvas, 141 x 213.7 cm.
Walker Art Gallery,
National Museums
Liverpool

The Proscribed Cavalier

Apart from Cope's picture in the Peer's Corridor in the Palace of Westminster
the scene of *King Charles raising his Standard at Nottingham* was also painted by
Augustus Leopold Egg (Walker Art Gallery, Liverpool). Egg had first submitted
a drawing of the subject to the Royal Fine Arts Commission in 1852, but he
received no premium. Unlike Cope, he shows a singularly gloomy King under
an equally gloomy sky. Despite the enthusiasm of a small band of assembled
cavaliers, Egg does not manage to suggest anything but an unhappy resolution
to the King's move.[29] Another canvas in the Liverpool collection, Charles
Landseer's *Eve of the Battle of Edgehill* (fig.35), also purports to represent the
King at war. Landseer's picture of 1845 shows a council of war, but there is little
in the picture that suggests either urgency or military preparation. Thackeray
sharply, and irreverently, commented on it that 'nobody seems to have anything
particular to do, except the royal martyr, who is looking at a bone of ham that
a girl out of the inn has hold of … The King in this attitude (with the baton
in his hand, simpering at the bacon aforesaid) has no more of the heroic in him
than the pork he contemplates and he deserves to lose every battle he fights.'[30]

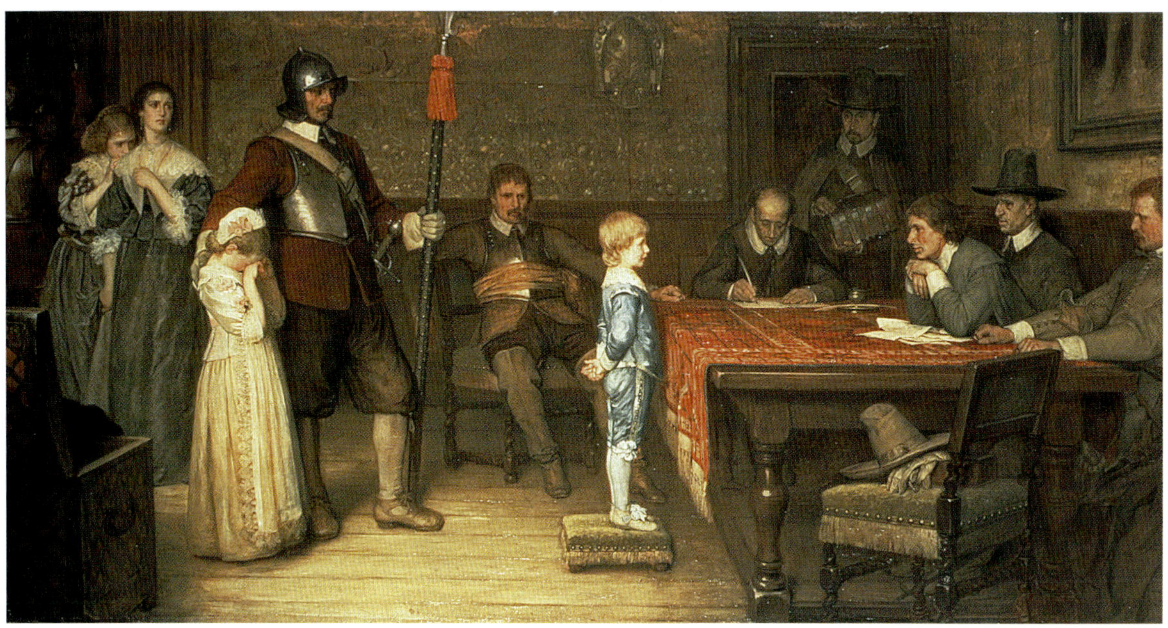

36 William Frederick
Yeames, *And When Did
You Last See Your Father?*,
1878, Oil on canvas,
131x251.5 cm.
Walker Art Gallery,
National Museums
Liverpool

The most dramatic of the mid-Victorian paintings that show episodes from the Civil War and the early days of the Commonwealth depict not real events and recognisable historical characters in Van Dyke costumes, but invented ones. The situations that these invented characters find themselves in serve to stress the sharply divided politics of the period. The most lastingly celebrated of all these is William Frederick Yeames's *And When Did You Last See Your Father?* of 1878 (fig. 36). The picture may have taken time to establish itself in the popular memory, but it was once so famous as to be re-presented as a waxwork tableau at Madame Tussauds, a tableau which first appeared in the Marylebone Road galleries in 1933, was re-formatted in 1980, and which finally disappeared in only 1989.[31] For Yeames, who wished to paint his nephew 'of an innocent and truthful disposition' in 'a situation where the child's outspokenness and unconsciousness would lead to disastrous consequences, ' a country house occupied by Puritan inquisitors 'during the Rebellion in England' seemed to offer an ideal subject. The oppositions are stark. We are not just observing innocence challenged by experience, or male military might persecuting women and children, but the whole fictional panoply of Civil War England.[32] The distressed aristocratic women are attired in silks and lace, while the figure of the centrally placed boy-hero is dressed in blue silk. He and his bright, fancy dress almost certainly derive from Van Dyke via Gainsborough's famous *The Blue Boy*, though he might strike some modern observers as a clone of Little Lord Fauntleroy. Opposed to the boy and his family are the dull colours of the representatives of the military and religious might of the new order. His chief inquisitor, who leans towards him across the table, is decidedly *not* Oliver Cromwell, though his sober dress may have suggested the idea to many sentimental admirers of the picture. What we do have is a parade of everything the popular imagination once readily associated with Cromwell's regime: the armed ironsides, the buff-jackets, the breastplates, the cropped heads, the tall, pointed Puritan hats and the plain, white pilgrim-father linen collars. The real drama of the picture lies in its evocation of the old and the new, in its sense of revolutionary change and in its suggestions of class conflict. The tension implied by the picture's title is of course crucial but, as the picture shows, some issues are already resolved. The Roundheads have won, and the Cavalier family are obliged to endure the consequences of having backed the wrong side. Might may not be right, but it is certainly mighty. Yeames's *And When Did You Last See Your Father?* is a picture about proscription. Its real resonance for Victorian admirers, and for subsequent generations, stems from the fact that it not only evoked a tense period in British history, but that it also suggested vivid modern parallels. Those parallels were to be found in a whole variety of nasty, oppressive and generally foreign regimes, some of which were even to claim some form of kinship with the Cromwellian revolution.

John Everett Millais exhibited his *The Proscribed Royalist, 1651* (fig. 37) at the Royal Academy in 1853. He showed it with *The Order of Release* (see fig. 84, p. 215), another scene that shows the consequences of taking sides in a military conflict and of ending up on the wrong one. *The Order of Release* depicts a brave Highland wife delivering her husband from a Redcoat prison after the 1745 Jacobite Rising. We cannot, however, be certain of the relationship between the hidden cavalier and the well-dressed woman whose hand he gratefully kisses in *The Proscribed Royalist*. Commenting on the picture when it was shown at the retrospective exhibition of Millais's works in 1898, M. H. Spielmann wrote:

> This drama admits of several interpretations. It is the daughter succouring the father – the mistress her lover – the sister her brother –

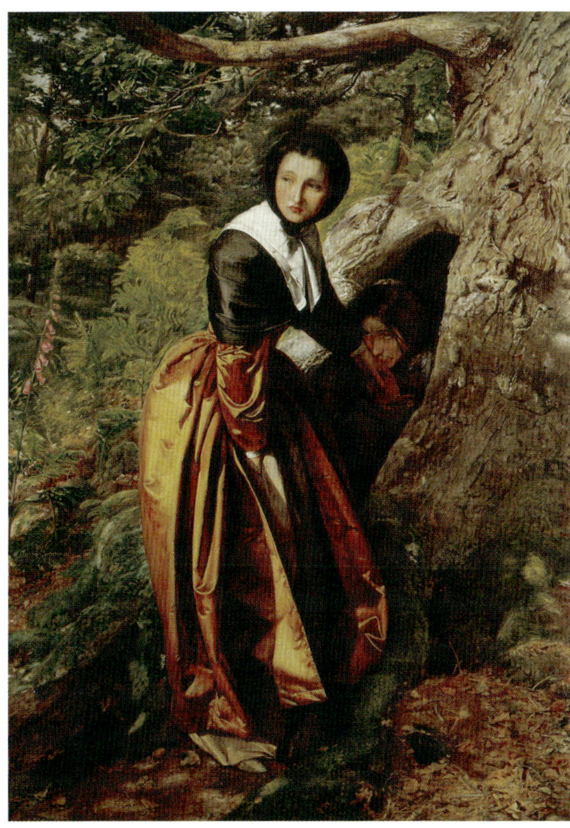

37 John Everett Millais, *The Proscribed Royalist*, 1853, Oil on canvas, 102.9 x 73.6 cm. Private collection

in that reign of terror when to harbour a Cavalier meant condemnation, when every rustle of leaf of squirrel sounded like a footfall, and the shadow of every branch seemed like that of man – of a spy.[33]

Where Spielmann got his absurd idea of a Cromwellian 'Reign of Terror' from we cannot be sure, but what he rightly suggests is that we have to read a great deal into the picture, and not only concerning the precise nature of the link between the man and the woman. This is a picture which, like William Shakespeare Burton's striking *A Wounded Cavalier* (fig.38) of 1856, shows the dangers of commitment, whether that commitment be emotional, familial or political. When he began his picture in 1852, Millais must have been aware that he was offering a retrospect on a period two hundred years anterior to his

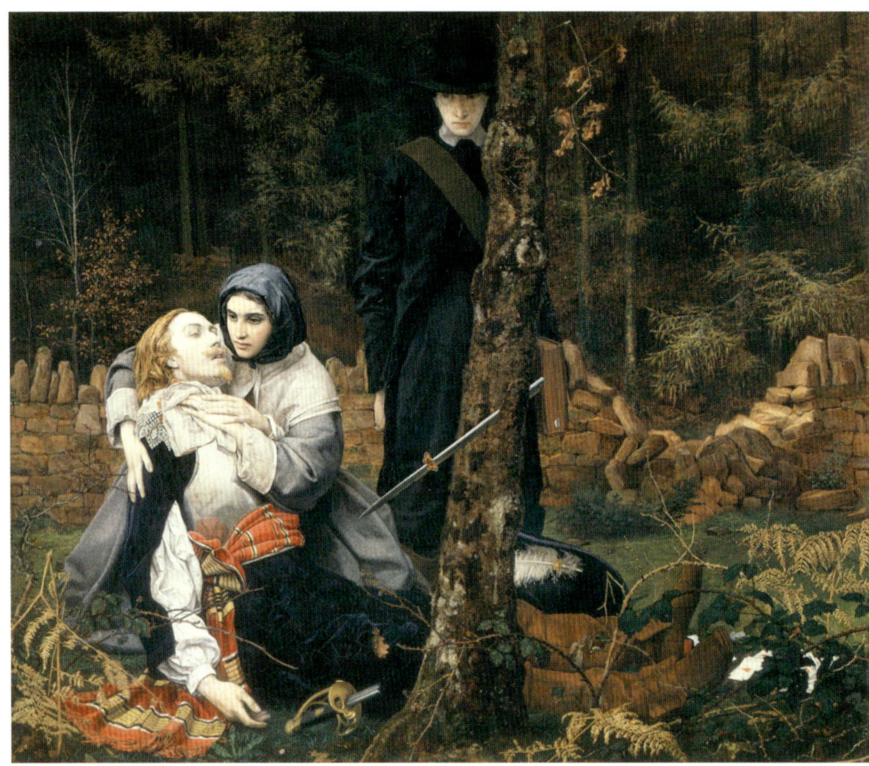

38   William Shakespeare Burton, *The Wounded Cavalier*, 1855–56, Oil on canvas, 88.9 x 104.1 cm. Guildhall Art Gallery, City of London

own. The fact that he gives the date '1651' alerts us both to this fact and to the likely literary sources that lie behind the painting. The Battle of Worcester, in which Charles II had vainly attempted to regain his father's throne, had been fought on 3 September 1651. With his army in disarray, the defeated Charles had been obliged to escape from Worcester in disguise, seeking asylum in loyal houses and, most famously, in an hospitable oak tree. Those Cavaliers who had fought with the new king were very likely to have found themselves among the ranks of the 'proscribed,' but many other active Royalists of an older generation had had their estates sequestered and their persons threatened as 'malcontents.' The young family of one such 'malcontent' figures in Frederick Marryat's enduringly popular *The Children of the New Forest* (1847). It is perhaps extraordinary that Marryat, a seaman to his tarry fingertips, should have written such a landlocked novel, but this address to 'the junior reader' clearly caught the mood of the time. This is a starkly pro-Cavalier novel in which

Cromwellians are generally cast as mean-spirited baddies in high-crowned hats. The chief exception to this rule is the sympathetic Parliamentarian Intendent of the New Forest who gives the boy-hero, Edward Beverley, a clear exposition of the ambiguities of his position:

> I will now answer for myself and thousands more. You are too young a man to have known the cause of the insurrection, or rather opposition to the unfortunate King Charles. He attempted to make himself absolute, and to wrest their liberties from the people of England; that his warmest adherents will admit. When I joined the party which opposed him, I little thought that matters would have been carried so far as they have been. I always considered it lawful to take up arms in defence of our liberties, but at the same time I equally felt that the person of the king was sacred. (Chapter 16)

Both the Intendent and Edward agree that the execution of the king was 'murder,' though Edward remains at a loss as to how any decent man could bring himself to rebel against his lawful sovereign. *The Children of the New Forest* is the story of four singularly resourceful aristocratic siblings, orphaned when their father dies at the Battle of Naseby and consequently deprived of their rightful inheritance. The children are obliged to take refuge in a remote sylvan cottage in the New Forest, once royal property but now sequestered by Parliament. The Forest provides them with a vegetable-garden, good pasturage, ample game, ponies and even stray cattle and they survive as efficiently, and improbably, as the shipwrecked Swiss Family Robinson. Much of the narrative is taken up with accounts of how Edward and his brother Humphrey master the arts of deer stalking, cattle rustling, animal husbandry and carpentry, but there are digressions when Edward absents himself to fight with the new King Charles at Worcester and when he later joins the exiled Royalists in Paris and the Low Countries. It all ends happily, of course, with Edward married to the noble Intendent's daughter and their inheritance restored in 1660, but the nub of the story is concerned with the woods as a refuge and with the New Forest acting as a kind of Shakespearian Arden. There is a good deal of Bible reading in *The Children of the New Forest*, but Marryat does not distract his 'junior readers' with the religious controversies of the seventeenth century. Nevertheless, it is in the Forest that the wrongfully disinherited Beverleys find a kind of spiritual contentment and a new rustic dignity without ever questioning their ingrained commitment to the Cavalier cause.

The date '1651' in the title of Millais's painting almost certainly echoes that of Sir Walter Scott's novel *Woodstock; or, The Cavalier*. The novel, which carries the subtitle *A Tale of the Year Sixteen Hundred and Fifty-One*, has an aged 'malcontent,' Sir Henry Lee, as a central character and his proscribed son, Eustace, as its hero. The year 1826, which saw the appearance of Scott's novel, was also notable for the commercial success of Horace Smith's *Brambletye House; or, Cavaliers and Roundheads*. This too presents readers with an ageing malcontent baronet who makes no attempt to restrain the royalist passions of his proscribed son, Jocelyn Compton. Though set in 'the latter years of Oliver Cromwell's Protectorate,' we realise that Jocelyn's proscription has resulted from his having fought for the Stuart cause at Worcester. Both novels have active roles for the fugitive Charles II, but neither contains a scene that might have directly suggested the subject of Millais's painting. Indeed, as *Woodstock* shows, it is not to the hero that any amatory interest attaches but to the wandering hands and eyes of the restless young King. As we know that Millais took his fellow artist, Arthur Hughes, as the model for the Cavalier concealed in the cleft oak-tree, there can, of course, be no hint that the fugitive is meant to be Charles or that the woman's anxious sideways glance is the consequence of an unexpected and stolen kiss. It would seem that, as with Yeames's painting, we are looking at a fictional event with no obvious precedent either in history or literature. Like Yeames, Millais was doubtless attracted by the stark oppositions of 1651 and by the dramatic opportunities presented by perils and dangers inherent in the times. The very currency of themes derived from the Civil War is evidenced not just by Scott's and Smith's novels, but also by the popularity of Vincenzo Bellini's opera *I Puritani* ('The Puritans'), first staged in Paris in January 1835 and performed in London at the King's Theatre in the following May. Further revivals of the opera, which Millais may have seen, took place at Covent Garden in 1851 and 1852.[34] Act 3 of *I Puritani* does, however, contain a secret liaison between the proscribed Royalist, Arturo Talbot, and his confused Puritan beloved, Elvira Walton. Elvira, betrothed to Arturo, has become mentally distracted because her beloved has contrived the escape of Queen Henrietta Maria from Plymouth disguised in Elvira's bridal veil. The secret reconciliation of the lovers takes place in a grove where, despite Arturo's capture by his Roundhead pursuers, he is operatically saved from death by a fortuitous pardon.

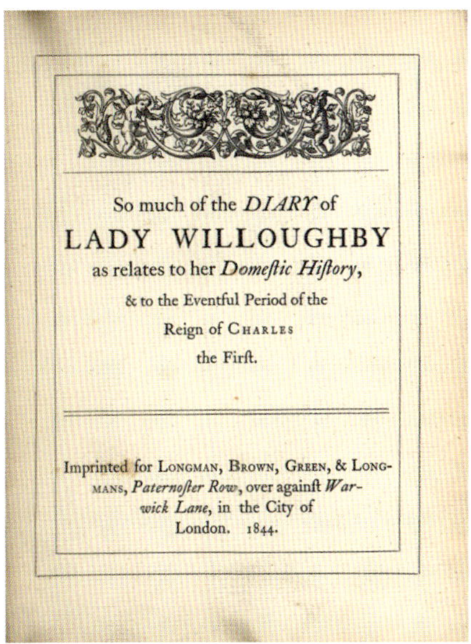

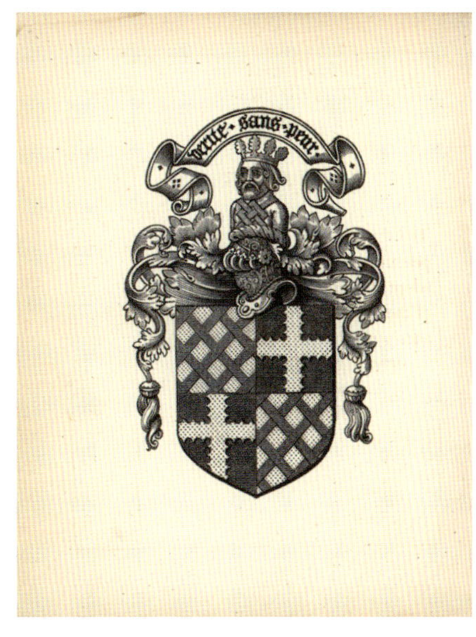

39 Title Page from *Lady Willoughby's Diary*, 1844. Private collection

40 Page ornament from *Lady Willoughby's Diary*, 1844. Private collection

That stories of Cavaliers and Roundheads had a particular currency in the 1840s and 50s is also evidenced in the pages of two profoundly different works: the fictitious *Lady Willoughby's Diary* of 1844 (figs.39, 40) and Charles Dickens's *Bleak House* of 1852-53. *Lady Willoughby's Diary* or, to give it its full title, *So Much of the Diary of Lady Willoughby as relates to her Domestic History, & to the Eventful Period of the Reign of Charles the First*, became celebrated amongst twentieth-century book collectors as the first book printed in the revived Caslon type (a claim which has since been doubted).[35] Its real merits do indeed lie in the quality of its production (it is printed on fine paper and still has a strong typographical impact) but its lasting fascination is due to the fact that the enterprising London publisher, Longmans, wanted to produce a book that not only read like a seventeenth-century memoir but actually looked like one too. The creator of 'Lady Willoughby,' who reveals herself in her second volume (*Some Further Portions of the Diary* of 1848) to be a friend of John Evelyn, was clearly inspired by the first appearance in print of Evelyn's diary in 1818-27. Even so, the *Diary* offers a telling slant on history told from an aristocratic woman's point of view. Like a thoroughly modern liberal couple, the Willoughbys have been drawn to the Parliamentary cause because they oppose the arbitrary government of the King. When, however, Parliament has enforced its will and holds the King captive, Lady Willoughby graphically describes her husband's concerns for Charles's future well-being:

> And the *King*, deare *Husband*, I asked, is he safe, and will he depart the Countrey? No man knoweth, he reply'd: he will not be permitted to leave the Country, if Guards and strong Castles can prevent. He is safe, so far as concerns his Life: he may be deprived of Power or even of his Crowne, but on no Plea can they take his Life: and yet who shall say where they will stop? I would lay down my Life to know him to be safe: we have fought and striven, and have set a Stone rolling that haply will crush all that come in its way, Laws, *Parliament*, or even the *King* himselfe. My *Husband* leant downe his Head on the table, & hid his Face on his arme, and so remained overwhelmed by the prospect of misery before us.[36]

The Willoughbys are clearly a devoted, and indeed, a devout couple, but the political consequences of their moderate opposition to King Charles's personal rule lead first to a crisis of conscience and then to direct opposition to the new regime.

The retrospect on another aristocratic seventeenth-century couple in *Bleak House* tells a very different story. Readers of the novel are made aware of the ominous associations of the Ghost's Walk at Chesney Wold long before the story of the haunted terrace is retold by Mrs. Rouncewell, the fiercely loyal housekeeper at the Dedlock family's country estate. Her account opens clumsily but, for the radical Dickens, tellingly with Mrs Rouncewell's awkward fumbling with politically correct facts:

> In the wicked days of King Charles the First – I mean, of course, in the wicked days of the rebels who leagued themselves against that excellent king – Sir Morbury Dedlock was the owner of Chesney Wold. (Chapter 7)

Sir Morbury was, needless to say, 'on the side of the blessed martyr' but his wife 'who had none of the family blood in her veins, favoured the bad cause.' This Lady Dedlock was reputed to have spied on Cavalier assemblies at Chesney Wold and to have reported plans to the 'rebels'. The childless Sir Morbury and his lady are ill-matched both socially and emotionally and their relationship is further strained when her brother is killed in battle by a near kinsman of his. So offended is she that she regularly lames cavalier horses in the house's stables, but being surprised by her husband when about her nefarious nocturnal activities the wicked baronet struggles with his wife, a horse lashes out and she is permanently lamed in the hip. Thus she is obliged to spend the rest of her unhappy life silently and uncomplainingly hobbling up and down the terrace, holding on to the stone balustrade. When finally she is struck down by death she looks 'fixedly and coldly' on the baronet and proclaims: 'I will die here where I have walked. And I will walk here, though I am in my grave. I will walk here until the pride of this house is humbled. And when calamity, or when disgrace is coming to it, let the Dedlocks listen for my step.' *Bleak House* is conspicuously concerned with issues of the 1850s and *not* the 1650s. Nevertheless the story of the curse laid on Sir Morbury Dedlock's successors must have struck Dickens as both exemplary and timely. The modern Dedlocks, proud, self-satisfied and, with other establishment families, slowly strangling the body-politic, are portrayed as a relic of an increasingly defunct social order. They have to be shamed into retreat. But Dickens is implying more: in the seventeenth century they constituted a house divided against itself, and houses so divided cannot stand. The story of Sir Morbury Dedlock might represent the larger state of England during the Civil War, just as the complex story of the modern Dedlocks, as it is told in *Bleak House*, speaks of the Condition of England in the nineteenth century. Dickens is touching on the horrors of division as they broaden out from a family to the nation as a whole. With father pitted politically against son, brother against brother, husband against wife, historic England had tottered. The drama implicit in civil division certainly appealed to artists in search of a good plot or a charged romance, but the very nature of that drama also gave rise to a shiver of fear. When the American Civil War broke out in 1861 that shiver had become a horrid, but vaguely familiar, reality to many observers on this side of the Atlantic.

His Highness

The sunken stretch of grass on the western flank of Westminster Hall is sometimes known as Cromwell's Green. On it stands a statue of the Lord Protector by Hamo Thorneycroft (fig.41) which was unveiled in November

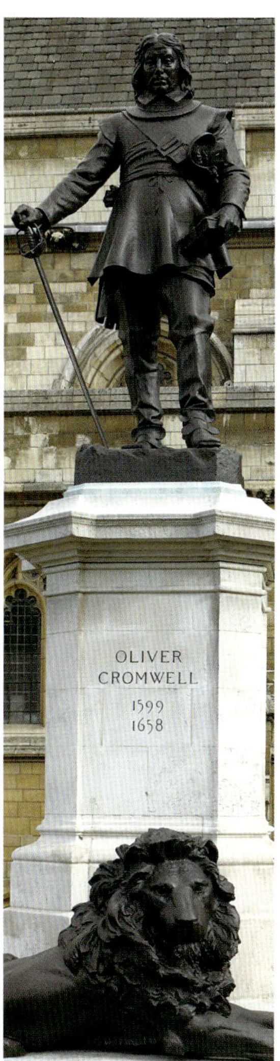

41 Hamo Thorneycroft, Cromwell, Westminster Hall Green, 1897, Bronze statue, 304. 8 cm high. Palace of Westminster Collection

1899. The huggermugger unveiling ceremony was performed by the sculptor and one of his assistants during a Parliamentary recess. Only four other people were present, one of whom was the police constable on duty.[37] In his posthumous life, as in his physical life, Cromwell proved to be a deeply contentions figure. The Palace of Westminster had taken its time in commemorating one of its most famous and dynamic members, though it was on a pole at the south end of Westminster Hall that the regicide Cromwell's severed head was displayed for some twenty years after his corpse had been disinterred from the Abbey and dragged to Tyburn for a symbolic 'execution.' An *amende honorable* might have been offered in the 1840s, when the idea of a monument was discussed by the Fine Arts Commission, but nothing came of the plan. In the 1860s Manchester took what must have seemed a typically radical lead by including a stone head of Cromwell amongst those of the Kings and Queens of England on the new Assize Courts (1859-64) and by placing a marble bust by Matthew Noble (1861) in the Sculpture Gallery of its new Town Hall. A second statue of Cromwell, also by Noble, was presented to the citizens of Manchester by a private donor and was erected in 1875 near the Anglican Cathedral on the spot reputed to be where the first victim of the Civil War was killed (the statue has been moved to Wythenshawe Park).[38] Despite the fact that the issue of commemorating Cromwell in Parliament had been periodically raised in the House of Commons nothing positive was done until the Liberal Prime Minister, Lord Rosebery, took up the scheme in 1895. Where opposition to the scheme had once come from Conservatives, by the 1890s it was the Irish Nationalists who most vocally opposed the idea. Cromwell had never been forgiven either for his ruthless sequestrations or for his actions at the siege of Drogheda. Herbert Gladstone had warned the artist that 'the Irish, except Ulster, were going to fight hard against the erection of the Cromwell statue' and he added 'the Scotch have equally good reason to object … but they are different and will not probably.'[39] It was a singularly heated debate in the Commons over the actual siting of the statue that finally forced the already beleaguered Rosebery's resignation from the premiership in 1896. The Commons having refused to vote any funds towards the project, it was Rosebery who footed the entire £3000 bill. Thorneycroft's bronze statue stands on its sunken lawn, at a safe distance from the pavement, presumably to secure it against any public (or Irish) abuse. It shows the hatless Lord Protector looking down, seemingly lost in thought, in a pose purposefully unlike that he

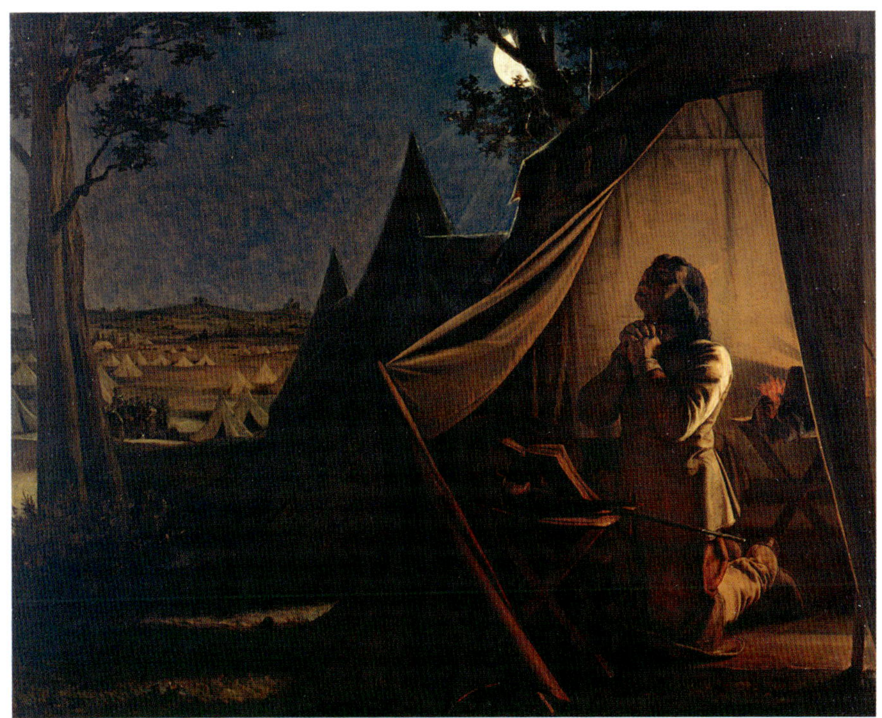

42 Augustus Egg, *Cromwell Before Naseby*, 1859, Oil on canvas, 101.6 x 127cm. Royal Academy of Arts, London

had assumed in Delaroche's *Cromwell Uncovering the Coffin of Charles I.* Here he stands, stolid but untriumphant, with a sword in his right hand and Bible in his left. At the foot of the plinth is a watchful seated lion of which Rosebery had expressed the hope that it would be 'more confident, not too dolorous.'[40]

Hamo Thorneycroft's choice of artefacts is indicative of how Cromwell's reputation had developed in the nineteenth century. In 1859 Augustus Leopold Egg had represented him in *Cromwell before Naseby* (fig.42) as a devout soldier of the Lord, rapt in earnest prayer. The kneeling figure is viewed through the opening in a tent, a Bible is open on a folding camp-stool before him, propped up on his drawn sword. The brooding man-of-destiny Cromwell appears again in Ford Madox Brown's *St Ives, AD 1630. Cromwell on his Farm* (fig.43). This painting was first conceived of as a watercolour study in 1853–56 when Brown felt socially isolated, misunderstood and rejected by the art establishment. It shows the great man in civilian dress with, as one critic styled it, 'a saturnine visage.' Where Hamo Thorneycroft had painstakingly studied contemporary

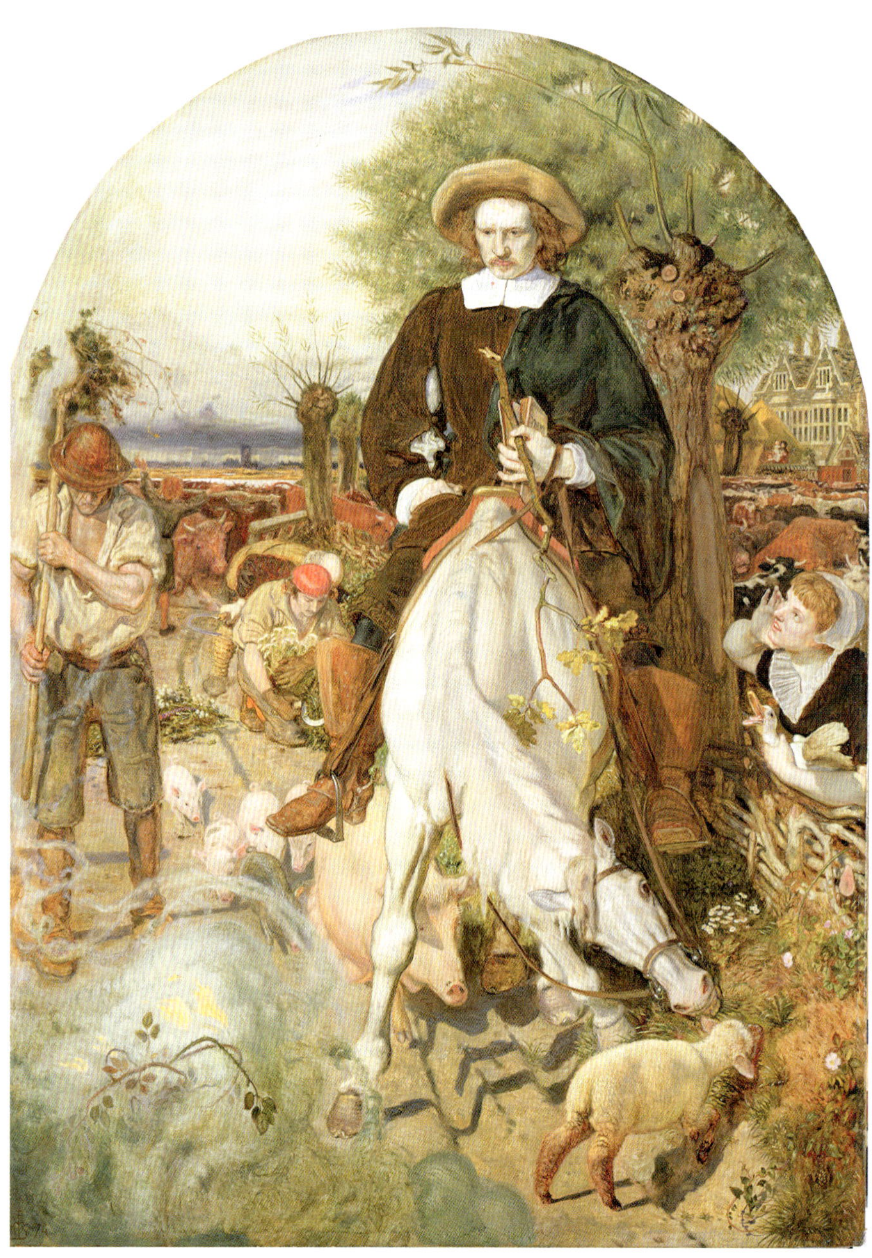

43   Ford Madox Brown, *St Ives, AD 1630. Cromwell on his Farm*, 1874,
      Oil on canvas, 143 x 104.3 cm. Lady Lever Art Gallery, National Museums Liverpool

portraits of Cromwell, Brown simply used his own face as the model for his withdrawn, meditative hero. When he repainted the picture in oils in 1874, he continued to represent a Cromwell who has the painter's own features and who shares his personal dejection.[41] In a depressed state in 1853 Brown had taken up Carlyle's edition of Cromwell's *Letters and Speeches* (1846) and read it with something approaching relish. Ford Madox Hueffer describes the artist's gloom with a touch of wryness:

> The spectacle of a man holding himself apart from his fellows and steeping himself in Carlyle and gloom is … one capable of being burlesqued: the mood had, perhaps, its self-conscious side, and as such it must have appeared to Madox Brown's deserted companions a fit subject for the squibs of Rossetti in his buoyant moods.[42]

The self-absorbed Brown therefore identified himself with a Cromwell who still had to wait to realise his true vocation and his proper destiny. Brown was particularly taken with Carlyle's account of the period when Cromwell had returned, in a low state of mind, to his estates near St. Ives following Charles I's dismissal of Parliament in 1629. Carlyle describes Cromwell in retirement at St. Ives 'hoping to walk with integrity and humble devout diligence through this world; and by his Maker's infinite mercy, to escape destruction, and find Salvation, in Divine Worlds.' He also describes the low-lying and unspectacular Huntingdonshire landscape that seems to reflect both Cromwell's and Brown's cast of mind: 'The lands he rented are still there, recognisable to the Tourist; gross, boggy lands fringed with willow trees.'[43] Despite the gloomy mood of the painting, we are bidden to interpret the very intensity of Cromwell's expression as he gazes at a smoky bonfire. He has ridden abstractedly past farm-labourers at their work, a beckoning serving woman, an intrusive sow and a lamb that seems likely to be squashed by the hooves of the advancing horse. All importantly, this Cromwell holds a half-open Bible in his left hand and, as one of his letters tells us, he has come across two verses from Psalms 89: 'Lord, how long? Wilt thou hide Thyself for ever?' and 'And shall Thy wrath burn like fire?' Here then is the Man of Destiny, not yet called to be a soldier or a justified rebel, who, like a Hebrew Prophet, awaits the Divine call to shift English history in a new direction.

Ford Madox Brown represents Cromwell for a receptive mid-Victorian audience as a hero in the making. He would not have been recognised as such by the majority of the men and women of the preceding century. Take, for example the brief account of the Lord Protector offered to the alert schoolboy in Mavor's schoolboy text *The Young Man's Companion, or Youth's Instructor; being a Guide to the Various Branches of Useful Knowledge* in 1824:

> Oliver Cromwell was the son of a private gentleman … From accident or intrigue he was chosen member for Cambridge in the Long Parliament: but he seemed at first to possess no talents for oratory, his person being ungraceful, his dress slovenly, and his elocution homely, tedious, obscure and embarrassed. He made up, however, by zeal and perseverance, what he wanted in natural powers; and being endowed with unshaken intrepidity and much dissimulation, he rose through the gradations of preferment to the post of lieutenant-general … On December 16 [1653] he was invested with the title of Lord Protector of the Commonwealth of England, Scotland and Ireland … [and] acted in the most arbitrary and oppressive manner where his own interest was concerned … His favourite daughter, Mrs Claypole, died on August 6, 1658, of a languishing disorder, during which she is said to have awakened the horrors of his guilty conscience. He was from that time wholly altered, grew more reserved and suspicious; not indeed without reason, for he found a general content prevail throughout the nation. He wore armour under his clothes, and always kept a pistol in his pocket … A tertian ague came at last to deliver him from this life of horror and anxiety. He died on the 3rd of September … and his death was considered remarkable by one of the most violent tempests which had blown in the memory of man. He was then fifty-nine years old, and had usurped the government nine years.[44]

Mavor's Cromwell is a dissimulating scoundrel and usurper, a dictatorial tyrant haunted by his conscience like a latter-day Richard III. He dies in his bed, a guilty thing, as a thunderstorm rages to underline the displeasure of the heavens. It was against such a background of popular distaste that Carlyle was to declare Cromwell the exemplary hero. He was acclaimed not only as the hero of his own time but as the timeless champion of a new order of things.

Carlyle may have been Cromwell's most vocal and articulate defender in the first half of the nineteenth century, but he was by no means his first or only apologist. In *Woodstock* (1826) Sir Walter Scott had endowed him with dignity and a spirit of wise generosity. Take, for example, Cromwell's noble defence of his policy once Charles II has been proscribed after the Battle of Worcester:

> Cromwell sighed deeply as he answered, 'Ah … in this troubled world, a man, who is called like me to work great things in Israel, had need to be, as the poets feign, a thing made of hardened metal, immovable to feelings of human charities, impassible, resistless … the world will hereafter, perchance, think of me as being such a one as I have described, "an iron man, and made of iron mould" – Yet they will wrong my memory – my heart is flesh, and my blood is mild as that of others … and canst thou think it is a light thing to me, that, the blood of this lad's father [Charles I] lying in some measure upon my head, I should now put in peril that of the son? They are of the kindly race of English sovereigns, and, doubtless, are adored like to demigods by those of their own party. I am called Parricide, Blood-thirsty Usurper, already for shedding the blood of one man, that a plague might be stayed – or as Achan was slain that Israel might thereafter stand against the face of their enemies … Truly … it is a great thing … to be lifted above the multitude; but when one feeleth that his exaltation is rather hailed with hate and scorn than with love and reverence – in sooth it is a hard matter for a mild tender-conscienced infirm spirit to bear – and God be my witness, that rather than do this new deed I would shed my own best heart's-blood in a pitched field, twenty against one.' (Volume 3, Chapter 9)

This is the humane soldier and the politic statesman who justifies his statecraft with passionate, immediate and informed reference to Scripture. With the Bible in his left hand and the sword in his right, Scott's fearless Cromwell forges a way ahead in defence of justice, principle and religion.

A similarly upright Cromwell emerges from Horace Smith's *Brambletye House*, but in 1840 Smith published a far more substantial and wholly sympathetic fictionalised account of the Lord Protector in his *Oliver Cromwell: An Historical Romance*. Smith's Whig narrative looks askance at Charles I's court, is especially venomous about the shifty and untrustworthy Henrietta Maria, and is disparaging about most of Charles's cavaliers. There is a particularly unforgiving description of Prince Rupert at the Battle of Newbury:

> A tall, strongly-built, and splendidly-accoutred man, superbly mounted on a jet black barb … Yet were his features coarse and ill-favoured, marked with a supercilious sneer, and an expression ill-humoured, haughty, and imperious. His hair, which flowed far down his shoulders, was harsh and quite uncurled. His figure too, though tall and powerful, was graceless – his body corpulent and gross, betraying symptoms of debauchery and licence, as plainly as his countenance reflected a mind despotic, brutal, and self-willed. (Volume 2, Chapter 5)

This is as antipathetic and unromantic a view as one could wish for, though it runs counter to the evidence in the portraits of Rupert painted by Lely and to his received reputation for flashy gallantry. This 'Puritanical' distaste for Cavaliers as a whole allows for a uniformly benign light to fall on all of King Charles's principled enemies. They sing psalms before battle, they pray earnestly, they debate matters of theology and politics with educated vigour, and they justify themselves from the Scriptures with alacrity. No character is more prayerful and Bible-soaked than the virtuous Cromwell. Despite, or perhaps because of, the intensity and integrity of the Protector's Protestant faith, Smith makes great play with the legend that the young Cromwell had been granted a vision of his future greatness in which he was told that he would be a king in all but name. Here is Cromwell describing his vision to the novel's fictional hero, Edgar Ardenne:

> 'Fancy! *Fancy* I saw a vision,' cried Oliver impatiently. 'I tell you, Edgar Ardenne, as plainly as mine eyes behold you now, I saw that dusky form – as clearly as mine ears drink in your doubting accents, so clearly did I feel the tones of its immortal voice. How should I fancy such things? I was then but a boy – a wayward, headstrong and most ill-conditioned schoolboy. It was a sabbath night and I lay wide awake, plotting I know not what of orchard-breaking, or of hen roost robbing for the morrow – when suddenly a strange and thrilling fear crept over me – I knew that I was not alone, though I saw nothing. I felt as though a pair of mighty wings were spread above me, chilling my very soul – I would have cried aloud, but my voice choked within me – I would have risen up and

fled, but could not move a finger … It was a night of murky darkness, but suddenly a faint and pallid light filled the whole chamber, not emanating from one brighter point, but uniform as daylight, though very dull and ghastly. My curtains were drawn suddenly asunder, and a tall misty shape stood in the opening. I tell you I did see it perfectly and plainly, for I did not faint, though my flesh quivered aguelike – and the cold sweat stood in beads on my brow – and my hair bristled, as instinct with life. There it stood while I reckoned twenty, and then a deep slow voice, of strange and solemn harmony, rolled forth without an effort – "Arise! arise," it said, "thou shalt be first in England!" It then vanished, and all again was darkness, but the voice was tingling in mine ears when the next sun was high in the heaven.' (Volume 2, Chapter 8)

Smith's Cromwell has been endowed with prophetic vision and, it seems, mystically anointed by God to be a David or a Solomon without having the title of King. When Ardenne suggests that the vision might be untrustworthy or, more dangerously, devilishly expressive of enthusiasm or of suppressed ambition, Cromwell coolly responds that he feels what he saw was akin to the legendary dream accorded to Marcus Junius Brutus, and then resorts to a Davidic prayer for humility:

'But thou, Lord, knowest – thou beholdest – yea! thou readest the most inward thoughts of this thy servant – continue me then, O thou merciful and mighty One, continue me thine instrument; and shield me from the power of the evil one; and be thy word a lantern to my feet; and keep me, even as I now am – thine, O Lord, thy servant and thine only!'

When, in the closing pages of the novel, death approaches Smith's fevered Cromwell this vision of greatness continues to haunt him – but so does the spectre of a 'blood-stained and headless trunk.' 'King! King!' shouts the devoutly Republican Cromwell, 'there be *no* kings in England – the *man*, the *man* Charles Stuart!' He is calmed by the solicitous Ardenne and by the twin balms of prayer and reflection. Then, as a great storm rumbles over London and thunder claps break the 'melancholy silence,' Cromwell breathes his last and Ardenne offers him a heartfelt eulogy in the Shakespearian or, at the very least, Miltonic mode:

There passed the spirit of the greatest man England has ever seen! Peace to his soul! His faults die with him! – but never – never, while the round world endures, shall his fame be forgotten, or the good he hath done his country, pass away. Weep, England, weep! Your benefactor is no more – and I foresee much strife, much anarchy, much blood! But he, who hath gone hence, hath sown the seed of thy prosperity, thy freedom, and thy glory; and thou shalt reap the harvest, thou and thy sons for many a deathless age, when he who is nothing – and I who mourn above him shall be dust rendered unto dust and ashes unto ashes! (Volume 3, Chapter 4)

In the unlikely event that Shakespeare or Milton had been given the opportunity to write an historical novel they would probably have rendered this dramatic deathbed scene infinitely more expressive, more stately and more poignant. Nevertheless, one suspects that even Sir Walter Scott at his most romantically charged could not have done it better. It is certainly utterly distinct from the artist David Wilkie Wynfield's pious representation of *The Death of Oliver Cromwell* of 1867 (Victoria and Albert Museum) which shows a serene deathbed with Cromwell's female relatives praying at the foot of the bed and a bevy of earnest kneeling Puritan ministers beseeching the mercy of the Almighty in an adjacent chamber.

We cannot be certain that Carlyle knew Smith's novel, but many of his own convictions about Cromwell find echoes in the novel, and certain aspects of the novel are in turn amplified in Carlyle's edition of the *Letters and Speeches*. Both men certainly seem to have shared a profound and unquestioning admiration for Cromwell's character and for his lasting influence over the constitutional development of Britain and the wider world. Cromwell is the undoubted star of the last of Carlyle's lectures 'On Heroes, Hero-Worship and the Heroic in History' delivered on 22 May 1840. The lecture was appropriately on 'the last form of Heroism; that which we call Kingship.' Having attempted to define what he means by the word 'King,' Carlyle proceeds to set up a series of theses and antitheses, gods and false gods, heroes and men of straw. Most effective is his characterisation of Archbishop Laud as some fuddy-duddy man of the past, a man who resembles 'a College-Tutor, whose whole world is forms, College-rules; whose notion is that these are the life and safety of the world.' Against the pathetically hidebound figure of Laud, trapped by the past, stands the dynamic mould-breaker, Cromwell:

Everywhere we have to note the decisive, practical *eye* of the man; how he drives towards the practical and practicable; has a genuine insight into what *is* fact. Such an intellect, I maintain, does not belong to a false man: the false man sees false shows, plausibilities, expediences: the true man is needed to discern even practical truth … by whatever name you might call him, the acknowledged Strongest Man in England, virtually the King of England, requires no magic to explain it![45]

This is the Cromwell who triumphantly marches through the pages of Carlyle's edition of the *Letters and Speeches* as the representative of 'our English genius against the world,' and as the soul of the Puritan revolt which proved to be 'a revolt transcendentally memorable, and an epoch in the World's history.'[46]

Avenging the Slaughtered Saints: Milton and Cromwell

Cromwell's 'virile personality' seems to have stirred Ford Madox Brown's imagination as much as it did Carlyle's. In 1877 Brown returned to a Cromwellian subject in his *Cromwell, Protector of the Vaudois* (fig. 44), a painting that shows the Lord Protector exercising his influence in the interest of the persecuted Waldensian Protestants of Piedmont in 1655. Significantly, the radical Brown contemplated a parallel painting showing *John Brown rescuing Negro Slaves* but he never completed the scheme.[47] Brown had taken up residence in Manchester at the time and, in common with many Non-conformist Mancunians, he was well aware of how powerfully the Waldensians and the American slaves, both victims of oppression, figured in the Protestant Victorian consciousness. Unlike African Americans, however, the Waldensians, who had been guaranteed their liberty in modern Piedmont in 1853, were always destined to be relatively small beer when it came to the great issues of human rights (it has been estimated that in 1868 there were only 28 ordained ministers of the sect in the entire Kingdom of Italy).[48] Nevertheless, Cromwell intervention on their behalf in the 1650s was seen as a landmark not only in the Protector's foreign policy but also in Britain's championship of minority rights in the larger world. The significance of the Waldensians for British Protestants was largely sentimental and historical, but few readers of John Milton could ever forget the fact that he had addressed one of his finest sonnets,

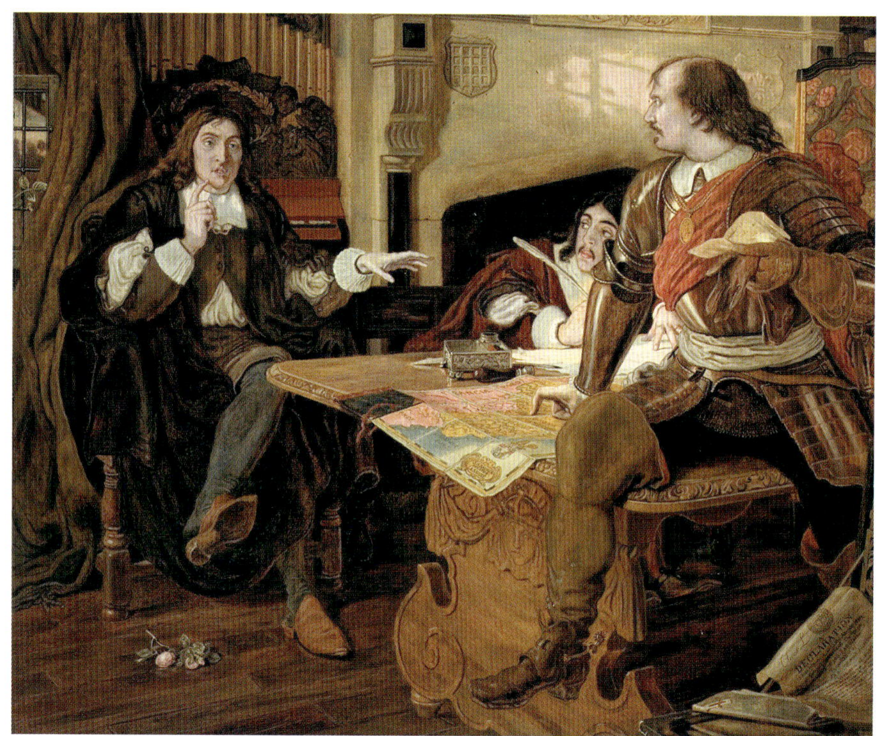

44 Ford Madox Brown, *Cromwell, Protector of the Vaudois*, 1878, Oil on canvas, 78.7 x 96.5 cm. Nottingham Castle Museum

'Avenge, O Lord, thy slaughtered saints,' to a call for Divine vengeance to fall on those who had perpetrated the massacre of April 1655. Brown's painting shows Cromwell in armour, apparently just returned from reviewing his troops, suddenly confronted with the news from Piedmont and determined on a vigorous response to any Popish assault on good Protestants, regardless of their nationality. Across the table from him sits a blind and quiet Milton who is translating Cromwell's angry words into a diplomatic despatch in Latin while Andrew Marvell writes it down from his fellow-poet's dictation (a re-translation of the letter into English had been published by Carlyle). A map of Savoy is spread on a table on which the 'virile' Cromwell sprawls, but there are roses at Milton's feet and behind his head is his chamber organ with its keyboard ready for the musical poet's touch. This then is not only a picture of Cromwell as the heroic defender of the Protestant cause; it is also, crucially, a representation of the culturally acceptable face of the Cromwellian regime.

John Milton's reputation as a poet had stood high in the eighteenth century, though responses to him as a man of affairs, notably Samuel Johnson's, were far less generous and apologetic. A handsome monument to the poet, incorporating a bust by Rysbrack, had been erected in Poet's Corner in Westminster Abbey in 1737 by Christopher Wren's Whig successor at the Office of Works, William Benson. The inscription, composed by Benson, does however refer rather more to the donor than to poet himself and certainly makes no direct reference to his politics. This was shortly before the much larger wall-monument to Shakespeare, designed by William Kent, was erected by public subscription in 1741. Though neither poet was actually buried in the Abbey, it was deemed fitting that both should be memorialised in what was increasingly regarded as the English Pantheon. Shakespeare, however, was never held guilty of crimes against the state and the busts of three Kings adorn the sculpted plinth on which he leans. Milton, the defender of regicide and of the English Republic, and the doughty foe of episcopacy, must have seemed to cut a far more awkward figure in this Coronation church and Royal Peculiar where the Establishment met to pray. It seems that the Christian poet, whose genius was apparent in *Paradise Lost*, was allowed to have redeemed the Puritan apologist's glaring civil sins. Those sins, mortal for eighteenth-century commentators, seem to have been reclassed as merely venial by their Victorian successors.

Milton, as friend of and Latin Secretary to Oliver Cromwell, had figured marginally in Scott's *Woodstock* and far more prominently in Horace Smith's *Brambletye House* and *Oliver Cromwell*. Scott deftly defuses any anti-Miltonic sentiments by putting an eruption of exaggerated spleen into the mouth of the staunch Royalist, Sir Henry Lee: 'John Milton, the blasphemous and bloody-minded author of the *Defensio Populi Anglicani*! – the advocate of the infernal High Court of Fiends! – the creature and parasite of that grand imposter, that loathsome hypocrite, that detestable monster, that prodigy of the universe, that disgrace of mankind, that landscape of iniquity, that sink of sin, and that compendium of baseness, Oliver Cromwell' (Volume 3, Chapter 1). By contrast, when the narrator of *Brambletye House* glimpses Milton and Marvell at work in the Library at Whitehall, he describes them as 'men worthy to sit enthroned in that costly library, and to be surrounded by the great and kindred intellects of the world' and as 'men who have become the certain heirs of never-dying fame'(Volume 1, Chapter 6). In the opening chapter of Smith's *Oliver Cromwell* the Protector himself characterises Milton as 'that pure-minded Christian', 'that most zealous patriot' and 'that sanctified, elected vessel.' When, four chapters later, we encounter the 'elected vessel' himself, the poet is praised as 'an ardent votary of liberty, in its most liberal and extended sense' and as 'a dreamer of those bright Utopian visions concerning perfect commonwealths and absolute equality of men, which, in whatever age or country, never have been, never can be, realized.'

The supposition that Milton's intellectual stretch overreached the bounds of possibility seems to have earned his prose works a general pardon amongst liberal-minded nineteenth-century readers. One antipathetic mid-Victorian critic, Thomas Arnold junior, was, however, prepared to take a stand against an increasing acceptance of Milton as the 'votary of liberty.' Clearly reacting against his eminent father's consistent liberalism, the younger Arnold expresses not only a suspicion of Milton's idea of liberty but also a nagging doubt about the universal benefits of liberty itself:

> There is much that is unspeakably noble and beautiful in Milton's plan … but it was straining the bow too far … besides, it was but a small section of the English people (perhaps it can never, in the nature of things, be more than a small section of any people) that was educated up to relish, or right use, of so large a freedom as Milton desired. Accordingly, after the death of the great captain, who had led them by a strange and terrible march far away from the beaten track known to their fathers, the people subsided into their old ways and notions at the Restoration, and the time of reaction began.[49]

Arnold was probably attempting to counteract the opinions of most persuasive nineteenth-century critic of Milton, the great Whig historian, Thomas Babington Macaulay. Macaulay's essay, 'Milton,' a long review of the translation into English of the *de Doctrina Christiana*, was first published in the *Edinburgh Review* in August 1825. When Macaulay's collection of *Critical and Historical Essays* appeared in 1843 'Milton' took pride of place, and remained in that prominent position in the many subsequent editions of what was an essential *vade mecum* of progressive historical opinion. In his essay Macaulay consistently reiterates the view that no diminution of the poet's intellectual enterprise is evident either in his prose or his verse. To see any aspect of Milton's thought as unworthy of him was both unhistorical and demeaning:

His public conduct was such as was to be expected from a man of spirit so high and of an intellect so powerful. He lived at one of the most memorable eras in the history of mankind, and at the very crisis of the great conflict between Oromasdes and Arimanes, liberty and despotism, reason and prejudice. That great battle was fought for no single generation, for no single land. The destinies of the human race were staked on the same cast with the freedom of the English people. Then were first proclaimed those mighty principles which have since worked their way into the depths of the American forests, which have roused Greece from the slavery and degradation of two thousand years, and which, from one end of Europe to the other, have kindled an unquenchable fire in the hearts of the oppressed, and loosed the knees of the oppressors with an unwonted fear.[50]

Macaulay is determined to prove that the Civil War, the Commonwealth and the Protectorate were the essential prelude to the Glorious Revolution when England expelled a tyrant and secured 'the solemn recognition of popular rights, liberty, security, toleration.' Those who oppose these fundamental Whig principles, on which the modern constitution is founded, stand for darkness not light (hence Macaulay's Zoroastrian references to the fraternal battles of Oromasdes and Arimanes). They therefore refuse to acknowledge Milton's pre-eminent position as the advocate of personal and public liberty. Milton had made a considered and forward-looking choice when he took sides:

> The choice lay, not between Cromwell and liberty, but between Cromwell and the Stuarts. That Milton chose well, no man can doubt who fairly compares the events of the protectorate with those of the thirty years which succeeded it, the darkest and most disgraceful in the English annals.[51]

The contention that the reigns of Charles II and James II were the 'darkest and most disgraceful' in English history is not allowed to be a matter of dispute. This is the Whig theory of history at its most sweeping, evangelical and grandiose. Macaulay feels that he has both history and historical justice on his side, and that all opposition can dismissed as at best footling and at worst devilish. One can see why he admired Milton's reasoned, puritanical arrogance so much. Here is Macaulay summing up his hero's character and achievement:

> There are few characters which have stood the closest scrutiny and the severest tests, which have been tried in the furnace and have proved pure, which have been weighed in the balance and have not been found wanting, which have been declared sterling by the general consent of mankind, and which are visibly stamped with the image and superscription of the Most High. These great men we trust that we know how to prize; and of these was Milton. The sight of his books, the sound of his name, are pleasant to us … Nor do we envy the man who can study either the life or the writings of the great poet and patriot, without aspiring to emulate, not indeed the sublime works with which his genius has enriched our literature, but the zeal with which he laboured for the public good, the fortitude with which he endured every private calamity, the lofty disdain with which he looked down on temptations and dangers, the deadly hatred which he bore to bigots and tyrants, and the faith which he so sternly kept with his country and with his fame.[52]

Here we have Milton, washed clean of the taints of bigotry, chauvinism, regicide and republicanism, and presented to the modern age as a secular saint. He may be stamped with the 'image and superscription of the Most High,' but he is otherwise serenely free of any sectarian bias or any hint of heresy. Yes, he was a man of his time, and, yes, he zealously espoused the causes of his time, but he nevertheless transcends history.

When, in the late 1840s, it was proposed to decorate the 'Poets' Hall,' now known as the Upper Waiting Hall, in the Palace of Westminster it was ordained that the room should exhibit painted scenes from the work of eight English and Scottish poets: Chaucer, Spenser, Shakespeare, Milton, Dryden, Pope, Scott and Byron. In the original scheme the painter John Callcott Horsley was commissioned to paint a fresco illustrative of Milton's twinned poems *L'Allegro* and *Il Penseroso*. It was, however, Macaulay who intervened to insist that Milton's art should not be represented by such relatively minor works, and that a scene from *Paradise Lost* might form a more fitting tribute to his genius. Even Macaulay, it seems, did not have the gall to suggest that an exemplary scene from political invectives, such as *Areopagitica* or *The Tenure of Kings and Magistrates*, might have been even more appropriate to the Houses of Parliament. As a consequence Horsley's tame mural shows *Satan Touched by*

Ithuriel's Spear while Whispering Evil Dreams to Eve (fig.45), a scene from Book IV of *Paradise Lost*.[53] It is a noble theme, but it cannot be said that Horsley's top-heavy painting does it much justice. Thus, as in the nearby Abbey, Milton had found a proper place among the poets rather than among the polemicists. Nevertheless, it is testimony to the very contentiousness of the politics of the Civil War in nineteenth-century England that this other Milton, the champion of liberty and the embattled Cromwellian propagandist, could not be represented in the decorative scheme for the new Parliament building. Despite Macaulay's spirited advocacy, his writings still rubbed against sensitive historical wounds and like certain of Delaroche's paintings they appeared to attack 'the nervous system of the public.' But then, as we have seen, a proposal half a century later to commemorate Milton's great patron could actually serve to humble a Prime Minister and bring down an administration.

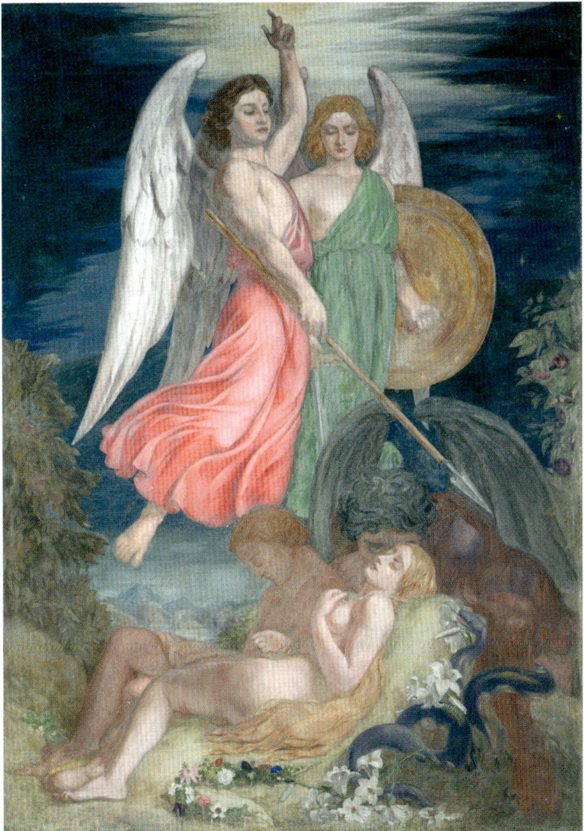

45 John Callcott Horsley, *Satan Touched by Ithuriel's Spear while Whispering Evil Dreams to Eve*, 1848, Fresco, 246.4 x 175.3 cm. Palace of Westminster Collection

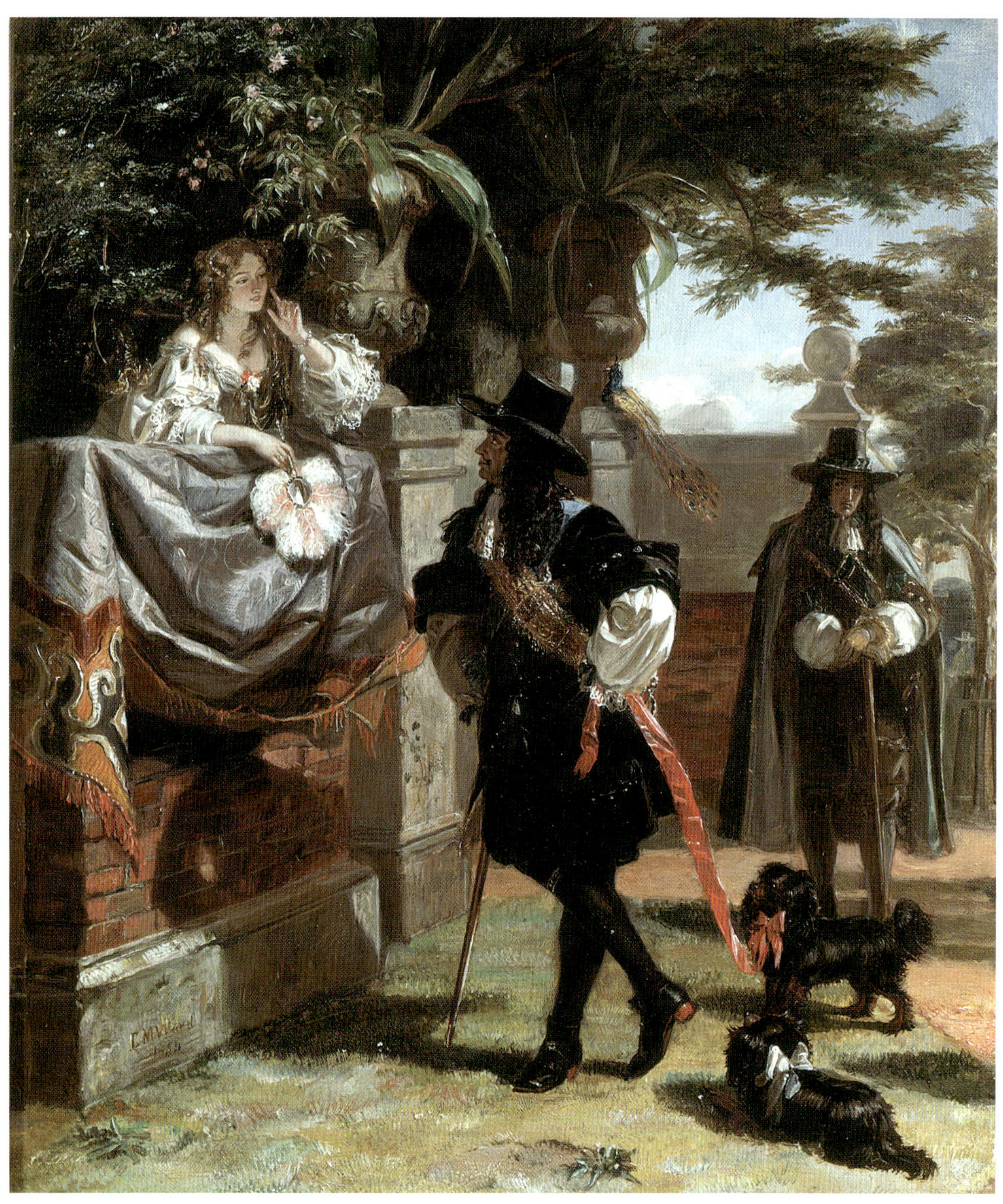

46 Edward Mathew Ward, *An Interview between Charles II and Nell Gwynn, as Witnessed by Evelyn*, 1854, Oil on canvas, 34.8 x 29.8 cm. Victoria and Albert Museum

III

THREE KINGS AND TWO QUEENS

From the Restoration to Queen Anne

Until 1859 any devout Anglican venturing into his or her parish church on the twenty-ninth of May would have been bidden to render thanks for 'the wonderful deliverance of these Kingdoms from THE GREAT REBELLION, and all the Miseries and Oppressions consequent thereupon.' The faithful were also asked to bless the Almighty for His 'miraculous providence' in the year 1660 in having restored their 'then most gracious sovereign Lord, King *Charles* the Second, notwithstanding all the power and malice of his enemies' and in having granted 'the publick and free profession of thy true Religion and Worship, together with our former Peace and Prosperity.' The last collect of the day offered further thanks to God for disappointing and overthrowing 'the wicked designs' of those rebels who were defined as 'high-minded men, who, under the pretence of Religion, and thy most holy Name, had contrived, and well-nigh effected the utter destruction of this Church and Kingdom.' By the time the Church of England relegated this 'Restoration' service to its liturgical lumber-room it is likely that relatively few church-goers would have felt able to wholeheartedly echo its sentiments.

Given his Whig prejudices, that otherwise sound Protestant, Thomas Babington Macaulay, would probably have been constitutionally disinclined from ever referring to 'Good King Charles's Golden Days.' The character of the restored King, as described in the first volume of Macaulay's *History of England* (1848), was not one to inspire confidence (fig.46). Indeed, for Macaulay, very soon after his Restoration, Charles came to embody a growing disillusionment with the Stuart dynasty. His reign is not so much golden as leaden:

> The restored King was at this time [1660] more loved by the people than any of his predecessors … His return had delivered the country from an intolerable bondage … He had received from nature excellent parts and a happy temper … He passed through all varieties of fortune, and had seen both sides of human nature. He had, while very young, been driven forth from a palace to a life of exile, penury and danger … From such a school it might have been expected that a young man that wanted neither abilities nor amiable qualities would have come forth a great and good King. Charles came forth from that school with social habits, with polite and engaging manners, and with some talent for lively conversation, addicted beyond measure to sensual indulgence, fond of sauntering and of frivolous amusements, incapable of self denial and of exertion, without faith in human virtue or in human attachment, without desire of renown, and without sensibility to reproach … Honour and shame were scarcely more to him than light and darkness to the blind.[1]

This view of Charles II was shared by many of Macaulay's Victorian contemporaries, though their distaste was generally founded on moral rather than political principles. 'Mrs Markham's' enduringly popular *A History of England … For the Use of Young Persons,* which first appeared in 1823, describes a cynical Charles II in deeply unsympathetic terms:

> He had a good figure, and, though his features were harsh, there was something agreeable in his countenance; and his cheerful, easy, and graceful deportment made him altogether a very engaging person. He had a great deal of cleverness, shrewdness and wit; and with common application, might have been anything he pleased. But he loved amusement, and hated business, and to live idly and merrily was all he cared for. His good-humour proceeded merely from the selfish principle of driving away care: his freedom from ambition was only the love of ease. He had no wish to be a great, or a good monarch, and he only valued his country because he found in it a dwelling place. He had a good head, but a bad heart, or rather

he had no heart at all: he was devoid of feeling, and only feared foes and valued friends as they could injure or serve him. His constitutional good nature was all he had to recommend him; and this concealed, for a time, his entire want of better qualities.[2]

This allows Charles the one quality he was popularly remembered for – his merriness – but it seems to doubt if, in Charles's case, this actually *was* a quality. Charles Dickens is equally scathing about the King and his reign in his *A Child's History of England* (1851–54):

There never were such profligate times in England as under Charles the Second. Whenever you see his portrait, with his swarthy, ill-looking face and great nose, you may fancy him in his Court at Whitehall, surrounded by some of the very worst vagabonds in the kingdom (though they were lords and ladies), drinking, gambling, indulging in vicious conversation, and committing every kind of profligate excess.[3]

Readily resorting to an ironic register, Dickens then proceeds to list examples of the King's 'merriness' (which includes hanging, drawing and quartering ten living regicides and disinterring the bodies and Cromwell and his family). This 'merry monarch,' Dickens concludes, sold England 'like a merry Judas, over and over again.'[4]

In the popular English imagination the reign of Charles II was memorable more for its negative aspects than for its positives. The charter given to the Royal Society in 1660 or the foundation of the Royal Hospitals at Kilmainham in Dublin in 1680 and at Chelsea in 1682 went largely unnoticed in history books. Instead, most people remembered the restoration period for three things in particular, and all of them were disasters. The King and his court were depraved and frivolous; London suffered from what was to prove the last epidemic of bubonic plague in 1665, and, a year later, the City was almost completely destroyed in the Great Fire. In Scotland the King was remembered, and generally disparaged, for his duplicity, for the re-introduction of an Anglican hierarchy, and for the consequent rising of the Covenanters. In Ireland he probably was not much remembered at all, except for not being Oliver Cromwell. Amongst Protestant Nonconformists in all three Kingdoms his regime was notorious for the discriminatory legislation represented by the Test,

Corporation, Conventicle and Five Mile Acts. 'Mrs Markham' is determined that her children should recall the relationship between the King's character and the moral depravity of the Kingdom and its wider culture: 'His bad conduct had a pernicious influence not only on the times in which he lived, but on those that followed … even the public taste was corrupted … many of the books written at that time were polluted with the same vicious spirit that so generally prevailed in society.' The only redeeming features of the reign seem to be the publication of *Paradise Lost* (a poem by 'a poor, blind Puritan … which for sublimity and purity has never been excelled') and the rebuilding of London in a 'more agreeable and more healthy' manner after its wholesale expurgation by incineration:

> The dirt was burnt out which used to harbour the infection. The old wooden houses, with windows not made to open, could never be purified by fresh air; the want of which, and the want of cleanliness, were enough to harbour and encourage infectious disorders.[5]

One is almost led to the conclusion that England might have been a happier place if the dissolute King and his court had similarly been consumed in a sanitary bonfire of the vanities. Dickens cannot quite bring himself to see the Great Fire of London as retribution for national depravity, but when he writes of the rebuilt City as more regular, cleanly and healthy than the old wooden one he none the less looks for parallel modern instances of urban desuetude:

> It [London] might be far more healthy than it is, but there are some people in it still – even now, at this time, nearly two hundred years later – so selfish, so pig-headed, and so ignorant, that I doubt if even another Great Fire would warm them up, to do their duty.[6]

As ever in his work, the indifference, inefficiency and decadence of political institutions are to blame, whether they be unelected seventeenth-century monarchs and their debauched courts, or smug modern Lord Mayors, Aldermen, do-nothing Parish Boards and a whole variety of Circumlocution Offices.

Instrumental in confirming, and to some degree tempering, such prejudices about the Restoration period were the publication in 1818-19 of *Memoirs Illustrative of the Life and Writings of John Evelyn* and in 1823 of *Memoirs of Samuel Pepys, Esq. F.R.S … deciphered by the Revd. John Smith.*[7] John Evelyn's *Diary*, which covered the years 1644-1706, had, until 1818, remained an unconsidered manuscript that had been scrappily preserved at his family home in Surrey. On its appearance in two printed volumes it proved so steadily popular that new editions were called for in 1827, 1854, 1859 and 1879. It was the success of the publication of Evelyn's *Diary* that stimulated work on the far more substantial journal of Samuel Pepys that had been preserved with the rest of his library at Magdalene College, Cambridge. Unlike Evelyn, Pepys had written both voluminously and in a shorthand which required translation. Given the scurrilous nature of some of the material, and the very length of the manuscript, Pepys's *Diary* had to be edited in order to render it becoming for the more fastidious amongst early nineteenth-century readers. The original transcript, covering the years 1660-69, ran to some fifty-four volumes. When published, the severely abbreviated text, edited by Lord Braybrooke, was greeted with real enthusiasm. Pepys was acclaimed by Francis Jeffrey, the editor of the *Edinburgh Review*, as having the most 'indiscriminating, insatiable and miscellaneous curiosity that ever prompted the researches, or supplied the pen, of a daily chronicler.'[8] Braybrooke brought out further, slightly expanded, editions in 1828, 1848-9, 1851 and 1854, and a new editor, the Reverend Mynors Bright, produced a new transcription for what was yet another incomplete version of the *Diary* in 1875-79.

The differences between these two great diaries were very evident to their first readers. The sweep, the time-span, and the sharp critical judgments of Evelyn's journal gave it an immediate *rapport* and it is not surprising that both the author of *Lady Willoughby's Diary* (1844) and Elizabeth Penrose ('Mrs Markham') refer severally to the man and to his social observation with obvious approval. By contrast, Pepys's *Diary* was admired for its particularity, its domestic detail, its gossip and its vivid account of both trivial and national events. Together, the diaries offered a radically new and immediate way of looking at both public and private history, and indeed at the inter-relation of the public and the private. Both diarists mix easily with the great men of their times and they witness both radical social developments and public disasters. In their very different ways both almost certainly influenced the generation of Victorian novelists who embarked on confessional, first-person narratives in the 1840s and 50s: Charlotte Brontë with *Jane Eyre* in 1847, Charles Kingsley with *Alton Locke* in 1850, Dickens with *David Copperfield* in 1849-50, and, above all, Thackeray with his seventeenth-century historical novel, *Henry Esmond* of

1852. What is certain is that the appearance of Evelyn's and Pepys's *Diaries* in the 1820s established new stars in the literary firmament. Two relatively forgotten public figures had been belatedly transformed into indispensible commentators on their times.

The *Diaries* of Evelyn and Pepys rendered the affairs of the Restoration court and the suffering of Londoners from the Plague and from the Great Fire uniquely vivid to Victorian readers. Both diarists were intimate with Kings and counsellors, but they also left a record of their dealings with servants and tradesmen and they described how they took their ease, how they stimulated their minds, how they diverted and entertained themselves, and how they took their daily bread and relished their claret. They also described the extent to which they were acquainted with grief and, moreover, with the pervasive nature of epidemic disease and sudden death. Even Daniel Defoe's celebrated *Journal of the Plague Year* (1722) could not quite rival the immediacy of their records of the late seventeenth century.

Pestilence and Fire

The revival of a public fascination with the decidedly dark side of Restoration England during the nineteenth century is evident in three, contrasted, but once popular, paintings: William Powell Frith's *Claude Duval* (fig.47) of 1860; Frank William Warwick Topham's *Rescued from the Plague* (fig.48), 1898, and Paul Falconer Poole's *Solomon Eagle Exhorting the People to Repentance during the Plague of London* (fig.49), 1843. The notoriously 'gallant' highwayman, Claude Duval, had come to England from France in the train of the Duke of Richmond in 1660. Some people believed that he was Richmond's illegitimate son. He certainly seems to have acquired a veneer of good manners from somewhere for when he took to the road he rapidly gained a reputation both for daring and for a chivalrous attention to his female victims. He had been captured in London and hanged at Tyburn in 1670, though during his confinement at Newgate his first biographer, William Pope, recounts that he was visited by a good number of ladies of fashion. Frith's painting, which was engraved soon after it was first exhibited, shows the masked highwayman in a particularly celebrated encounter. A travelling coach has been stopped on a stretch of heathland by a group of five highwaymen and its singularly

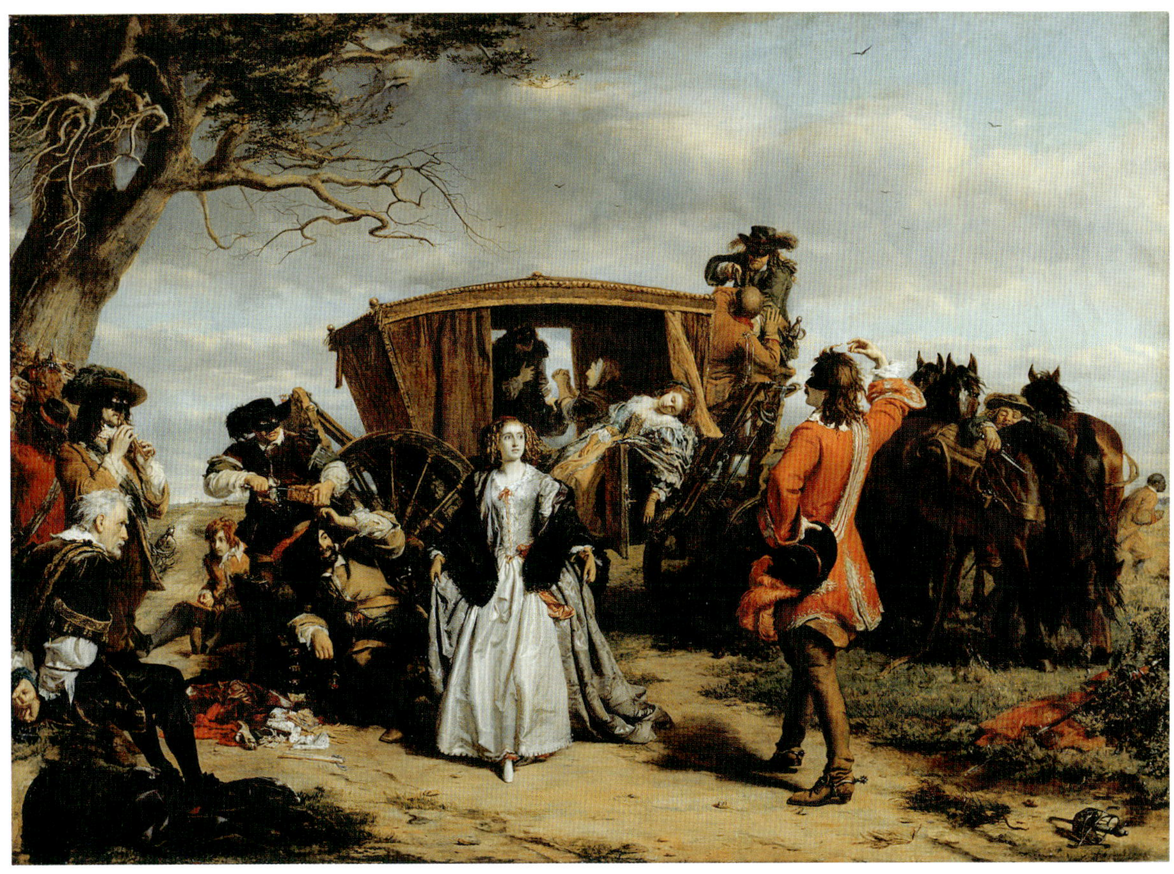

47 William Powell Frith,
Claude Duval, 1860,
Oil on canvas,
108.8 x 153 cm.
Manchester Art Gallery

disgruntled, and evidently rich, owner has been trussed up. One young female has been overcome with the vapours and an elderly woman traveller begs for mercy from one of Duval's gang. While the other highwaymen are actively involved in relieving their victims of any valuables, Duval, to the accompaniment of a flageolet, is about to begin dancing what William Pope described as a 'coranto' with a particularly well-dressed, and evidently enchanted, courtly lady.

It is likely that Frith's attraction to the subject was two-fold. Here was an opportunity to display his skill in representing the costumes and manners of Charles II's court. But he was also intent on exposing the inherent dangers of travel in the seventeenth century, and here was what can be interpreted as a

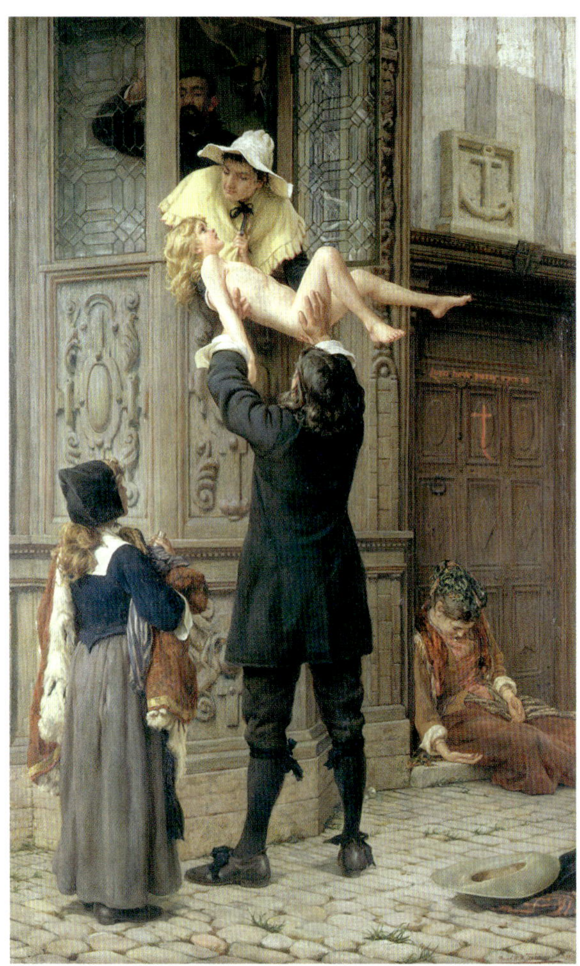

48   Frank Topham, *Rescued from the Plague, London*, 1898, Oil on canvas, 182.9 x 114.3 cm. Guildhall Art Gallery, City of London

complement to Frith's depiction of modern travel, *The Railway Station* of 1862. In the earlier picture rich travellers are victimised by a 'gallant' highwayman. The implication is that, however elegant the situation may appear, what we are in fact witnessing is a sordid robbery and a distressingly commonplace historical hazard. In *The Railway Station*, we have jumped two centuries. The curtained travelling-coach in *Claude Duval* has now been replaced by a steam locomotive and its crowded public carriages. Here, to the right of the picture, a criminal is being apprehended by police officers as he is about to board the train. Gone is the elegant exchange of salutes, and Duval's theatrical gallantry

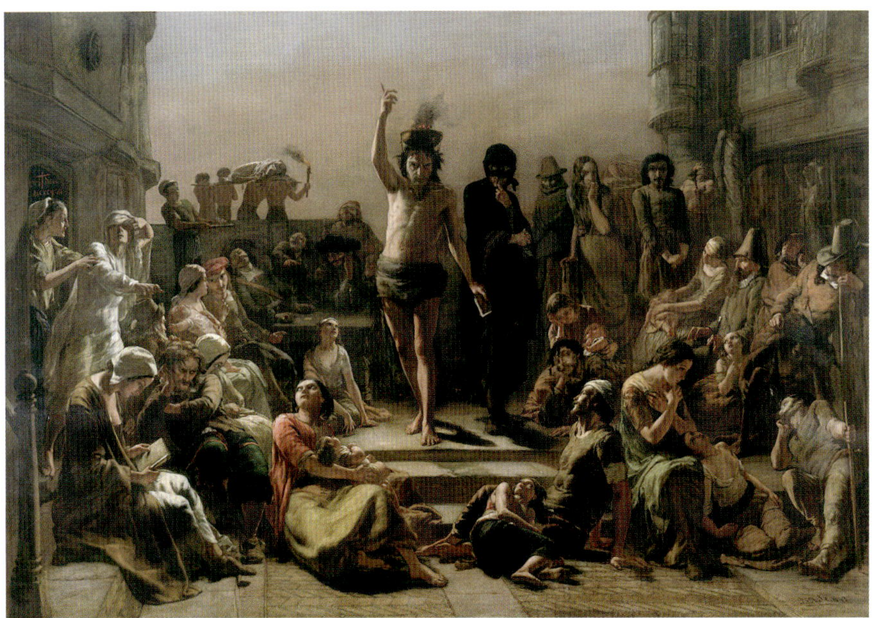

49 Paul Falconer Poole, *Solomon Eagle Exhorting the People to Repentance during the Plague of London*, 1843, Oil on canvas, 173.2 x 241 cm. Sheffield Galleries and Museums

has been supplanted in the modern age by a well-dressed criminal's evident terror of the law. Taking the two pictures together, we can safely assume that, far from decrying the loss of romance, Frith is rejoicing in the relative dullness of ordered life in the nineteenth century.[9]

Frank Topham's *Rescued from the Plague* and Poole's *Solomon Eagle* may have owed something of their erstwhile popularity as images of the seventeenth century to the accounts of the Plague in Evelyn's and Pepys's *Diaries*, but they are equally indebted to an early Victorian novel: William Harrison Ainsworth's *Old Saint Pauls* of 1841. Topham shows a blond, naked young girl being lowered by her anxious mother and father from an elaborate Elizabethan casement window into the arms of a waiting gentleman. In the street a woman waits with clothes ready for the child, though near them another woman lies slumped by a door inscribed with a cross and the legend 'Lord Have Mercy Upon Us.' The child's family have evidently been locked into to a plague-infected house and her rescuers are illegally spiriting her away, leaving her clothes behind her. The scene was based on Pepys's account of a saddler in Gracious Street, who, having lost all his other children to the Plague, delivers his last surviving daughter 'stark naked into the arms of a friend.' The drama of the picture may also have been suggested by the scene in Book 3, Chapter 6 of Ainsworth's novel in which Amabel Bloundel is rescued from her parents' house by Leonard Holt. Ainsworth's *Old Saint Pauls* is, however, certainly the inspiration of Paul Falconer Poole's *Solomon Eagle Exhorting the People to Repentence* (fig.49). This is a busy, crowded canvas that teeters on the verge of absurdity. The semi-naked Eagle, crowned with a smoking brazier, gesticulates to what looks like an inattentive audience in a London street. Eagle's would-be congregation look up with blank expressions at this eccentric latter-day prophet as if the Plague has already drained most signs of vigour from them. It is like a parody of John the Baptist preaching in the wilderness. Ainsworth had described the preacher as 'a tall gaunt man, with long jet-black hair, hanging in disordered masses over his shoulders.' His eyes are 'large and black' and they blaze 'with insane lustre.' His looks, Ainsworth somewhat lamely adds, were 'so wild and terrific, that it required no great stretch of the imagination to convert him into the genius of the pestilence.' (Book 1, Chapter 2). The novelist represents his sermon as consisting of a string of doom-laden biblical quotations but then pictures him suddenly starting off and 'shrieking … "awake! sinners, awake! – the plague is at your doors! – the grave yawns for you ! – awake and repent!"' One could only wish that Poole had attempted to show a little more wakefulness on the part of the stricken Londoners.[10]

Harrison Ainsworth's *Old Saint Pauls: A Tale of the Plague and the Fire* is a typical ragbag of historical information, architectural reconstruction and exaggerated plotting. Like Ainsworth's other early novels it enjoyed real popularity. It was first published as a weekly serial in the *Sunday Times*, then as a three-decker novel (both in 1841), then again serialised in monthly parts in 1842-43, then published in volume form in 1847, 1857, 1884 and 1891 and, despite the radical decline in Ainsworth's literary fortunes, it remained in and out of print until well into the twentieth century.[11] Amongst its most passionate admirers were the young Holman Hunt and Macaulay, who is recorded, extraordinarily enough, as 'devouring' the 'pregnant pages of Ainsworth' and as having found himself 'lost in amazement that [these] wonderful historical novels have not an abiding place in every house.'[12] *Old Saint Pauls* certainly does have its memorable episodes, but Ainsworth is at his most effective when he evokes the pre-Fire London when he describes the great gothic cathedral with its new portico by Inigo Jones ('though beautiful in itself, [it] was totally out of character with the edifice, and, in fact, a blemish to it'). Here is Ainsworth's delineation of the city as it is viewed from the cathedral's tower in the early summer of 1665 by his central character, Leonard Holt:

> From the elevated point on which he stood, his eye ranged over a vast tract of country bounded by the Surrey hills, and at last settled upon the river … its surface was spotted with craft, while innumerable vessels of all shapes and size were moored to its banks. On the left he noted the tall houses covering London Bridge; and, on the right, traced the sweeping course of the stream as it flowed from Westminster. On this hand, on the opposite bank, lay the flat marshes of Lambeth: while nearer stood the old bull-baiting and bear-baiting establishments, the flags above which could be discerned above the tops of the surrounding habitations … The whole city of London was spread out like a map before him, and presented a dense mass of ancient houses, with twisted chimneys, gables and picturesque roofs – here and there over-topped by a hall, a college, a hospital, or some other lofty structure … The spires and towers of the churches shot up in the clear morning air, — for, except in a few quarters, no smoke yet issued from the chimneys. On this side, the view of the city was terminated by the fortifications and keep of the Tower. (Book 2, Chapter 6)

Unable to resist the knowing intrusion, Ainsworth reminds us that 'ere fifteen months had elapsed the whole mass … would be swept away by a tremendous conflagration'. Nevertheless, Leonard Holt's view of mediaeval and Tudor London, informed as it is by Wenceslaus Hollar's engravings, presented many sentimental Victorian readers a vision of lost glory. It must have brought a lump to the throat of those who had persuaded themselves that Gothic England was the *beau ideal* from which the modern world had fallen away. The 'picturesque' London that Holt observes is a city like nineteenth-century Rouen or Amiens, with its wooden merchants' houses, its gothic churches and halls, and towering above it one of the great mediaeval cathedrals of Europe. Although the appearance of the Gothic St. Paul's had been meticulously recorded in William Dugdale's *The History of S. Paul's Cathedral* in 1658, a volume which must have been well known to the novelist, nearly all the elements of the old London that surrounded it had been irretrievably and unrecordedly lost in the Great Fire. Although King Charles, who stirs himself into action when the Fire is at its height, declares that he would not have the 'august cathedral' injured for half his kingdom, even he cannot save it. Instead, he is obliged to watch its destruction and that of the crazed Solomon Eagle, who we learn has actually started the Fire, and who finally flings himself headlong 'into the flaming abyss' of the burning cathedral. Ainsworth (with occasional nods to Samuel Pepys) vividly describes the arching wall of flames as they approach and then encompass the building. The novel ends with a classic case of Ainsworth's tidy and progressive optimism. Leonard Holt, who has managed to save the King's life, is married to his beloved, and ennobled, and 'by sedulously cultivating his talents … was enabled to reflect credit upon the high rank to which it had pleased a grateful sovereign to elevate him.' He is also blessed with an extraordinarily long life for, Ainsworth insists, 'he lived to see the new cathedral completed by Sir Christopher Wren, and often visited it with feelings of admiration, but never with the same sentiments of veneration and awe that he had experienced, when, in times gone by, he had repaired to OLD SAINT PAULS.'

Sic Monumentum Requiris

Wren's St. Paul's was not in fact completed until October 1708, when the last stone of the new cathedral was laid by its architect's two sons. Their father, aged seventy-six, apparently watched the ceremony from ground level. Wren was the only survivor of the original office of works that had supervised its construction since it was begun in 1675.[13] Once completed, the new St. Paul's seems rapidly to have effaced memories of the old building. It, and its great dome, were almost universally admired until nineteenth-century critics began to carp at its style and to mourn the destruction of its predecessor. Had the old building survived, one wonders quite what horrors would have been perpetrated by late-Georgian or Victorian 'restorers' once they had removed Inigo Jones's portico and set to work to undo all 'impure' additions to its decayed fabric.

In 1841 in his *True Principles of Pointed or Christian Architecture*, A. W. N. Pugin had dared to suggest that there was something fundamentally *false*, and therefore immoral, about the structure of Wren's masterpiece (figs. 50, 51). This

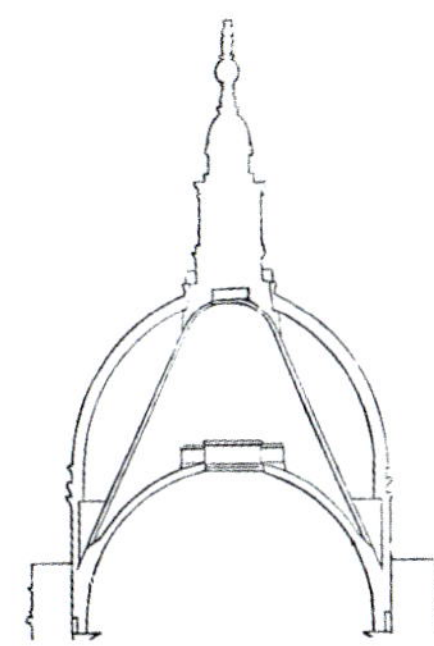

nexed section, the upper part of St. Paul's is mere imposing show, constructed at a vast expense without any legitimate reason.

From the various symptoms of decline which I have shown to have existed in the later pointed works, I feel convinced that Christian architecture had gone its length, and it must necessarily have destroyed itself by departing from its own principles in the pursuit of novelty, or it must have fallen back on its pure and ancient models. This is quite borne out by existing facts. Now that the pointed style is reviving, we cannot successfully suggest any thing new, but are obliged to return to the spirit of the ancient work.

Section of the Dome of St. Paul's. Indeed, if we view pointed architecture in its true light as Christian art, as the faith itself *is perfect, so are the principles on which it is founded.* We may indeed improve in mechanical contrivances to expedite its execution, we may even increase its scale and grandeur; but we can *never successfully deviate one tittle from the spirit and principles* of pointed architecture. We must rest content to *follow*, not to *lead*; we may indeed widen the road which our Catholic forefathers formed, but we can never depart from their track without a certainty of failure being the result of our presumption.

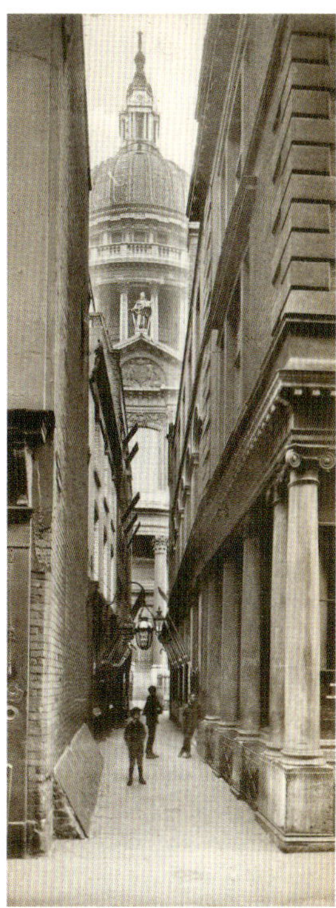

is how Pugin's first biographer, Benjamin Ferrey, summarises the argument against St Paul's:

> The writer next proceeds to criticise 'St. Paul's,' London, and ridicules the miserable expedients adopted to disguise those essential supports of the building which in Gothic constructions are made the means of light and elegant decoration. In St. Paul's, one half of the edifice is built to conceal the other. This system of shams and unrealities is Pugin's abhorrence. He does not fail to point out its fictitious dome as one of the greatest defects in the metropolitan cathedral. The author takes high ground in his argument, and indeed maintains that 'if we view pointed architecture in its true light as Christian art, as the faith itself is perfect, so are the principles on which its architecture is founded.'[14]

Despite the fact that Pugin originally addressed his remarks to a group of sympathetic Midlands Catholics at St. Marie's College, Oscott, Ferrey is reiterating what to many readers must have seemed like architectural heresy. Pugin knew that

50 Cross-section of St. Paul's Cathedral, illustration in *The True Principles of Pointed or Christian Architecture* by Augustus Welby Northmore Pugin, 1841. Private collection

51 St Paul's Cathedral, photograph, late 19th century. Private collection

he was dismissing a Protestant structure, which many of his listeners might well have regarded as merely a schismatic conventicle, but his censures remained calculatedly provocative. His problem is not with Wren's structural ingenuity but with the fact that Wren had not been prepared to build in the Gothic, or truly 'Christian', style. Ferrey records that when Pugin visited Rome in 1851 he explored St. Peter's 'in a state of rage,' exclaiming betimes: 'Why they can't even carry out decently their own miserable style.' When he returned to England he told friends that he got out of the Baroque Eternal City as soon as he possibly could, 'for every hour he was there he felt endangered his faith.'[15]

Pugin's moral distaste for Wren's St. Paul's was extravagant, but his scruples about the structural inventiveness of the design (which he dismisses as 'shams and unrealities') were shared by at least one far less factional architectural critic. James Fergusson in his *History of Modern Architecture* (1862) was prepared to acclaim St. Paul's as Wren's masterpiece and as 'the largest and finest Protestant cathedral in the world, and, after St. Peter's, the most splendid church created in Europe since the revival of Classical Architecture.' Nevertheless, he complains that 'it was a mistake artistically to rest the dome on eight instead of four arches, though constructively there is some mechanical advantage in so doing.' A similar observation is made about Wren's ingenious solution to the problem of supporting his great dome: 'The introduction of a cone to carry the lantern was a master-stroke of mechanical skill; but there is perhaps no instance in Monumental Architecture where the mechanical exigencies have been allowed so completely to govern the artistic as this and we cannot but feel we are verging so nearly on the limit of stability as to give rise to a feeling of falsehood or insecurity utterly destructive of all grandeur in this building.' Wren, Fergusson, concludes 'was more of an engineer than an architect, and, consequently, always preferred the display of his mechanical skill to the expression of his artistic feelings.'[16]

Generally, however, nineteenth-century writers seem either to have taken St. Paul's for granted or to have been intensely proud that such a masterpiece should grace the British capital. The author of *Black's Guide to London and Its Environs* (1875) proclaimed it 'not only by far the finest building in the Italian style in London, but the finest in Britain.' For some the smoke-blackened cathedral and its dome had become synonymous with sooty modern London. Even its 'smoky coat,' so familiar to Victorian visitors, struck some commentators as appropriate, given the fact that the reconstruction of the cathedral had been financed by a tax levied on the household coal brought into the port of London. John Forster records that for the boy Dickens 'the cupola of St. Paul's, looming through the smoke, was a treat that served him for hours of vague reflection afterwards.'[17] Augustus Hare, who generally prefers the time-worn to the modern in his astute commentaries on European cities, similarly waxes lyrical about the cathedral in his *Walks in London* (1890):

> … dark and grand, St. Paul's Cathedral occupies the platform on top of the hill. Sublimely impressive in its general outlines, it has a peculiar sooty dignity all of its own, which, externally, raises it immeasurably above the fresh, modern-looking St. Peter's in Rome … When you near it, the mighty dome is lost, but you have always an inward all-pervading impression of its existence, as you have seen it a thousand times rising in dark majesty over the city; or as, lighted up by the sun, it is sometimes visible from the river, when all minor objects are obliterated in mist. The colonnade surrounding the dome is incomparable: by blocking up every fourth intercolumniation, Wren not only obtained an appearance of great strength but an invaluable variety of light and shadow. And, apart from the dome, the noble proportions of every pillar and cornice of the great church cannot fail to strike those who linger to look at them, while even the soot-begrimed garlands, which would be offensive were they clean, have here an indescribable stateliness.[18]

In all weathers, and from all angles, Wren's 'Italianate' masterpiece seems to have struck Victorian visitors as utterly habituated to London. Even the antiquarian John Timbs, the author of *Curiosities of London* (1855), appears to have been so struck by the variety and beauty of the cathedral as to have been able to expunge all memories of its mediaeval predecessor from his consciousness. The effect of the building, he writes is 'truly magnificent … viewed from Cheapside, it presents an imposing mass, and the western front, with its campanili and the majestic dome, is a stupendous termination to the vista of Ludgate-hill; whilst from Blackfriars Bridge, the graceful dome appears in impressive contrast with the less harmonious body of the building.'[19]

St. Paul's rises majestically above and beyond a fantasy conglomeration of Wren's other buildings in the great classical architect, C.R. Cockerell's *A Tribute to the Memory of Sir Christopher Wren* (fig. 52). This composite drawing was

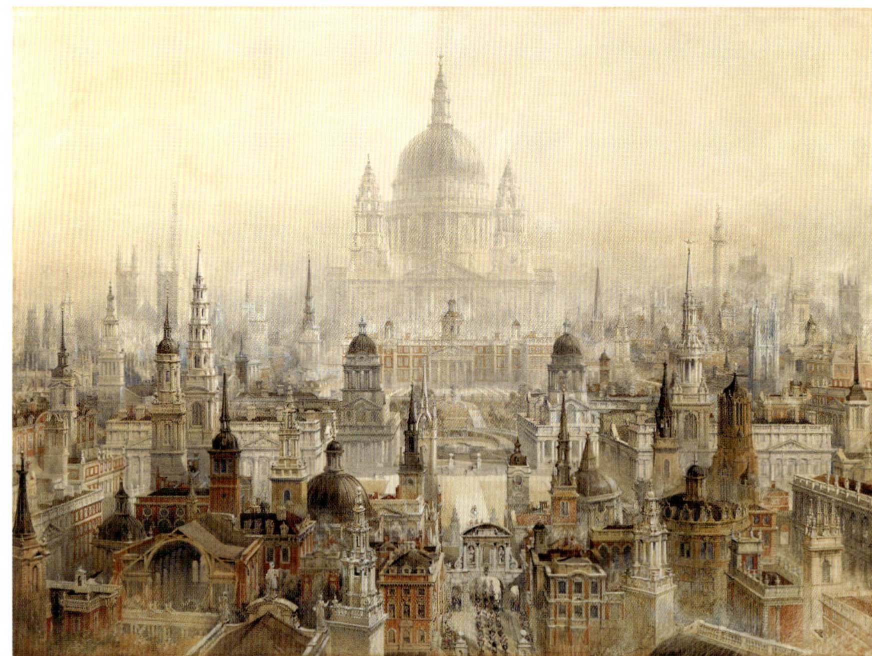

52 Charles Robert Cockerell, *A Tribute to the Memory of Sir Christopher Wren*, 1838, Watercolour over pencil, 99 x 132cm. Exhibited at the Royal Academy 1838. RIBA Library Drawings & Archives Collections

exhibited at the Royal Academy in 1839 and is still regularly reproduced in architectural handbooks. Cockerell, who had been appointed surveyor to the fabric of St. Paul's in 1819, was a consistent and profound admirer of Wren's work and in the lectures he gave as Professor of Architecture at the Royal Academy he reiterated his admiration in the face of criticism from the more ardent Goths. 'Character,' he told his students, was the basis of Wren's art 'and poetry has appeared in all [his] conceptions.'[20] In his last lecture, delivered in 1856, Cockerell stressed that St. Paul's was 'without a rival in beauty, unity and variety' and argued that the double windows in the apse allowed light to penetrate 'as in Gothic churches.' Indeed, he insisted, perhaps to persuade the Goths of the justice of his arguments, that Wren had created 'a gothic structure clothed in classical garb.'[21] His great watercolour *Tribute* shows a disproportionate St. Paul's, unencumbered by the clutter of houses and business premises that surrounded it in actuality. It soars above a reduced representation of the unbuilt Winchester Palace which closes the vista at the end of an avenue that has passed through Temple Bar and between the towers of the Greenwich Hospital. To the sides cluster parts of Hampton Court, Chelsea Hospital and the Sheldonian Theatre, but the whole composition is given its true vigour by

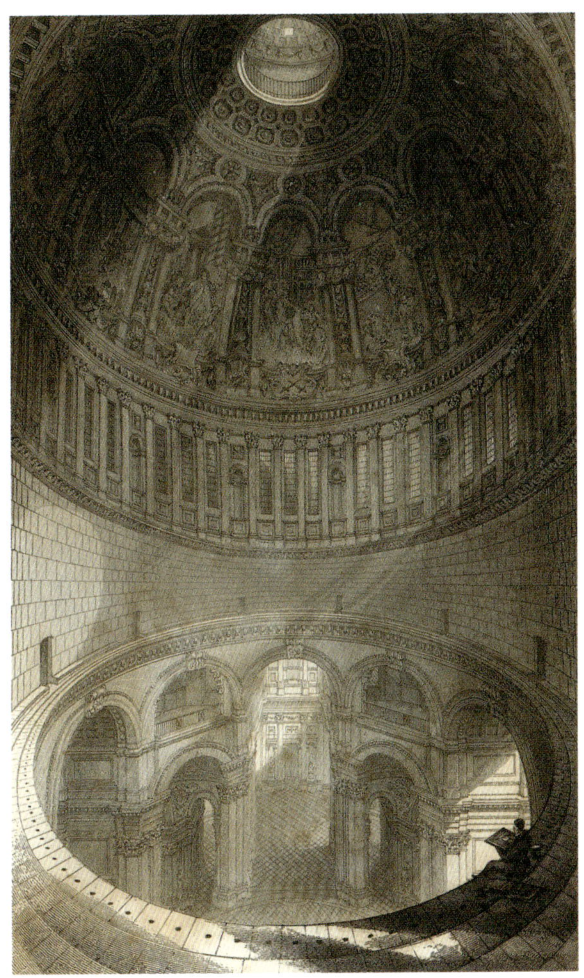

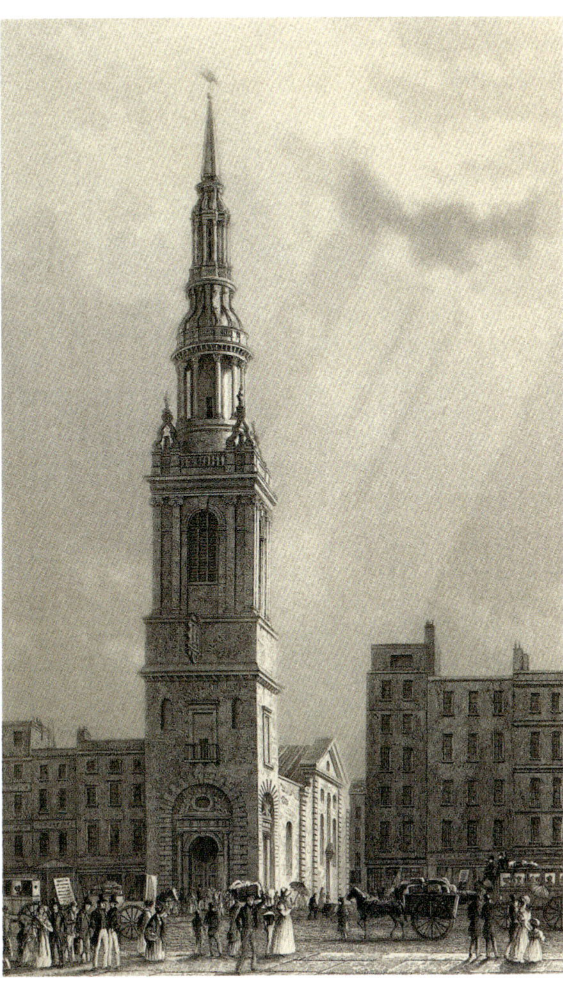

the inventive spires of no fewer than thirty three of the City parish churches rebuilt by Wren after the Great Fire. Cockerell is showing us a contrived vision of the heavenly city, one in which each element has been conceived of by the fertile brain of a single divinely inspired artist.

In 1839, the year in which Cockerell exhibited his *Tribute to the Memory of Sir Christopher Wren*, the architect George Godwin published a very different kind of tribute to Wren's genius. Godwin's two-volume, *The Churches of London: A Description of the Ecclesiastical Edifices of the Metropolis*, was richly illustrated with engravings after drawings by Frederick Mackenzie and Robert William Billings.

53 St Paul's Cathedral, engraved illustration in *The Churches of London* by George Godwin, 1839. Private collection

54 St Mary-le-Bow, engraved illustration in *The Churches of London* by George Godwin, 1839. Private collection

The volumes exquisitely capture a now lost view of the Victorian City of London (though, despite Godwin's broad title, the text does not venture beyond the boundaries of the City). Apart from precious representations of what are now long-demolished churches, the engravings variously show an utterly vertiginous view of the Whispering Gallery at St. Paul's (without its railing, and with an artist sketching on its rim, his legs dangling into space) (fig. 53); the unrestored, pew-cluttered interior of St. Bartholomew-the-Great; St. Bride's, Fleet Street at the end of an avenue of Regency shops; and St Mary-le-Bow towering above the tall houses of a busy Cheapside (fig. 54). What is extraordinary is that Godwin evidently felt no qualms about praising Wren's City churches when so many other Victorian commentators, including Dickens, were beginning to disparage them as dull, dusty, unfrequented, and quaintly redundant. Godwin is even prepared to single out Wren's wonderfully varied spires for special praise. He carefully analyses the slightly eccentric tower of St Mary Somerset (nowadays a free-standing structure, having been deprived of its church), he bemoans the loss of the urns which crowned the steeple of Christchurch, Newgate Street (they are now replaced, but the church is a sad ruin) and he waxes eloquent over the spire of St Mary-le-Bow:

> Wren has contrived, in all his churches, to preserve this character [of a distinct building] for his steeples as much as possible, by commencing them in all cases … directly from the ground. In the beautiful example before us … we obtain the campanile for the most part in its proper shape – distinct and unattached, whereby the effect of its great height is increased, and its form, as the small proportion which the base bears to the height is more apparent, becomes picturesque and striking. To describe, or criticise at length, the steeple of Bow church would now be supererogatory. Opinion has stamped it as one of the most successful works of its class, both as regards design and construction and with this opinion we perfectly agree; indeed, we may add, that did Wren's reputation as an architect, rest solely on this one building, it would in our opinion, be perfectly secure.[22]

Godwin's *The Churches of London* is more than a Victorian celebration a series of partially overlooked, and increasingly threatened, historic London buildings. It now forms a unique record of the extent to which Wren's City churches once served as elegant landmarks in the vibrant and densely populated core of the city. It was not to be outshone until George H. Birch published his superbly illustrated photographic survey *London Churches of the XVIIth and XVIIIth Centuries* in 1896.

In his description of St Paul's Cathedral Godwin repeats the common early-Victorian complaint that the interior of the great church was 'cold and meagre.' The reason for this coldness lay not simply in the fact that Wren had never been given the opportunity of selecting an appropriate decorative scheme, but also in the refusal of the eighteenth-century bishop of London, Richard Terrick, to countenance the offer by the founder-members of the Royal Academy to provide wall-paintings. As Godwin puts it, the Academicians' generous offer was deemed to 'savour of Popery, and likely to produce clamours,' and was abruptly abandoned. By the time that C.R. Cockerell was appointed Surveyor, the interior of the Cathedral was grimy as well as cold and in 1821 the building was redecorated for the first time since its consecration. Cockerell repainted the pilasters in the chancel in the blue selected by Wren, and contemplated cleaning Sir James Thornhill's grisaille murals in the dome, but no funds for the latter were forthcoming from the Dean and Chapter. It was not until the latter half of the nineteenth century, and with the appointment of Deans who were not only sympathetic to the principles of the Oxford Movement but also relatively unafraid of the taint of 'Popery,' that any new decorative schemes came to fruition. By that stage, however, the problem lay not in finding images of a soundly Protestant nature but in harmonising High Victorian styles with Wren's architecture. The idea was that the Cathedral should be 'completed' but, without any clear indication as what its original architect would have wanted, modern artists seem to have been determined to impose their own distinctive styles on the structure. To relieve the 'coldness' colour became the key. Between 1872 and 1875 Wren's and Cockerell's now dingy blue and gold decorations were stripped away and new mosaic figures of four Old Testament prophets, designed by Alfred Stevens (fig. 55), and the four Evangelists, by George Frederick Watts, gradually filled the eight spandrels of the dome. The mosaics, by Salviati & Co. of Venice, were

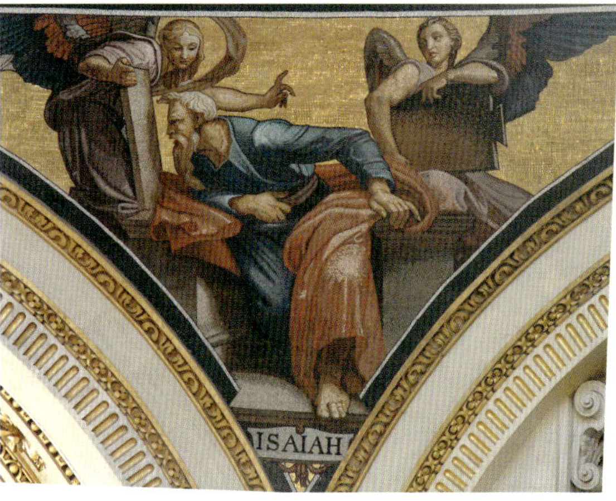

55 Alfred Stevens, Mosaic of the Old Testament Prophets: Isaiah, designed 1872–75, completed 1891. St Paul's Cathedral

only completed in 1891. In 1872 the great organ case, which had blocked off the choir, was divided in two, thus opening a new vista to the high altar. In the closing years of the century new coloured glass windows, designed by the German Nazarene painter, Schnorr von Carolsfeld, were fitted at the East End, mosaic decoration by Sir William Blake Richmond was applied to the saucer domes and the aisle vaults, and, above all, a new altar was placed at the east end of the Choir and a vast marble reredos, designed by George Frederick Bodley, was installed behind it in 1891. Thus the interior of the choir of St. Paul's was 'completed'; or rather, it was utterly transformed by Bodley's staid and heavy Baroque reredos and by Richmond's florid experiments with art nouveau mosaic. The effect was remarkable and sumptuous, but it must be admitted that it had more of the Victorian 'Wrennaisance' drawing room about it than of a church that Wren himself might have recognised. The completed scheme never won consistent admiration and when the glass was blown out and the reredos damaged during the Second World War, another generation of designers seems to have rejoiced in dismantling much of it.[23]

The Constitutional Crisis

One of the many *canards* raised about interference by the Catholic, James, Duke of York, was that he had been instrumental in denying Wren the opportunity of realising his first centrally planned design for St. Paul's. This design, which survives as the 'Great Model' preserved in the existing cathedral, was not given its royal warrant, so the story went, because James 'wanted a building more suited to the Catholic ritual than this church would have been.'[24] The story is absurd, for the so-called 'Warrant Design' that Wren produced as an alternative to the centrally planned church might well have been clumsy but it at least showed a response to the requirements of the *Anglican* as opposed to the *Catholic* liturgy. As a sound Anglican, and as the nephew of a Laudian bishop, Wren readily acknowledged that cathedral clergy needed a choir divided from the nave, and spaces convenient for Morning Prayer and for a Consistory Court. The nave of the old St. Paul's had been a particularly notorious public space and the Restoration Dean and Chapter had insisted on reserved areas for the practice of dignified worship. The idea of James's 'Catholic' interference has now been replaced with the equally absurd argument that the English 'establishment' was either too 'conservative' or too 'gothic minded' to countenance Wren's first radical plans and therefore forced him into an awkward compromise. As Wren's nineteenth-century admirers knew, a close study of his completed masterpiece reveals the nature of his genius, not his genius for compromise.

Nevertheless, Whig historians of the eighteenth and nineteenth centuries were agreed that every example of James's interference was motivated either by his Catholic principles or by an instinct for autocratic rule. Those Victorian readers who knew their Pepys would have known that the diarist painted a very different picture of the Duke of York compared to the antipathetic one offered by standard history books. The assiduous reformer of Charles II's navy was not the manipulative interferer of popular myth. Nevertheless, few convinced Protestants needed much persuasion to recognise in James the greatest threat to the security of reformed religion in England since the days of Mary Tudor. The decency, even conscientiousness, of the man was always likely, it was argued, to be compromised by his professed Catholicism. James was, moreover, a Stuart with an inherited propensity to tyranny. For her child-readers 'Mrs Markham' is explicit about both aspects of James's nature:

> James was in the fifty-third year of his age, when he succeeded to the throne of England. He had not his brother's talent and brilliancy, but he was a man of much perseverance and steady application to business. He had been brought up by his mother a Papist, and had acquired from his religion a harshness and bigotry which does not appear to have belonged naturally to his character. He meant to act rightly, and to be, according to his own ideas, a good king. But he mistook, or, to speak more properly, he did not regard, the feelings, opinion or character of the people he had to govern.

'Mrs. Markham's' even-handedness seems to have had the right effect on her own children for in the ensuing 'conversation' young George confidently proclaims that it was, 'to be sure, very wrong of James to want to make all people Papists, whether they would or no; and yet, somehow or other, I can't help thinking that he meant well.'[25] What lies behind the suppositions made by the Markham family is that no true Papist ever meant England well, and that, somehow, the new King's religious principles firstly led him astray and then, inexorably, into losing the goodwill of his Protestant people. The assumption is that, as all good Whigs would have believed, James had resigned his kingship rather than having been deprived of it. Macaulay, who spent a great deal of his *History of England* exploring the theory that the succession of William and Mary was both a moral necessity and totally legitimate in constitutional terms, is explicit about the defects in James's character:

> Though a libertine, James was diligent, methodical and fond of authority and business. His understanding was singularly slow and narrow, and his temper obstinate, harsh, and unforgiving. That such a prince should have looked with no good will on the free institutions of England, and on the party which was particularly zealous can excite no surprise.[26]

Once James publically professes his Catholicism, Macaulay is able to identify him as the desperate disease threatening future English well-being:

> His nature was haughty and imperious … But he was almost as much debased by superstition as his brother by indolence and vice. James was now a Roman Catholic. Religious bigotry had become the dominant sentiment of his narrow and stubborn mind, and had so mingled itself with his love of rule, that the two passions could hardly be distinguished from each other.[27]

For Macaulay, much of the restless political manoeuvring and instability at the Court of Charles II stemmed from the Catholic Duke of York's very existence. Moreover, James's sole motivation in encouraging those uncertainties and difficulties was his religion. Essentially his policy had one sole object: the promotion of himself as the champion of the Catholic Church in England and of Catholicism as the one true faith.

It might seem odd, therefore, that when Macaulay helped to determine the subjects of the series of paintings that decorate the Commons Corridor in the Palace of Westminster, James, either as Duke of York or as King, is conspicuous for his absence. This might be interpreted as a subtle indication of his *de facto* abdication. James has written himself out of history, even as a sinister, behind-the-scenes eminence. But then, we should remind ourselves, Oliver Cromwell is equally unrepresented in the parallel series of frescoes in the Peers Corridor. Cromwell's and James's considerable constitutional significance are merely implied, but are otherwise left unpictured. Edward Matthew Ward's

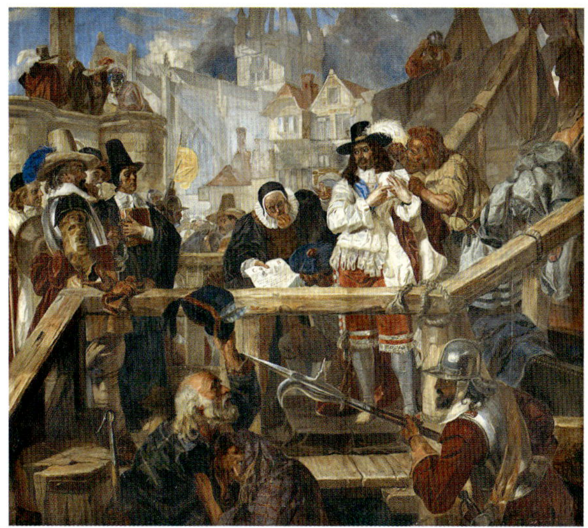 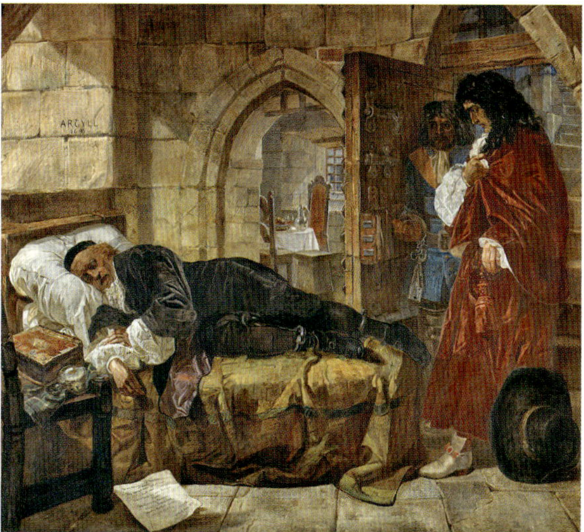

eight paintings in the Commons Corridor were originally commissioned in 1849 and were executed in the years 1853–68. As in the Peers Corridor, the subjects present viewers with an ostensible balance of political sympathies. The paintings, which deal with the years 1650–1689, pair insistently 'royalist' scenes with others that show men and women opposed to royal 'tyranny.'[28] Unlike the Peers Corridor, however, the Commons Corridor boasts two complementary scenes drawn from Scotland's violent and factious seventeenth-century history: *The Execution of the Marquis of Montrose* (fig. 56) and *The Last Sleep of Argyle* (fig. 57). James Graham, first Marquis of Montrose, Charles I's lieutenant-general in Scotland, had been finally defeated at Invercarron and betrayed to the Covenanters. He was condemned and executed by hanging in the Grassmarket at Edinburgh in May 1650. The Marquis, ever the well-dressed cavalier, stands at the foot of the famously high scaffold, with St. Giles's in the background. Extraordinarily enough for Edinburgh, the High Kirk is lit by an uncommonly bright sun. An aged highlander in the foreground raises his tartan bonnet in salute, but he is aggressively thrust aside by the pike of an armed soldier. *The Last Sleep of Argyle* shows an infinitely calmer scene, with the soberly dressed Earl asleep in his cell in Edinburgh Castle on the morning of his execution in June 1681. Argyle, a determined opponent of James II, is reported to have been asked on the scaffold whether or not he died a Protestant. 'Yes,' he replied, 'and a cordial

56 Edward Mathew Ward, *The Execution of the Marquis of Montrose*, 1857, Fresco, 207 x 237.5 cm. Palace of Westminster Collection

57 Edward Mathew Ward, *The Last Sleep of Argyle*, 1858, Fresco, 207 x 237.5 cm. Palace of Westminster Collection

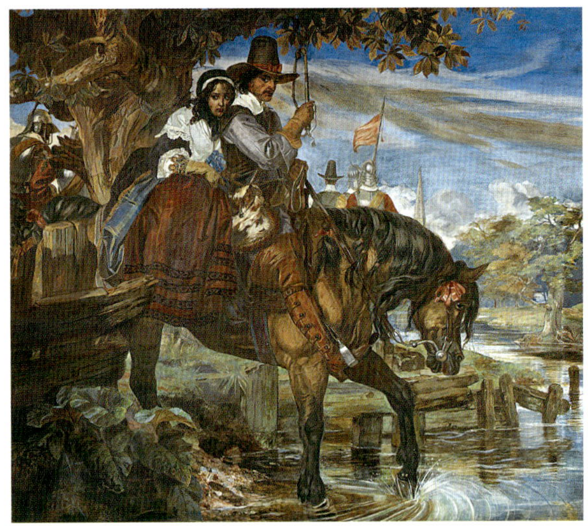

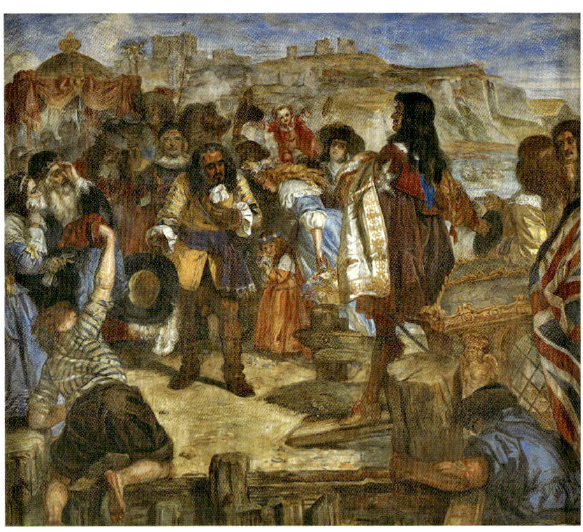

58   E.M.Ward, *Charles II Assisted in his Escape by Anne Lane after the Battle of Worcester*, 1861, Water glass painting

59   E.M.Ward, *The Landing of Charles II at Dover in 1660*, 1864, Water glass painting

60   E.M.Ward, *General Monk declaring for a Free Parliament*, 1868, Water glass painting

61   E.M.Ward, *The Acquittal of the Seven Bishops*, 1867, Water glass painting

62   E.M.Ward, *The Lords and Commons Presenting the Crown to William and Mary in the Banqueting House in 1688*, 1857, Water glass painting,

63   E.M.Ward, *Alice Lisle Concealing the Fugitives after the Battle of Sedgemoor*, 1857, Fresco

hater of popery, prelacy, and all superstition.' Ward shows him about to be awoken by his gaolers, peacefully sleeping the sleep of the just (and the justified) with a Bible at his bedside.

Two of Ward's English scenes show Charles II (a favourite subject of the painter; his far more frivolous canvas, *Charles II and Nell Gwynn*, had already proved popular, see fig.46). The first picture shows the refugee king '*assisted in his Escape by Anne Lane after the Battle of Worcester*' (fig.58). Here a wigless and anxious Charles, disguised as a groom, is mounted with Anne Lane behind him. Their horse moves tentatively across a stream while Roundhead soldiers search for the fugitive in the background. *The Landing of Charles II at Dover* (fig.59) moves us forward ten years to a representation of the joyous welcome accorded to the King at his restoration. The beach scene shows General Monk bowing ingratiatingly to Charles and an Anglican cleric casting his eyes thankfully to heaven. Aged aristocrats look on in happy satisfaction and a sailor lad waves his cap in welcome. The preceding scene, *Monk Declaring for a Free Parliament* (fig.60), puts the Restoration into its constitutional context, but the three remaining paintings explore the dilemmas and crises of the 1680s. Two of them, *The Acquittal of the Seven Bishops* (fig.61) and *The Lords and Commons Presenting the Crown to William and Mary* (fig.62), show significant public events. The third, *Alice Lisle Concealing the Fugitives after the Battle of Sedgemoor* (fig.63), is decidedly more private and was derived from an incident made much of by Macaulay in his *History*. Alice Lisle, a Hampshire gentlewoman of Roundhead sympathies, had

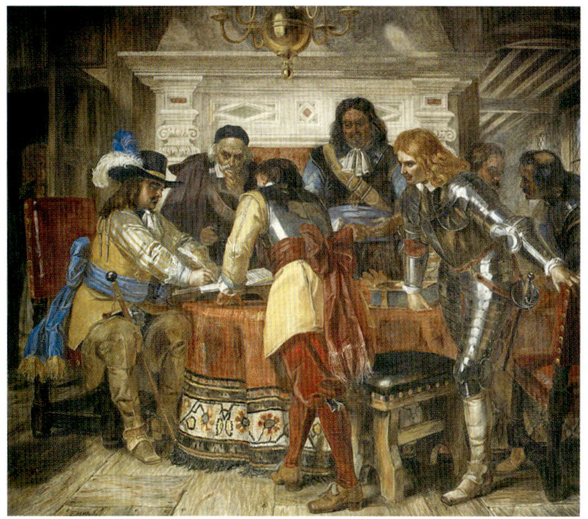

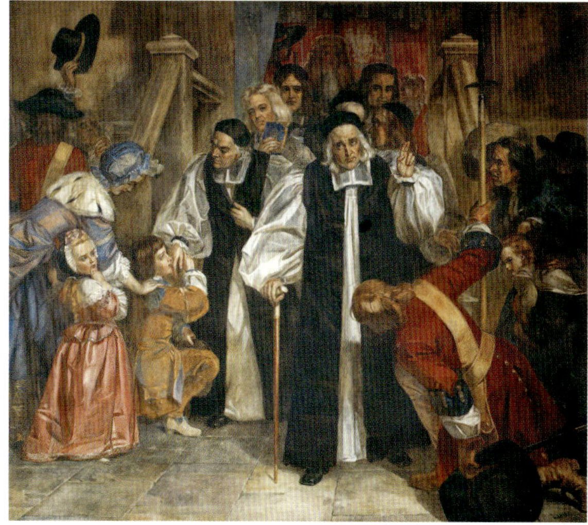

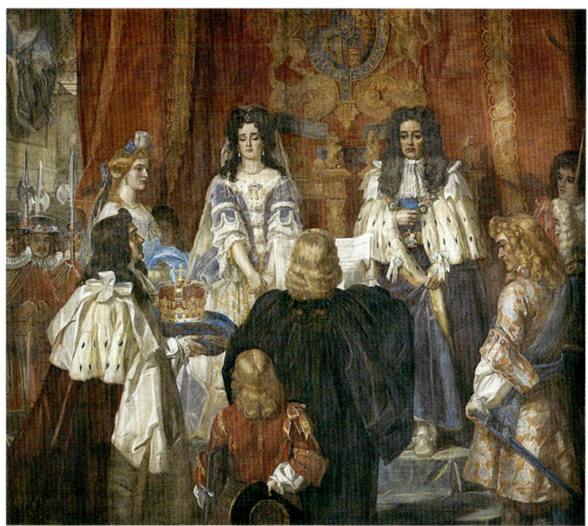

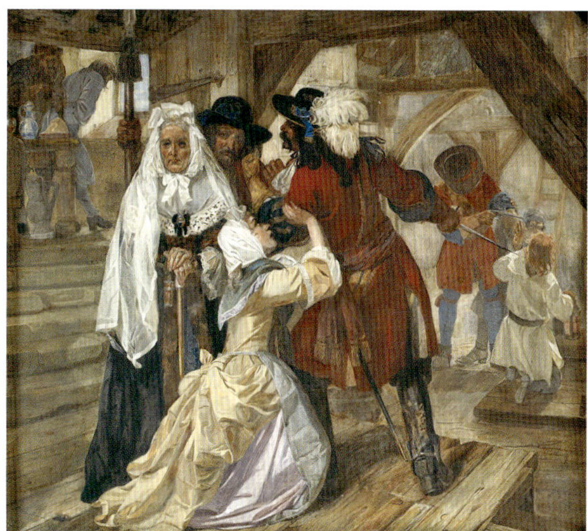

Figs. 58–63:
All 207 x 237.5 cm.
All Palace of Westminster
Collection

nevertheless 'shed bitter tears for Charles the First' and had protected 'many cavaliers in their distress.' Having recklessly extended her hospitality to those who had rebelled against James II, she was accused of treason after the defeat of Monmouth's rag-tag army and was tried by the notorious Judge Jeffreys (who proved himself more than usually volatile and abusive on the bench). Alice was found guilty and condemned to be burned to death. Only after direct appeals to the King was the sentence commuted to beheading and she was executed at

Winchester in 1685. Ward shows us not the brutal circumstances of Alice Lisle's trial and death but the moment that she is apprehended. She stares resolutely forward as the King's soldiers ignore the appeal of a kneeling female relative and as her illegal guests are discovered and arrested. Ward's *The Acquittal of the Seven Bishops* celebrates the release of the bishops in June 1688 following their being found innocent of the charge of seditious libel brought by James II's government (the bishops had protested at the King's insistence that they sanction the reading of his 'Declaration of Indulgence' in churches and had been imprisoned in the Tower). The painting shows the seven prelates, led by Archbishop Sancroft with his hand raised in blessing, descending a staircase watched by a kneeling soldier and an evidently jubilant group of well-dressed men and women.

For Macaulay, the climactic scene in the series must have been Ward's representation of the ceremonial acceptance of the crown by William and Mary in February 1689 (fig.62). Neither monarch looks particularly enthralled by the solemn occasion. Indeed, Mary has an air of cultivated boredom, quite unbecoming in a princess, and the unprepossessing William gives the impression of not quite grasping the drift of the Speaker's constitutional demands. It would be improper to suggest that their expressions suggest that they are serenely untroubled by their joint act of usurpation. Only the figure to their right, who we take to be Mary's younger sister Anne, seems to be both sufficiently solemn and alert to what is happening. Macaulay had described this momentous ceremony in his *History* as the consummation of the English Revolution. He then adds the comment:

> When we compare it with those revolutions which have, during the last sixty years, overthrown so many ancient governments, we cannot but be struck by its peculiar character. Why that character was so peculiar is sufficiently obvious, and yet seems not to have been always understood either by eulogists or censors.[29]

The consummation may have been devoutly wished for by the British nation, but, as E. M. Ward awkwardly represents them, its two royal protagonists look distinctly underwhelmed by the whole occasion.

THE 'BLOODY ASSIZE' AND THE KING'S BOOT

If King James II is conspicuous for his absence from the paintings in the Commons Corridor his influence, both for good and ill, is pervasive in one of the most popular of Victorian historical novels, R[ichard] D[oddridge] Blackmore's *Lorna Doone: A Romance of Exmoor* (1869). In the best tradition established by Sir Walter Scott, Blackmore's novel intermixes regional matters with issues of national concern. Few Victorians needed to be reminded of the extravagant and reckless career of Charles II's illegitimate son, James, Duke of Monmouth, or of his armed rebellion in July 1685 aimed at toppling his Catholic uncle. Above all, legends were spun around Monmouth's defeat, his humiliating escape in disguise, his capture and execution, and the brutal suppression of his erstwhile supporters in arms. Nineteenth-century travellers to the counties of Dorset and Somerset were directed to the site of Monmouth's landing (Lyme Regis), to that of his defeat (Sedgemoor), and to that of his capture near Woodlands (Murray's *Handbook* for 1869 records that the ash tree under which the Duke was discovered was still 'scored with the names of numerous visitors').[30] Murray's *Handbook*, amplifying its comments with appropriate citations from Macaulay's *History*, also pointed visitors to the site of the Bloody Assize in Dorchester, to the display of Judge Jeffreys' chair in the Town Hall, and to the location of his lodgings in High West Street (in the 1860s it was Dufall's glass shop).[31] In the description of Taunton in Somerset Murray goes to some lengths to describe the savage retribution exacted by the victorious General Kirke, and later by Jeffreys, on those suspected of having supported the rebellion:

> Executions, without the form of a trial, commenced. The sign-post of the White Hart served as a gallows … It was believed in London that Kirke put 100 prisoners to death in the week that followed the battle. This irregular massacre was soon followed by no less cruel, but more judicial, acts of barbarity. Jeffreys' 'Bloody Assize' began … On the judge's arrival, he declared in his charge that it would not be his fault if he did not depopulate the place – a threat which he did his best to carry out. In vain did Bp. Ken write to the King to implore mercy for his misguided diocese, complaining that it was impossible to walk along the highways without seeing some ghastly spectacle, and that the whole air of Somersetshire was tainted with

death. The judicial massacre went on unabated. Even the poor children, who had presented the colours to Monmouth, had to purchase their pardon by bribes to the Queen's maids of honour, who employed as their agent, not the famous Wm. Penn, as Lord Macaulay has erroneously maintained, but one George Penne, a leading dealer in this infamous traffic. At length, to the relief of the inhabitants, the chief justice proposed 'to jog homewards' having transported 385 persons and hung 97.[33]

Not many modern guidebooks would have the temerity, let alone the ready information, to correct the most eminent historian of the day. Nevertheless, Murray's *Handbook* expresses a real sense of outrage at the excesses committed in the West Country after Sedgemoor. It was drawing both on long and unhappy local memories and on an established demonology that had been fostered by generations of Whig historians. Kirke and Jeffreys were but the willing tools of a King determined to impose his royal will, and his alien religion, on all of his subjects, however humble they might be.

In Chapter 11 of Volume 2 of *Lorna Doone* the narrator, John Ridd, explains the popular rumblings current in the West of England against the policies of the ailing Charles II:

> Disaffection to the King, or rather dislike of his brother, James, and fear of Roman ascendency, had existed now for several years, and of late were spreading rapidly; partly through the downright arrogance of the Tory faction, the cruelty and austerity of the Duke of York, the corruption of justice, and confiscations of ancient rights and charters; partly through jealousy of the French king, and his potent voice in our affairs; and partly (or perhaps one might even say, mainly) through that natural tide in all political channels, which verily moves as if it had the moon for its mistress.

Earlier in the novel Ridd had been warned by the pernicious Jeffreys to 'keep from everything which leads beyond the sight of thy knowledge' and not to find himself 'a tool for the other side.' This 'honest and simple' Ridd, as Jeffreys cynically describes him, never does cross to 'the other side.' He is something of an apolitical figure, caught up in troubled times both at home on Exmoor and in the capital. He stoutly holds to the Tory concept of loyalty to 'Church and King,' but he is acutely aware of the national rifts and suspicions that mark the accession of James II. Even after his unhappy experience of the bloody battlefield at Sedgemoor, and his expressions of distress at the nature of the judicial massacres that follow Monmouth's rout, Ridd's loyalty is unquestioning. He does, however, allow a deep unease to creep into his accounts of his interviews with the King. James, who fondly supposes that the well-built Ridd harbours Catholic sympathies, makes his own narrow religious prejudices perfectly clear:

> 'I am well pleased,' said His Majesty, with a smile which almost made his dark stubborn face look pleasant, 'to find that our greatest subject, greatest I mean in bodily form, is also a good Catholic. Thou needest not say otherwise. The time shall be, and right soon, when men shall be proud of the one true faith.' Here he stopped, having gone rather far; but the gleam in his eyes was such that I durst not contradict. (Book 3, Chapter 16)

The King's long-term plans for Ridd, having knighted him and married him to the wealthy and aristocratic Lorna, are made plain at the end of the novel. But, as the new 'Sir John,' explains, greater events have prevented their realisation:

> His Majesty, well-disposed towards me for my previous service, and regarding me as a good Catholic, being moved moreover by the Queen, who desired to please Lorna, consented without much hesitation, upon the understanding that Lorna when she became of full age, and the mistress of her property … should pay a heavy fine to the Crown, and devote a fixed portion to her estate to the promotion of the holy Catholic faith, in a manner to be dictated by the King himself. Inasmuch, however, as King James was driven out of his kingdom before this arrangement could take effect; and another king succeeded, who desired not the promotion of the Catholic religion, neither hankered after subsidies (whether French or English), that arrangement was pronounced invalid, improper and contemptible. (Book 3, Chapter 21)

The King is exposed as venal, but so are his henchmen. Ridd admits, with a heavy heart, that though James's proposed subsidy to Catholic causes has not been exacted, the sweeteners already paid to Judge Jeffreys in order to smooth his way to social promotion and marriage, have proved to be non-returnable.

As he appears in the pages of *Lorna Doone*, James II has a myopic view of the destiny of English Catholicism. More unpleasantly, he reveals an inherent tendency to spite and cruelty. It is very likely that Blackmore took his cue for describing James as he does from the pages of Macaulay's *History*, though he goes far further in implying that the King possessed an unpleasant sadistic streak. In his first interview with the King John Ridd is rewarded for capturing two would-be robbers. James's unconcealed delight derives from the knowledge that, thanks to Ridd's bravery, he now has his hands on two proven political enemies who may well hold information about other dissidents. He orders a pair of 'boots,' Scottish instruments of torture, the design of which he had personally 'improved'. He oils the 'boots' himself and expresses the worry that 'there was no man in London quite competent to work them'. Then, rejoicing in the fact that he now has two victims to practice on, the King announces that 'he would try one or two, rather than wait for his pleasure, till the torturer came from Edinburgh.' This is the same King whom Macaulay records enjoying the humiliation of his traitorous nephew. James, who had agreed to see the defeated Monmouth alone, was determined not to pardon him. As the historian implies, though the King's intransigence was perfectly proper, the very fact of his having granted Monmouth an interview, when all prospect of a pardon had been ruled out, was commonly interpreted as 'an outrage of humanity and decency.' The pitiable Monmouth, with his hands tied behind his back with a silken cord, 'threw himself on the ground,' and crawled to the King's feet:

> He wept. He tried to embrace his uncle's knees with his pinioned arms. He begged for life, life at any price … By the ties of kindred, by the memory of the late King, who had been the best and truest of brothers, the unhappy man adjured James to show some mercy. James gravely replied that this repentance was of the latest, that he was sorry for the misery which the prisoner had brought on himself, but that the case was not one for lenity … The poor terrified Duke vowed that he had never wished to take the crown, but had been led into that fatal error by others … He was pre-eminently the champion of the Protestant religion. The interest of that religion had been his plea for conspiring against the government of his father, and for bringing on his country

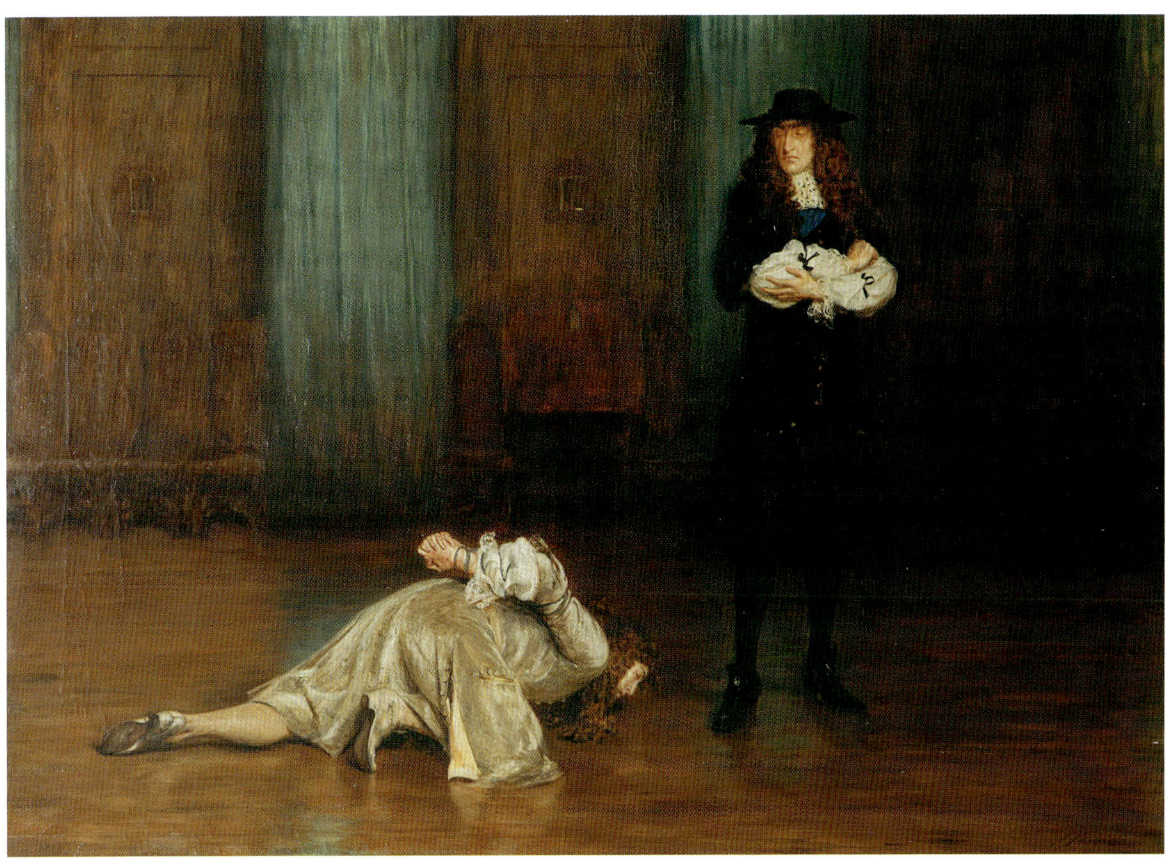

64 John Pettie, *The Interview between James II and the Duke of Monmouth*, 1882, Oil on canvas, 93.4 x 130.5 cm. Manchester Art Gallery

the miseries of civil war: yet he was not ashamed to hint that he was inclined to be reconciled to the Church of Rome. The King eagerly offered him spiritual assistance, but said nothing of pardon or respite. 'Is there then no hope?' asked Monmouth. James turned away in silence.[33]

James's cold pleasure, and his superior sneer as he watches the squirming Monmouth, was memorably caught by the artist John Pettie in his painting of 1882 of this last 'outrageous' interview, *The Interview between James II and the Duke of Monmouth* (fig.64).

Nevertheless, it is not the King's spite and potential sadism that we are most alerted to in Blackmore's novel, but that of his proxy, George Jeffreys. In addition to his evident pleasure in tormenting and cowing those brought

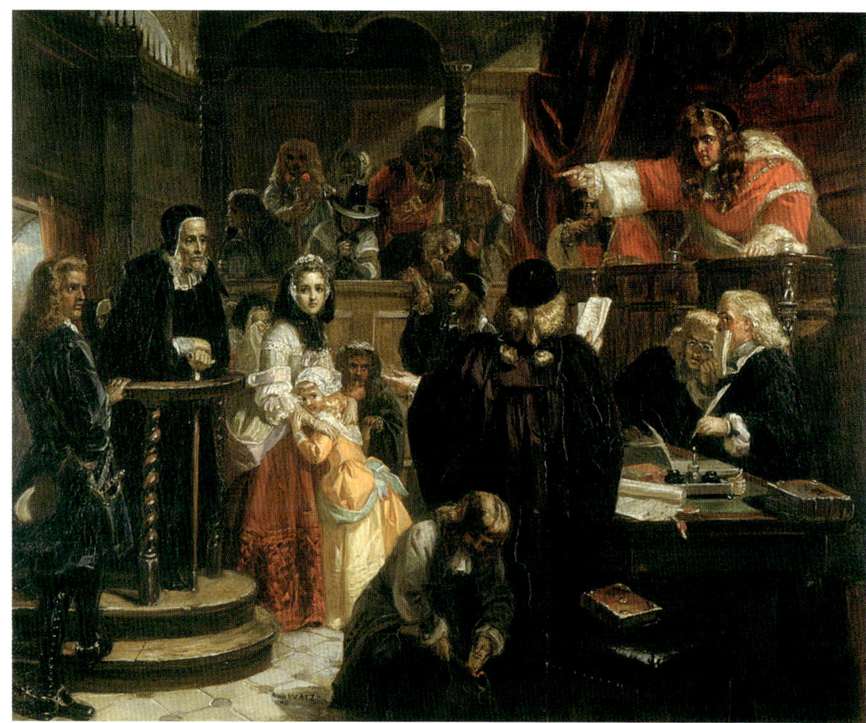

65   Edward Mathew Ward,
*Judge George Jeffreys on
the Bench Hurling Abuse
at Richard Baxter at his
Trial,* Oil on canvas,
42.2 x 52.2 cm.
Sheffield Galleries and
Museums

before him for justice, Jeffreys has an unpleasant propensity for both alcohol and venality. When we first meet him in the novel Ridd describes the Chief Justice as 'a thick-set, burly, and bulky man, with a blotchy broad face, and great square jaws, and fierce eyes full of blazes; he was one to be dreaded by gentle souls and to be abhorred by the noble.' This had become a received way of describing a man who, by the nineteenth century had acquired a reputation as a drunken monster. E. M. Ward had painted him, in *Judge Jeffreys on the Bench* (fig.65), raising himself from the bench, in order to point a bullying finger at an aged cleric in the dock. Naturally enough, Macaulay gave his readers a deeply unsympathetic sketch of Jeffreys' character:

Tenderness for others and respect for himself were feelings alike unknown to him. He acquired a boundless command of the rhetoric in which the vulgar express hatred and contempt. The profusion of maledictions and vituperative epithets which composed his vocabulary could hardly have been rivalled in the fishmarket or the beargarden. His countenance and his voice must always have been unamiable ... The glare of his eyes had a fascination for the unhappy victim on whom they were fixed. Yet his brow and his eye were less terrible than the savage lines of his mouth ... Even when he was sober his violence was sufficiently frightful. But in general his reason was overclouded and his evil passions stimulated by the fumes of intoxication.[34]

It is probably due to Macaulay's influence that the newly formed National Portrait Gallery acquired William Claret's portrait of Jeffreys in 1858 (fig.66). Claret's painting shows a man who is infinitely more becoming, and indeed more refined, than Blackmore, Ward or Macaulay would have us believe. Charles Dickens, who describes Jeffreys as a 'drunken ruffian' and a 'red-faced, swollen, bloated, horrible creature,' was even prepared to inform the readers of his *A Child's History of England* that 'none of the excesses of the French Revolution was worse than the Bloody Assize.'[35] Nevertheless, Dickens was clearly fascinated by this leering pantomime villain. It is extraordinary therefore to find him referring in his French Revolutionary novel, *A Tale of Two Cities* (1859), to Sydney Carton as bearing a resemblance to Claret's portrait. The drunken Carton, found slumped in his chambers after a night's revelry, has 'that rather wild, strained, seared marking about the eyes which may be observed in all free livers of his class, from the portrait of Jeffries [*sic*] downward' (Book 2, Chapter 4). Dickens, who may have known that Jeffreys, like the fictional Carton, had been educated at Shrewsbury School, plays with oppositions and balances throughout his novel. The association between the inebriate judge and the wastrel lawyer offers yet another twisted opposition. Given the fact that Carton's Christian name, Sydney, is almost certainly derived from that of the Whig hero, Algernon Sidney (who had been executed for his involvement in the Rye House Plot), Dickens appears to be curiously interweaving strands from two revolutionary periods.[36] Carton, the alcoholic barrister, will redeem himself through self-sacrifice. Jeffreys, on the other hand, is irredeemably trapped in the manifest corruption and violence of the period immediately anterior to an English revolution deemed to be 'Glorious' by those who engineered it.

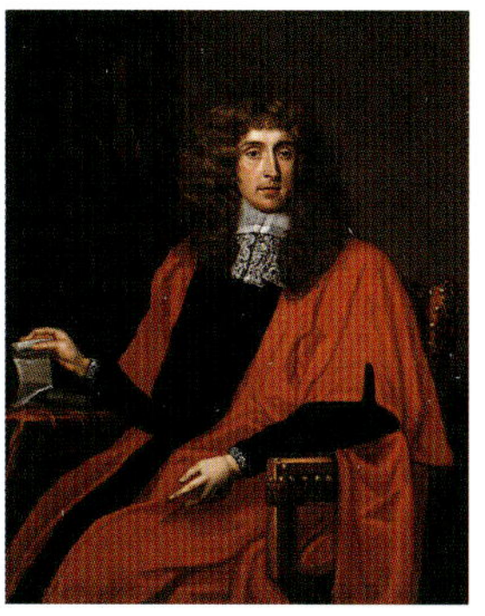

66 Attributed to William Wolfgang Claret, *Judge George Jeffreys, 1st Baron Jeffreys of Wem*, *c*1678–1680, Oil on canvas, 126.4 x 102.2 cm. National Portrait Gallery, London

WILLIAM AND MARY COME INTO THEIR OWN

In 1859 what were known as the 'Occasional Services' annexed to the Book of Common Prayer were dropped from its pages. These four services, for 5 November, 30 January (a Fast Day), 29 May, and, latterly, 20 June, commemorated the Gunpowder Plot, King Charles the Martyr, the Restoration of Charles II and the Accession of Queen Victoria respectively. Each had been introduced by an Act of Parliament and each was authorised by a special proclamation issued at the beginning of each reign, but by 1859 the Church of England had begun to recognise the political awkwardness attendant upon these annual commemorations.[37] The service for 'Gunpowder Treason' on 5 November had been altered in the time of King William III in order to remember the King's successful landing – thanks to a fortuitous 'Protestant Wind' – at Torbay on the same day in 1688. The collects for 'Gunpowder Treason' marked the delivery of James I and his Parliament from 'Popish treachery'; those added by William's order spoke of another delivery, this time from 'Popish tyranny and arbitrary power.' After the Litany the faithful were reminded of the blessed arrival of the Dutch fleet bearing the Dutch prince who had preserved the British nation 'from the attempts of our enemies to bereave us of our Religion and Laws' and who, by Divine Providence, had seen 'all opposition fall before him, till he became our King and Governour.' Thus was the so-called 'Glorious Revolution' sanctioned by Church and State.

Macaulay ended his great *History of England, From the Accession of James II* with the death of William III in 1701. Most of the history of the island anterior to the accession of James had been covered in a single chapter. The second chapter was given over to the eventful reign of Charles II, and Chapter 3 opened with Macaulay's celebrated, and wide-ranging, 'description of the state in which England was at the time when the crown passed from Charles the Second to his brother.' William landed in Chapter 9 and the succeeding sixteen chapters dealt with the new constitutional settlement and with the King's successful campaign in Ireland and his military challenges to Louis XIV. When its last volume was published in 1861, the completed *History* served to persuade readers that the year 1688 had marked the culmination of the great crisis in English life, a crisis which had steadily built up since the time of the Reformation and which had been left unresolved by the radical changes effected by the Civil War. A credulous Victorian reader might also have been given the impression that from William's reign onward nothing much of consequence had happened. This was, of course, what the 'Whig' interpretation of British history was all about, and it partly explains why the battles over Reform in the 1820s and 30s were so bitter. By the opening of the nineteenth century the 'ideal' constitution of Church and State, and the assurances about the liberty of the citizen defined in the Bill of Rights, had remained substantially intact for more than a century. It had, moreover, remained safe in the hands of a succession of temperate Protestant monarchs and of those Whig oligarchs who had taken on the burden of government. Most nineteenth-century Whigs had come to recognise that the reforms of the 1830s were the necessary consequence both of what had been decided in 1689 and of a new political situation. Tories, naturally enough, took the opposite view. Great Britain in 1830 presented a very different social and political landscape compared to the one described in Chapter 3 of Macaulay's *History*. The Nation was now one moulded by significant shifts in the composition of society, by the Industrial Revolution, by the loss of its first colonial empire and by the acquisition of a second, and by the vast changes brought about across the Channel by the French Revolution. Those of a more conservative disposition suspected all change: constitutional, social and, above all, revolutionary. One revolution, and a 'glorious' one to boot, was quite enough.

As his advocacy of reform in the 1830s shows, Macaulay was no constitutional conservative. In a famous speech to the House of Commons in March 1831 in support of the Reform Bill he parodied the manner in which a Jacobite orator might have argued for the political status quo in 1688:

> 'Why make a change of dynasty? Why trouble ourselves to devise new securities for our laws and liberties? See what a nation we are. See how population and wealth have increased since what you call the good old times of Queen Elizabeth. You cannot deny that the country has been more prosperous under the House of Stuart than under their predecessors. Keep that House then and be thankful.' Just such is the reasoning of the opponents of this bill … It is precisely because our institutions are so good that we are not perfectly contented with them; for they have educated us into a capacity for enjoying still better institutions.[38]

For Macaulay, the experience of history compelled reform in the present. The nineteenth century had a progressive impetus precisely because it had inherited a tradition of progress. Nevertheless, conservative-minded Victorian readers of the *History* might well have come away from a perusal of it with the fond idea that the British Constitution had somehow been established by heaven's command. The Settlement of 1689 may well have been determined by the special conditions of the late seventeenth century, and it had been forged thanks to the efforts liberty-loving Protestants, but its essentially providential nature was proved by the fact that it had worked well enough throughout the eighteenth century and had precluded further revolutionary disruption. Even more radical readers would have agreed that the Settlement and the Declaration of Rights of 1689 had worked their benign influence over the constitution of the United States and had firmly established the principle of representative government in two continents. In an important sense, therefore, Macaulay's *History of England* ended not just with the death of William III but with the equivalent of what twenty-first-century historians have styled 'the death of history.' Dickens put it another way in his own *History of England*, albeit one written for the use of children:

> I have now arrived at the close of my little history. The events which succeeded the famous Revolution of one thousand six hundred and eighty eight, would neither be easily related nor easily understood in such a book as this.[39]

In other words, history since 1688 is rather boring if you are a child. It told of powerful Whig ministries, of acts of parliament, civil rights and of the long, complacent afternoon of the Anglican ascendancy, not of wicked kings, Civil War, the bloody repression of dissent and embattled prelates. As far as many Victorians were concerned, monarchs, ministers and bishops stopped being both tyrannical and dangerous in 1688. The trouble for the popular historian was that they also stopped being interesting.

The generally temperate reigns of William and Mary suggested the advantages of being ruled by monarchs who lacked both flair and personality. William had proved himself to be constitutionally and politically tolerant, a gifted commander of his armies, an asthmatic promoter of his Dutch friends, and something of a philistine; Mary embroidered, collected blue-and-white china, admired tulips and patronised Henry Purcell. The couple were childless, but were, as far as the world knew or cared, devoted to one another (Macaulay's last paragraph piously recorded that a black silk ribbon found on William's body contained a gold ring and a lock of Mary's hair). Through their reign St. Paul's Cathedral continued to rise from its foundations to its glorious dome and the City of London at its feet enjoyed an unrivalled economic prosperity thanks to Britain's military and naval triumphs. The Bank of England was founded in 1694, Whitehall Palace was destroyed by fire and the War of the Spanish Succession saw Britain victoriously allied against France, but for most Victorian observers the joint reign was uneventful. Its greatest, and most lasting, cultural achievement, beyond the continuing work on St. Paul's and the music of Purcell, was the reconstruction by Sir Christopher Wren of the royal apartments at Hampton Court.

HAMPTON COURT

Queen Victoria opened the State Apartments and Gardens at Hampton Court Palace to the public in November 1838. Entry was free. None of her royal ancestors had lived in the Palace since the reign of George II, though significantly enough William, the Prince of Orange, driven from the Netherlands by French Revolutionary forces, had taken up residence in the vacated palace between 1795

67 South front of William III's Palace at Hampton Court

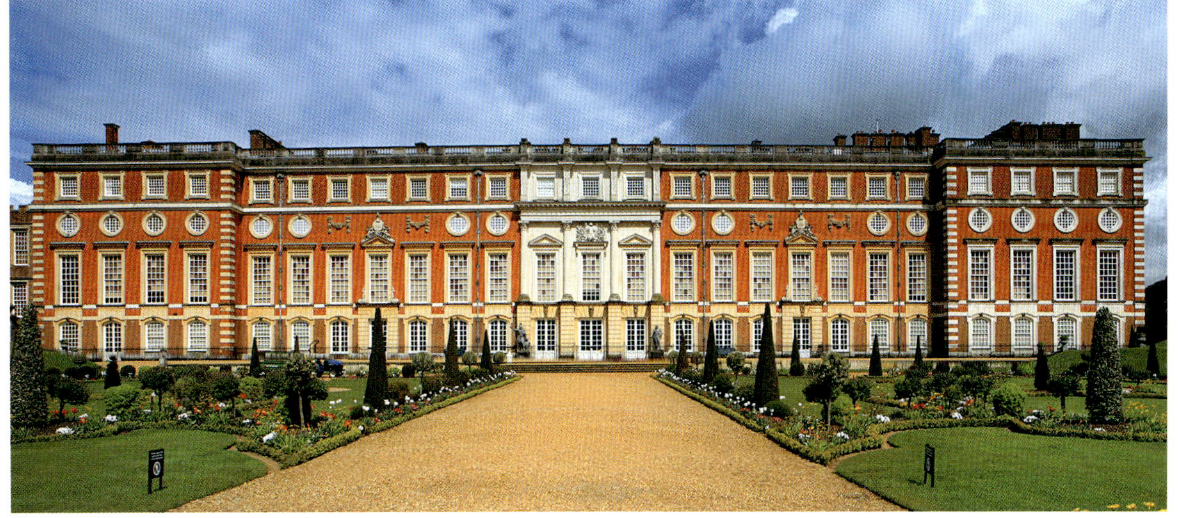

and 1813 (fig.67). Otherwise, it had been divided up as 'grace-and-favour' residences for former royal servants, members of noble families, and other distinguished persons who found themselves in reduced circumstances. Dr Johnson had apparently applied for one such apartment in 1776 but nothing seems to have come of his application. The great populariser of science, Michael Faraday, was however more successful in 1858 and remained in occupation until his death in 1867. In *Little Dorrit* Dickens's unbearable snob, Mrs. Gowan, has 'shady and sedate apartments' there, apartments that her cynical son later describes as 'that red-brick dungeon at Hampton Court,' and parts of the palace unseen by tourists remained similarly occupied until the latter years of the twentieth century. The 1838 opening of the State Apartments, with their rich display of pictures from the royal collection, and of the Palace Gardens, with the popular Maze, had rapidly established Hampton Court as one of the prime tourist attractions of London. Even in the first year of admission some 115,971 curious persons, drawn from all social classes, came to visit. James Thorne's highly informative *Handbook to the Environs of London* of 1876 noted that excursions to the Palace had proved especially popular in the years of the International Exhibitions of 1851 and 1862. By the 1870s the average number of annual visitors was 217,589 and, Thorne tells us, some 30,000 people passed through the Lion Gates on Whit Monday 1872.[40] The author of a later catalogue of the collections claimed in 1881 that some ten million had visited the Palace in the forty-three years since its opening.[41]

In 1834 King William IV appointed Edward Jesse 'Itinerant Deputy Surveyor' in the Office of Woods, Forests and Land Revenues. Despite this somewhat Ruritanian title, Jesse's chief responsibility was for the upkeep of Windsor Castle and Hampton Court and he rapidly acquired a detailed knowledge of the complex architectural history of both buildings. When Hampton Court was opened to the general public he set about the work of restoration and popular explication with exemplary thoroughness and in 1841 produced a handy pocket guidebook, *A Summer's Day at Hampton Court, being a Guide to the Palace and Gardens; with an Illustrative Catalogue of the Pictures According to the New Arrangement, Including Those in the Apartments Recently Opened to the Public.*[42] Jesse's *Guide* was initially addressed to visitors travelling to the Palace by the regular horse-bus service (the railway did not arrive until 1849) and it included a short account of William III's other suburban Palace at Kensington which was also on the route of the horse bus. What really interests him, however, is neither Kensington nor the Wren additions to Hampton Court but the old Palace, begun by Cardinal Wolsey and reconstructed by Henry VIII. Indeed the first sixty-four pages of his one hundred and forty-eight page guide are taken up with an account of the buildings and their royal residents before William and Mary. Although his comments on the pictures, ceiling paintings and tapestries in each of the Wren State Apartments are meticulous, Jesse seems to be far less engaged by the late-seventeenth-century architecture than he is by the parts of the palace still ascribed to Wolsey's anonymous architects. His comment on William and Mary's rebuilding is ambiguously telling:

> Hampton Court owes much of its present splendour to William III. He employed Sir Christopher Wren as his architect, and he built the present state-rooms, the two great staircases, and made various alterations, which need not be enumerated, as his style of architecture is perfectly distinct from that of Wolsey. It is to be regretted perhaps that his palace was ever interfered with.[43]

We sense that the 'regret' loomed larger in Jesse's antiquarian mind than did his 'perhaps'. Hampton Court as a whole evidently fascinated its thousands of visitors, but neither Wren's architecture, nor the memories of his royal patrons, seem to have been much appreciated. Other mid-nineteenth-century commentators appear to have been equally unimpressed by the seventeenth-century part of the palace. The author of Bohn's *Pictorial Handbook of London* of 1854, who had been so impressed by Inigo Jones's unbuilt plans for Whitehall Palace, considered that the 'Dutch taste and crotchets' of William and Mary had 'so influenced this work that it is unfair to regard the designs as his [Wren's]'.[44] James Thorne is equally condescending:

> William III, intending to make the palace his chief residence, commissioned Sir Christopher Wren to erect a new suite of State Apartments more in accordance with the taste of the day than the sombre rooms of the Tudor king. Wren demolished two of Wolsey's courts, and remodelled a third, and erected the long uniform southern and eastern fronts, towards the Thames and the gardens, in a semi-classic style, having no affinity to the older structure. Wren's building is, however, good of its

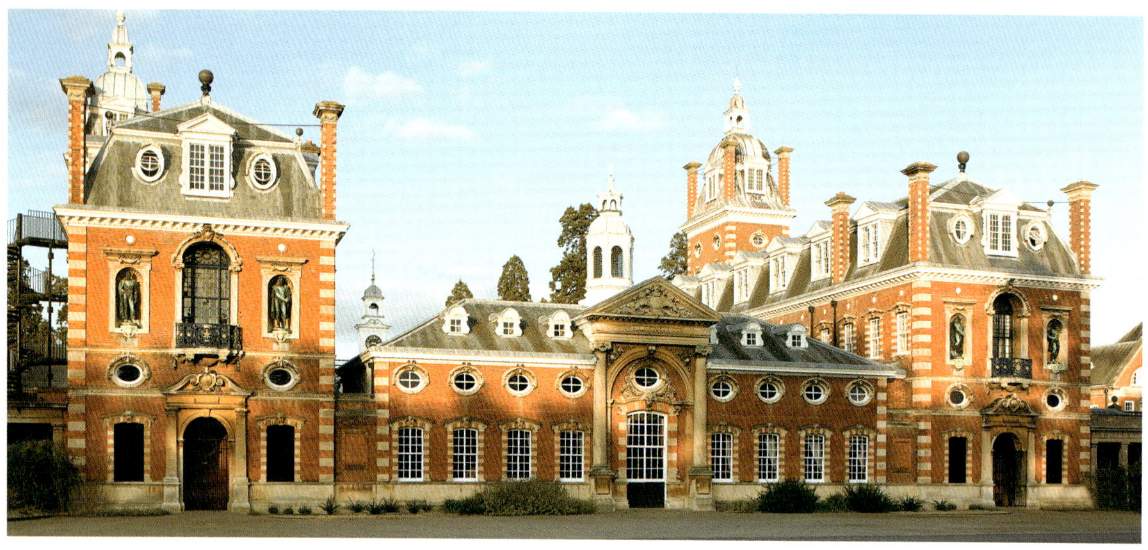

68   Wellington College,
Berkshire

kind. The elevations are imposing from their extent, and have much simple dignity of character.[45]

Clearly, Wren's domestic architecture, however grand and 'dignified' it appeared, had yet to find determined and discriminating admirers. Even James Fergusson, who had so stoutly defended the design of St. Paul's, quibbled over the fact that at Hampton Court Wren's basement was 'too low' and that what he called the 'bel étage' was 'destroyed by the circular windows over the principal ones.' The great merit of the design, Fergusson claimed, lay merely in its 'largeness, and being devoid of all affectation.' He was at least prepared to allow that Wren's work contrasted favourably with Wolsey's, though neither, he believed, was 'of the best age of its peculiar style, nor perhaps the best of its age.' This is damnation with faint praise, though at least the rebuilding of Hampton Court escapes the unrelievedly damnatory comment Fergusson makes about Wren's Chelsea Hospital ('It would not be easy to find a worse building anywhere').[46]

The impact of Wren's work at Hampton Court was only gradually felt on historians of English architecture and on latter-day architects. Indeed, the domestic architecture of Wren and his contemporaries was not properly celebrated until the appearance of John Belcher and Melvyn Macartney's superb photographic survey *Later Renaissance Architecture in England* of 1901. It was, however, the earlier discovery that red brick with stone dressings was not an aesthetic aberration, but something attractive to the eye, that began to change things. After the 1720s red brick had steadily been looked down on as a material that was both old-fashioned and more than a little showy. Later eighteenth-century London was a brick city, but its townscape was substantially constructed from the unassuming, dull yellowish stocks that proclaimed the quiet virtues of proportion and self-effacement. The reds and pinks of Wren's time seemed to assert their glaring individualism in a way that later generations would deem to be un-classical, even 'baroque.' Ironically, the fashion for red brick seems to have been reintroduced not by architects wedded to the classical or 'Italian' tradition but by ardent advocates of the Gothic style. Where Ruskin had proclaimed the delights of colour in Venetian architecture, men like William Butterfield broke into the grey uniformity of Margaret Street in the West End of London with his striking design for a diapered, red-brick church (1849-59) in the North German style. The earliest substantial building in the Wren manner, Wellington College of 1856-59 (fig.68), was conspicuously not in London, but in rural Berkshire. Here the architect, John Shaw, constructed a public school based not on mediaeval or Tudor models, but on courtyards and wings owing a greater debt to the plan of the Greenwich Hospital than to those of Winchester or Eton. The mansard roofs of Wellington College may derive from seventeenth-century French models, but the circular windows and the stone swags unfailingly recall Hampton Court. Only the insistently Gothic school chapel, added in 1860 by Sir George Gilbert Scott, broke into this innovative reprise of seventeenth-century themes. It may well be thanks to his work at Wellington College that Scott could generously refer in 1878 to the 'Queen Anne' style as 'really the domestic variety of the architecture of Sir Christopher Wren, and a very good style it really was.'[47] William Eden Nesfield's remodelling of a classical house at Kinmel Park in Denbighshire (Clwyd) from *c*.1868 shows a similar debt to Hampton Court. Kinmel is a grand country house and its monumental symmetry asserts a palatial rather than a vernacular pedigree. The work of John Shaw and Nesfield was pioneering, opening the way for Norman Shaw's far more daring experiments in the 1880s and for that *omnium gatherum* architectural movement known as the 'Queen Anne style.'[48]

The true herald of the 'Queen Anne' revival is a relatively modest London house overlooking the palace at Kensington much frequented by the Queen herself (fig.69). William Makepeace Thackeray, who built the house for his own

69   Late 19th-century
photograph of William
Makepeace Thackeray's
house at Palace Green,
Kensington.
Private collection

70   Title-page from *The
History of Henry Esmond*
by William Makepeace
Thackeray, 1852.
Private collection

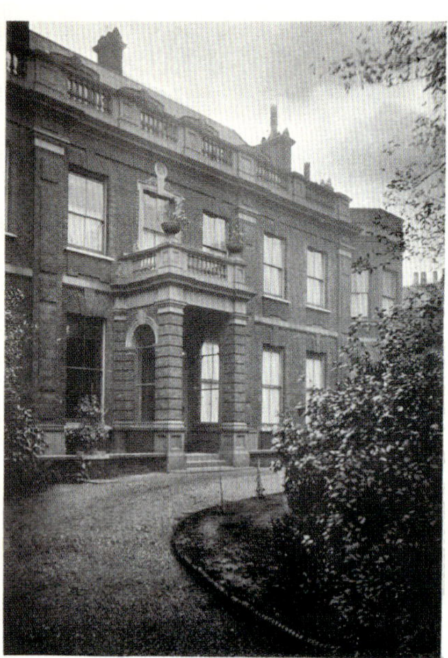

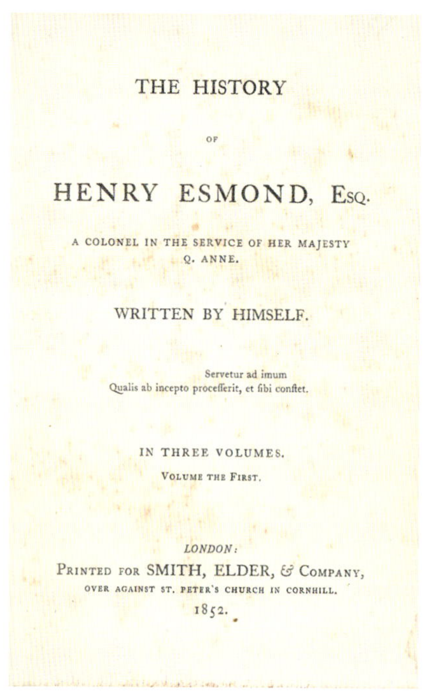

occupation in 1860–61, set one of the most memorable scenes of his novel,
Henry Esmond, in the adjacent palace gardens. Here, Thackeray supposes, the
ailing Anne has a secret meeting in the Cedar Walk with her half-brother,
James, the Jacobite Pretender to her throne. The novelist was sentimentally
attached to the historical associations of a Kensington which was still, when
he first knew it, little more than a village detached from London. He had
written *Vanity Fair* in a bow-fronted Regency house in Young Street and had
spent his middle years in a 'shabby genteel' house in Onslow Square. In *Esmond*
he had fondly imagined the semi-rural Kensington Square as it was in the
opening years of the eighteenth century when only the nearby palace gave
Kensington a distinct identity. 2 Palace Gardens, or 'Palazzo Thackeray' as the
publisher, John Blackwood, christened Thackeray's last London residence, was
built, following the novelist's own sketches, by Frederick Hering. It was,
moreover, to be 'the reddest house in all the town.' Thackeray's neighbour,
John Everett Millais, believed that, in a relatively short space of time, it had
changed the face of London by spreading a new fashion for the once despised

red brick.[49] The detached house on Palace Green has a relatively plain façade, enhanced by incised brick pilasters, and heavy keystones; the entrance porch, the central window above it, and the cornice have stone dressings. Despite its clear references to the past and its unambiguous redness, it is unmistakeably a house of its time. The house was finished in 1861 and Thackeray and his daughters moved in on 31 March. Inside, the furniture was predominantly early Georgian and the house's green walls were hung with seventeenth- and eighteenth-century portraits and landscapes. One of Thackeray's cousins describes 2, Palace Green as follows:

> The house was full of treasures. Old English looking-glasses – cabinets filled with Sèvres, Dresden and Chelsea china – quaint old high-backed chairs and settees – and many interesting pictures by Old Masters. Among them were a charming specimen of Mytens signed and dated 1665. One represented a girl in a pink silk dress, plucking a rose; another a child in yellow, with a crimson hat and feather, carrying apricots – a dog at her side. A large picture of Queen Anne, seated on a throne attended by an allegorical female figure of Peace, painted by De Troye in commemoration of the Treaty of Utrecht. A *Conversation champêtre* by Watteau. Portrait of a lady in a ruff, white head-dress, rich crimson and gold dress and gold chain, by Pourbus, 1604. Cupids sporting by Boucher. Portrait of a lady, in a blue dress and pearl necklace. A landscape with peasants and cattle on a wooden bridge, Old Cuyp. A curious panoramic view in the Low Countries with a grand encampment of Spanish troops by E Van de Velde.[50]

There was also a capacious wine cellar. 'Here,' the novelist told a friend, 'I am going to write my greatest work – A History of the Reign of Queen Anne.' Then, looking at his well-stocked bookshelves he added: 'I want to absorb the authorities gradually, so that when I come to write, I shall be filled with the subject, and can sit down to a continuous narrative without jumping up every moment to consult somebody.'[51] This proposed history of Queen Anne's reign had been 'a pet project' for some years and it was intended to be both an extension of, and a complement to, Macaulay's *History of England*. It was not to be realised. On Christmas Eve 1863 Thackeray was found dead in his bed in this, his 'lordly dwelling house,' a house that he rightly feared would prove to be a red-brick 'Vanity Fair.'

Henry Esmond and Good Queen Anne

Thackeray's period of residence at 2 Palace Green, short as it was, was crucial in helping to establish a fashion for late seventeenth-century architecture and for early eighteenth-century artefacts. The house also effectively launched Kensington's Victorian career as an artistic quarter, known not for French-style bohemianism, but for expensive, architect-designed houses with 'aesthetic' interiors in which choice antiques could be displayed. The new-found popularity of Queen Anne's reign was also considerably indebted to the success of Thackeray's earlier novel, *The History of Henry Esmond, Esq. A Colonel in the Service of Her Majesty Q. Anne. Written by Himself.* This mock autobiography appeared in three volumes in November 1852. As a three-decker, it was outwardly a typical enough product of the vogue for first-person narrated fiction in the 1850s. What made the book distinctive was the fact that it was printed in an eight-point Caslon typeface and that Thackeray employed seventeenth-century phraseology, spellings and abbreviations (fig.70). He also composed running-titles at the head of each page. This format marked a radical departure from the pattern established in *Vanity Fair* and *Pendennis*, both of which Thackeray had published as illustrated, monthly-part serials. *Esmond* is also a notably sober, even melancholic, historical narrative, one that purposefully disconcerted its original readers, both visually and thematically. As he announced in its dedication, the novel's style echoed the 'manners and language of Queen Anne's time' when social preoccupations and prejudices differed fundamentally from those of the 1850s. The narrative looks back on the remembered life of its protagonist, but it also offers a grander retrospect on a highly distinctive and politically disjunctive age.

The narrator of *Henry Esmond*, who addresses us almost detachedly in the third person, is a Jacobite both by persuasion and by family tradition. He stems from a family which, we are told, has pawned its plate and mortgaged its property in defence of Charles I and whose country seat at Castlewood has withstood a Parliamentary siege. As a melancholy undergraduate at Cambridge, nicknamed 'Don Dismallo' by his fellows, Esmond assiduously supports the exiled James II:

> [he] gave himself many absurd airs of loyalty; used to invite young friends
> to Burgundy, and give the King's health on King James's birthday; wore

> black on the day of his abdication; fasted on the anniversary of King
> William's coronation; and performed a thousand absurd anticks, of
> which he smiles now to think. (Volume the First, Chapter 10)

Esmond's amusement at the 'anticks' of his old self are habitually tinged with
a combination of nostalgia and a disillusion with the values he once held dear.
Take for example his astute comment on the self-destructive nature of the
Stuart dynasty:

> Ours is the most loyal people in the world surely; we admire our kings,
> and are faithful to them long after they have ceased to be true to us.
> 'Tis a wonder to any one who looks back at the history of the Stuart
> family, to think how they kicked their crowns away from them; how
> they flung away chances after chances; what treasures of loyalty they
> dissipated, and how fatally they were bent on consummating their own
> ruin. If ever men had fidelity, 'twas they; if ever men squandered
> opportunity, 'twas they; and of all the enemies they had, they themselves
> were the most fatal. (Volume the Second, Chapter 3).

At the foot of the page there is a Greek quotation from the *Odyssey* (1. 32–34)
reminding readers not to blame the gods for their misfortunes, but to see evil as
rooted in human hearts and bringing about sorrows 'beyond that which is
ordained.' The Esmonds have found their loyalty to the Stuarts steadily strained,
tested and undervalued over time and, as the novel shows, their sorrows continue
far into the reign of Anne. Henry's climactic disillusion is double. His unrequited
love for his cousin Beatrix is coupled with the knowledge that the Pretender (the
'Chevalier St. George') has completely wrecked a planned *coup d'état* on the death
of Queen Anne, having been distracted by trying to seduce the same Beatrix. Not
only does the Chevalier reveal a congenital relish for fornication, but the written
evidence of his dalliance is blasphemously concealed in that sacred text for Stuart
loyalists, the *Eikon Basilike* (supposedly the pious meditations of Charles I). The
Pretender takes the news of his failure with a typically nonchalant grace, expressed,
we are told, in French: 'Thus to lose a crown … to lose the loveliest woman in the
world; to lose the loyalty of such hearts as yours, is not this, my lords, enough of
humiliation?' At such a crisis, even the English language deserts a man who has
betrayed those who had risked so much to support his claim to the throne of his

ancestors. For Henry Esmond, at least, the accession of a Hanoverian king marks the end of his political and social ambition and he resolves to withdraw from England forever and settle on family lands in Virginia:

> With the sound of King George's trumpets, all the vain hopes of the weak and foolish young Pretender were blown away; and with that musick, too, I may say, the drama of my own life was ended. (Volume the Third, Chapter 13.)

The running-title at the head of the previous page had read '*Vivat Rex.*' Earlier in his narrative Esmond would have questioned who actually *was* the King: the legitimate James or the usurping George? Now he has an unambiguous answer. Both the man now identified as 'the Pretender' and Esmond's pretensions to love and politics are vanquished as a new era opens. Queen Anne was most famous in the nineteenth century, thanks to a much-quoted line of George Colman's, for being dead. Now, she and the ruling House of Stuart truly are defunct, the Jacobites have bungled, and the Elector of Hanover has peacefully succeeded to the throne.[52]

As the century developed *Henry Esmond* retained the early esteem accorded to it by its first readers. If never Thackeray's most popular novel, it was its author's firm favourite amongst his works and it was greatly admired by those of an 'aesthetic' bent. Three editions appeared within two years and for the new issue of 1868 George du Maurier provided eight full-page illustrations, adding twelve more for the 1884 edition. The case for seeing *Henry Esmond* as a pioneer 'art novel' could be based not solely on the walk-on parts allotted to Alexander Pope and Jonathan Swift but on the fact that Thackeray was intensely aware of the 'artifice' of his creation. His daughter quotes the novelist as saying that when he was composing *Esmond* he had been 'living in the last century for weeks' until he got to fancy himself 'almost as familiar with the one as with the other.'[53] Anne Thackeray Ritchie also describes the three-volume edition as appearing 'in periwig and embroidery.' She was referring to the novel's distinctive format, but her words could also be taken as a reference to its scrupulous representation of an eighteenth-century sensibility. One early reviewer, George Brimley, argued that it contained the essence of Thackeray's art, an art deeply imbued with the ethics and aesthetics of the previous century:

The moral antithesis of actual and ideal is the root from which springs the peculiar charm of Mr. Thackeray's writings; that mixture of gaiety and seriousness, of sarcasm and tenderness, of enjoyment and cynicism, which reflects so well the contradictory consciousness of man as a being with senses and passions and limited knowledge, yet with a conscience and a reason speaking to him of eternal laws and a moral order of the universe. It is this that makes Mr. Thackeray a profound moralist, just as Hogarth showed his knowledge of perspective by drawing a landscape throughout in violation of its laws. So, in Mr Thackeray's picture of society as it is, society as it ought to be is implied.[54]

In an important way, therefore, Thackeray had re-explored a disconcertingly eighteenth-century way of looking at life. *Henry Esmond* offered not an escape into the past, but an intimate representation of why the past was both like *and* unlike the present.

QUEEN ANNE

The acclaim accorded to Thackeray's representation of early eighteenth-century life in *Esmond* is testified to by the two costume paintings based on incidents in the novel by Augustus Egg, the most famous of which, *Beatrix Knighting Esmond* (1857, fig.71), was an early acquisition of the Tate Gallery. The novel was also approvingly quoted in W. H. Davenport Adams broad survey of 'Men and Manners, Life and Letters in England's Augustan Age' to which he blithely gave the title *Good Queen Anne* (1886). Davenport Adams insists that he did not know of a 'more picturesque description' of the Battle of Wynendael than that provided by Thackeray. It is a contention that is hard to contradict, given the paucity of accessible descriptions of that largely overlooked victory of General Webb's. Nevertheless, Davenport Adams knew that Thackeray had done his military and topographical homework and that Esmond's respect for Webb far outweighed his dislike of Marlborough. Elsewhere, the two volumes of *Good Queen Anne* provided late Victorian readers with a spirited account of literature, theatre, painting, politics and naval affairs in the twelve years of Anne's reign. It is possibly the first time that the word 'Augustan' was used in this context. The introductory paragraph is

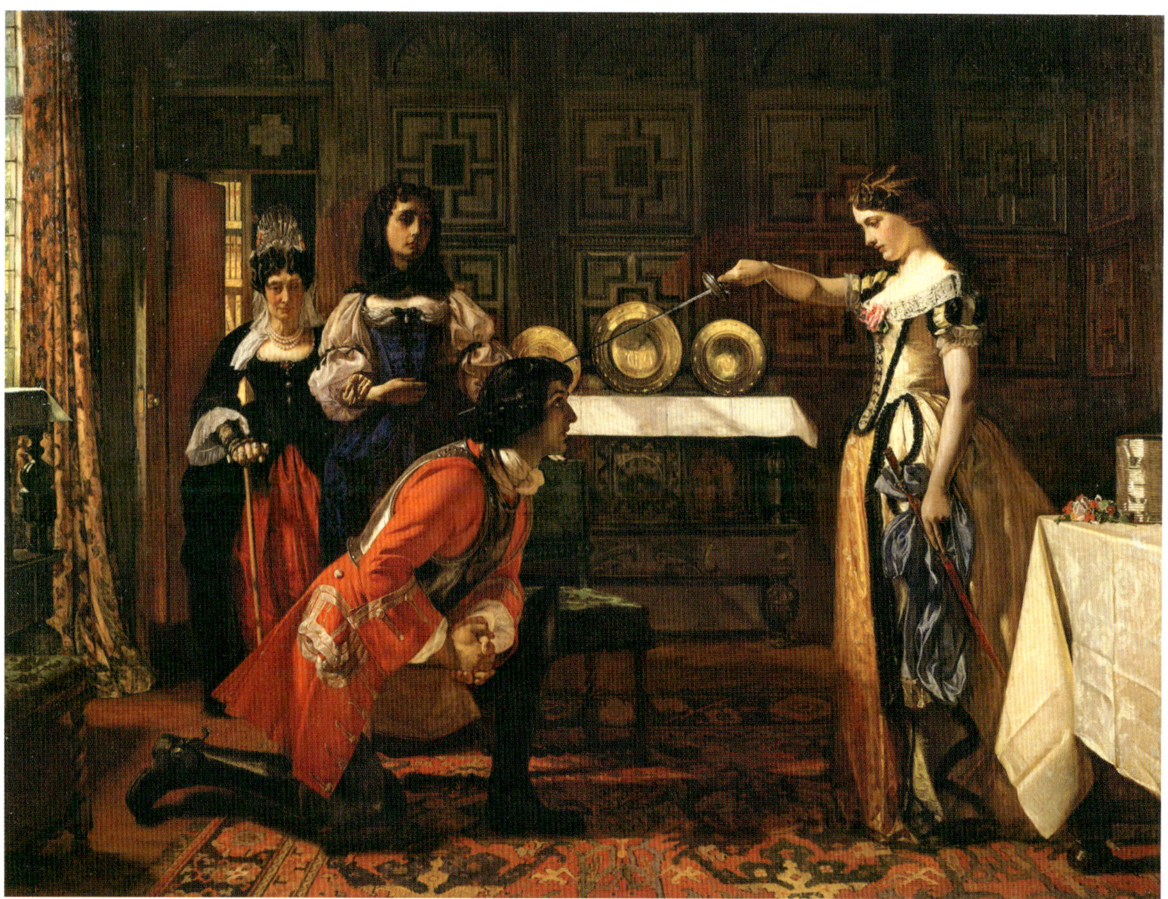

71   Augustus Egg, *Beatrix Knighting Esmond*, 1857, Oil on canvas, 86.9 x 117.1 cm. Tate, London

explicit in its claims for the cultural significance of the period:

> The reign of Queen Anne is one of the most interesting periods in our English history. It witnessed a remarkable development of intellectual activity, which permanently affected the tone and character of our literature. It witnessed the evolution of our constitutional system, and the greater definiteness of ministerial responsibility. It witnessed the foundation of our naval supremacy, and the origin of our military prestige. It witnessed the union of England and Scotland into a compact kingdom … it was crowded with great and remarkable men and women,

in politics, in letters, in art, in society – men and women who, through a variety of circumstances, are as familiar to us, or even more familiar than, the famous personages of times much nearer to us.[55]

Davenport Adams goes on to insist that 'no one will dispute' that Pope and Swift, Addison and Steele were known to late Victorian readers 'as intimately as the writers of the first half of the present century.' Even Queen Anne, so often cruelly dismissed as 'stodgy,' basks in a similarly flattering light and emerges, extraordinarily enough, as the nursing mother of the age, a generous-minded Victorian benefactress *avant la lettre*:

> A warm and faithful friend; with a genial temper and a heart full of kindly feelings; liberal, even to lavishness, in her charities; she honestly deserved – and this is no light praise – the fond epithet which her subjects spontaneously attached to her name, and is still remembered in history as
> 'GOOD QUEEN ANNE'.[56]

Despite such gushing tributes, Davenport Adams's survey of Anne's reign occasionally offers some astute criticism of early eighteenth-century art and literature. He sees Swift and Marlborough as, in their radically different ways, the most 'conspicuous' men of their age, and he writes observantly about both Pope and Defoe. It is only in his comments on contemporary painting and architecture that we can detect that his views are myopic by twenty-first-century standards. He singles out Sir Godfrey Kneller as an artist 'who claims a longer notice than I have accorded to any of his contemporaries' but then proceeds to give us gossipy biographical facts rather than any analysis of Kneller's achievement. James Gibbs is praised for having designed one 'really beautiful church' – St. Martin-in-the-Fields – but the rest of his works are merely listed without any enthusiasm or discrimination. The highly original London churches of Nicholas Hawksmoor and Thomas Archer are passed over without mention and far more notice is given to Vanbrugh the playwright than to Vanbrugh the architect ('for illustrations of contemporary manners Vanbrugh may be consulted with even more advantage than any of his dramatic contemporaries'). It is evident that Vanbrugh's architecture was clearly not to Davenport Adams's taste:

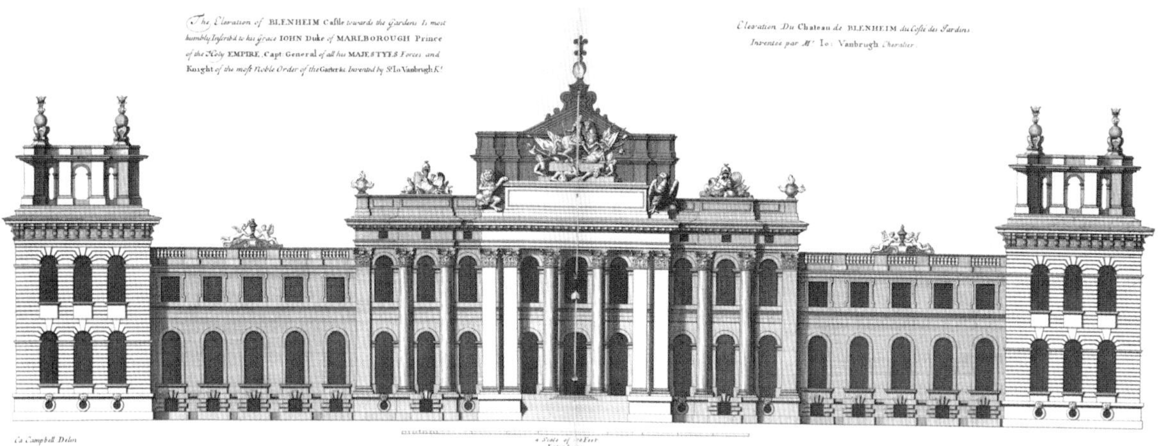

72 Blenheim Palace, plate
from *Vitruvius Britannicus*
by Colen Campbell,
1717. Private collection

His structures are distinguished by grandiosity rather than grandeur. They are boldly conceived, however, and solidly executed; and though ponderous in outline and frigid in detail, produce an impressive effect by their general massiveness.[57]

When he returns to a discussion of Vanbrugh later in his study, all he can find to say about Blenheim Palace (fig.72) − 'the worthiest monument of his architectural skill' − is that, thanks to the interfering Duchess of Marlborough, 'its erection brought him neither pleasure nor profit.'[58]

When we recall that in 1864 Dickens had referred to Thomas Archer's great 'Queen Anne' church of St. John's, Smith Square, as 'hideous' and resembling 'some petrified monster, frightful and gigantic, on its back with its legs in the air,' we should not necessarily be surprised to encounter Davenport Adams's deep unease with the style we now commonly refer to as 'English Baroque'.[59] In 1870 the assiduous historian, Philip Henry, 5th Earl Stanhope, had found it equally difficult to come to terms with Sir John Vanbrugh's architectural eccentricities. Stanhope's *The Reign of Queen Anne* (1870) gave Victorian readers what Thackeray had failed to do, a worthy continuation of Macaulay's *History of England* into the reign of William III's successor. Worthy it certainly is, but it completely lacks Macaulay's novelistic flair for analysing character, for capturing the feel of historical events, or for exploring the larger cultural environment in which those events take place. Stanhope merely mentions Vanbrugh in connection with Marlborough's victories:

> The Queen gave orders to construct at her expense a stately palace in the park of Woodstock which should bear the name of Blenheim and be a lasting record of her own and the nation's gratitude. Her Majesty having approved the model the work was at once commenced under the direction of Mr. Vanbrugh, afterwards Sir John. His merits as an architect were highly extolled in his lifetime but at present are more commonly viewed in the light of the sarcastic epitaph composed at his decease.[60]

He then proceeds to quote the much-repeated couplet: 'Lie heavy on him Earth, for he / Laid many a heavy load on thee.' It is just possible than Stanhope may have gleaned what he implies was the 'commonly' held view that Vanbrugh's architecture was unrelievedly ponderous from the somewhat ambiguous analysis of his achievement in James Fergusson's *History of the Modern Styles of Architecture* of 1862. Fergusson certainly detects merits in Vanbrugh's style, but he cannot quite bring himself to praise it, let alone admire it:

> Whether or not Sir John Vanbrugh derived his love of ponderosity from the Dutch blood that is said to have flowed in his veins, or from some accident of taste or education, it was at least innate and overpowering … Blenheim was to Sir John Vanbrugh what St Paul's was to Wren – the great opportunity of his life, and the work by which he will be judged and his name handed down to posterity … In designing his elevation he avoided all the faults that can be charged against Versailles, which was then the typical palace of the day … yet with all this, Blenheim cannot be called successful. The principal Order is so gigantic as to dwarf everything near it; and as it everywhere covers two stories, it is always seen to be merely an ornament. In the entrance front especially there is such a confusion of lines and parts as to destroy that repose so essential to grandeur, while the details are too large to admit of their being picturesque; and though the sky-line is pleasingly broken, it is by fantastic and not by constructive elements. If we add to all this that the details are always badly drawn, and generally capriciously applied, it will be easy to understand how even so grand a design may be marred.[61]

Fergusson's final dismissal of Blenheim as 'designed by some Brobingnagian architect for the residence of their little Gulliver' is equalled by a similarly fastidious distaste for Castle Howard ('its defects arise principally from the fact that Vanbrugh seems to have had no ideas of how to ornament a building except by the introduction of an Order'). Unsurprisingly, he has no eye at all for the yet more eclectic churches of Hawksmoor, dismissing St George-in-the-East with the words: 'the term vulgar expresses more correctly the effect produced than perhaps any other epithet that could be applied to it.' As with most of his contemporaries, Fergusson is blind both to the subtlety and originality of what are now regarded as the masterpieces of the English Baroque. The central architectural achievements of the reign of Queen Anne are dismissed as evidence of 'how unsettled men's minds were in matters of taste at this period.' No progress was to be hoped for, Fergusson adds, and 'the balance must before long turn steadily towards either originality or towards servility.'[62]

'QUEEN ANNE'

'Originality' was certainly what many of Fergusson's contemporaries in the architectural world were seeking. Nevertheless, what many truly original Victorian architects chose to call the 'Queen Anne' style in the 1870s was not remotely an architectural style that an informed subject of the last Stuart Queen would have recognised. In truth, it was a style that owed more to the tastes of Anne of Denmark than to the time of her royal great-grand-daughter. It was a bastard mixture of elements drawn from Kew Palace, Amsterdam merchants' houses, Flemish town-halls and any number of country rectories of the first third of the eighteenth century. What 'Queen Anne' houses had to have in common was that they were constructed in red brick, had fussy gables and sported white-painted sash windows. If anything the 'Queen Anne' style, as it was understood in the 1870s and 80s, owed more to the irregularity promoted by the Gothic revival than to the accepted principles of domestic architecture in 1700.[63] There might have been a touch of Wren here and there, but no reference to the ponderous vulgarities associated with Vanbrugh or Hawksmoor would have been deemed proper. In the United States, a republican 'Queen Anne,' with a penchant for tile-hanging, shingled gables and bay-windows with small panes of glass, took on an even wilder stylistic independence. In 1887, a leading proponent of the 'aesthetic' design in the home, J. Moyr Smith, wittily described the change in fashion in a 'prelude' to his *Ornamental Interiors, Ancient and Modern* in terms of a flirtation with a new goddess:

> The former worshippers of bright, original, intelligent, vivacious Gothica, turned their backs on her, to grovel in the dust before Queen Anne … One loved her for her homeliness, another for her dignity and picturesque grace; this admired her because she was so domestic and unpretending, that other because she was so rich and so queenly. She was pure English, pure Flemish, pure Italian … Her age was as varied as her other characteristics, for her dress and style showed that she must be the contemporary of Julius Caesar, of Francis I, William the Silent, the Grand Monarque, Napoleon Bonaparte, the Brothers Adam, Norman Shaw, and John J. Stevenson. Pretty little lodges, dignified mansions, tall, gawky street fronts and clumsy or picturesque temples called Board schools were erected in her honour, and she seemed to be installed as the architectural divinity, vice Gothica dethroned. The moral of this allegorical prelude is that the name of Queen Anne has been tacked on to things of very opposite styles, periods, and countries, with which the style of the real Queen Anne had no connection.[64]

What the new 'goddess' offered to a new generation of Victorians was yet more choice. Men and women of taste in the 1840s had rejected the 'Elizabethan' in favour of the purer forms defined by the Gothic revival, but there still remained those who, with equally refined artistic opinions, retained a loyalty to the 'Greek' and the 'Italianate'. The outcome of this long drawn out 'battle of the styles' was now further unsettled by a style that was attractive because it was, in fact, no defined style at all and which could be seen as derived from no obvious historical precedent. Nevertheless, one prominent Victorian Goth saw this new eclecticism not so much as a conscious rejection of the architectural principles that he had fostered but as a perverse adaptation of them. Towards the end of his successful career George Gilbert Scott wrote perceptively:

> The style now known [as Queen Anne] … embraces all varieties, from the close of the Elizabethan period to the middle of the eighteenth century, with a preference for that most resembling Elizabethan, so that it

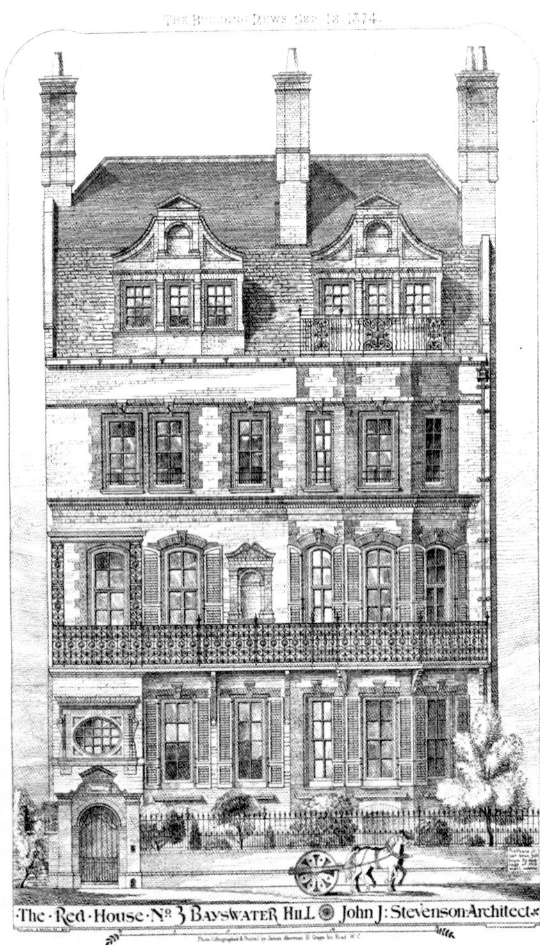

73 John James Stevenson, illustration of The Red House, *Building News*, 1880. Private collection

really brings in very much which is highly picturesque and artistic in character such as no 'Gothic man' would fail to appreciate … a so-called 'Queen Anne' house is now no more a revival of the past than a modern-gothic house.[65]

One of the most significant, and successful, of the younger men to join the 'Queen Anne folks' was Scott's own architect son, George Gilbert Scott, junior.[66] The younger Scott was in good company, for, as Moyr Smith had mentioned, temples to that tutelary goddess Queen Anne had already sprung up all over England. Flattering illustrations of these new buildings had, moreover, been reproduced in books and professional journals. The Scottish architect John James Stevenson built the striking 'Red House' on Bayswater Hill for himself in 1871-73 and illustrated it in *Building News* (fig.73). This Kensington house and its interiors were to have considerable impact on public taste but Stevenson's two-volume book, *House Architecture*, which appeared in 1880, was to have yet more currency. In the mid-1870s, however, the 'Queen Anne' style was far from the exclusive preserve of a Kensington élite. A new suburb for discriminating, comfortably-off, but by no means opulent, middle-class residents was developed at Bedford Park in west London. Yet again, the designs for these detached and semi-detached villas were illustrated in architectural journals. Most had small gardens separated from the road by palings and, though all boasted the distinctive characteristics of the 'Queen Anne' breed, each was different from its neighbour. When the first of the new buildings at Newnham College in Cambridge opened for its women students in 1875 it seemed perfectly proper that they were in the gabled, red-brick style so favoured by the intelligentsia. Newnham was particularly distinctive in that its architect, Basil Champneys, had eschewed the Gothic and the Tudor models deemed appropriate for recent men's colleges at Oxford and

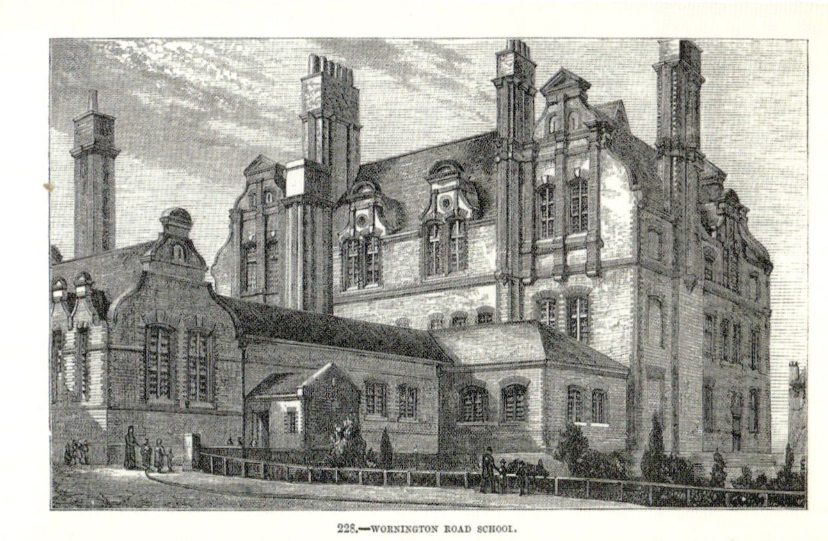

74 London Board School,
engraved illustration in
School Architecture by
Edward Robert
Robinson, 1877.
Private collection

Cambridge. Students' rooms led off well-lit corridors rather than staircases and they looked out onto gardens rather than across enclosed courtyards. The rooms were furnished with William Morris chairs and gate-leg tables and writing-desks in the eighteenth-century manner. In many ways, Newnham College was the most refined, and most immediately appealing, achievement of the 'Queen Anne' revival. The greatest public impact of the style was, however, the result of a very different educational innovation. The Elementary Education Act of 1870 (the 'Foster Act') gave aspiring architects the opportunity of changing what they often thought of as the drab London townscape for the better. All over the metropolis, and particularly in areas that were deprived both socially and aesthetically, new three- or four-storey Board Schools, well-lit and airy buildings, began to assert themselves in the terraced streets and over the often insanitary alleys of the inner suburbs. The two hundred and sixty schools constructed between 1870 and 1881 were built in red brick, or in London stocks dressed with red brick; some boasted broken gables, others had fanciful roof-lines and bulbous spires that would have flattered Bavarian castles. The architect of some of the best of these early schools (fig.74), Edward Robert Robson, described his mission in his proselytising book *School Architecture* in 1877, to provide schools for children whose manners, morals, habits of order, cleanliness, and punctuality, temper, love of study and of the school, cannot fail to be in no inconsiderable degree affected by the attractive or repulsive situation, appearance, out-door convenience and in-door comfort, of the place where they are to spend a large part of the most impressionable period of their lives.[67]

These schools were to have a moral purpose as well as an architectural functionality: train up a child in the way he should go and you may also endow him with a love of beauty. The Board Schools of the 1870s and 80s still leave their architectural mark on London, much as they did when Sir Arthur Conan Doyle gave Sherlock Holmes a happy insight as his train crosses a railway viaduct near Clapham Junction. The tall red schools strike Holmes as resembling 'brick islands in a lead coloured sea.' They are like lighthouses, he tells Watson, 'Beacons of the future! Capsules, with hundreds of bright little seeds in each, out of which will spring the wiser, better England of the future.'[68]

§

Bedford Park, Newnham College and the London Board Schools were in every sense a world away from the culture that had flourished in the reign of Queen Anne. A new suburb, free of the smoke of London, a college for the higher education of women, and universal state-funded elementary education, were utopian concepts utterly alien to the opening years of the eighteenth century. The very fact that an architectural style, and indeed a way of life loosely linked to Queen Anne's reign, should be associated with such radical social improvements is an indication of Victorian restlessness with many of the received ideas of the nineteenth century. Macaulay, the historian and the Whig politician, had insisted that progressive development was the key to the advance of modern British civilisation. The 'Queen Anne' movement did not represent a sentimental attachment to the past over the present but a conscious attempt to re-align civilisation away from the complacency, social deprivation, dreariness and sheer ugliness brought about by urbanisation and the industrial revolution. In some quarters the manners and modes of the early eighteenth century might have seemed preferable to those of Victorian England, but to most intelligent men and women neither nostalgia nor regret for some lost golden age offered feasible ways of looking at the present. At its core, industrialisation offered the modern world the kind of choices which were utterly inconceivable to former ages. Provided they were well enough off, the quaint or the curious could opt to live as mediaeval barons, Tudor princes or eighteenth-century gentlemen; but most Victorians chose not to. No matter how ardently a Victorian aesthete might have adulated the age of Queen Anne, none but the most eccentric would have happily opted to appear in public in perukes, let alone in the tall wired head-dresses, known as *commodes*, sported by court ladies in the 1690s. What Victorian men and women *did* choose, when they could afford it, was a distinctive life-style. For those late-Victorians who considered that they did have good taste, that life-style entailed intermixing domestic antiques with modern artefacts, oriental rugs with Morris wallpaper, blue-and-white porcelain with Doulton ware, Georgian furniture with nineteenth-century plumbing. For the liberal- or radical-minded, like Morris himself, the inevitable forward movement of society would eventually open up those choices even to those most disadvantaged by the economic and technological changes of the nineteenth century: the urban poor. The notion that a Clapham Board School in the 'Queen Anne' style might be a beacon for the future was far from fanciful. Most thinking men and women knew full well that life and thought in Queen Anne's England were stifling in comparison to the vibrancy of modern society, to the openness of party political debate, and to the adventurousness of intellectual enterprise in the latter half of Queen Victoria's reign. Glances back to the past offered alternative insights not viable alternative life-styles. Robert W. Edis, one of those self-appointed Victorian advisors on aesthetics that latter-day journalists vulgarly call 'life-style gurus,' got it just about right when he described in 1881 the potential and long-term benefits of the 'fashion dedicated to her most sacred Majesty, Queen Anne'. It was

> a fashion which had developed much of really good art character, and which, after all, properly applied, is really bringing us back to old English work. Amongst the more educated professors of the style, we find at present many pretty conceits, which are not worthy of the name of art; but we also find good construction and carefulness of design, which we may hail as forerunners of better times and more artistic work.[69]

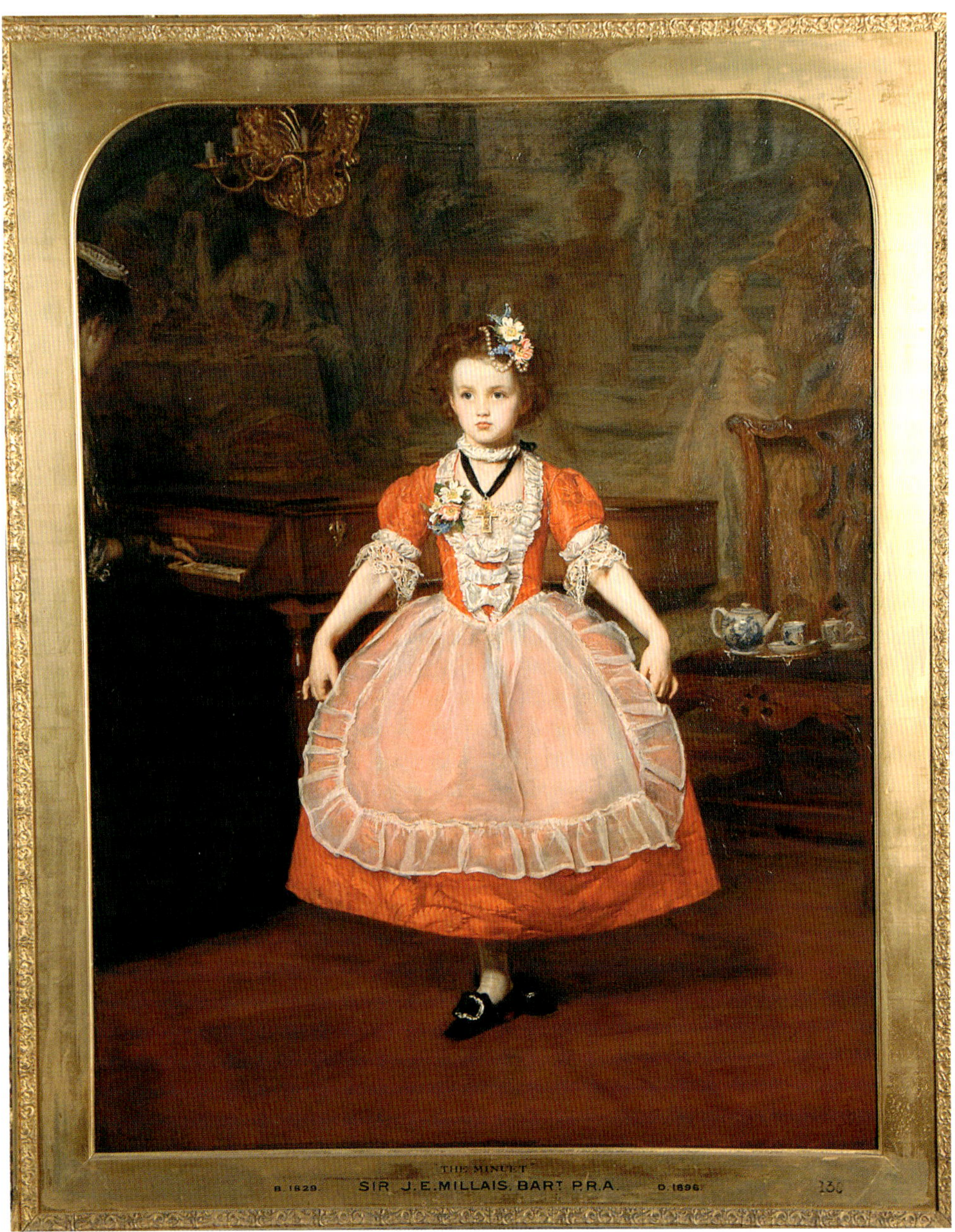

75   John Everett Millais, *The Minuet,* 1866, Oil on canvas, 110 x 85 cm. Elton Hall Collection

IV

THREE GEORGES

THE HANOVERIAN KINGS

John Everett Millais had an uncanny knack both for subtly turning his art in new directions and for finding a ready audience for it. In 1866 he dressed his eldest daughter, Effie, in a mid-eighteenth-century style red dress and posed her in front of a harpsichord. The eight-year-old Effie has flowers in her hair and on her frilled bodice. Her arms and feet are formally positioned ready for her to begin dancing a minuet. Millais exhibited the finished picture, known simply as *The Minuet* (fig.75), at the Royal Academy in the following year.[1] Its success was such that smaller versions of the painting were commissioned and a mezzotint of it was published in 1868. *The Minuet* precisely caught the fashionable mood of the time, for here was the 'Queen Anne' style translated into paint. Millais may well have known that in May 1850 Queen Victoria's two eldest daughters had performed a minuet at Osborne House in honour of their mother's birthday. Both girls were attired in costumes of the time of George II, though the elder, the Princess Royal, was dressed as a boy, complete with powdered wig and tricorne hat. The poses and costumes of the royal dancers were recorded for their fond parents in a watercolour by Franz Xaver Winterhalter.[2] In Millais's far less courtly picture the woman who is playing the minuet on the harpsichord has her back to us; she has a white cap on her head, but is dressed in black and wears black lace mittens on her hands. Given the shadow, and the angle from which we view her, it is difficult to determine if her dress is of eighteenth- or mid-nineteenth-century design. Behind her is a faded tapestry showing some kind of *fête champêtre* with an elegantly clad eighteenth-century dancer in a pose similar to Effie's. A brass wall-sconce contains half-burnt candles and a blue-and-white tea service has been placed informally on the seat of a late Georgian side-chair. The chair was apparently borrowed from Thackeray's daughter and had in all likelihood formed part of her father's collection of antiques. The strikingly clad Effie, in her red dress and muslin pinafore, seems to be stepping forward from a sober world of blacks and browns into a far brighter one. It is as if this representative of modern girlhood is moving from the shadowy eighteenth into the nineteenth century, and her movement is mediated by music. She is leaving behind her what had become, by the time the picture was painted, collectable artefacts and she advances towards us into the present. Effie may be dressed as a girl of the 1760s, but she is dancing for an audience of the 1860s.

In an interview published in the *Daily News* in 1884 Millais was insistent that he lived 'in an age of transition' and that the reason that historical and large genre paintings were no longer popular with artists was because there was a new demand 'for truth, for actuality.' Millais went on to expand on his point:

> The world is much older than it was thirty or forty years ago. It not only knows more in reality, but is more knowing in its attitude … I cannot help thinking that a great deal of confusion arises from the use of the adjectives 'historical' and 'real.' They have no scientific precision. Historical painting means different things, at different times, and in different months … Hogarth is a true historical painter, as well as a great satirist, for he has painted his time with marvellous strength and exactness. Realism, again is understood to signify all kinds of things by different people. One will understand it as a mere literal transcript of nature, another the same thing after being distilled or smelted in the artist's mind.[3]

Historical painting was becoming defunct, Millais argued, both because there was 'much less heart in the work' and, equally tellingly, because the public was now wary of buying pictures with historical subjects. In painting his young daughter in eighteenth-century costume Millais was eschewing a 'literal transcript' of the past. He was, rather, representing history as if it were 'real' in the living present. *The Minuet* was merely the first of a series of paintings in which Millais showed figures from the present somehow acting out the roles of characters from the past. They are emphatically modern rather than historical pictures, but they are equally not to be viewed as mere 'fancy-dress' paintings.

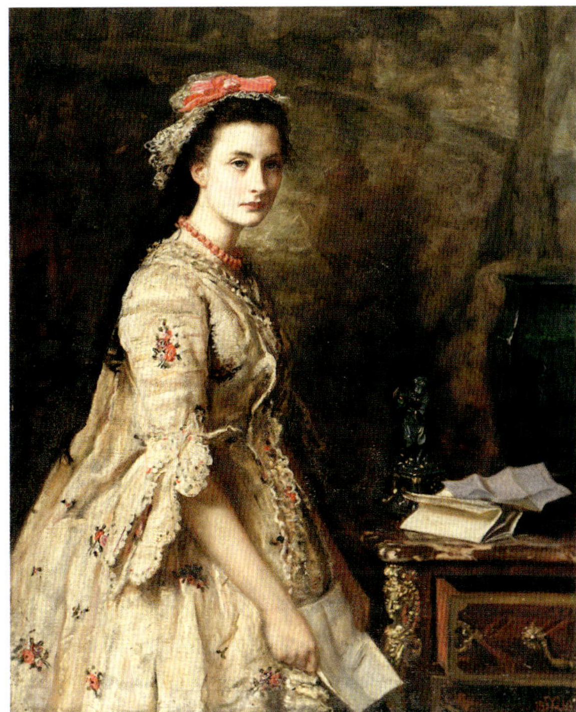

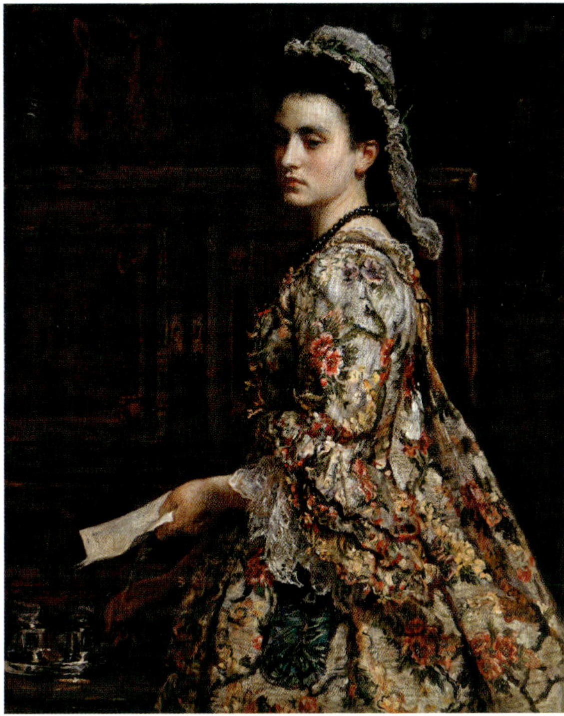

Millais's *Stella* and *Vanessa* (both 1868 (figs.76, 77) are cases in point. Both show modern women in eighteenth-century costume, but both paintings also serve to represent the two great women in the life of Jonathan Swift as living women, not as painted shadows. The same could be said of *Clarissa* of 1887 (fig.78), for here again the Victorian woman can be seen as standing for Richardson's heroine but not standing in for her. In an important way, Millais's pictures of eighteenth-century 'subjects' were a new departure in his art, one prompted by the shifting view of historical reality in the 1860s and 70s. Most proponents of the 'Queen Anne' movement declined to see the past as something to escape into. Instead, they aspired to reform the art and manners of the present with reference to the past. In 1885 Walter Armstrong observantly described what he saw as characteristic of Millais's recent paintings:

> For fifteen years Sir John has restricted himself to the life of his own
> time, and has put unity of effect in the forefront of his art. I say his own

76 John Everett Millais, *Stella*, 1868, Oil on canvas, 112.7 x 92.1 cm. Manchester Art Gallery

77 John Everett Millais, *Vanessa*, 1868, Oil on canvas, 113.7 x 91.4 cm. Sudley House, National Museums Liverpool

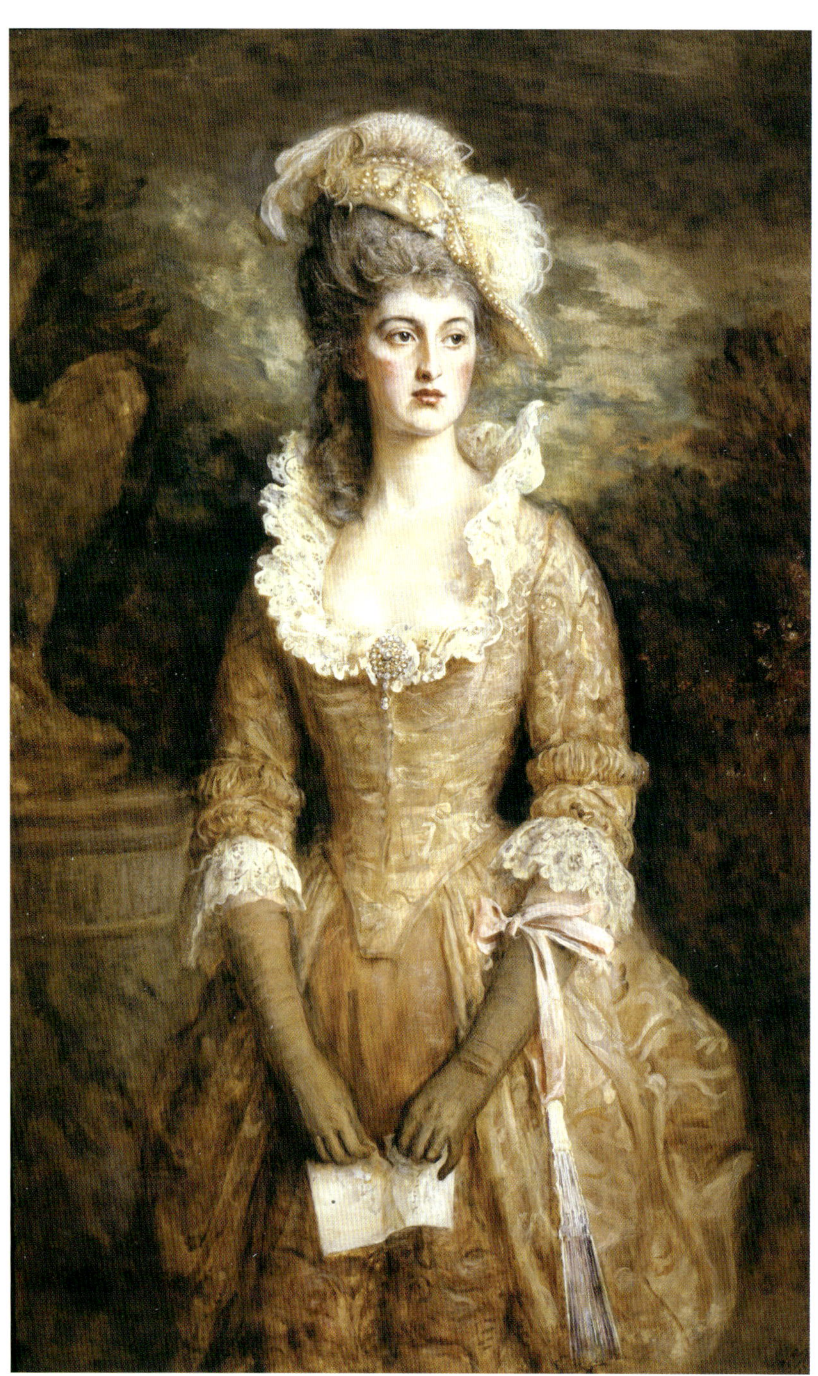

78 John Everett Millais, *Clarissa*,
    1887, Oil on canvas,
    146 x 94cm. Private collection

time advisedly, because in the few instances in which he has gone to a past century for a subject he has not in the least tried to make it a serious restoration. He has treated it on the lines of the novelist. He has given enough archaeology to satisfy our sense of fitness, and not an atom more. He has come to a full acceptance of the principle that Art should be content with the people and the life of which it knows the innermost thought. The painter who sets to work to produce the manners of a bygone age handicaps himself.[4]

Readers of Sir Walter Scott's novels in the 1820s had recognised Scott's distinctive genius for rendering historical characters real. Not only did his characters appear to speak like the men and women of the past, they also dressed in old costumes, they ate from old plates, slept in old beds, and moved in and out of antique rooms. Scott tended to write in the third person and he included extensive descriptions, integral to the fabric of each novel, of the landscapes, townscapes, palaces, manor houses, taverns and cottages that his characters variously frequent. Thackeray's *Henry Esmond* of 1852 was a very different kind of historical novel. Esmond, as a confessional first-person narrator, does not describe the clothes he wears, the rooms he lives in, the plates he eats from, or the beds he sleeps in, because he takes them for granted as commonplace and everyday things. They are essential to him as a man of his time, but only incidental to him as a writer of a retrospective memoir. As both Millais and Walter Armstrong imply, the historical painters of the generation after Scott had been determined to show the past as meticulously and accurately as they could. They studied architectural handbooks and guides to historical costume; they looked at antique knives, forks and spoons, and they noted how draperies were draped and how the light fell from diamond-paned casements. The painter of the 1870s, Millais and Armstrong claim, no longer needed painstaking research or a library of illustrated reference books to represent the past; he simply needs to be like Thackeray and his fellow novelists and to convey an impression of 'the innermost thought.' In Millais's *The Minuet* the 'archaeology' has retreated to the background while the truly interesting aspect of the painting, the vivid, dancing child in her red dress, holds our attention with her determined movement forward and her intent look in our direction. As with Millais's picture of his sons in the later *The Boyhood of Raleigh*, his daughter is living history 'distilled or smelted' in the artist's mind.

Remembering the First George

When Millais referred to the kind of historical painting that still flourished in the 1840s and 50s he also recalled the kind of subjects which had once been familiar to him as 'friends of his childhood.' These are subjects, predominantly drawn from early mediaeval history, that had been favoured by Daniel Maclise, Charles Robert Leslie and even by his Pre-Raphaelite brothers. Archaeologically correct costume pictures had not been banished from the Royal Academy by the 1880s, but they had certainly changed in style, and they increasingly represented moods or manners rather than specific historical incidents. With the growing fashion for representing eighteenth-century costume in the latter half of the nineteenth century there also appears to have been a paucity of events that were deemed worthy of representation. In a noticeable way, national history since the Glorious Revolution seems to have struck painters as undramatic, even 'eventless.' In suggesting that the 'real' now predominated over the 'ideal' in artists' minds, Millais also sensed that what his public sought was a greater stress on the present.

Edward Matthew Ward's *The South Sea Bubble* (fig.79), which had been exhibited at the Royal Academy in 1847, was representative of the old school of historical paintings. It shows a scene in Change Alley in the City in 1720 at the height of the great speculation which so marked the reign of George I. The imminent crash is yet to come, and Ward shows us a busy pawnbroker's shop next to a trader's table set out for convenience in the open air. Well-dressed ladies and gentlemen, and even a slightly anxious clergyman, are avariciously intent on the potential speculative growth of their bubbling investments. Given the subject, and given Ward's *penchant* for historical costume, it is surprising that the painting does not even glance at Hogarth. There are no nuances and no moral seems to be implied, yet alone drawn. What Victorian observers would readily have drawn from the picture, however, was the fact that it did have clear echoes in their own precarious and often unscrupulous financial world of speculation in railway shares and broken banks.

Apart from the failed Jacobite Rising in Scotland and parts of the north in 1715, the South Sea Bubble was by far the most memorable event of George I's twelve-year reign. For most Victorians, any sentimental attachment to the cause of the Stuart Pretenders seems to have been centred on the far more romantic (and disruptive) campaigns of Prince Charles Edward rather than of

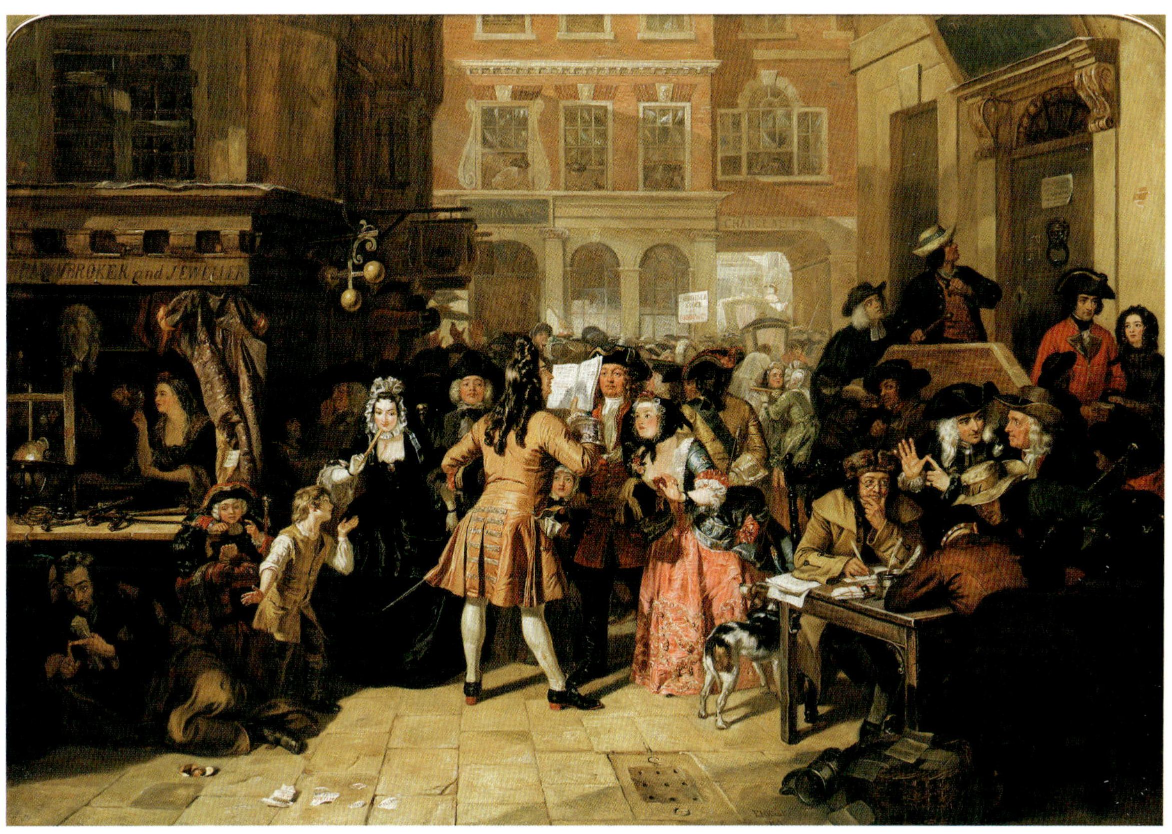

79   Edward Mathew Ward, *The South-Sea Bubble Scene in Change Alley in 1720*, 1847, Oil on canvas, 129.5 x 188 cm. Tate, London

his father's spectacular failure thirty years earlier. Few commentators appear to have found the new Hanoverian King attractive, let alone interesting, but schooled as they were by Macaulay they accepted the dull George I's right of inheritance to a now essentially Protestant throne. 'Mrs. Markham's' son, the King's namesake George, expresses a real enthusiasm for the House of Stuart in his conversation with his mother (though he seems to forget that, if he were indeed a Scot, he would refer to James the Eighth rather than James the Third). His patient mother feels obliged to suggest rather deeper pitfalls in his juvenile lack of wisdom:

> *George.* I don't at all wonder that the Scotch wanted to have their own king. Oh! If I had lived in those times, what a Jacobite I would have been! James the Third should have been my king.

> *Mrs. Markham.* I suspect that you would not have had a very good one. The Pretender was a man of very inferior abilities, and of a mean, selfish character. And after he had been in Scotland, and his adherents had seen that he was not the high-minded hero they had fancied him to be, his cause visibly declined.[5]

George is not to be completely squashed by this riposte and reverts to his rebellious Jacobitism at the end of the conversation: 'I dare say George I was a better king than James would have been, still, those Scotch Highlanders were fine, brave fellows, and worth all the English Whigs and Tories put together.'[6] It must be admitted that Mrs. Markham had not made out a particularly inspiring case in favour of King George. She has told her children that he was 'a man of plain, steady understanding, grave in his manner, and simple in his habits, and had the reputation of being a sagacious politician.' She has also let slip the fact that he brought no Queen to England with him and tells her children that this was because he 'either had, or supposed himself to have, so much reason to be displeased with her conduct, that he shut her up in the castle of Ahlden … where she remained during the rest of her life.'

'Mrs Markham' does not go into further embarrassing details concerning George I's unfortunate domestic life, though they appear to have been familiar enough to her fellow Victorians. In the first of his lectures on 'The Four Georges,' delivered in America in the winter of 1855, Thackeray was far more forthcoming. Here he is describing the situation at the court of Hanover, when the 'cold, selfish libertine' George was still heir to the Electoral throne and his unloved wife, Sophia Dorothea, was embroiled in an affair with the Swedish Count Königsmarck:

> The characters in the tragedy, on which the curtain was now about to fall, are about as dark a set as eye ever rested on. There is the jolly prince, shrewd, selfish, scheming, loving his cups and his ease (I think his good humour makes the tragedy but darker); his princess, who speaks little but observes all; his old, painted Jezebel of a mistress; his son, the Electoral prince, shrewd too, quiet, selfish, not ill-humoured, and generally silent … there is poor Sophia Dorothea, with her coquetry and her wrongs, and her passionate attachment to her scamp of a lover … and there is Lothario … than whom … one can't imagine a more handsome, wicked, worthless reprobate …

The prince was absent when the catastrophe came. The princess had had a hundred warnings; mild hints from her husband's parents; grim remonstrances from himself … On the night of Sunday, the 1st of July, 1694, Königsmarck paid a long visit to the princess, and left her to get ready for flight. Her husband was away in Berlin; her carriages and horses were prepared and ready for the elopement. Meanwhile, the spies of Countess Platen, had brought the news to their mistress. She went to Ernest Augustus, and procured from the Elector an order for the arrest of the Swede. On the way by which he was to come, four guards were commissioned to take him. He strove to cut his way through the four men, and wounded more than one of them. They fell upon him; cut him down … he was dispatched presently; his body burnt the next day; and all traces of the man disappeared … The princess was reported to be ill in her apartments, from which she was taken in October of the same year, being them eight-and-twenty years old, and consigned to the castle of Ahlden, where she remained a prisoner for no less than thirty-two years. A separation had been pronounced previously between her and her husband. She was called henceforth the 'Princess of Ahlden', and her silent husband no more uttered her name.[7]

This is the stuff of the most extravagant of Italian operas and of the most torrid of French melodramas, and it might have provided any number of sensational subjects for a Victorian painter, but no English artist would have dared venture in that direction. Sophia Dorothea was, after all, great-great-great grandmother of Queen Victoria and, to all intents and purposes, the uncrowned Queen-Consort of the first Hanoverian King of Great Britain and Ireland. Sagacious and grave King George may have seemed to those who flatteringly described his reign in England, but his earlier life in Hanover was far from boring.

When he was contemplating the subject of his lectures on *The Four Georges* Thackeray told his mother in 1852 that if he hoped for preferment hereafter he had 'best keep a civil tongue in [his] head … I should be sure to say something impudent if I got upon that subject.'[8] By 1855 he evidently felt that such acts of *lèse majesté* were likely to be ignored in republican America. His success across the Atlantic emboldened him to repeat the lectures privately in England and, in November 1856, publicly in Edinburgh (where his passing comments on Mary, Queen of Scots were hissed, though no such reaction greeted his multiple criticisms of George I).[9] He then went on to give the lecture series in Glasgow, Hull, Derby, Liverpool and Manchester, and in January and February 1857 he delivered the four lectures four times over in London. He then took them on the road yet again, as he styled it, in the role of 'the wandering puller down of kings.' Though he believed that he had managed to offend influential members of the Whig aristocracy ('the halls of splendour are to be shut to me'), he evidently felt that by 1860 *The Four Georges* was sufficiently palatable to appear, with illustrations, in the pages of the *Cornhill Magazine*.[10] It was published in book form the year after.

Although much of the antipathy stirred up by *The Four Georges* was directed at Thackeray's comments on the fourth George, the tone for the four lectures was decidedly set by the mood of amused cynicism evident in the first. Thackeray, whose fascination with life at the petty courts of eighteenth- and early nineteenth-century Germany is evident in *Barry Lyndon* and in *Vanity Fair*, was clearly well-acquainted with the history and the scandals of any number of real life Pumpernickels. In the lecture on George I he not only claims that he had made it his business to visit Hanover ('that ugly cradle in which our Georges were nursed') but that he was familiar with 'contemporary books of travel in the early part of the last century.' The landscape of eighteenth-century Germany strikes him as 'awful – wretched wastes, beggarly and plundered; half-burned cottages and trembling peasants gathering piteous harvests.' Through these barren landscapes a princely carriage 'flounders through the ruts' on its way to an 'enormous, hideous, gilded, monstrous marble palace' with a fanciful name such as Wilhelmslust, or Ludwigsruhe, or Monbijou, or, in the case of Hanover, Herrenhausen. Having told us how much he relished the 'small-beer chronicles' of German court-life, he goes on to catalogue the Electoral servants at Herrenhausen, from the high chamberlain, down to the four pastrycooks, the seven officers of the wine and beer cellars and the fourteen postillions. He also gives us their annual salaries. In 'the good old times,' however, all this pretension stood in stark contrast to the situation of 'common men' who were 'driven by herds, and sold to fight the emperor's enemies on the Danube, or to bayonet King Louis's troops of common men on the Rhine.'[11] This is the petty but heartless world that produced a German Elector who in 1714 found himself elevated to the throne of England:

When the crown did come to George Louis he was in no hurry about putting it on. He waited at home for awhile; took an affecting farewell of his dear Hanover and Herrenhausen: and set out in the most leisurely manner to ascend 'the throne of his ancestors,' as he called it in his first speech to Parliament. He brought with him a compact body of Germans, whose society he loved, and whom he kept around the royal person. He had his faithful German chamberlains; his German secretaries … his two ugly, elderly German favourites, Mesdames of Kielmansegge and Schulenberg, whom he created respectively Countess of Darlington and Duchess of Kendal … One seems to be speaking of Captain Macheath, and Polly and Lucy. The king we had selected; the courtiers who came in his train … I protest it is a wonderful satirical picture.[12]

Nevertheless, like his own Esmond before him, Thackeray finds himself constrained to accept that this unappealing German is a better bet as a King than the rejected Stuart alternative:

He was not a lofty monarch, certainly: he was not a patron of the fine arts: but he was not a hypocrite, he was not revengeful, he was not extravagant. Though a despot in Hanover, he was a moderate ruler in England. His aim was to leave it to itself as much as possible, and to live out of it as much as he could … He kept his compact with his English subjects; and if he escaped no more than other men and monarchs from the vices of his age, at least we may thank him for preserving and transmitting the liberties of ours.[13]

This may well strike us as merely grudging praise, but it is in many ways typical of Thackeray's sardonic historical judgements. If not exactly a 'puller down of kings,' he was certainly possessed of the kind of sharpness of observation that refused to suffer either fools or heroes gladly. Significantly though, what he observes of George I is a long way from the *saeva indignatio* by which certain of the King's own more embittered subjects judged both him and his self-seeking ministers.

SWIFT, ADDISON AND POPE

Thackeray's much acclaimed earlier series of public lectures, *The English Humourists of the Eighteenth Century*, was first delivered in London in the spring of 1851. His audience at Willis's Rooms in King Street, St. James's, included amongst the 'duchesses and great ladies' and the 'bishops, bigwigs and parliament men' a sprinkling of the most eminent minds of his time: Charlotte Brontë, Harriet Martineau, George Henry Lewes and the historians Henry Hallam, Thomas Carlyle and Thomas Babington Macaulay. Such was the fashionable prestige Thackeray attracted that, as Charlotte Brontë complained, his third lecture had to be postponed because 'duchesses and marchionesses' had pressed him to avoid a clash between it and Royal Ascot.[14] Nevertheless, what Thackeray had to say in these lectures was not always flattering either to the authors he discussed or to the refined sensibilities of his audience. He generalised and he spoke *ad hominem*, pointing to foibles and eccentricities. The lectures on the *English Humourists* embody the novelist's own refusal to recognise Carlylean heroes when he can more readily identify a weak-kneed fool. No man, as he consistently reminded his audiences, was a hero to his valet, and one of Thackeray's many literary personae was that of a knowing valet-de-chambre.

The first lecture in the series dealt with Jonathan Swift, a writer whose life was familiar to most early Victorians through Sir Walter Scott's short biography of 1821. In *Henry Esmond* Thackeray would tell his readers that Esmond regarded Marlborough and Swift as 'the two greatest men of that age,' but the original audience at the lecture were to be given a very narrow view of this 'greatness.' Many of them might well have supposed that Thackeray would have been naturally attracted both to Swift the wit and to Swift the moralist, and that he would express a degree of fellow-feeling for him. They were to be disappointed. Thackeray seems to be bewildered by his subject, and he describes him with a sense of repulsion tinged with sadness. He is clearly disturbed by the Dean's cramped emotional life and by his complex relationships with 'Stella' and 'Vanessa':

> And yet to have had so much love, he must have given some. Treasures of wit and wisdom and tenderness too, must that man have had locked up in the caverns of his gloomy heart, and shown fitfully to one or two

whom he took in there. But it was not good to visit that place. People did not remain there long, and suffered for having been there. He shrank away from all affections sooner or later. Stella and Vanessa both died near him, and away from him. He had not heart enough to see them die … An immense genius: an awful downfall and ruin. So great a man he seems to me, that thinking of him is like thinking of an empire falling.[15]

Thackeray emerges as equally troubled by what he sees as the 'Emperor' Swift's more outlandish works. The *Drapier's Letters* are 'master-pieces of dreadful humour and invective' but the proposition they contain 'is as monstrous and fabulous as the Lilliputian island.' 'As is the case with madmen,' Thackeray adds, 'certain subjects provoke him, and awaken fits of wrath. Marriage is one of these.' When he discusses 'A Modest Proposal' he sees Swift as a man 'who enters the nursery with the tread and gaiety of an ogre.' Most fastidiously of all, Thackeray cannot bring himself to find the fourth book of *Gulliver's Travels* in the least palatable. Swift, in his view, oversteps the mark, and the lecturer approaches the ogre with unequivocal expressions of *odi et amo*:

> As for the humour and conduct of this famous fable, I suppose there is no person who reads but must admire; as for the moral, I think it horrible, shameful, unmanly, blasphemous; and, giant and great as this Dean is, I say we should hoot him. Some of this audience mayn't have read the last part of Gulliver, and to such I would recall the advice of the venerable Mr. Punch to persons about to marry, and say 'Don't.' When Gulliver first lands among the Yahoos, the naked howling wretches clamber up trees and assault him, and he describes himself as 'almost stifled with the filth that fell about him.' The reader of the fourth part of Gulliver's Travels is like the hero himself in this instance. It is Yahoo language; a monster gibbering shrieks, and gnashing imprecations against mankind, – tearing down all shreds of modesty, past all sense of manliness and shame; filthy in word, filthy in thought, furious, raging, obscene.[16]

Thackeray almost seems to be assuming a Swiftian voice, but his invective is directed back at the Dean. On one level he seems entirely to miss the point of Book Four of *Gulliver*. His Swift un-mans himself, and thereby denies his humanity. On another level, Thackeray understands Swift's pessimism completely, but simply cannot swallow its implications. As a good pre-Darwinian, even the cynical Thackeray refuses to accept that humankind, as the pinnacle of divine creation, might properly be represented as irredeemably bestial. Swift, the essential Augustinian, implies that the fallen and depraved Gulliver requires Grace in order to grasp redemption. Perhaps to the surprise of many of his readers Thackeray emerges here as the eternally hopeful, and unashamed, Pelagian.

Thackeray was not alone in finding aspects of Swift's work unacceptable and best left unread. In 1853 the Scottish critic, William Spalding, the author of *The History of English Literature … for the Use of Schools and Private Students*, told his readers that all of Swift's prose works were masterpieces of 'bare, strong, Saxon English,' but warned that none was 'quite destitute either of his keen wit or his ferocious ill-nature.' Spalding sharply added that despite being 'one of our shrewdest observers' Swift possessed a celebrity 'which through his moral perversities, is not much more enviable than the notoriety a man would obtain by being exposed on the pillory.'[17] Thomas Arnold junior, writing in 1862, describes a Swift who imagines himself 'to be living among a set of creatures who in different ways were monstrous caricatures of humanity, in order better to represent mankind in a light ridiculous or hateful.' Almost with a sigh of relief, he then comments: 'this sinister and satirical purpose – so altered are the times – cannot awaken much of our interest now.' *Gulliver's Travels*, he concludes, was now read only by children who found it a source 'of pure amusement … without reference to the allegorical meaning.' One supposes that these Victorian children were spared the allegory of its fourth Book by those fond parents who provided them with expurgated versions.[18] Some twenty years later we find the plodding W. H. Davenport Adams reiterating the invective and the incomprehension:

> Of the fourth part … my estimate must be unfavourable. The extravagance of the idea is not redeemed by the force and vehemence which have in them an element of savagery. The coarseness of the satire is not less conspicuous than its cynicism; and there must have been a radical unsoundness in the intellect which created the Houhynhyms and the Yahoos, the former as impossible as the latter are bestial. … Was ever anyone the better for studying it?[19]

Swift might well have been delighted by the fact that he continued to excite quite so much controversy one hundred and fifty years after his death. It should not surprise us, however, that Victorians of all ages so notably failed to respond to the more shocking aspects of his work. Even after the active revival of interest in the eighteenth century in the 1860s, Swift did not fit in with the acceptable image of a refined humanist culture. It was not that Swift was seen as some kind of angry Goth but that, at his most aggressive, his satire served to undermine all pleasant assumptions about the nature of life, whether that life was lived under a periwig or a shiny Victorian top hat.

Joseph Addison's work was evidently much more to Victorian taste. The adulatory tone was set by Macaulay in his review of Lucy Aiken's biography of the essayist in July 1843. For the reviewer, Addison had emerged from Aiken's study as embodying

> the just harmony of qualities, the exact temper between the stern and the humane virtues, the habitual observance of every law, not only of moral rectitude, but of moral grace and dignity …[20]

Here then is the exemplary, reliable, well-behaved schoolboy as opposed to the naughty, clever, delinquent Swift. Later in the essay, Macaulay goes on to develop a contrast between 'the three most eminent masters of the art of ridicule during the eighteenth century': Voltaire, Swift, and the gently virtuous Addison:

> Voltaire is the prince of buffoons. His merriment is without disguise or restraint. He gambols; he grins; he shakes his sides; he points the finger; he turns up the nose; he shoots out the tongue. The manner of Swift is the very opposite to this. He moves laughter, but never joins in it. He appears in his works such as he appeared in society. All the company are convulsed with merriment, while the Dean, the author of all the mirth, preserves an invincible gravity, and even sourness of aspect, and gives utterance to the most eccentric and ludicrous fancies, with the air of a man reading the commination service.
>
> The manner of Addison is as remote from that of Swift as from that of Voltaire. He neither laughs out like the French wit, nor, like the Irish wit, throws a double portion of severity into his countenance while laughing inwardly; but preserves a look peculiarly his own, a look of demure serenity, disturbed only by an rich sparkle of the eye, an almost

> imperceptible elevation of the brow, an almost imperceptible curl of the lip … We own that the humour of Addison is, in our opinion, of a more delicious flavour than the humour of either Swift or Voltaire.[21]

Knowing that Macaulay was in his audience at Willis's Rooms, Thackeray made an appreciative nod to this essay in his second lecture in the *English Humourists* series. For Thackeray too, Addison has a special charm and 'a wit that makes us laugh, and leaves us good and happy' and he happily confesses that 'we cherish, and love him, and owe as much pleasure to him as to any human being that ever wrote.' The man moreover was 'one of the kindliest benefactors that society has ever had.'[22] His comparison with Swift is, however, far crueller than Macaulay's:

> He came in that artificial age, and began to speak with his noble, natural voice. He came, the gentle satirist, who hit no unfair blow; the kind judge who castigated only in smiling. While Swift went about, hanging and ruthless – a literary Jeffries – in Addison's kind court only minor cases were tried; only peccadilloes and small sins against society: only a dangerous libertinism in tuckers and hoops; or a nuisance in the abuse of beaux' canes and snuff-boxes.[23]

For both Macaulay and Thackeray, Addison is some kind of Victorian *manqué*, a gentlemanly and humane wit whom they might have cultivated in club-land. Addison seems to have spoken directly to both of them, and they both responded with unadulterated, manly affection. Here, having dropped the sardonic valet-de-chambre pose, is the damp-eyed, sentimental Thackeray again:

> We love him for his vanities as much as his virtues. What is ridiculous is delightful in him: we are so fond of him because we laugh at him so. And out of that laughter, and out of that sweet weakness, and out of those harmless eccentricities and follies, and out of that touched brain, and out of that honest manhood and simplicity – we get a result of happiness, goodness, tenderness, pity, piety; such as, if my audience will think their reading and hearing over, doctors and divines but seldom have the fortune to inspire.[24]

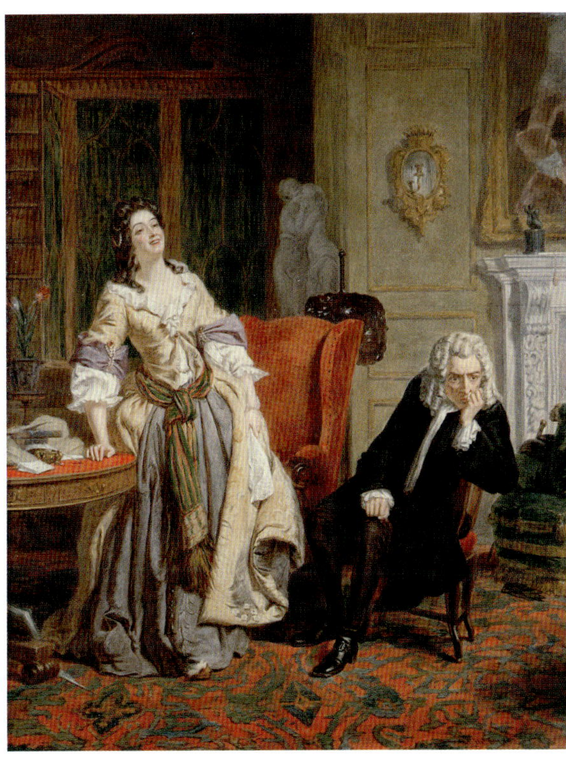

80   William Powell Frith,
The Rejected Poet, 1863,
Oil on canvas, 91.5 x
71cm. Wolverhampton
Art Gallery

One is tempted to think that Thackeray protests too much. What still surprises
is that this professed distruster of heroes should, at this point in his lectures,
be wallowing in a warm bath of hero-worship.

No Victorian would readily have accorded hero-status to Alexander Pope.
W. P. Frith's once celebrated painting of the poet being ridiculed by Lady
Mary Wortley Montagu (*The Rejected Poet*, fig.80) summed up a common
enough assumption that Pope cut a rather sad figure. Frith's picture shows
Lady Mary laughing as she leans back confidently, while the dejected poet sits
crumpled on a low chair. Behind them a copy of the Roman sculpture of
Cupid and Psyche adds an irony to Pope's humiliating rejection. Thackeray
retold the story in his fourth lecture on the eighteenth-century humourists:

He wrote flames and raptures and elaborate verse and prose for Lady
Mary Wortley Montagu; but that passion probably came to a climax in
an impertinence and was extinguished by a box on the ear, or some

such rebuff, and he began on a sudden to hate her with a fervour much more genuine that that of his love had been. It was a feeble, puny grimace of love, and paltering with passion.[25]

The words 'feeble' and 'puny' echo through a good deal of nineteenth-century comment on Pope's life, especially when they refer to his physique, but the words 'hate' and 'fervour' figure equally prominently as adjectives in studies of his poetry. For some commentators, notably those who wrote under the shadow of the more heady Romantic critics, Pope, the sharp-tongued satirist, was no poet at all. This post-Romantic complaint had been reiterated, and then given an even more ambiguous response, by William Spalding in 1853:

> It has gravely been asked whether Pope was a poet. They who put the question, expecting to compel an answer in the negative, must have fallen into some confusion in their use of words. But, if they ask, with a similar design, whether he was a great poet, or a poet of the first order, we shall tell the truth in answering them as they wish. We might perhaps say, further, that the works that he has given us do not possess nearly all the value, which his fine genius might have imparted to them.[27]

Spalding is inclined to argue that though true greatness eludes Pope, a definable, intellectual genius is indeed apparent in his work. Not long after, Joseph Angus, 'Examiner in English Language, Literature and History to the University of London,' summed up the ambiguity in Pope's reputation in his *Handbook of English Literature* of *c.*1860:

> His character and the character of his poetry … have been warmly assailed, and as warmly defended. His character was undoubtedly a collection of contradictions. He appreciated excellence, and has admirably described it; yet he was guilty of meanness which it is impossible to defend. He was a steadfast and even a tender friend, a dutiful and loving son; yet his fierceness and petulance and jealousy were unbounded and inexcusable. As a poet he is one of six[,] to scenes from whose works is assigned an honourable place in our new Houses of Parliament – his compeers, Chaucer, Shakespeare, Milton, Spenser and Dryden. Yet he is not to be compared with Shakespeare or with Milton. He has none of the universality of the first, none of the

sublimity of the second. He never describes man or nature; and there is but little of insight or power in his delineations of virtue.[26]

A far more spirited defence of Pope's poetry is offered by his co-religionist, Thomas Arnold, though Arnold seems hard pressed to find clear evidence of Pope's Catholic profession in his work. Nonetheless, Arnold recognises something truly distinctive in the poet's achievement: 'In Pope … we have at last a poet who made his art his first consideration, who rated his function as a man of letters at its true dignity, and refused to subordinate it to those political and party considerations which had hitherto, with English writers, been paramount to everything else.' In common with other half-hearted admirers, Arnold recognises the particular merits of both *The Rape of the Lock* ('the most faultless of Pope's works … a most telling satire upon the frivolous fashionable crowd which breathes the atmosphere of courts') and of *The Essay on Man* ('the reader will notice how highly condensed, and even elliptical, the form of expression often is in the finest works of Pope').

As many critics recognised, however, Pope's verse was never easily fitted into the kind of poetic categories beloved by Victorian anthologists. Only one minor lyric ('Happy the man') appears in Francis Turner Palgrave's *The Golden Treasury* in 1861. This 'Ode on Solitude' was, by the poet's own account, 'written at about twelve years old.' In two popular illustrated anthologies, *Early English Poems: Chaucer to Pope* of 1863 and Robert Aris Willmott's *English Sacred Poetry* of 1861, Pope was represented by the somewhat atypical 'Sacred Eclogue,' *The Messiah* of 1712. His major poems were evidently considered too long, too unwieldy, or too didactic to sit easily with verse concerned with cultivated emotion or with the inspirational beauties of the natural world. Nevertheless, Thackeray for one was prepared to tell the audience of his fourth lecture that the closing lines of *The Dunciad* could safely stand comparison with those of any poet in English:

In these astonishing lines Pope reaches, I think, to the very greatest height which his sublime art has attained, and shows himself the equal of all poets of all times. It is the brightest ardour, the loftiest assertion of truth, the most generous wisdom, illustrated by the noblest poetic figure, and spoken in words the aptest, grandest, and most harmonious. It is heroic courage speaking: a splendid declaration of righteous wrath and war … It is a wonderful and victorious single combat, in that great battle, which has always been waging since society began.[28]

This stout defence of Pope at his most articulate and determined might well have appealed to Byron. Nevertheless, it took another twenty years of the nineteenth century before Pope's reputation as a major poet was re-established amongst the thinking classes.[29] Leslie Stephen's essay 'Pope as a Moralist' appeared in the first volume of *Hours in a Library* in 1874 and the poet was to figure, slightly awkwardly, in Stephen's ground-breaking study of philosophy, theology and economic and political theory, *The History of English Thought in the Eighteenth Century* in 1876. In the 1880s Stephen also contributed a biography to the 'English Men of Letters' series. Despite the fact that the late nineteenth-century poet Francis Thompson was to typify Stephen's critical methods as 'natively prosaic and unimaginative' he does manage to offer a clear case both for Pope's intellectual enterprise and for the quality of his verse. In the 1874 *Hours in a Library* essay Stephen knew that he faced an uphill struggle in his defence of the poet:

> His writings resemble those fireworks which, after they have fallen to the ground and been apparently quenched, suddenly break out again into spluttering explosions. The waters of a literary revolution have passed over him without putting him out. Though much of his poetry has ceased to interest us, so many of his brilliant couplets still survive that no dead writer, with the solitary exception of Shakespeare, is more frequently quoted at the present day. It is in vain that he is abused, ridiculed, and often declared to be no poet at all. The school of Wordsworth regarded him as the embodiment of the corrupting influence in English poetry; and it is only of late that we are beginning to aim at a more catholic spirit in literary criticism.[30]

Although Stephen lacks his father-in-law Thackeray's passion when it comes to defending Pope, he firmly believes that not only was the 'school of Wordsworth' wrong but also that its influence on literary taste was properly fading. 'Good sense,' Stephen later remarks, 'is one of the excellent qualities to which we are scarcely inclined to do justice at the present day,' and it is on Pope's 'good sense,' and intellectual 'equilibrium, stirred by no vehement gales,' that he bases his re-assessment. The nineteenth century, Stephen argues, has persisted in misunderstanding Pope for nobody 'has ridiculed more happily the absurdities of which we sometimes take him to be representative.' If late-Victorian readers sought to delight in essentially 'decorative' or 'pseudo-classical' eighteenth-century styles, he warns them that they will not find much comfort in Pope. Stephen, the professed agnostic, likes the unsentimental, no-nonsense aspect of his subject and he especially admires the 'pantheism' that Pope had derived from his philosophical mentor, Bolingbroke:

> Pantheism, in fact, is the only poetical form of the metaphysical theology current in Pope's day. The old historical theology of Dante, or even of Milton, was too faded for poetical purposes; and the 'personal Deity,' whose existence and attributes were proved by the elaborate reasonings of the apologists of that day, was unfitted for poetical celebration by the very fact that his existence required proof. Poetry deals with intuitions, not with remote inferences, and therefore in his better moments Pope spoke not of the intelligent moral Governor discovered by philosophical investigation, but of the Divine Essence immanent in all nature, whose 'living raiment' is the world.[31]

Despite his justification of this sentiment, one suspects that Stephen has drifted into precisely the kind of Wordsworthianism that he has set out to argue against. Stephen's essay ends with him quoting Pope's 'pantheistic' 'Universal Prayer,' which, when it was first published, Pope appended to the *Essay on Man*. Stephen sees it as 'the utterance of a tolerant, reverent, and kindly heart' and, more importantly, as utterly unlike the kind of hymn that Victorian admirers of Keble's *The Christian Year* would appreciate. Leslie Stephen's Pope is unequivocally a man of the first half of the eighteenth century, but, unlike the angry, petulant cripple who had been caricatured of most early Victorian critics, he has emerged from the cloudy vapours of Romanticism as a clear, sensible and rational voice for modern times.[32]

Leslie Stephen's determined advocacy of Pope's rationality was unlikely to have influenced the publisher Leonard Smithers when he commissioned Aubrey Beardsley to provide eight illustrations for a new edition of *The Rape of the Lock* in 1896 (figs. 81, 82). In *Hours in a Library*, Stephen had warned readers against seeing Pope as in any way 'filigree,' but this was precisely the quality he praised in *The Rape of the Lock* when he wrote about the poem in his short biography of Pope. It was another convert to the refined beauties of eighteenth-century verse, Edmund Gosse, who persuaded Beardsley to contribute to Smithers' handsome

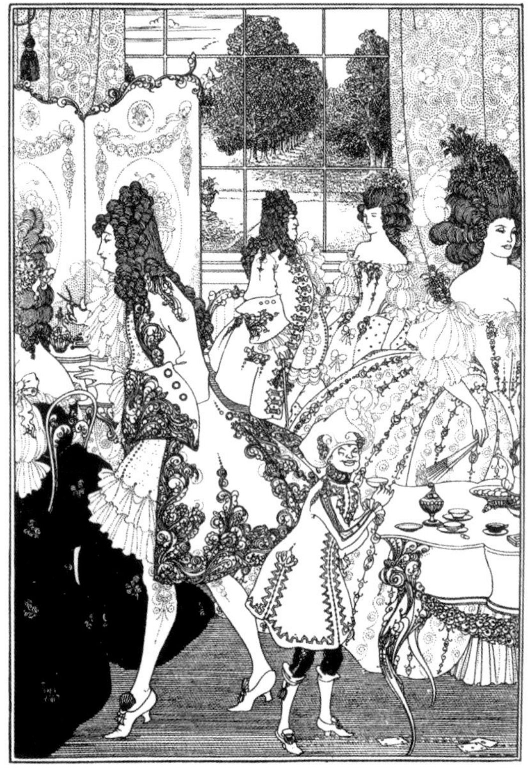

409 The Rape of the Lock (409)

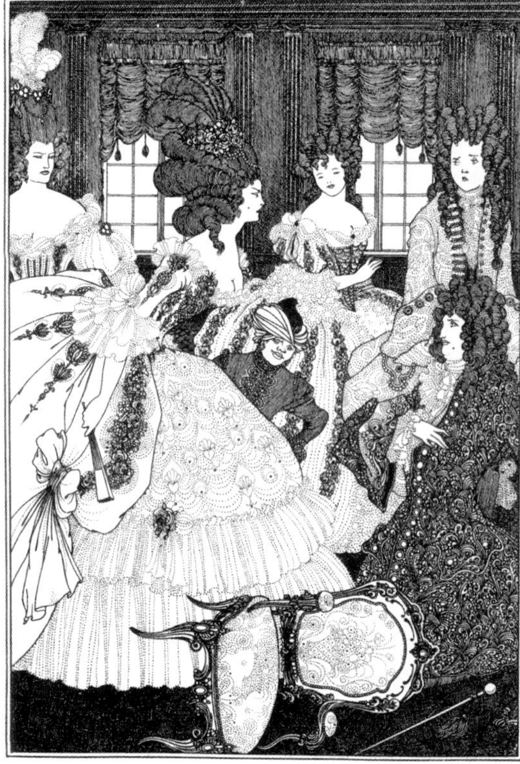

410 The Battle of the Beaux and the Belles, for *The Rape of the Lock* (411)

81, 82 Aubrey Beardsley, illustrations in *Rape of the Lock by Alexander Pope*, 1896. Private collection

quarto edition. The success of the volume, both in terms of its artistic merits and its sales, was, however, testimony to the pleasure taken in 'filigree' poetry by a new generation of readers who were actively questioning the received values of mid-Victorian culture. Beardsley's illustrations first appeared in large format, but were later issued by John Lane as a miniature edition (1901). They are amongst Beardsley's most assured and detailed masterpieces of black-and-white drawing and they clearly appealed to a discriminating *fin-de-siècle* audience. Three of the most striking drawings show a young turbaned pageboy. He appears first with Arabella in 'The Barge'; he grins at us, sipping from a shallow cup, just as her lock is about to be severed in 'The Rape'; and he emerges impishly from behind the heroine's voluminous (if anachronistic late-eighteenth-century) skirts, in 'The Battle of the Beaux and the Belles.' This blackamoor figure has no original in Pope's poem, but for Beardsley he takes on something of Pope's narrative role as an amused, slightly detached, observer. It is just possible that when Hugo von Hofmannsthal, who knew a good deal about English art, was preparing the libretto for Richard Strauss's rococo fantasy *Der Rosenkavalier* in 1911 he was thinking of these *Rape of the Lock* drawings. Just before the curtain falls in the last act of the opera, Sophie has dropped her handkerchief. In the last bars, a little black page, Mahomet, runs in to retrieve it. Thanks to Beardsley's mediation, Mahomet has moved with decorative ease from Queen Anne's Hampton Court to Maria Theresa's Vienna.

CELEBRATING HANDEL

Thackeray was clearly delighted by the story that when Sir Robert Walpole announced to the new King George II that his royal father had died at Osnabrück the new monarch declared: 'Dat is one big lie.' Thus, unpropitiously, in June 1727 began the thirty-three year reign of the second Hanoverian king. In that same year another German George, Georg Friederich Händel, had been naturalised as a British citizen, taking the anglicised name George Frideric Handel. He was taken to English hearts infinitely more readily than the new king, and he has never lost his place there. A statue of the composer, an Apollo *en déshabille*, by Louis François Roubiliac, had been erected in a niche in the Great Grove at the Vauxhall Gardens in 1737 and it remained there until Vauxhall closed in 1840 and the Garden's contents were auctioned off (it is now in the Victoria and Albert Museum). Many Victorian music lovers assumed that Handel *was* so utterly English that he had, virtually single-handedly, allowed the British nation to hold its head up high amongst other more prolifically musical nations. As Samuel Butler proudly noted: 'Handel was not an Englishman by birth, but no one was ever more thoroughly English in respect of all the best and most distinguishing features of Englishmen … He chose England … and what does this involve, if not that England … is the most musically minded country in the world?'[33] In their native Germany, the music of Bach had been all but eclipsed until Mendelssohn revived it the 1830s, but in England Handel's pre-eminence as a composer had never been challenged. Few nineteenth-century choral meetings took place without the performance of some chorus of Handel's, and few concert rooms failed to be emblazoned with his name. When Handel died in London in April 1759 he was interred in Westminster Abbey and some three thousand mourners attended his funeral service in this English Valhalla.[34] His musical links with the Abbey were to remain intimate in the hundred years following his death. In 1761 Roubiliac's great monument to the composer was unveiled in the South Transept. A theatrical Handel stands surrounded by musical instruments while an angel in the clouds plays a harp. He looks inspired. Before him lies a large sheet of music bearing the opening words and melody of the aria from *Messiah*: 'I know that my Redeemer liveth.' Thus, enshrined in Poets' Corner, he and his great aria seem to affirm their shared Englishness. Close to his monument are busts of Thackeray and Macaulay. The remains of Charles Dickens occupy the grave next to Handel's and Dr Johnson lies nearby.

In that same year of Handel's naturalisation the composer received a commission to write four anthems for the Coronation of the new King in Westminster Abbey. Their performance at the ceremony in October 1727 required about one hundred and sixty musicians as well as the Abbey's choir but, though rehearsals had gone well, the choir managed to omit one anthem entirely and they sang *Zadok the Priest* at the wrong point in the service. Nevertheless, *Zadok* and the other anthems have remained integral to each succeeding coronation service, not excepting that of Queen Victoria in June 1838. Since the late eighteenth century they, and certain of Handel's oratorios, have also steadily maintained their popularity with both amateur and professional choirs. *Zadok* figured as the opening piece at the first posthumous 'Handel Commemoration' in Westminster Abbey in 1783. The event, attended by members of the Royal Family, took place over three days and climaxed with a performance of *Messiah*. These 'Commemorations' virtually became annual events.[35] After 1791, however, these 'Grand Performances' moved to St Margaret's Church, and in 1796 and 1797 they were held in the Chapel Royal at the Banqueting House in Whitehall (on the latter occasion, when the Nore mutiny was encouraging the idea that a more general revolutionary spirit was abroad, the rumour circulated that the King and the Royal family were to be blown up in the Chapel *à la* Guy Fawkes).

George III's illness precluded his direct patronage in the opening years of the nineteenth century, but it was against a background of rivalry from provincial music festivals, notably at York, Birmingham and Edinburgh, that a 'Royal Music Festival' was triumphantly resumed in Westminster Abbey in 1834 under the patronage of King William IV and Queen Adelaide (fig. 83). The Vice Patrons were the Royal Dukes, and the 'Presidents' included thirteen dukes, seven marquises, and nineteen earls (including the Prime Minister, Earl Grey). The successful organisation of the great event became such a matter of pride that a special commemorative programme was published. The interior of the Abbey was transformed with galleries and boxes, and one thousand three hundred two-guinea tickets were allocated for seats in the nave and aisles, while a further one thousand four hundred people were accommodated under the galleries at a price of one guinea. These handsome tickets for the rehearsals and the actual performances were printed on embossed card in a different colour for each of the four days (they were reproduced in the commemorative programme). The King and Queen attended every performance 'in grand state' and the programme proclaimed that 'never was beheld a more splendid display of Royalty, Rank, and Fashion' and that nothing could 'be more impressive than the scene, at the conclusion of the introductory symphony to the Coronation Anthem, on the first day, when Their Majesties, and the whole brilliant assembly, rose simultaneously, as the orchestra, consisting of upwards of six hundred voices and instruments, poured forth its powerful volume of sacred harmony.'[36] Music from Handel's oratorios dominated the 1834 festival, with selections from *Samson* on the first day, *Israel in Egypt* on the second, *Judas Maccabaeus* on the third and *Messiah* on the fourth. Haydn's *Creation* was sung in English on June 24th, and a *Kyrie* from his 'Second Service' (the word *Mass* was clearly unacceptable) on the day following. This second performance also included the *Credo* from Mozart's 'First Service,' but any overtly catholic spirit was duly tempered by a rendition by the tenor John Braham, accompanied by the chorus and the two-hundred- and-twenty-four man orchestra, of 'Luther's Hymn.'

The links between Handel's oratorios, massed choirs, over-stuffed orchestras and royal patronage flourished as the nineteenth century developed. When Queen Victoria, who as heir to the throne had attended the 1834 Festival, formally opened the Great Exhibition in May 1851 it was deemed fitting that the occasion should be solemnised not simply by a prayer from the Archbishop of Canterbury but also by the 'Hallelujah Chorus.' The chorus was performed, as the Queen noted in her

83 Royal Music Festival Programme, 1834. Private collection

journal, 'with 200 instruments and 600 voices, which sounded like nothing.'[37] We must assume that the Queen meant that the grand forces involved had sung in such sacred harmony that numbers did not count, and not that their voices were lost in the crystal spaces. When the Crystal Palace was rebuilt at Sydenham it became the celebrated venue for even greater Handel Festivals. The first was held in 1857 when a huge chorus of young persons drawn 'from every large town in England,' of 'the highest respectability,' and possessing 'an intellectual and personal enjoyment of the sublime strains they were to render,' were specially trained under a 'new system of choral singing.'[38] Over the three days of the Festival there were performances of *Israel in Egypt*, *Judas Maccabaeus* and *Messiah* before an audience that included the Queen and Prince Albert, of whom it was noted that the Queen beat time with her fan while Albert followed the music with a score in his lap. During this first Festival it was reported that 'the volume of sound was dispersed and lost in the prodigious space.' As a consequence, a false roof was introduced at the Crystal Palace for the second Great Handel Festival in 1859, a celebration marking the Handel centenary. Some 81,319 attended, including George Eliot and George Henry Lewes who came, in the pouring rain, to *Messiah* on 20 June.[39] Thereafter highly successful Handel Festivals were held triennially, with a special celebration in 1885 to mark the bicentennial of the composer's birth. These Triennial Festivals continued to flourish into the twentieth century, the last taking place in 1926. Thanks largely to the amount of timber introduced into the building to accommodate such huge concerts, the Crystal Palace burned to the ground in 1937. The event seemed to many to mark the end of an era. It certainly began to mark the end of the rescored, hyper-inflated performances that are dismissed by fastidious modern observers as more characteristically Victorian than genuinely Handelian.

Handel's oratorios, and particularly *Messiah*, were admired by nineteenth-century music-lovers because they discovered in them the kind of emotional fulfilment that they seem to have missed in other early eighteenth-century music. Nourished as they were by the symphonies, concerti and the operatic innovations of their contemporaries, the Romantic and post-Romantic composers, Victorian concert audiences seem to have craved stimulation and massive sonority. They were accustomed to large and versatile orchestras, and they relished both singing in, and listening to, massed choirs. Their tastes were variously pandered to at concerts of modern music by visiting conductors such as Berlioz and Wagner. Nevertheless, in what remained a profoundly religious age, Victorian music-lovers seem to have found the oratorios of Handel uniquely expressive of the sorrows, joys, and triumphs of their faith. Moreover, these religious emotions were expressed in the solid language of the Authorised Version of the Bible (or something akin to it), not in trilling Italian or Popish Latin. Performances of Handel's oratorios, whether in a secular or a religious context, whether in London or in Birmingham, united Catholics and Protestants and happily blurred divisions between Anglicans and Dissenters. But the vast popularity of *Judas Maccabaeus* or *Messiah* in Victorian England seems to have eclipsed the works of Handel that had been most appreciated by his English contemporaries when he first arrived in London: his Italian operas. Regardless of the quality of the music, the shapely, stately formality of Handel's operas seemed irredeemably artificial and old-fashioned in Victorian eyes. For the most part, the operas had to wait until the second decade of the twentieth century to find appreciative editors, let alone capable singers and audiences prepared to take pleasure in them. The one exception to this was *Acis and Galatea*, an opera in English originally performed to a select aristocratic audience at Cannons, but familiar to much wider audiences through its multiplicity of airs and melodic delights. *Acis and Galatea*, rescored for greater forces than Handel could ever have envisaged, was briefly staged at Drury Lane by William Charles Macready in February 1842. It had elaborate sets by the marine painter, Clarkson Stanfield, and its imaginative production seems to have charmed audiences, but Macready closed it prematurely. One discriminating member of those audiences, Edward Fitzgerald, was entranced by the evening and he described it to a friend:

> You enter Drury Lane at a quarter to seven: the pit is already nearly full: but you find a seat, and a very pleasant one … the musicians come up from under the stage one by one: 'tis just upon seven: Macready is very punctual: Mr T. Cooke is in his place with his Marshal's baton in his hand: he lifts it up: and off they set with old Handel's noble overture. As it is playing, the red velvet curtain … draws apart: and you see a rich drop scene, all festooned and arabesqued with River Gods, Nymphs and their emblems: and in the centre a delightful, large, good copy of Poussin's great landscape … where the Cyclops is seen seated on a mountain, looking over the sea. The overture ends, the drop scene rises, and there is the seashore, a long curling bay: the sea heaving under the moon and breaking upon the beach,

and rolling the surf down – the stage! … The choruses were well sung, well acted, well dressed, and well grouped: the whole thing creditable and pleasant. Do you know the music? It is of Handel's best: and as classical as any man who wore a full-bottomed wig could write.

Nevertheless, Fitzgerald, who was never an admirer of *Messiah* in its Crystal Palace garb, was in many ways an atypical nineteenth-century observer. For him, Handel lacked true sublimity but triumphed musically when he was avowedly secular:

his Hallelujah chorus is a chorus not of angels but of well-fed earthly choristers, ranged tier above tier in a Gothic cathedral, with princes for audience, and their military trumpets flourishing over the full volume of the organ. Handel's gods are like Homer's, and his sublime never reaches beyond the region of the clouds. Therefore I think that his great marches, triumphal pieces, and Coronation Anthems, are his finest works.[40]

The Handel beloved of the Victorians, including Fitzgerald, was a man they had formed in their own image and a composer whose thumping tunes could be pleasurably rolled out for appropriate high days, holidays, choral festivals and after-dinner entertainments. Ripped out of their original contexts, *Zadok the Priest* and the Hallelujah Chorus graced state occasions and 'See, the conqu'ring Hero comes' was appropriated for military bands and grand organ recitals alike. Many an unprofessional male voice tackled 'O Ruddier than the Cherry' and many delicate amateur hands essayed 'The Harmonious Blacksmith' on a drawing-room piano. That last piece, the E major air and variations from Handel's Harpsichord Suite no. 5, had a particular afterlife of its own. The story that Handel had been inspired by hearing the rhythms of a village forge at Cannons was probably apocryphal, but it suited Victorian anecdotalists. The nickname was evidently so familiar when Dickens wrote *Great Expectations* in 1860 as to allow him to play yet another variation on it. The air's nickname so appeals to the slightly whimsical Herbert Pocket that he suggests that as 'Philip' is not a particularly becoming Christian name for Pip, another might fit him better:

'We are so harmonious, and you have been a blacksmith – would you mind it?'
'I shouldn't mind anything you propose,' I answered, 'but I don't understand you.'

'Would you mind Handel for as familiar name? There's a charming piece
of music by Handel, called the Harmonious Blacksmith.'
 'I should like it very much.'
'Then, my dear Handel,' said he turning round as the door opened …

Thereafter, for Herbert at least, Pip is 'Handel,' *tout court*.

REBELLION AND RIOT

Handel composed his bellicose oratorio *Judas Maccabaeus* in the immediate
aftermath of the defeat of Prince Charles Edward Stuart and his army at
Culloden in April 1746. The oratorio was designed to flatter the conquering
hero of the battle, William Augustus, Duke of Cumberland, and thus to greet
him on his triumphant return to London. Such was Handel's rush to appeal
to an audience rejoicing in Cumberland's success that, for later performances,
he borrowed what was to become its most famous number, 'See, the
conqu'ring Hero comes,' from his earlier oratorio *Joshua*.[41] For the vast
majority of English men and women and for the many Scottish lowlanders
who supported the Protestant cause and the Hanoverian dynasty, the victory
of George II's second son was a victory for the *status quo*. In 1860, in one of
his essays on the painter William Hogarth, George Augustus Sala describes
Hogarth's modest allegiance to the Hanoverian throne. What Sala says of
Hogarth probably stood for many of his fellow Englishmen:

> Of the German kings who were good enough to come from Herren-
> hausen, and sit on our throne – the kings who were always scampering
> over to the Vaterland, who talked French at court, and did not know
> enough of the English language to deliver their own royal speeches, nay,
> scarcely knew to what rank in the State their servants were eligible –
> Hogarth could not have been a great admirer … He simply hated
> Jacobitism as the vast body of the middle classes hated it, for the reason
> that, to his mind, the success of the Stuart cause was associated with
> *soupe maigre*, fricasseed frogs, and foreign ascendancy, with surreptitious
> warming-pans, popery, brass-money, and wooden shoes.[42]

For Jacobites and sentimentalists on both sides of the border, however, Culloden was an unmitigated disaster. It marked both the effective end of the Stuart pretension to the throne of Great Britain and the beginning of the end for the ancient social loyalties that bonded Highland Scotland together. For the succeeding century alternative kings were now decidedly 'over the water,' and they were in all likelihood no' comin' back again.

To most Victorians Jacobitism was familiar not as a political doctrine, or as a distinctly Scottish protest against the Union and a German dynasty, but as minstrelsy, melancholy and the stuff of romance. The lost Stuart cause was an historic rather than a living threat to the *status quo*, and the House of Hanover was secure on the throne of its ancestors. So secure did Queen Victoria feel that in June 1845, one hundred years after the rising, she hosted a *bal costumé* at Buckingham Palace at which guests were required to wear fancy costumes in the style of the Court of George II. The Queen and Prince Albert, accompanied by the Duke and Duchess of Nemours, danced a formal minuet as the ball opened. Prince Albert, resplendent in red velvet costume and powdered wig, who might well have recalled the *élan* of Prince Charles Edward Stuart far more than the dumpy George II, had declined to shave off his moustache for the occasion.[43] No commentator, whether Scots or English, seems to have found this Fancy Ball in the least bit distasteful, let alone politically insensitive. In a sense Jacobitism, and the more potent Scottish element in its symbolism, had long been neutralised. Sir Walter Scott's *Waverley* of 1814 had explored the case for and against the Young Pretender, and had argued for the social and economic benefits of the Union. Modern Scotland, the novelist told his readers, had been transformed since 1745. Under Scott's tutelage, King George IV had sported the kilt on his celebrated visit to Edinburgh in 1822 and had toasted his northern Kingdom in whisky (though Sir Walter, having begged for the King's glass as a souvenir, promptly managed to break it). Responsive both to honour and to history, George had also paid for Antonio Canova's superb marble monument to the exiled Stuarts in St. Peter's in Rome. George's niece, Victoria, fell in love with Scotland. She and Albert followed the deer in specially designed tartan plaids, danced the Highland Fling, and were woken in the mornings by a piper. At Balmoral they decorated the furniture and floors of their mountain retreat with revived tartan patterns, some of which had been banned by George II's government after Culloden in an attempt to extinguish Highland identity.

It was under Scott's influence, and as the editor's 'constant and unbiased friend,' that James Hogg published his *The Jacobite Relics of Scotland; Being the Songs, Airs, and Legends of the Adherents to the House of Stuart* in 1819. It was both a work of national pride and a labour of love, but it was far from being an act of protest. 'Our Jacobite songs and tunes,' Hogg told his readers, 'are the best that the country ever produced.' He then added that they were 'a delightful though rude epitome of the history of our country during a period highly eventful, when every internal movement was decisive toward the establishment of the rights and liberties which we have since enjoyed.' These are not the words of a grudging Unionist, let alone of an elegist for a lost Scotland. Indeed, Hogg is prepared not only to include an appendix containing Scottish Whig (that is, anti-Jacobite) songs, but the general introduction to his volume is fulsome in its praise for the sympathy and liberality of George III and his heir:

> Besides the great measure of restoring the forfeited estates to the chiefs, our venerable sovereign shewed, on every occasion, how little his heart was capable of nourishing any dislike against those who had acted upon principle against the authority of his house. The support which he afforded to the exiled branch of the Stuarts will form a bright trait in his history … The same kindness to the memory of those who hazarded themselves in the cause of the Stuarts has been inherited by the present administrator of royal authority [the Prince Regent] … He was heard to express himself one day before a dozen of gentlemen of both nations, with the greatest warmth, as follows: 'I have always regarded the attachment of the Scots to the Pretender – I beg your pardon, gentlemen – to Prince Charles Stuart, I mean – as a lesson to me whom to trust in the hour of need.'[44]

Later in his introduction Hogg avers that 'the rival claims of Stuart and Brunswick are not more to the present generation than those of Bruce and Balliol, or York and Lancaster.' Given this balanced, temperate tone, it is more than a little shocking to experience the vivid spleen and the raucousness of many of the Jacobite lyrics in the collection. The third song in the anthology ('Lesley's March to Scotland') is rabidly anti-Presbyterian: 'March! – march – scourges of heresy! / Down with the kirk and its whilliebaleery!' Song XXV disparages the Acts of Succession and Union in no uncertain terms, and looks for a true Catholic Stuart to replace the dead 'Lutheran,' Queen Anne:

> I'll sing you a song, my brave boys,
>   The like you ne'er heard of before;
> Old Scotland at last is grown wise,
>   And England shall bully no more.
> Succession, the trap for our slav'ry,
>   A true Presbyterian plot,
> Advanced by by-ends and knav'ry,
>   Is now kicked out by a vote,
> The Lutheran dame may be gone,
>   Our foes shall address us no more;
> If the treaty should never go on,
>   She for ever is kick'd out of door.

At least the balance is redressed in the last ballad in the collection, an avowedly Whig fantasy describing Bonnie Prince Charlie's ('Perkin's') despair over the dubious quality of his rag-tag army. 'Perkin' addresses a last-minute recruit:

> 'For if they join battle, they'll make a short stay,
> That you may have time, sir, to scour away;
> Then as fast as they can they'll all follow after,
> That they may not be kill'd, or die in a halter.'

> 'Ah me!' then cried Perkin, 'this rascally mob
> Are fit but the henroosts and orchards to rob.
> Alas, I'm undone! My cause must go down,
> For I'm sure these can never obtain me the crown,

> Surrounded by them, like a cheat I should look:
> My doom I can read, sir, without any book.
> Such an army as this, 'tis a thousand to one,
> Will bring me to Tyburn, instead of a throne.'

Hogg's collection is hard-headedly unsentimental. It can have afforded little pleasure either to nostalgic nineteenth-century Jacobites or to any hopeful music publisher in search of the kind of romantic Scottish airs that echoed through so many Victorian drawing-rooms.

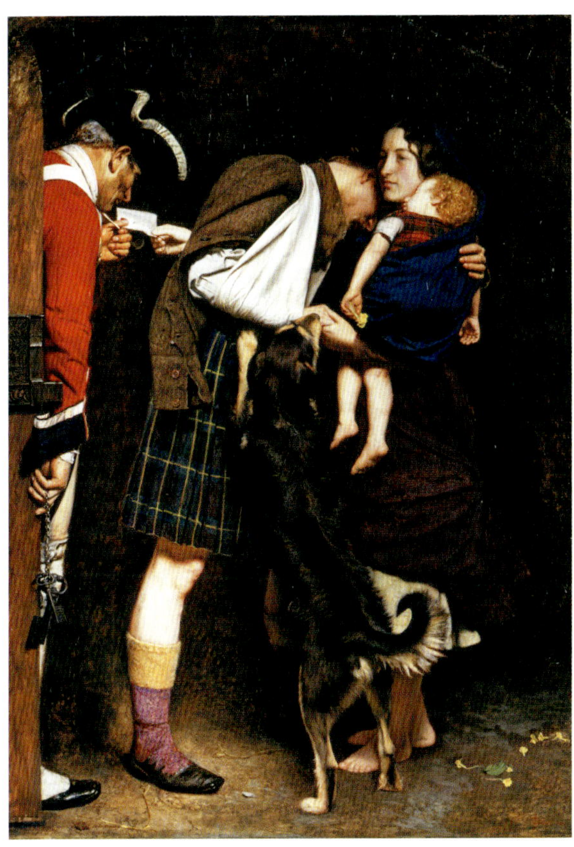

84 John Everett Millais, *The Order of Release 1746*, 1853, Oil on canvas, 102.9 x 73.7 cm. Tate, London

Many of those drawing-rooms could have been hung with engraved versions of Millais's often sentimental paintings illustrative either of the Jacobite rebellions or of Sir Walter Scott's fictional accounts of Scotland in the period. *The Order of Release 1746* (fig.84), first exhibited in 1853, appeared as a mezzotint three years later; *The White Cockade* of 1862 was engraved in 1878, and the saccharine *An Idyll of 1745* (fig.85, 1884), showing a drummer-boy in Hanoverian uniform playing his fife to entertain three Highland girls, was etched by W. Hole in 1897. As M.H. Spielmann remarks in *Millais and his Works* these pictures show the artist declaring his sympathy 'romantic, of course, not therefore political – with the Jacobites.'[45] The fact that the period following the suppression of the Jacobite Rebellion *was* political had haunted not just Sir Walter Scott and his literary circle: it was to figure in many late-century

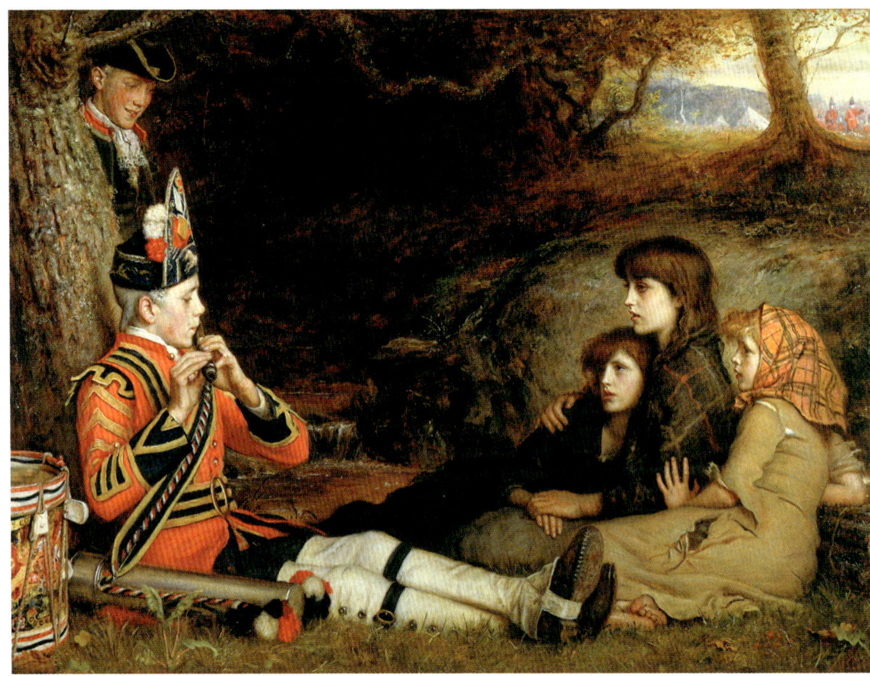

85 John Everett Millais, *An Idyll of 1745*, 1884, Oil on canvas, 140 x 191cm. Lady Lever Art Gallery, National Museums Liverpool

paintings by John Pettie. Three of Robert Louis Stevenson's most striking novels, *Kidnapped* of 1886, its sequel, *Catriona*, of 1893, and *The Master of Ballantrae* of 1889, also deal with the aftermath of the defeat of the Young Pretender. All three novels are concerned with inheritance, both in the narrow family sense of the term, and with Scotland's larger historical inheritance of political and civil insurgency. *Kidnapped* is set in 1751 when the consequences of the government's confiscation of Highland estates after the Rebellion are biting hard. When David Balfour first encounters the illegally returned Jacobite exile, Alan Breck Stewart, he explains what he understands of his new acquaintance's situation:

> At that period (so soon after the forty-five) there were many exiled gentlemen coming back at the peril of their lives, either to see their friends, or to collect a little money; and as for the Highland chiefs that had been forfeited, it was a common matter of talk how their tenants could stint themselves to send them money, and their clansmen outface the soldiery to get it in, and run the gauntlet of our great navy to carry

> it across. All this I had, of course, heard tell of; and now I had a man
> under my eyes whose life was forfeit on all these counts and upon one
> more; for he was not only a rebel and a smuggler of rents, but had taken
> service with King Louis of France. And as if all this were not enough,
> he had a belt of golden guineas round his loins. Whatever my opinions,
> I could not look on such a man without a lively interest. (Chapter 9)

Balfour's 'lively interest' adds a further complication to his already complicated
life. He is no Jacobite himself (notice he says 'our great navy'), but he is forced
by circumstances to find common cause with Breck. He is also drawn into an
appreciation of the sufferings of the Highland clans under the British military
'occupation.' Clan chiefs are either in exile or in hiding; their factors are
suspect; the Gaelic language is spoken guardedly and, the kilt and plaid having
been banned, the 'lowland habit' is worn under duress. Balfour sympathetically
describes the enforced peculiarities of male attire on the Isle of Mull:

> Some went bare, only for a hanging cloak or great coat, and carried
> their trousers on their backs like a useless burthen; some had made an
> imitation of the tartan with little parti-coloured stripes patched together
> like an old wife's quilt; others, again, still wore the highland philabeg,
> but by putting a few stitches between the legs, transformed it into a pair
> of trousers like a Dutchman's. All those makeshifts were condemned
> and punished, for the law was harshly applied, in hope to break up clan
> spirit; but in that out-of-the-way, sea-bound isle, there were few to make
> remarks and fewer to tell tales. (Chapter 15)

Despite his real reservations, he later even joins in a treasonable toast to 'The
Restoration':

> Thereupon we all touched glasses and drank. I am sure I wished no ill
> to King George; and if he had been there himself in proper person, it's
> like he would have done as I did. No sooner had I taken out the dram
> than I felt hugely better, and could look on and listen, still a little mistily
> perhaps, but no longer with the same groundless horror and distress of
> mind. (Chapter 23)

This moment epitomises the ambiguity of *Kidnapped*. As in Scott's *Waverley*, we have a hero who is an outsider to much of the political intrigue described in the novel. Here, though, instead of Scott's uninformed Englishman out of his depth in Highland Scotland, we have in Balfour a Scots Lowlander who is drawn two ways. His basic loyalties are to the Kirk and a Protestant King but, confronted by Alan Breck and the cause he has espoused, he is romantically drawn to an alternative Scotland. This was the kind of cultural division that Stevenson was to explore again in *The Master of Ballantrae* where two brothers take different political sides and pursue radically different destinies.

Scotland, like England, had experienced a murderous civil war in the mid-seventeenth century, but the issues over which it had been fought were infinitely less well defined than those which divided English royalists from English parliamentarians. The 'civil war' which seems to have fascinated Scottish writers far more was that fought out, occasionally bloodily, in the eighteenth century. This 'war' had been occasioned by the Act of Succession, which excluded the senior line of the Stuart family from the throne of an ostensibly united Kingdom, and by the Act of Union, which tied Scottish political institutions to English ones. Some Scots, who believed that their nation had been coerced into Union, fondly believed that the restored Stuarts might save them from the signal dishonour brought upon the once independent northern Kingdom. Others, who believed purely and simply in the dynastic rights of the House of Stuart, were persuaded that an alien, secular sanction had deprived a legitimate royal house of its divinely ordained right to rule. The eighteenth-century Scotland that so enthralled Sir Walter Scott's successors was a nation divided not just by questions of legitimacy and religion, or by an historic antipathy to England, but by cultural fault-lines that separated the Highlands from the Lowlands, clan chieftains and Catholic crofters from Protestant Lairds and Presbyterian townsmen, disappointed Jacobites and confident Whigs. As Scott, Hogg and Stevenson readily recognised, post-1745 Scotland had boomed, thanks to the peace and prosperity secured by the Union. In the course of the eighteenth century it had also become a predominantly industrious, ordered and stable Protestant society. Its troubles lay in its margins. Until the opening decades of the nineteenth century, neither cerebral Whig Edinburgh nor commercial Glasgow was far, either historically or geographically, from the lawless, tribal, Gaelic-speaking, and still residually Jacobite, 'other' Scotland. That was what the great nineteenth-century writers of Scotland saw as defining the culture from which they sprang. This was also what made them distinct from their English contemporaries. Romanticism, unnaturally coupled with industrialisation, had moulded Scotland into a modern European nation. The process had first required the neutering of the 'other' and then safely and picturesquely viewing it through tartan lenses.

When Stevenson wrote *Kidnapped*, his title still exclusively described the act of seizing and then selling a victim into 'slavery' as an indentured labourer on a plantation in one of the southern states of America. Evidently, the disorder in many parts of Scotland in the mid-eighteenth century made the practice both common and lucrative. Certainly, for Stevenson's unscrupulous villains, it offered a ready solution to a dispute about inheritance which stopped short of murder. Probably due to the European success of the novels of James Fenimore Cooper eighteenth-century America seems to have held an ambiguous place in the imaginations of cis-Atlantic writers. The New World was pictured both as a populous sea-board and a tractless wilderness. The Republic that emerged from the Revolution was both a land of liberty and opportunity and a place where men and women could disappear (sometimes voluntarily). As readers of Defoe's *Moll Flanders* also knew, the colonies had in addition provided a convenient dumping ground for convicts and the unwanted dregs of British society. As all earnest Victorian abolitionists recognised, the curse of black slavery lived on in the liberty-loving republic for a generation after it had been abolished in the British Empire. Like a Scotland unburdened with a fraught history, eighteenth-century America was recognisably 'civilised' but there was a conspicuous rawness about its civilisation, and its edges were decidedly perilous. Like Scotland it was 'kith-and-kin,' but like Scotland it did things differently. For most Victorian writers, looking back to the century of the Revolution, America was all frontier, all possibility.

Both Dickens and Thackeray were well acquainted with the eastern United States. Both had either given readings or successfully lectured in a land thirsty for sophistication and yet perfectly confident in its own values. Both men went to make money. Thackeray visited the United States twice, lecturing on the *English Humourists* during his first visit in 1852-53 and on *The Four Georges* in his second in 1855-56. Like Dickens before him, he was disgruntled at America's failure to comply with international copyright. When he first arrived in New York in 1852 he was particularly annoyed to see reprints of the newly published *Esmond*, priced at a mere 50 cents. The London edition had been expensively set up in old style type; the New York piracy was printed 'in the ordinary type,' and, what was worse, was littered 'with new-fangled American spelling.'[46] Nevertheless, Thackeray seems to have responded happily to the country where he had imagined the Esmond family settling for their Indian Summer in 1718. There, with his mind preoccupied with eighteenth-century England, he delighted in discovering relics of the Revolution and in seeking out the virtually ubiquitous portraits and busts of George Washington. He was particularly fascinated to discover two crossed swords hanging on a wall in a house in Beacon Street in Boston: one had belonged to the owner's grandfather, who had fought with Washington; the other, to his wife's grandfather, who had fought for King George. They were to figure in the opening paragraph of Thackeray's somewhat ungainly sequel to *Esmond*, *The Virginians: A Tale of the Last Century* (1857–59).

Where *Henry Esmond* is melancholy and centred on its often marginalised narrator, *The Virginians* is spirited and divided between accounts of the lives of the two Warrington brothers, one who proves to be a loyalist, the other a supporter of American independence. Thackeray himself seems to have regretted that he did not make more of the American Revolution in his narrative. Though his original intention had been to lay his scene in Virginia, and to describe the progress of the War through the experiences of the two brothers, in the end he set rather too much of it in George III's England. As a result, Dr Johnson was to figure in the narrative nearly as significantly as Benjamin Franklin. This imbalance may stem from Thackeray's concern to avoid any prospective references to the profound constitutional dilemmas facing the United States in the years immediately preceding the Civil War. These dilemmas would certainly have touched on the future of the fictional Warrington/Esmond plantation in slave-holding Virginia. By the time he began his novel Thackeray seems to have persuaded himself that he had only a limited sympathy with the more radical Abolitionists. In 1856 he described Charleston, South Carolina, as 'like Europe with an aristocracy and a very pleasant society, ruling patriarchally over its kind black vassals.' Charleston's white citizens had proved 'hospitable, tolerably lettered, keeping aloof from politics as almost all gentlemen of the States are forced to do.' When, in the same letter, he describes the condition of the slaves he had encountered he is unrepentant about his prejudices: 'I have no doubt that … negroes have never been so well off as those now in America. This does not make slavery right: but – but I can't mend it, and so leave it.'[47] But Thackeray may have had an even larger problem with white America. By the end of his second tour he was distinctly out of love with vital aspects of the United States. He wrote home from St. Louis with a fastidious distaste for the American 'rabble':

> How this country whiggifies me. The rabble supremacy turns my gorge. The gentlemen stand aloof from public affairs, and count no more than yonder Irish bog trotter who is driving a pig before the window or those two illiterate blaspheming ruffians who were cutting their gums with their penknives in the bar – I couldn't bear to live in a country at this stage in its political existence – In fine I want to get home more and more.[48]

Thackeray had hoped to find a land of high-thinking and principled Anglo-Saxon gentlemen, descendants of Virginian grandees like his own Henry Esmond or the upright George Washington whom he so esteemed. Instead, he found a mongrel nation that struck him as unworthy of their Colonial inheritance. *The Virginians* opens with a recall of a seemingly lost idyll:

> The gentry of Virginia dwelt on their great lands after a fashion almost patriarchal. For its rough cultivation, each estate had a multitude of hands – of purchased and assigned servants – who were subject to the command of the master. The land yielded their food, live stock and game. The great rivers swarmed with fish for the taking … Their hospitality was boundless. No stranger was ever sent away from their gates. The gentry received one another, and travelled to each other's houses, in a state almost feudal. The question of Slavery was not born at the time of which we write. To be the proprietor of black servants shocked the feelings of no Virginian gentleman; nor, in truth, was the despotism exercised over the negro race generally a savage one. The food was plenty; the poor black people lazy and not unhappy. (Chapter 2)

This is complacency in the extreme. Thackeray's vision of Colonial Virginia looks to us like a perverse admixture of Jane Austen's Hampshire, Turgenev's Russia, and a Romantic fantasy of the Middle Ages, relocated in an Arcadian landscape. His choice of the word 'patriarchal' tells us a great deal, but this is no Abrahamic campsite or the Promised Land. This Arcadia thrives on exploitation. The 'question' of slavery may not have been born in eighteenth-century Virginia, but the embarrassing *fact* of slavery manifestly had and, for the vast majority of Victorian observers, it tainted the whole concept of American liberty.

Generally Thackeray tends to avoid these embarrassments. George Warrington has a black servant, Gumbo, whom he brings to England with him and who proves to be much like any other Thackerayan servant: resourceful, comic and faithful, though never particularly vocal. The main problem that American readers of *The Virginians* seem to have had with the novel was not the issue of slavery but the representation of the man whose heroism they regarded as unchallengeable: George Washington.[49] Thackeray the man was an unstinted admirer of the General; Thackeray the novelist could never quite surrender himself to hero-worship. The young Washington we meet in the first part of the novel is humourless, gauche, and somewhat commonplace. Towards the end of the narrative, however, Thackeray's 'loyalist' character, George Warrington, gives a stout defence of a man whom he regards as a totally honourable military opponent:

> What a constancy, what a magnanimity, what a surprising persistence against fortune! Washington before the enemy was no better nor braver than hundreds that fought with him or against him … but Washington the Chief of a nation in arms, doing battle with distracted parties; calm in the midst of conspiracy; serene against the open foe before him and the darker enemies at his back; Washington inspiring order and spirit into troops hungry and in rags; stung by ingratitude, but betraying no anger, and ever ready to forgive; in defeat invincible, magnanimous in conquest, and never so sublime as on that day when he laid down his victorious sword and sought his noble retirement: – here indeed is a character to admire and revere; a life without a stain, a fame without a flaw. (Chapter 39)

If such praise can issue from the mouth of an enemy, and from a fellow-Virginian who has a personal grudge against the man, one wonders what nineteenth-century Americans can have found to complain about. Perhaps, it was just another case of Thackeray overstepping a mark in the belief that *lèse majesté* was an offence only in monarchies.

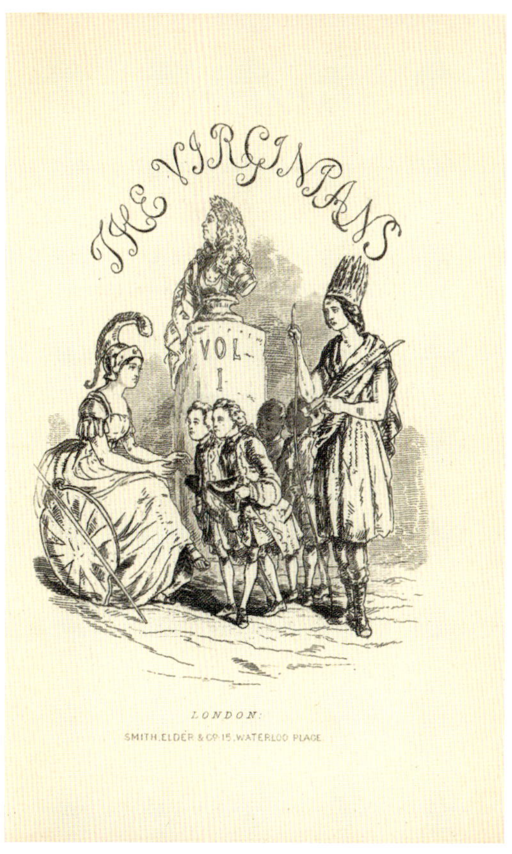

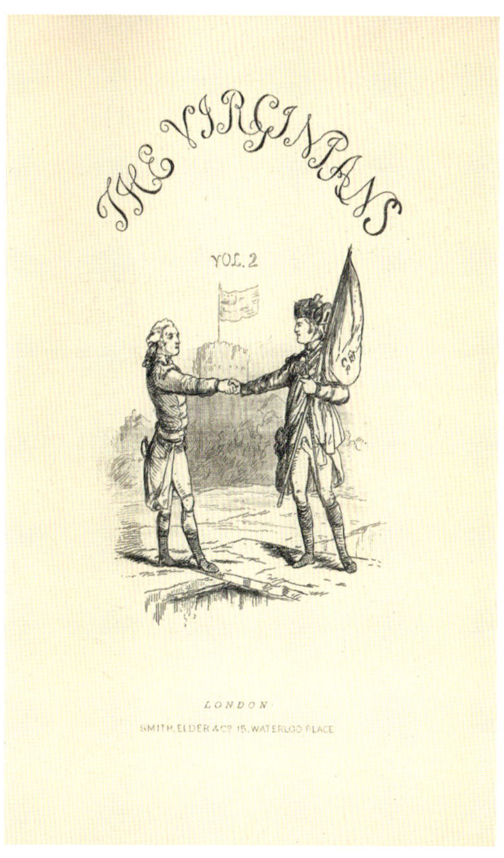

In *The Virginians* Thackeray also makes a brave stab at seeing the American War of Independence as a fraternal struggle between two branches of the Anglo-Saxon race. The title-page to the novel's first volume (fig.86) carried an engraved drawing by the novelist. Here, under a laurelled bust of George II, two boys are being presented by an emblematic figure of America to a seated Britannia. The boys are attended by their two black servants. The title-page of volume two, however, carried a very different device (fig.87). It was the one that had appeared on the monthly-part cover and it shows George Warrington, carrying a semi-furled Union Jack, bidding farewell to his brother, Harry. They are standing on a sea-shore and behind them the Stars and Stripes flies bravely from a tower. The American victory is assured, and the departing loyalist graciously cedes dominion to the citizen of a new republic. Thackeray's narrative had attempted to persuade readers that American independence had

86, 87 Title-page from *The Virginians* by William Makepeace Thackeray, vols. 1 and 2, 1857–59. Private collection

been determined by natural justice and by a shared inheritance of constitutionally defined liberties. In justifying his own position, the loyalist George Warrington describes his fraternal attempts at reconciliation with his American brother, Henry:

> I did not try to urge upon him (I had done so in vain many times previously) our British side of the question, the side which appears to me the best. He was accustomed to put off my reasons by saying 'All mighty well, brother, you speak as an Englishman, and have cast in your lot with your country, as I have with mine.' To this argument I own there is no answer, and all that remains for the disputants is to fight the matter out, when the strongest is in the right. Which had the right in the wars of the last century? The King or the Parliament? The side that was uppermost was the right, and on the whole much more humane in their victory than the Cavaliers would have been had they won. Nay, suppose we Tories had won the day in America: how frightful and bloody that triumph would have been! What ropes and scaffolds one imagines, what noble heads laid low! A strange feeling this, I own: I was on the Loyalist side, and yet wanted the Whigs to win. (Chapter 40)

This was a commonly enough held view amongst Victorian liberals. What is extraordinary, however, is the degree to which Thackeray allows George Warrington to echo the views of his grandfather, Henry Esmond. Like Esmond, the thoughtful George is a Loyalist and a Cavalier by instinct and by persuasion, and, like him, he has fought bravely for a lost cause. Like Esmond, he evokes other lost battles and lost causes, but without rancour or nostalgia. As most Victorians would readily have acknowledged, the American War of Independence was resolved by a clear victory and by the formally recognised separation of Great Britain from its former Colonies. No such formal resolution marked the end of armed conflict between Royalists and Parliamentarians, or between Hanoverians and Jacobites on the islands of Britain and Ireland. In neither case was independence or separation an option. Thackeray hedges his political bets in *The Virginians*, and he allows both sides in the struggle, winners and losers, to express their convictions amicably. There were no such easy resolutions when Thackeray's Victorian contemporaries used historical fiction to explore the untidy state of domestic politics.

The American Revolution was far from bloodless, but when victory was assured on the American side, the Revolution consolidated itself without a descent into chaos and further blood-letting. Liberal-minded Europeans looked on America's peaceful transition from a raw republic to a mature republic with a mixture of admiration and envy. They well knew that the element in the 'class-less' American population that Thackeray had cruelly characterised as 'the rabble' was infinitely more vociferous and numerous in Europe. When it manifested its resentments in class-ridden England it struck some commentators as infinitely more sullen and threatening. Nearly all Victorians, whatever their politics, looked back on the urban violence of the French Revolution with an especial dread. The September Massacres in Paris, the arbitrary justice meted out in the streets by *sans culottes*, and the denunciations of class enemies before the Revolutionary Tribunal, loomed large as nightmares haunting the post-revolutionary generations. Dickens was to explore these nightmares in *A Tale of Two Cities* in 1859, but from the beginning of his career as a writer he had contemplated writing a novel concerned with the chaotic few days of urban disruption in eighteenth-century England: the Gordon Riots of 1780. The riots, stirred by the machinations of Lord George Gordon, were supposedly a protest against the minimal relief granted to George III's Roman Catholic subjects. Though Catholic chapels were to prove primary targets for the London mob's intemperate anger, the more widespread damage left London scarred and temporarily ungovernable. When he finally got down to writing *Barnaby Rudge: A Tale of the Riots of 'Eighty* in 1841 Dickens was well informed about the violence of the Reform riots of the early 1830s and was probably equally well aware of the more recent manifestations of Chartist unrest in the English provinces. He also knew Sir Walter Scott's vivid account of the so-called 'Porteous Riots' in Edinburgh of 1736 in *The Heart of Midlothian* (1818).

Barnaby Rudge is a tale about intemperance, intolerance and madness. Its central fictional character, Barnaby, is a troubled imbecile; its most important historic character is the dangerously deranged Lord George Gordon. Barnaby is caught up in the riots which rage uncontrollably about him; Gordon inspires them and delights in their progress. For Dickens, however, the problems of eighteenth-century society go far deeper than an urban propensity for riot. More than being simply an expression of a repugnance for mob rule, *Barnaby Rudge* is also an extended critique of aristocratic privilege and of what the novelist saw as the excessive influence exerted by the upper classes in Georgian England.

Barnaby's instability and powerlessness in the face of events veering out of control are reflected by parallel traits in the aristocratic Gordon. Similarly, the odious Sir John Chester's prejudices are echoes of those of one of Dickens's great bugbears, the fourth Earl of Chesterfield, the author of the *Letters written by the Right Honourable Philip Dormer Stanhope, Earl of Chesterfield to his Son* (1774). Dickens's contemporaries tended to vilify Chesterfield for his notorious neglect of Dr Johnson, but the novelist himself seems to have had a particular distaste for the *Letters*. He clearly regarded their influence as pernicious and their author as a supercilious villain. In Chapter 23 Sir John Chester is given an extraordinary apostrophe to a writer he regards as 'his country's pride':

> I thought I was tolerably accomplished as a man of the world … I flattered myself I was pretty well versed in all those little arts and graces which distinguish men of the world from boors and peasants, and separate their character from those intensely vulgar sentiments which are called the national character. Apart from any natural prepossession in my own favour, I believed I was. Still, in every page of this enlightened writer, I find some captivating hypocrisy which has never occurred to me before, or some superlative piece of selfishness to which I was utterly a stranger. I should quite blush for myself before this stupendous creature, if, remembering his precepts, one might blush at anything. An amazing man! A nobleman indeed! Any King or Queen may make a Lord, but only the Devil himself – and the Graces – can make a Chesterfield.

This is a gross distortion, of course, but Dickens was evidently grossly offended not just by Chesterfield's advocacy of dissimulation and serpentine self-promotion but also by his patrician assumptions about the virtues of 'good-breeding.' Like the diabolic 'Machiavel' invented by the Elizabethans, Dickens's Chesterfield is a convenient cynosure for everything he disliked about the surface charms that had been avidly cultivated by the more worldly aristocrats of the eighteenth century.

In *Barnaby Rudge*, as in *A Tale of Two Cities*, Dickens sees the resentments of the *lumpenproletariat* as rooted in the repressive nature of the old 'aristocratic' legal system which attempted to control dissent amongst the lower orders. Again, the narrative approaches caricature when it represents those who support the rigorous penal code of the 1780s. Ned Dennis, the public hangman who having joined the riots finally dies on the scaffold, is given a blackly comic defence of the death penalty in discussion with the sinister Gashford:

> 'I'm a constitutional officer that works for my living, and does my work creditable. Do I, or do I not?'
>
> 'Unquestionably.'
>
> 'Very good. Stop a minute. My work is sound, Protestant, constitutional, English work. Is it, or is it not?'
>
> 'No man alive can doubt it.'
>
> 'Nor dead neither. Parliament says this here – says Parliament,"If any man, woman, or child, does anything which goes again a certain number of our acts" – how many hanging laws may there be at this present time, Muster Gashford? Fifty?'
>
> 'I don't exactly know how many,' replied Gashford, leaning back in his chair and yawning; 'a great number though.'
>
> 'Well, say fifty. Parliament says, "If any man, woman, or child, does anything again any of them fifty acts, that man, woman, or child, shall be worked off by Dennis." George the Third steps in when they number very strong at the end of a sessions, and says, "These are too many for Dennis. I'll have half for myself and Dennis shall have half for himself."'
> (Chapter 37)

Dennis then proceeds to tell the true story of Mary Jones, a nineteen-year-old mother who was hanged at Tyburn in 1771, 'with an infant at her breast,' for having been found guilty of attempting to steal four pieces of muslin from a shop in Ludgate Hill. 'That being the law and practice of England,' Dennis adds, 'Is the glory of England.' It then emerges that his real worry about conceding rights to Catholics is that if 'these Papists gets into power' they might begin to 'boil and roast instead of hang' and thereby render him unemployed.

As *Barnaby Rudge* vividly shows, the stringent penal code so treasured by Dennis is applied in full force once the Gordon Riots are suppressed. The State recovers its equanimity through cold-blooded, but nonetheless shocking, retribution and, as Dickens describes it, it is the most vulnerable who experience the worst the law can impose. Two wretches, found guilty of firing Lord Mansfield's house in Bloomsbury Square, are hanged in front of its ruins:

> Two cripples – both mere boys – one with a leg of wood, one who dragged his twisted limbs along by the help of a crutch, were hanged in this same Bloomsbury Square. As the cart was about to glide from under them, it was observed that they stood with their faces from, not to, the house they had assisted to despoil; and their misery was protracted that this omission might be remedied. Another boy was hanged in Bow Street; other young lads in various quarters of the town. Four wretched women, too, were put to death. In a word, those who suffered as rioters were, for the most part, the weakest, meanest, and most miserable among them. (Chapter 77)

This is the notorious 'bloody code' in action. Readers of 1841, who were still horribly familiar with public executions, were however well aware of the radical reduction of offences which carried the death penalty during Sir Robert Peel's period as Home Secretary in the years 1824-29. Nevertheless, Dickens wants to remind his readers that any nostalgia for the past was not only morally hazardous, it was founded on idle sentiment. However questionable the morals and practices of the present might appear, the eighteenth-century example offered no alternative vision. In his parody of the song 'A Fine Old English Gentleman', written at the same time as *Barnaby Rudge*, he savaged the 'Young England' mentality that looked back to 'the good old times':

> The good old laws were garnished well with gibbets, whips and chains,
> With fine old English penalties and fine old English pains,
> With rebel heads and seas of blood once hot in rebel veins,
> For all these things were requisite to guard the rich old gains
> Of fine old English Tory times,
> Soon may they come again.

Dickens's satire refers not simply to the 'bloody code' but also to the executions which followed the suppression of the Jacobite rebellion of 1745. As he reminded readers of *A Tale of Two Cities*, severed heads had regularly been exposed on Temple Bar in London. The last such gory relics were the heads of the rebels Townley and Fletcher, who had been decapitated in 1746. Though the last head apparently blew down in a gale in 1772, Dickens's acquaintance

Samuel Rogers (who died at the age of 92 in 1855) remembered having seen 'a black shapeless lump' on a spike of Temple Bar in his youth.[50] Thus, once in a while, the darker side of the eighteenth century still flickered into life in an age that fondly hoped it had happily left much of that darkness behind.

HOGARTH AND FIELDING

In 1843 Dickens paid the painter William Powell Frith £40 for two canvasses based on subjects from his novels. One showed *Kate Nickleby at Madame Mantalini's*; the other *Dolly Varden, looking back at her lover* (fig.88). Dickens hung both pictures in his dining room at Gad's Hill Place, but when he died in 1870 the two pictures fared very differently at the subsequent auction. The *Kate Nickleby* fetched £210, but the picture of the *Dolly Varden* from *Barnaby Rudge*, described in the sale catalogue as 'a masterpiece,' went for the extraordinary sum of £1,050. The reason for this stark disparity in price had little to do with the artistic merit of the two pictures but lay in the fact that by the early 1870s, Dolly Varden's eighteenth-century style dress was about to take on a fashionable life of its own. Frith had in fact made a series of paintings of Dolly Varden, Dickens's being the third version (the second version is in the Victoria and Albert Museum). The subject attracted the painter because it gave him the opportunity to paint a costume that contrasted with 'the ugliness of modern dress,' and he apparently used his grandmother's wedding dress as a model. He consequently showed Dolly as a smiling coquette dressed in a cherry-coloured mantle, a white silk dress, pinafore and a hooped-up chintz overskirt. Frith's paintings helped foster a new dress style for younger women described as 'a form of Polonaise, its essential feature being its material, chintz or cretonne, the underskirt being bright silk or cotton.' The 'Dolly Varden Hat,' which complemented the dress, had a crown surrounded by ribbon trimming and was decorated with what were described by contemporary writers as 'follow-me-lads' streamers.[51] Frith's picture does not, however, show its subject in anything like the 'Dolly Varden Hat' and her dress is predominantly of wedding dress colours. It would seem, therefore, that the real inspiration for the fashion was Dickens himself and his illustrator 'Phiz' (Hablot Knight Browne). Browne's engraved illustrations to Chapters 21 and 22, for example, show Dolly dressed very much in the manner adopted in the 1870s. The 'Dolly Varden' was conspicuously English in its appeal, perhaps as a

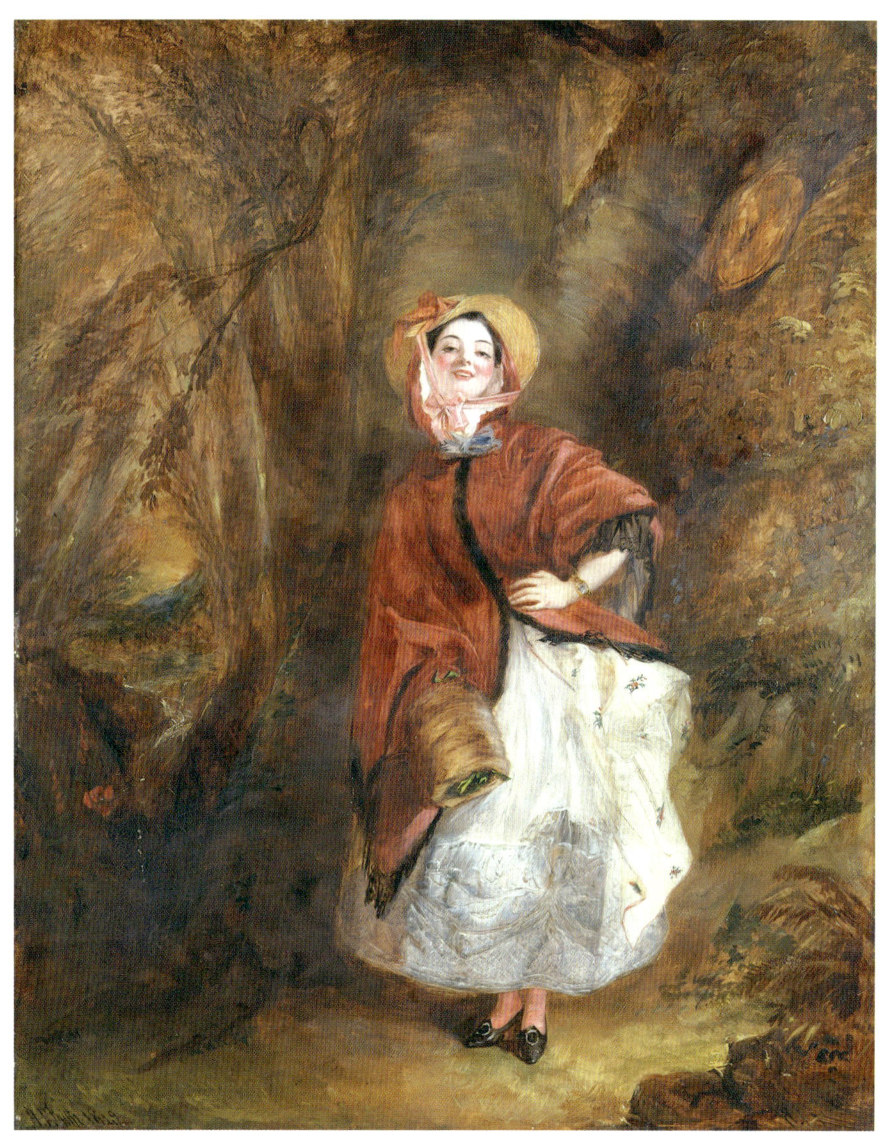

88 William Powell Frith,
Dolly Varden, 1842, Oil on
canvas, 54.6 x 44.5cm.
Victoria & Albert
Museum

consequence of the temporary eclipse of the Parisian salons after the collapse of
Napoleon III's government and the occupation of the city in 1870-71 by
victorious German troops. As Millais's *The Minuet* of 1864 also suggests, the vogue
for anything that could remotely be described as 'Queen Anne' (that is,

eighteenth century) could certainly include costume. The society magazine *The Queen* described the ideal wearer of the 'Dolly Varden' as if she were a version of Dickens's 'gay' Dolly herself. She would display her 'simple beauty, her trimness, her tinge of pertness and coquetry, her briskness, and under all these her modesty, her constancy, her truth, and her purest of pure hearts.' Dolly was effectively now the type 'of our national, our English maidenhood.'[52]

Dickens's illustrators, most notably 'Phiz' and George Cruikshank (who only worked on *Sketches by 'Boz'* and *Oliver Twist*), fixed visual impressions of the novelist's characters in his readers' minds which have lasted into the twenty-first century. The 'Dolly Varden' fashion is but the most conspicuous example of how the representation of a certain costume became inseparable from the way in which readers imagined a character. 'Phiz,' in particular, had for most of his career a close relationship with the author he illustrated, and Dickens appears to have been both very precise and very demanding in his instructions. In one crucial area, however, 'Phiz' had freedom of invention: he could add telling physical details in his illustrations that offered wry extra comment on the scene verbally described by Dickens. Particularly subtle in this respect is the illustration to Chapter 31 of *Dombey and Son* (1846–47) which shows the new Mr. and Mrs. Dombey arriving back at their grand house following their wedding. The leading characters are much as Dickens defines them, but 'Phiz' has added details in the background that indicate that the marriage will be less than serene and will ultimately be doomed to failure. The footmen at the door appear to be passing unfavourable comment on the couple; there is a noisy street-band and, amid the curious bystanders, is a pair of fighting (or sexually aroused) dogs. In the distance a Punch and Judy show in the street does not promise a happy match, and the funeral procession at the far right of the picture suggests an even unhappier augury. The illustrator's invention is both true to the spirit of Dickens and to the idiosyncrasies of the artist's own style. Original readers would also have detected that such visual commentary was profoundly indebted to the example of William Hogarth.

Dickens was a dedicated admirer of Hogarth. Prints of the artist's work decorated his homes and served as daily reminders to him of Hogarth's invention. His ready familiarity with Hogarthian imagery is evident throughout his fiction and the very word 'progress' in the subtitle of *Oliver Twist* ('The Parish Boy's Progress') recalled two of the most famous of Hogarth's narrative sequences. In his 'Author's Preface' to the third edition of the novel he described the artist as 'the moralist, and censor of his age – in whose great works the times in which he lived, and the characters of every time, will never cease to be reflected.' Elsewhere Dickens's debts to Hogarth are subtly glancing. When, for example, the infant Paul Dombey is baptised in what is probably the new parish church of St Marylebone, the christening party has to wait for the end of a 'dismal' wedding between a bride who was too old and a bridegroom too young. The scene might well have been drawn directly from the equivalent picture in *The Rake's Progress* (where, incidentally, Hogarth had used the *old* Marylebone church as his setting). The steady appreciation of Hogarth's work stretched far beyond Dickens, however. Hogarth's images directly fed the visual imaginations of a whole range of Victorian writers and painters alike; they echoed them; they played with them; they relocated them and, above all, they responded to them as if they had an immediacy for their own time. William Powell Frith, for example, paid direct tribute to Hogarth's *Four Times of the Day* in his unfinished *Morning: Covent Garden* and its companion pieces, *Noon: Regent Street* and *Night: Haymarket* (all 1862) and in his two wonderful narrative series, *The Road to Ruin* (1878) and *The Race for Wealth* (1882). When the former was displayed at the Royal Academy the pictures proved so popular that 'the policemen and the rail' were required to protect them from an admiring public.[53] Like Hogarth's, Frith's images obtained even wider currency thanks to the circulation of well-engraved reproductions of the original paintings.

During the opening half of the nineteenth century some of Hogarth's most famous paintings had begun to enter public collections. In 1837 Sir John Soane had bequeathed his eclectic collection to the nation, a collection which included both *The Rake's Progress* and *The Election* (which Soane had purchased for £598 and £1732 respectively). Visitors to Soane's house in Lincoln's Inn Fields were required to acquire tickets from the new museum's trustees, and both access and the days of opening were considerably restricted. Nevertheless, the Hogarths were regarded as a major attraction, despite what one guidebook described as the 'ingenious contrivances' which enabled them all to be displayed in the relatively constricted space in the Picture Room.[54] In 1839 when the newly established National Gallery opened in its Trafalgar Square building it was able to display both Hogarth's *Marriage à la Mode* and the artist's self-portrait with his pug. These pictures had been purchased in 1824, but it was to take another sixty years before any more of the artist's works entered the national collection.[55] In the 1850s the pictures were moved temporarily to Marlborough House, which is where Thackeray, who regarded *Marriage à la Mode* as 'the most important and highly wrought of Hogarth's comedies,' urged audiences at his lectures on the *English Humourists* to go and see them. *Marriage à la Mode* seems generally to have been interpreted as predominantly didactic in intent and as a pertinent morality tale. In 1834 the *Penny Magazine* saw the series as showing the kind of ruin that would only cease when all social classes 'learn to seek for happiness in the exercise and cultivation of the higher qualities in their nature.'[56] Thackeray's friend, Sir Henry Cole, told readers of his penny guide to the National Gallery in the 1840s that the paintings were likely to 'speak to the comprehension' of working men, while 1888 Edward T. Cook's *A Popular Handbook to the National Gallery* instructed visitors that 'as an accurate delineation of the surroundings of the high life of the eighteenth century, the pictures have never been assailed,' adding that they were '*historical* paintings of the utmost value.' To clinch his point Cook quoted Ruskin's precept that Hogarth rose 'not by painting Athenian follies, but London follies.'[57]

'Apart from the intrinsic merit of his pictures,' Cook's *Handbook* also advises visitors that 'Hogarth should be especially interesting as the first man of genius in the native British School.' He then proceeds to give readers a brief biographical sketch and a somewhat patronising critique of his art:

> He is often described as being 'more of a satirist than an artist'; but this is hardly so. He was a satirist because he was so faithful an artist … Hogarth had … a direct moral intention in his holding up of nature's glass; and herein is perhaps the secret of his greatness. But whilst the greatest English artists have never followed art for the sake of pleasure only, on the other hand no great artist ever followed art without pleasure. Hogarth is no exception to this rule.[58]

This sounds like a devout Ruskinian aphoristically hedging his bets. As Cook well knew (for he quotes both authorities), Hogarth's reputation did not really need defending. Some eighteen paintings by Hogarth, nearly all from private collections, had been displayed in the 'Paintings by Modern Masters' section of the great 'Art Treasures of the United Kingdom' held at Manchester in 1857. Earlier in the century both Charles Lamb and Thackeray had published deeply appreciative critiques of his achievement, though both writers seem to have been more inclined to *read* Hogarth's paintings rather than analyse their visual effects. Lamb had put the case in the extreme, claiming in his essay *On the Genius and Character of Hogarth* that the artist's 'graphic representations are indeed books' and that they 'have the teeming, fruitful, suggestive meaning of *words*'. Thackeray, on the other hand, seems to have most relished Hogarth as an unequalled social chronicler:

> To the student of history, these admirable works must be invaluable, as they give us the most complete and truthful picture of the manners, and even the thoughts of the past century. We look, and see pass before us the England of a hundred years ago … We may depend upon the perfect accuracy of these strange and varied portraits of the bygone generation.[59]

It was under Thackeray's editorship of the *Cornhill Magazine* in 1860 that George Augustus Sala published his nine articles on 'William Hogarth: Painter, Engraver, and Philosopher.' The essays are vivid, observant, sparklingly written, and full of modern instances. Sala sees Hogarth in a context that is both historic and contemporary. In his ninth essay he defends his own contention that 'Hogarth was *not* capable of the dignified in art' by insisting that the artist's lack of 'dignity' was more than compensated for by his mastery of 'seriousness.' His defence calls upon the supporting evidence of a string of examples drawn from nineteenth-century painting:

> He could be serious indeed; terribly and truly serious. Hang up the gambling-house scene, the duel in the bedroom scene, the harlot's death scene, or *Gin Lane*, by the side of Scheffer's *Faust and Mephisto on the Blocksburg*, of Delaroche's *Cromwell looking on the body of Charles I.*, of Décamp's *Morte*, of Edwin Landseer's *Shepherd's Chief Mourner* – and William Hogarth will keep his ground for solemn truth, for sober tragedy, for the reality, the domesticity of grief and terror.[60]

Hogarth is, therefore, rightfully accorded his place amongst the most esteemed modern painters. In a later essay Sala moves beyond Hogarth's emotional impact to acclaim his genius as a colourist. He again provides a specific context:

> His colour is deliciously pure and fresh; he never loads, never spatters paint about with his palette knife; never lays tint over tint till a figure

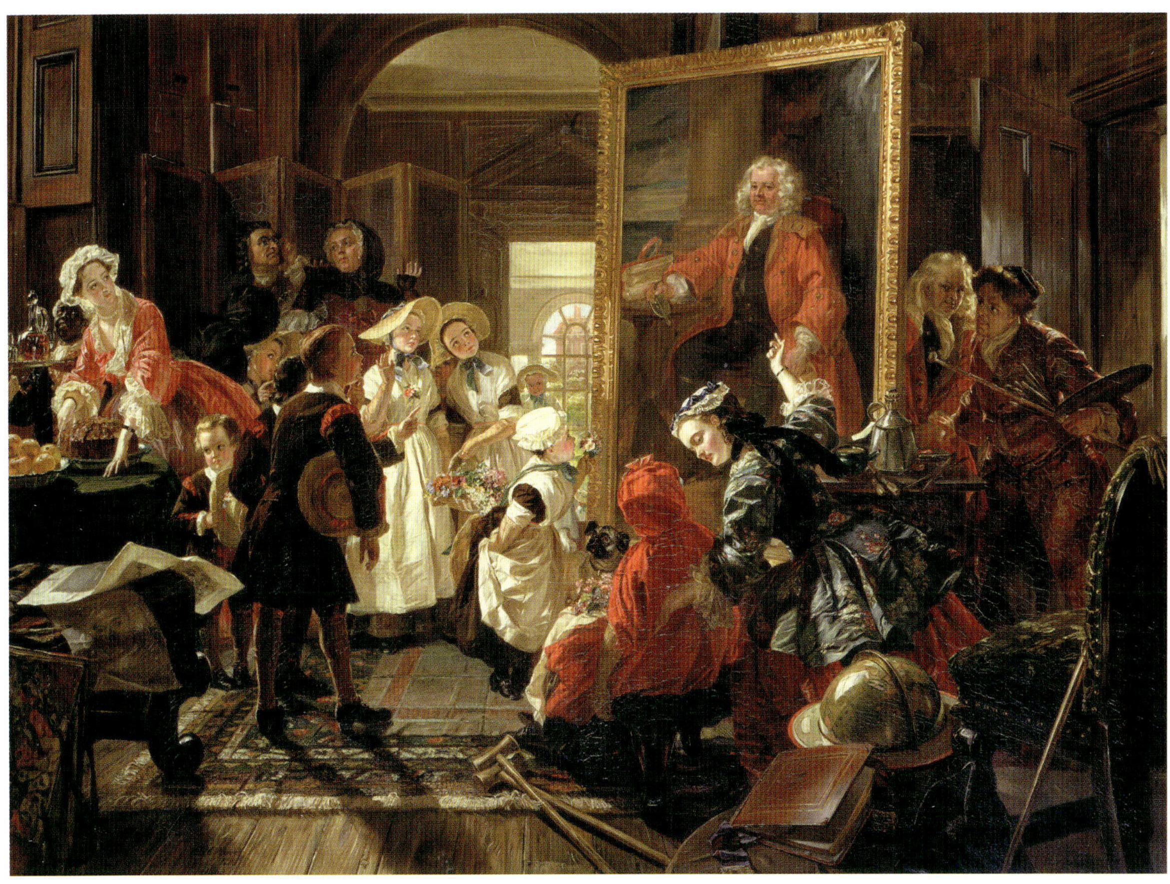

89 Edward Matthew Ward,
*Hogarth's Studio in 1739 –
Holiday Visits of the
Foundlings to View the
Portrait of Captain Coram*,
1863, Oil on canvas,
120.6 x 165.1 cm.
York Art Gallery

has as many vests as the gravedigger in *Hamlet*. Whites, grays, carnations
stand in his pictures and defy time; no uncertain glazings have changed
his foregrounds into smears and streaks and stains. He was great at
Manchester in 1857; great at the British Institution in 1814, when not
less than fifty of his works were exhibited, great in body, richness,
transparency; he is great, nay, prodigious, in the English section of the
National Gallery, where gorgeous Sir Joshua, alas! runs and welters and
turns into adipocere; and Gainsborough … grows pallid and threadbare,
and Turner's suns are grimed, and even Wilkie cracks and tessellates.[61]

A quotation from one of Sala's *Cornhill* essays accompanied the exhibition in 1863 of Edward Matthew Ward's fine painting: *Hogarth's Studio in 1739 – Holiday Visits of the Foundlings to View the Portrait of Captain Coram* (fig.89). Ward's painting had a particular currency beyond Sala's essays, for in 1857 Hogarth's great portrait of Coram had been lent to the Manchester Art Treasures exhibition by the Foundling Hospital. Ward's love of exactly representing historical costume is again very evident, though there would have been relatively little change in the clothes worn by the foundling children who are admiring the finished portrait. The smallest boy, however, has his eyes on a cake and a bowl of oranges provided by his generous host. A crippled girl to the fore has put her crutches down in order to have the excellence of the picture of Coram explained to her by a fashionably dressed woman. Hogarth's pug, Trump, can be glimpsed behind her. In the shadows to the right, stands Hogarth himself, palette in hand, waiting with uncharacteristic anxiety for responses to his art (or perhaps to his open hospitality). We are presented with Hogarth the painter and Hogarth the generous patron of the Foundling Hospital. But Ward gives us more. This a picture of a singularly well-appointed artist's studio and, more importantly, it is a painter's tribute to a fellow artist and to the inspirational quality of art itself.

The one painting of Hogarth's that clearly most attracted and absorbed Thackeray was one that must also have been very familiar to Ward. This was the self-portrait with the pug, Trump, acquired by the National Gallery in 1824. Here was the man himself and, looking at the picture, Thackeray evidently felt that he could come face to face with a man after his own heart:

> In the National Gallery most of us have seen … the portrait of his own honest face, of which the bright blue eyes shine out from the canvass and give you an idea of that keen and brave look with which William Hogarth regarded the world. No man was ever less of a hero; you see him before you, and can fancy what he was – a jovial, honest, London citizen, stout and sturdy; a hearty, plain-spoken man, loving his laugh, his friends, his glass, his roast-beef of Old England, and having a proper bourgeois scorn for French frogs, for mounseers, and wooden shoes in general, for foreign fiddlers, foreign singers, and, above all, for foreign painters, whom he held in the most amusing contempt.[62]

One suspects that Hogarth might have been rather taken with this tribute. It was, after all, an echo of many of the things he said about himself.

Thackeray seems to have identified himself as much with Henry Fielding as he did with Hogarth, but he had one considerable reservation: Fielding's work 'was not good reading for women, & only for a small race of men.'[63] This was a commonly held prejudice amongst Victorian commentators. Although Thackeray told his audience in his lecture on Fielding in the *English Humourists* series that he loved to recognise 'the brave and gentle heart' and the 'intrepid and courageous spirit' of 'the English Harry Fielding,' he had earlier attempted to define the problem raised in Victorian minds by that spirit:

> The world does not tolerate now such satire as that of Hogarth and Fielding, and the world no doubt is right in a great part of its squeamishness; for it is good to pretend to the virtue of chastity even though we do not possess it; nay, the very restraint which the hypocrisy lays on a man, is not unapt, in some instances, to profit him. But any man who has walked through Regent Street of a night, or has been behind the scenes of the Opera, or has even been to a theatre, and looked up to that delectable part of the house, the second tier of boxes, must know that the *Rake's* and *Harlot's Progress* is still by no means concluded … The same vice exists, only we don't speak about it; the same things are done, but we don't call them by their names.[64]

In 1850 Thackeray had famously informed readers of his novel *Pendennis* that since Fielding's death 'no writer of fiction … has been permitted to depict to his utmost power a *man*. We must drape him, and give him a certain conventional simper.' Here at least he seems to be admitting that moral squeamishness is an unhappy restriction upon the modern English writer. But Thackeray knew his readers, and through long experience of his own mother's Evangelical Christianity he was very familiar with the pervasive cultural force of 'middle-class morality.' Thackeray may have rued the strength of the modern 'hypocrisy' that precluded the composition of a modern *Tom Jones*, but his contemporaries did not necessarily notice that such 'hypocrisy' was problematic. Charlotte Brontë, for one, felt that Thackeray had gone too far in his defence of *Tom Jones* in his lecture. She was clearly recalling her late brother Branwell's less than exemplary life and his susceptibility to temptation:

> Had Thackeray owned a son, grown or growing up, and a son brilliant but reckless – would he have spoken in that light way of courses that lead to disgrace and the grave? … Had I a brother yet living, I should tremble to let him read Thackeray's lecture on Fielding … Not that for a moment I would have had Thackeray *abuse* Fielding, or even pharisaically to condemn his life; but I do most deeply grieve that it never entered into his heart sadly and nearly to feel the peril of such a career, that he might have dedicated some of his great strength to a potent warning against its adoption by any young man. I believe temptation often assails the finest manly natured, as the pecking sparrow or destructive wasp attacks the sweetest and mellowest fruit, eschewing what is sour and crude.[65]

Charles Dickens too, who revered Fielding devoutly enough to name one of his sons after him, was wary of admitting to his readers that the moral atmosphere of *Tom Jones* was wholesome. In Chapter 4 of *David Copperfield* the hero describes the 'small collection of books' that he devours in the period of his boyhood neglect. They are, we guess, the same books that the boy Dickens read and they include *Tom Jones*. 'They did me no harm,' David insists, 'for whatever harm was in some of them was not there for me; *I* knew nothing of it.' In case we miss which of the books he is referring to, he stresses that, though he had imaginatively 'impersonated' the characters in these books, he had been 'a child's Tom Jones, a harmless creature.' Too young therefore to be tempted, and we assume too innocent to understand what Fielding was talking about. It is very possible that Thackeray was commenting on this very passage in *David Copperfield* when he has his own admirable character, Colonel Newcome, admit that he read both *Joseph Andrews* and *Tom Jones* as a boy, when he 'kept other bad company, and did other low disgraceful things' (*The Newcomes*, Chapter 4). The aged Colonel claims that he was 'a wild young rebel' then, but as a man of mature years even the thought of the 'ruffian' Tom Jones makes his blood boil.

If mid-Victorian boys seemed to have been warned away from reading Fielding, it was generally assumed that mid-Victorian women would find him coarse and unpalatable. But it was not any supposed incitement to promiscuity that appears to have offended George Eliot; rather it was Fielding's delight in prolixity. In the opening of Chapter 5 of the first book of *Middlemarch* (1871) Eliot compares her own narrative art to Fielding's, and her own preliminary comments on the world to the long initial chapters to each of the Books into which *Tom Jones* is divided. This is where, she tells us, Fielding seems to 'bring his armchair to the proscenium and chat with us in all the lusty ease of his fine English.' But it is neither the domestic armchair nor the theatrical proscenium that strike her as problematic, so much as the awareness that no Victorian novelist can afford the same lengthy digressions from the line of the narrative:

> Fielding lived when the days were longer (for time, like money, is measured by our needs), when summer afternoons were spacious, and the clock ticked slowly in the winter evenings. We belated historians must not linger after his example; and if we did so, it is probable that our chat would be thin and eager, as if delivered from a camp-stool in a parrot-house.

This may strike some twenty-first-century readers of the far-from-succinct *Middlemarch* as perverse. Nevertheless, what Eliot seems to be saying is that her perception both of time and of the novelist's craft is radically different from Fielding's. Time in her modern, industrialised and mechanised world moved faster than in the mid-eighteenth century, and latter-day readers were likely to be more impatient with philosophical speculations on what she styles 'the tempting range of relevancies called the universe.' Such modern speculations might indeed prove as thinly inarticulate in the modern world as they would in the parrot-house. Eliot caricatures Fielding as a venerably benign colossus, one whose stature was now conditioned by her present. Fielding's fiction does not, therefore, provide the modern novelist with an imitable model. Eliot's admiring biographer, Leslie Stephen, seems to have sought to echo her arguments in his *English Thought in the Eighteenth Century* in 1876. Stephen too sees Fielding as exemplary of his time, and his fiction as representative of an old-fashioned, but, in its way, admirable enough, art:

> For insight into the motives of his contemporaries; for a power of seeing things as they are; for sympathy with homely virtues; and contempt for shams and hypocrites, Fielding is as superior to some later writers of equal imaginative force as they are superior to him in width of sympathy and delicacy of perception. His art is thus the most faithful representative of his age; he gives its coarseness and its brutalities, and sometimes with too little consciousness of their evils, though no one ever satirised more powerfully the worst abuses of the time. But he also represents the

strong, healthy common sense and stubborn honesty of the sound English nature, with a certain massive power of grouping and colouring which is peculiar to himself.[66]

This then is a big-boned, plain-speaking, overtly comic Fielding, but one who lacked the nuanced delicacy that later-nineteenth-century critics like Stephen expected of the novels of their own time. Fielding was too defiantly 'English,' but was all too often deemed to be deficient in what later Victorians most admired in the high culture of the preceding century. For Margaret Oliphant, writing in 1882, Fielding was essentially 'robust' and he wrote books that 'were not meant for women.'[67] For the over-fastidious George Meredith in his *An Essay on Comedy* of 1877 Fielding was merely a 'humourist' working in the 'bad tradition of comedy.'[68] Far more damning was the common enough critical assumption that Fielding's defiant Englishness defined him as inferior to his subtler, neater, and infinitely more cynical French contemporaries. Whether didactically seated in his armchair or relishing the low-life of country inns and London streets, Fielding had signally failed to represent the crafted, genteel, narrative subtlety that had a distinct appeal for those late-Victorians who felt that their own art cried out for more refinement.

Dr Johnson as Hero

Horace Walpole, whom Macaulay typified in one of his essays as 'the most Frenchified writer of the eighteenth century,' had little love for Fielding's work. Fielding had, Walpole complained in 1785, 'no idea of grace' and was 'perpetually disgusting.' He had, moreover, concentrated on the more unpleasant side of life: 'His innkeepers and parsons are the grossest in their profession, and his gentlemen are awkward when they should be at their ease.'[69] Walpole would, however, have found some support for his claim that Fielding lacked 'grace' in Samuel Johnson's antipathetic response to a novelist whom he felt appealed to 'a more superficial observer.' In a famous exchange with Boswell, Johnson claimed that Samuel Richardson, a writer who had dived 'into the recesses of the human heart,' was the more satisfying novelist. Boswell records:

> In comparing those two writers he used this expression; 'that there was
> as great a difference between them as between a man who knew how

a watch was made, and a man who could tell the hour by looking on the dial-plate.' This was a short and figurative state of his distinction between drawing characters of Nature and characters only of manners.[70]

Boswell, who was far from inclined to agree with Johnson's prejudice, goes on to insist that he found the 'moral tendency of Fielding's writings … ever favourable to honour and honesty, and cherishes the benevolent and generous affections.' He thus gives the impression of having the last say in an argument which he doubtless would not have been allowed to win in Johnson's presence.

Such exchanges lie at the core of Boswell's *Life of Johnson* and they were one of the reasons why the biography was so admired by Victorian commentators. For Macaulay it was 'assuredly a great, a very great work.' He then went on to justify this bold claim with a series of disarming observations concerning Boswell's intellectual and emotional limitations:

> We are not sure that there is in the whole history of the human intellect so strange a phænomenon as this book. Many of the greatest men that ever lived have written biography. Boswell was one of the smallest men that ever lived, and he has beaten them all … All the caprices of his temper, all the illusions of his vanity, all his hypochondriac whimsies, all his castles in the air, he displayed with a cool self-complacency, a perfect unconsciousness that he was making a fool of himself, to which it is impossible to find a parallel in the whole history of mankind.[71]

Here, therefore, was a book great in spite of its author. Boswell was a talentless writer, we are told: he was 'a dunce, a parasite, and a coxcomb' but his 'quick observation and a retentive memory' gave him an edge over more able men. What made his book great, of course, was the enthralling picture it gave of its subject. Boswell had given Johnson not just immortality, but a happily congenial posthumous presence:

> What a singular destiny has been that of this remarkable man! To be regarded in his own age as a classic, and in ours as a companion! To receive from his contemporaries that full homage which men of genius have in general only received from posterity! To be more intimately known to posterity than other men are known to their contemporaries!

That kind of fame which is commonly the most transient is, in his case, the most durable. The reputation of those writings, which he probably expected to be immortal, is every day fading; while those peculiarities of manner and that careless table-talk the memory of which he probably thought, would die with him, are likely to be remembered as long as the English language is spoken in any quarter of the globe.[72]

Macaulay is claiming that Boswell's *Life of Johnson* made Johnson uniquely familiar to the generations that came after him. Macaulay reiterated this point in the short biography of Johnson that he contributed to the *Encyclopædia Britannica* in 1856:

Since his death the popularity of his works … has greatly diminished … An allusion to his Rambler or his Idler is not readily apprehended in literary circles. The fame even of Rasselas has grown somewhat dim. But though the celebrity of his writings may have declined, the celebrity of the writer, strange to say, is as great as ever. Boswell's book has done for him more than the best of his own books could do.[73]

That Johnson's works seemed more than a little old-fashioned by the third decade of the nineteenth century is made delightfully clear in Miss Jenkyns's preference for them over Dickens's in the first story in Elizabeth Gaskell's *Cranford* (1851). That Johnson himself was a familiar reference point, however, is evident in the second *Cranford* story when Miss Matty remarks of Mr Holbrook's book-lined counting-house that 'it must be like one of the great Dr. Johnson's rooms.' When it is pointed out that Mr Holbrook is 'a great reader' and 'an eccentric' ('clever people always are') we sense the degree to which the spirit of Johnson haunts the imaginations of the faded Cranford ladies. Thanks to Boswell, the great man lived and argued as if he were some admired but slightly remote contemporary of theirs.

Boswell's Johnson was as an admirable figure, never heroic in the narrow sense of the term, but equally never commonplace. As Macaulay splendidly put it:

no human being who has been more than seventy years in the grave is so well known to us. And it is but just to say that our intimate acquaintance with what he would himself have called the anfractuosities

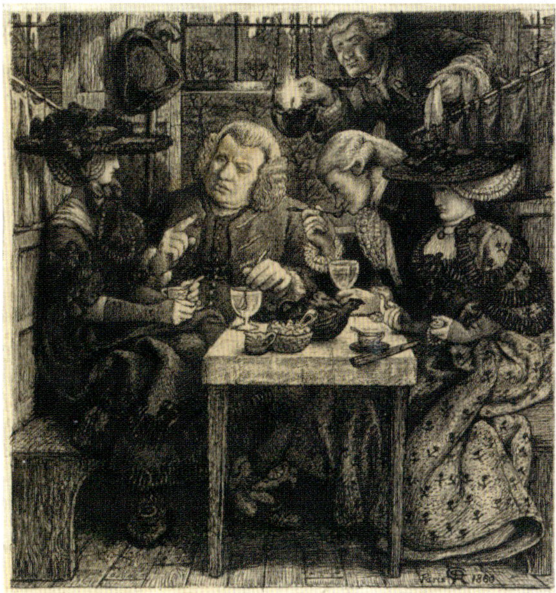

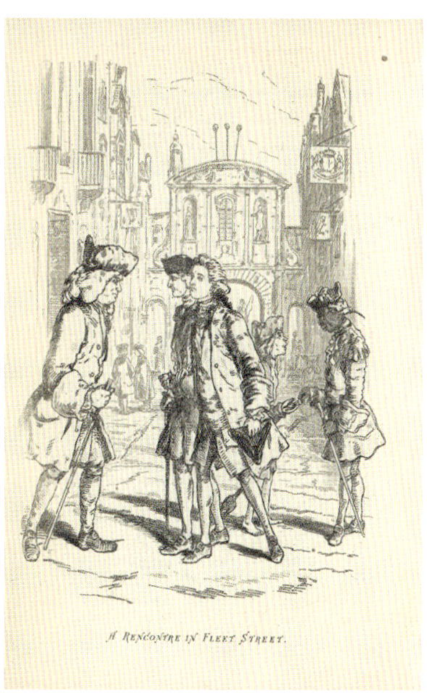

of his intellect and of his temper, serves only to strengthen our conviction that he was both a great and a good man.

What Macaulay is also implying is that, far more so than any novel by Fielding or any painting by Hogarth, the *Life of Johnson* had rendered cultural life in late eighteenth-century London singularly familiar to the nineteenth century.

The easy intimacy with which some Victorians approached the slightly gauche, unheroic Johnson is evident in Dante Gabriel Rossetti's intense pen and ink drawing *Dr Johnson at the Mitre* (fig.90). The drawing, with which Rossetti was sufficiently pleased for him to make a watercolour replica a year later, shows Johnson seated in a stall at the Mitre Tavern, accompanied by Boswell and two ladies. The Doctor is outlining his thoughts, raising his right finger in the process, and stirring a glass with a spoon in his left hand; one of the ladies, tea-cup in hand, looks intently at Johnson; the other has an air of impatience. Boswell, meantime, sips his drink from a spoon, while a waiter tends the overhead lamp. Rossetti took the incident from Boswell's account of the visit to Johnson of 'two women from Staffordshire … to consult him on the subject of Methodism, to which they were inclined.' 'Come,' Johnson said, 'You pretty fools, dine with Maxwell and me at the Mitre and we will talk over that subject.' After dinner,

90 Dante Gabriel Rossetti, *Dr Johnson at the Mitre*, 1860, Black ink on paper, support 22.2 x 21.7 cm. The Fitzwilliam Museum, Cambridge

91 Plate illustrating Samuel Johnson in *The Virginians* by William Makepeace Thackeray, 1857-59. Private collection

'he took one of them on his knee and fondled them for half-an-hour together.' The dining companion on this occasion was in fact not Boswell but Dr William Maxwell, but Rossetti evidently found the biographer more suitable as an ineffective chaperon than a clergyman (though Johnson has as yet made no move to take a lady on his knee).[74]

When Johnson is briefly observed as a passing figure in Thackeray's *The Virginians* he cuts an ungainly, and decidedly unfashionable figure: a 'great big awkward pock-marked, snuff coloured man' of whom Lord March remarks, 'he has never changed the shape of that hat of his for twenty years' (Chapter 25). Johnson is encountered again in Chapter 36 and Thackeray himself provided an illustration of 'this shabby-looking big man' crossing The Strand in front of Temple Bar, which is still clearly adorned with severed Jacobite heads (fig.91). It is on this occasion that Harry Warrington is warned about the problem with literary men by the obsequious lawyer, Mr Draper: 'the less you have to do with that kind of person, the better. The business we have in our office about them literary men is not very pleasant, I can tell you.' Thackeray's first readers may well have recalled at this point that the novelist himself had spoken of men of letters in a very different way in the concluding paragraph of the last of his *English Humourists* lectures:

> Does society look down on a man because he is an author? I suppose if people want a buffoon they tolerate him only in so far as he is amusing; it can hardly be expected that they should respect him as an equal. Is there to be a guard of honour provided for the author of the last new novel or poem? … The great world, the great aggregate experience, has its good sense, as it has its good humour. It detects a pretender, as it trusts a loyal heart. It is kind in the main: how should it be otherwise than kind, when it is so wise and clear-headed? To any literary man who says, 'It despises my profession,' I say, with all my might – no, no, no. It may pass over your individual case … but it treats you as you merit in the main. If you serve it, it is not unthankful; if you please it, it is pleased; if you cringe to it, it detects you, and scorns you if you are mean; it returns your cheerfulness with its good humour; it deals not ungenerously with your weaknesses; it recognizes most kindly your merits; it gives you a fair place and fair play.[75]

This is as stout a defence of both the 'man of letters' and of his public as we could wish for. In this lecture Thackeray was addressing the case of Oliver Goldsmith, a writer he particularly admired and one who had found an honoured place in Dr Johnson's circle. He is also, of course, speaking from his own experience as a writer while, at the same time, making common cause with the eighteenth-century writers whom he sees as enjoying 'an unceasing tribute of applause, admiration, love [and] sympathy.' What especially links him to the writers of the previous century, however, is the awareness that all of them had been obliged to depend on their readers for a living. As Thackeray's audience would have been keenly aware, the key 'man of letters' was the one who had been obliged to forge his career without the patronage of the villainous Lord Chesterfield: Samuel Johnson.

In May 1840, in the last of his highly influential lectures on *Heroes and Hero-Worship*, Thomas Carlyle had chosen to speak on the subject of 'The Hero as Man of Letters.' For Carlyle this last kind of hero was the quintessentially modern man:

> He is new, I say; he has hardly lasted above a century in the world yet. Never, till about a hundred years ago, was there seen any figure of a Great Soul living apart in that anomalous manner; endeavouring to speak-forth the inspiration that was in him by Printed Books, and find place and subsistence by what the world would please to give him for doing that … He, with his copy-rights and copy-wrongs, in his squalid garret, in his rusty coat; ruling (for that is what he does), from his grave, after death, whole nations and generations who would, or would not, give him bread while living, – is rather a curious spectacle! Few shapes of Heroism can be more unexpected.[76]

This is full-blooded Romanticism and it would seem to require, as illustrations of the contention, Byronic rebels or at the very least hungry bohemians scribbling away in their Parisian attics. In fact, Carlyle's three examples of heroic writers are all successful eighteenth-century men who shared a relatively humble birth: Johnson, Rousseau and Burns. It is Johnson for whom Carlyle harbours a particular affection and on whose head he heaps the greatest praise:

> As for Johnson, I have always considered him to be, by nature, one of our greatest English souls. A strong and noble man; so much left

undeveloped in him to the last: in a kindlier element what might he not have been, – Poet, Priest, sovereign Ruler! On the whole, a man must not complain of his 'element,' of his 'time,' or the like; it is thriftless work doing so. His time is bad: well then, he is there to make it better! – Johnson's youth was poor, isolated, hopeless, very miserable. Indeed, it does not seem possible that, in any the favourablest circumstances, Johnson's life could have been other than a painful one … Yet a giant invincible soul; a true man's.[77]

What we see here is Carlyle casting Johnson in the role of the hero, not only of his own time but also of the new age. He is not the man of the moment, or the man of destiny, but he remains the modest modern hero who masters both the moment and his particular destiny. He is above all a writer who struggles to realise his calling, and moreover one who is aware that his calling is to work within the framework of a divinely order universe:

Very curious how, in that poor Paper-age, so barren, artificial, thick-quilted with Pedantries, Hearsays, the great Fact of this Universe glared in, forever wonderful, indubitable, unspeakable; divine-infernal, upon this man too! How he harmonised his Formulas with it, how he managed at all under such circumstances: that is a thing worth seeing. A thing 'to be looked at with reverence, with pity, with awe.' That Church of St. Clement Danes, where Johnson still *worshipped* in the era of Voltaire, is to me a venerable place.[78]

This devout, coping, ultra-capable, self-made Johnson is wrenched out of his time and steadily remoulded into an extraordinary shape by Carlyle's heady rhetoric. Finally, almost unrecognisably, he is clothed in the fluttering mantle of a prophet:

Johnson was a Prophet to his people; preached a Gospel to them, — as all like him always do. The highest Gospel he preached we may describe as a kind of Moral Prudence: 'in a world where much is to be done, and little is to be known,' see how you will *do* it! A thing well worth preaching … such Gospel Johnson preached and taught; — coupled, theoretically and practically, with this other great Gospel, 'Clear your mind of Cant!' Have no trade with Cant: stand on the cold mud in the frosty weather, but let it be in your own *real* torn shoes; 'that will be better for you,' as Mahomet says!

This is no longer the awkward, shabby, familiar Johnson of Boswell's biography, but a man transfigured. This too is an eighteenth-century figure required to serve as the heroic inspiration to another, post-Romantic age. He has, as Carlyle sees it, passed through a veil, but not into any hidden inner sanctum. The veil in this case is one formed by forces that Johnson himself would not have recognised: Revolutionary and Romantic thought. But, as the man of sense rather than of sensibility, he has endured 'that waste of Scepticism in religion and politics, in life-theory and life-practice' and, heroic to the end, 'To the Spirit of Lies, bearing death and hunger, he would in no wise strike his flag.'

§

Carlyle's Johnson may seem to latter day readers to have precious little to do with the real Samuel Johnson.[79] Like Effie Millais dancing to an unheard minuet, or like the Mahlerian forces playing Handel in the Crystal Palace, this Carlylean re-invention typifies how Victorian culture sought to overlay that of the century before. In order to make that culture part of its own, many Victorians were determined to prove that it was noble to realise what was essentially an act of imperialism. They were enforcing assimilation. As a rule, they did so with supreme confidence. Where certain elements in eighteenth-century culture proved uncomfortable, as Jonathan Swift did, they tended to adopt an air of incomprehension. Where they recognised what they suspected were incitements to immorality or coarseness, as with the case of Fielding, they exposed them as avidly as seventeenth-century Puritans might. Where they detected that there might be cultural fault lines, as with the rumblings of Jacobitism and urban riot, or with Hogarth's graphic representations of the sordid nature of moral decay, they loudly asserted fellow-feeling. It was only with the questioning of the core values that had moulded High-Victorian England in the last twenty years of the nineteenth century that Victorian observers began to idealise the supposed refinements of a literature and a visual culture that were distinctly unlike their own.

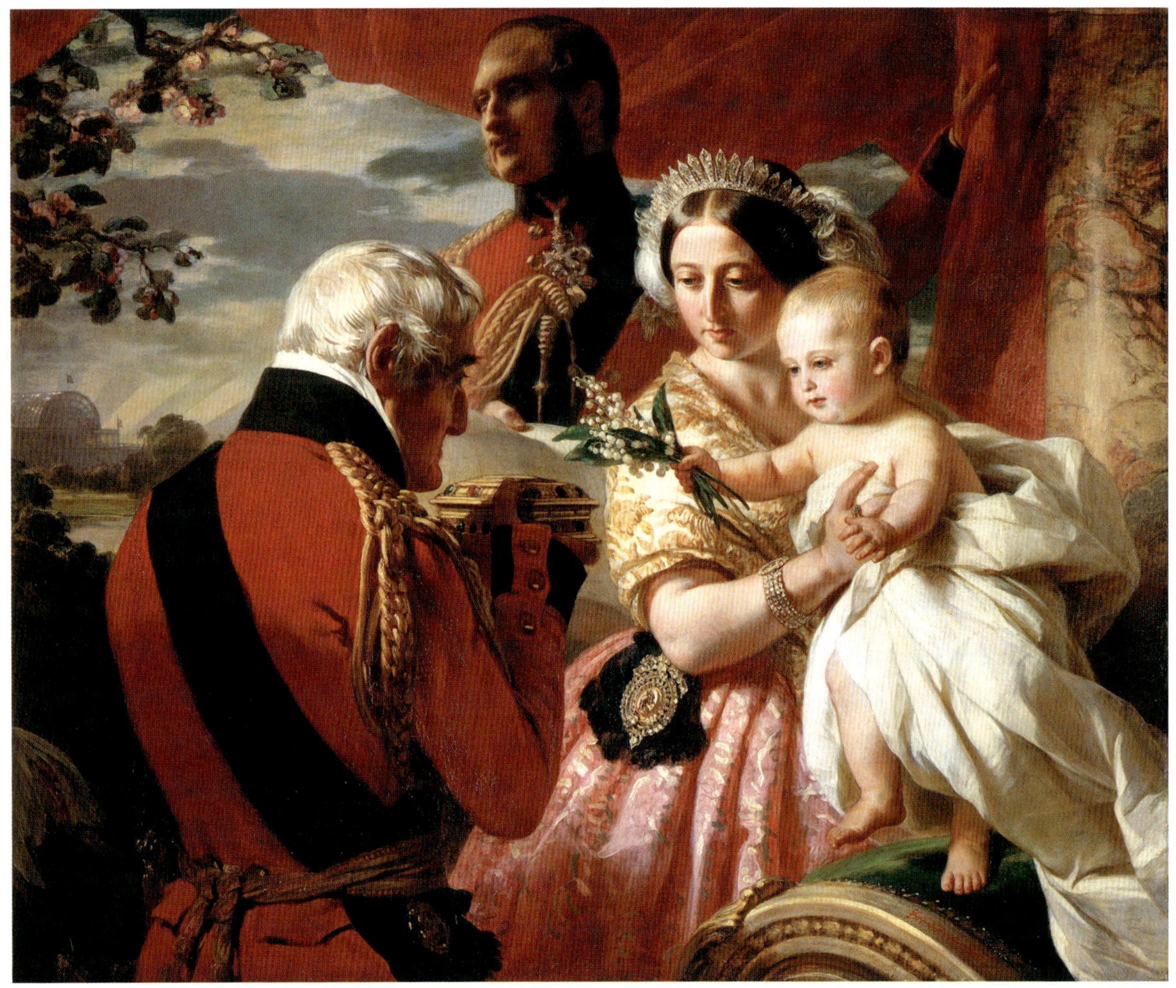

92 Franz Xaver Winterhalter, *The First of May 1851*, 1851, Oil on canvas, 106.7 x 129.5 cm. The Royal Collection

V

THE QUEEN'S WICKED UNCLES

The Regency, George IV and William IV

Thackeray concluded his lecture on the reign of George III with an extended reference to the King's descent into madness. Conscious that he was delivering the lecture to an American audience, and that American memories of the King were decidedly less happy than British ones, he rhetorically drew out a literary moral that he evidently hoped would moisten even the most unforgiving eye:

> 'O brothers,' I said to those who heard me first in America – 'O brothers! Speaking the same dear mother tongue – O comrades! enemies no more, let us take a mournful hand together as we stand by this royal corpse, and call a truce to battle! Low he lies to whom the proudest used to kneel once, and who was cast lower than the poorest: dead, whom millions prayed for in vain. Driven off his throne; buffeted by rude hands; with his children in revolt; the darling of his old age killed before him untimely; our Lear hangs over her breathless lips and cries 'Cordelia, Cordelia, stay a little!'
>
> > 'Vex not his ghost – oh! Let him pass – he hates him
> > That would upon the rack of this tough world
> > Stretch him out longer!
>
> Hush! Strife and Quarrel, over the solemn grave! Sound trumpets, a mournful march. Fall, dark curtain, upon his pageant, his pride, his grief, his awful tragedy.

Hard as it is to imagine poor Princess Amelia lying dead in the King's arms like Cordelia, let alone the Royal Princes cast in the roles of Goneril and Regan, Thackeray's parallel with *King Lear* is a telling one. When he was preparing his lecture in New York he wrote to the retired Shakespearean actor, William Charles Macready, describing how he had 'polished him [George III] off with an image taken from the death scene of an old king whom you … used to know in times when you wore crowns.'[1] It was Macready who, in January 1838, had staged *King Lear* for the first time since the seventeenth century without the adaptations made by Nahum Tate. Shakespeare's tragedy, which had been pronounced too searing for stage performance by Dr Johnson, had also become, during the period of the King George's illness, a play fraught with embarrassments (even with Tate's unfortunate alterations). John Forster, who saw Macready as Lear, declared that he had not only 'banished the disgrace' of Tate's happy ending but had offered 'the only perfect picture that we have had of Lear since the age of Betterton.'[2] Thus, in Shakespearean guise, Thackeray's George III became by association both an object of pity and a tragic hero. Where American and French revolutionaries had but recently proclaimed the innate guilt of royal tyrants, Thackeray pleads for tolerance and sympathy for the fallen hero, a man tragically ennobled by his loss of dignity.

When George III breathed his last on 29 January 1820 he had been on the throne for nearly sixty years. Though his son had acted as Regent since 1811, most of the High Victorian generation had been born in the old king's reign and in an age when the coins of the realm still bore his bull-necked profile. Queen Victoria, who never met her grandfather but who was to out-reign him, was born in 1819. Her most important Prime Ministers were all senior to her but, like her, were Georgians by birth: Melbourne had been born in 1779, Palmerston in 1784, Peel in 1788, Derby in 1799, Disraeli in 1804, and Gladstone in 1809. Amongst her eminent Victorian subjects, and perhaps the people we most readily think of as typically *Victorian*, were those equally born the subjects of George III: Faraday in 1791, Herschel in 1792, Carlyle in 1795, Macaulay in 1800, Newman in 1801, Robert Stephenson in 1803, John Stuart Mill, Elizabeth Barrett Browning and Isambard Kingdom Brunel in 1806, Darwin and Tennyson in 1809, Elizabeth Gaskell in 1810, Thackeray and George Gilbert Scott in 1811, Dickens, Robert Browning and Pugin in 1812, Trollope in 1815, Charlotte Brontë in 1816, Emily Brontë in 1818, George Eliot, Ruskin, Frith and Charles Kingsley in 1819. The majority of these eminences spent a formative part of their youth either under the Regency of George, Prince of Wales, or in his ten-year reign as King George IV. For most of them these years marked something of a transition, both in their own lives and in the larger experience of the Kingdom.

In the famous essay *De Juventute*, published in the *Cornhill Magazine* in 1860, Thackeray saw the beginnings of the railway system in 1830 as the opening of a new era:

> We who have lived before the railways were made, belong to another world. In how many hours could the Prince of Wales drive from Brighton to London, with a light carriage built expressly, and relays of horses longing to gallop the next stage? … It was only yesterday; but what a gulf between now and then!

By 1860 the world was moving at what the subjects of George IV would have regarded as a heady and even unholy speed, but the 'great gulf' to which Thackeray refers also existed in human minds. Regency childhoods seemed not only distant to those who looked back on them, but infinitely slower in pace. In the intervening years assumptions and manners had changed as radically as had machines and fashions. On one level it might strike us as strange that so many of Dickens's novels are set back in the stage-coach age, or that George Eliot should dwell so affectionately on the period of a childhood passed amid the changes wrought during the so-called 'Age of Reform.' On another level, we become aware that both Dickens and George Eliot used their fiction to explore the multiple shifts in perception experienced by their generation. The retrospect offered in their novels was rarely nostalgic, but it did offer a space for readjustment and for coming to terms with how the immediate past had shaped the present. The child, Wordsworth had told them, was father to the man. So too the Regency years, and the subsequent reigns of George IV and William IV, moulded a very distinctive and peculiarly energetic generation.

'Mrs Markham,' who had originally concluded her history with the end of the reign of George III, was to add two more chapters before she herself died in 1837. Her new chapters describe political, social and military affairs in the reigns of George IV and William IV, but she also feels obliged to describe some of the cultural changes that had taken place. Although she glances at industrial innovation, and at advances in transport and engineering, her real interest seems

to lie not in an account of the burgeoning of Birmingham or Manchester but in
the reconstruction of the more elegant parts of Regency London:

> One of the principal features of this period was the great improvement in
> the streets and buildings of the metropolis. Those who have known
> London, or at least the west end of London, in later years, can form no
> idea of what it was at the beginning of the century. Narrow streets and
> shabby houses filled the space now occupied by Regent-street. What is
> now the Regent's Park consisted then only of pasture fields, with sheds
> for cattle, and a few mean buildings. There was then no Zoological Garden,
> no Colosseum, no villas, no beautiful shrubberies, no agreeable drives. St
> James's Park was only a long meadow surrounded by trees, with a long
> and straight canal in the middle; and Hyde Park and Kensington Gardens
> were almost the only places where the inhabitants of London could gain
> any respite from the smoke and noise and closeness of the town.
>
> Steam-boats were first brought into use in Great Britain, on the
> Clyde, in 1812. Gas-lights began to be generally introduced into London
> in 1815 and 1816. The suspension-bridge over the Menai was commenced
> in 1819, and new London Bridge in 1824.[3]

As Mrs Markham's daughter, Mary, remarks in the subsequent 'Conversation':
'Since George IV made the Regent's Park for us, I think we may forgive him
for shutting himself up in his own.' Not all Victorians would have readily
agreed with her. Apart from some brief comments on the King's singularly
unhappy marriage, there is relatively little else about his character beyond the
references to his sequestered last years. Mrs Markham is slightly more
forthcoming about the disposition of William IV, who, she tells us, was said to
have been 'a remarkably engaging child' and one who retained through life
'an open simplicity of disposition and manners, which the habits, or rather the
seductions of the world, tend in general too much to check or destroy.' The
worldly seduction of the future king by Mrs Jordan, and the birth of numerous
Fitz-Clarences goes unmentioned, but otherwise he is seen as a commonplace
monarch who was 'too ready to yield a good-humoured compliance with the
wishes or advice of those who were immediately about his person.' Much is
made of the Reform Act (to which the King readily complied) and of the
advent of the railways, of the scourge of Asiatic cholera and of the destruction

of the old Palace of Westminster (over which disasters the King had no control whatever). It is illuminating, however, to turn to the additional instruction given by a supplementary 'Mrs. Markham', her supposed daughter-in-law, a role adopted by Mary Howitt after Elizabeth Penrose's death in 1837. Significantly, this new 'Mrs Markham' is, like so many of her eminent Victorian contemporaries, a 'Georgian,' having been born 'on the very day that George III died.' She offers her young readers even less about the characters of George IV and his brother than her predecessor. Having disposed of personal details, she writes infinitely more fully about the state of the nation in their respective reigns. We are told, for example, of the Cato Street conspiracy, of Catholic Emancipation, of the failed economic speculations of 1824, and of 'the restless, dissatisfied state of the public mind' and how that restlessness and dissatisfaction were described by Cobbett ('a man of great good sense but violent prejudices'). Gone is the first 'Mrs. Markham's' delight in Regent's Park; her successor is far more taken with the potential of steam-powered locomotion. Like any good Victorian she waxes fulsome about the new railways:

> The wonderful success of these enterprises and the facilities and advantages which railroads afford for travelling have now made them universal, not only in these islands but over the whole civilized world. By this means commerce is greatly extended, and nations since they have been able to see more of each other, have become much better friends. It is by the commercial and friendly intercourse which has been brought about to such a vast extent by means of steam during a time of peace, that we may hope, under the Divine blessing, for the more firm establishment of peace between the different nations of the earth.[4]

This new Mrs Markham is far more of a liberal than the old one. As such she recognises that it is not the character traits (or even the sexual morality) of kings that matters any more, but the reforms wrought about by their governments and the progress made by the Kingdom at large.

Nevertheless, for many other early- and mid-Victorians the extravagant life of George IV remained the object of condemnation. This was the man of whom *The Times* cruelly commented on his death 'there never was an individual less regretted by his fellow creatures than this deceased king.'[5] Though a tone of deference to the Queen's royal uncle was nearly always maintained, George was generally, if unfairly, regarded more as a profligate waster of public funds than as a discriminating patron of the arts. However much he may have tried to cast himself in the roles of Augustus and Maecenas, he was all too often dismissed as a cross between a slightly ridiculous Nero and an obese Trimalchio. Augustus was said to have found Rome a city of brick and left it a marble one. George found London brick and left it disguised under a layer of stucco. The West End, rebuilt to the designs of John Nash, was disparaged by unsympathetic Victorian commentators as little more than a tasteless, gimcrack creation. The King's reconstruction of Buckingham Palace, unfinished and uninhabitable at the time of his death, came in for particular criticism. Peter Cunningham's *Handbook of London* commented in 1850:

> When the grant was given by Parliament it was intended only to repair and enlarge the old Buckingham House; and therefore the old site, height and dimensions were retained. This led to the erection of a clumsy building, and was a mere juggle on the part of the king and his architect – knowing as they did that Parliament would never have granted the funds for an entirely New Palace. On Her Majesty's accession several alterations were effected – a dome in the centre, like a common slop-basin, turned upside down, was removed.[6]

When Cunningham wrote this the Palace was a mere twenty-five years old, and Queen Victoria had already been obliged to extend it in order to accommodate both her growing family and her official guests. What should have proved an architectural heirloom for George's successors had initially been a white elephant. A building that should have enhanced and dignified London had turned out to be a Palace only in name. Like the King who commissioned it, Buckingham Palace was seen as a sham, and as little more than expensive theatrical posturing.

Thackeray was inclined to be kinder than most about the King's self-indulgence, but he nevertheless ends his lecture on the fourth George with a pointed comparison between the so-called 'First Gentleman of Europe' and the respectably sober George Washington:

> Which is the noble character for after ages to admire;– yon fribble dancing in lace and spangles, or yonder hero who sheathes his sword after a life of

spotless honour, a purity unreproached, a courage indomitable, and a consummate victory? Which of these is the true gentleman? What is it to be a gentleman? Is it to have lofty aims, to lead a pure life, to keep your honour virgin; to have the esteem of your fellow citizens, and the love of your fireside; to bear good fortune meekly; to suffer evil with constancy; and through good or evil to maintain truth always? Show me the happy man whose life exhibits these qualities, and him we will salute as gentleman, whatever his rank may be; show me the prince who possesses them, and he may be sure of our love and loyalty.[7]

Rhetorical these questions may be, but each seems to have a ready answer to it: King George never quite matches the gentlemanly model established by President George. Earlier in his lecture Thackeray had identified the central problem in discussing George both as Prince of Wales and as King: he was more show than substance. Thackeray, who recalls that in his own youth 'almost every dining room had his [George IV's] portrait,' now recognises him only as a series of unbecoming fashion statements and vain gestures:

To make a portrait of him at first seemed a matter of small difficulty. There is his coat, his star, his wig, his countenance simpering under it … I look through all his life, and recognize but a bow and a grin. I try and take him to pieces, and find silk stockings, padding, stays, a coat with frogs and a fur collar, a star and blue ribbon, a pocket handkerchief prodigiously scented, one of Truefitt's best nutty brown wigs reeking with oil, a set of teeth and a huge black stock, under waistcoats, more under waistcoats and then nothing … He is dead but thirty years, and one asks how a great society could have tolerated him? Would we bear him now? In this quarter of a century, what a silent revolution has been working! It has separated us from old times and manners![8]

The bewigged and perfumed Prinny in his expensive, well-pressed clothes looks intolerably-old fashioned in the glare of an 1860s gas-light. Much of the tenor of Thackeray's complaint had been voiced some eighteen years earlier when Dickens had described the dancing-master, Mr Turveydrop, in *Bleak House* (fig.93):

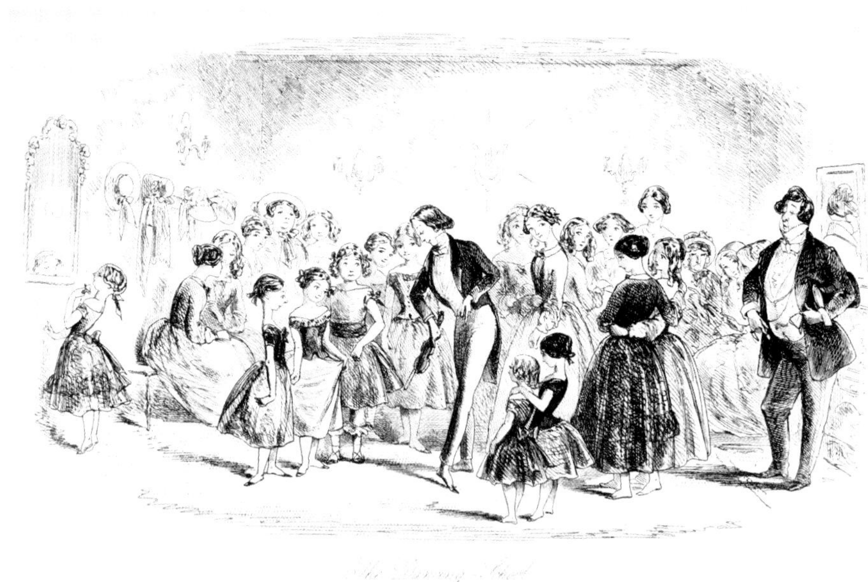

93 'The Dancing School', lithograph illustration by Hablot Knight Browne (Phiz) in *Bleak House* by Charles Dickens, 1853. Private collection

He was a fat old man with a false complexion, false teeth, false whiskers, and a wig. He had a fur collar, and he had a padded breast to his coat, which only wanted a star or a broad blue ribbon to be complete. He was pinched in, and swelled out, and got up, and strapped down, as much as he could possibly bear. He had such a neckcloth on (puffing his very eyes out of their natural shape), and his chin and even his ears so sunk into it, that it seemed as though he must inevitably double up, if it were cast loose … he had an eye-glass, he had a snuff-box, he had rings, he had wristbands, he had everything but any touch of nature; he was not like youth, … he was not like anything in the world but a model of Deportment. (Chapter 14)

Turveydrop, who so adulates the Prince that he has christened his son in his honour, has modelled himself so utterly on an empty ideal, that he too is nothing but a lie. Dickens therefore belittles the memory of the Regent by equating him with a grossly indolent dancing-master. If Thackeray persuades us to look on the decrepit Lear-like George III with sympathy, he and Dickens seem to agree to dismiss the spendthrift George IV, without either an apology or a deferential nod, as an object of ridicule.

Bath and Brighton

No British cities exemplify the contradictions and ramifications of Victorian taste better than the histories of Bath and Brighton in the nineteenth century. Both cities had been created by the immediate ancestors of Victorian Britons as pleasure resorts, but the Bath beloved of the Georgians was to find relatively little favour in the eyes of their successors. The staid delights of the inland spa were steadily eclipsed by a new taste for the sea-side. Thanks to the whims of George III, who preferred Weymouth, and the Prince Regent, who made Brighton very much his own, Bath was largely abandoned by men and women of fashion in the early nineteenth century and left to its own limited devices. The city, once reliant on wealthy visitors both for its prosperity and for its *cachet*, was, by the 1840s relegated to dowager status. Brighton, by contrast, not only burgeoned under the patronage of George IV, it survived his decline and death, and continued to flourish under a far more diverse generation of patrons: the Victorian middle classes. Much to the delight of those fastidious early twentieth-century critics, who loathed everything tainted by Victorian taste, Bath remained sleepily intact as a Georgian creation. The infinitely more eclectic Brighton, never much the resort of the fastidious, was in 1850 merely a sprawling series of stucco squares, terraces and villas surrounding the Regent's absurdly exotic Pavilion. By the end of the century, however, its architectural heritage had been stamped with an assertively Victorian identity. Where Bath proclaimed a palatial uniformity, Brighton rejoiced in an individuality that was distinctly Victorian in tone.

Despite the fact that Dickens seems to have visited Bath frequently, he had no love for the city. In the 1840s he went there as the friend of Walter Savage Landor, but he never shared Landor's conviction that this was the English Florence. Landor liked to think that it was during one of these visits to his house in St. James's Square that Dickens had first conceived of his character, Little Nell. In a mood as fanciful as the one that compared Bath to Florence, Landor was later to declare that he would happily have burned his rented house to the ground so that 'no meaner association should ever desecrate the birthplace of Nell.'9 He never, however, seems to have paused to think *why* Dickens might have first thought of the death-haunted Nell in Georgian Bath. The novelist himself was quite explicit in his letters that he found the city unrelievedly deathly. In 1857 he declared that he hoped never to have to visit 'that dreary old Bath' again, though he was not to keep to his resolution. Ten years later he succumbed to financial temptation and gave a Public Reading in the Assembly Rooms, but insisted that he had hated his audience.[10] In a letter of February 1869 he explained his antipathy further. Bath reminded him, he said, of a cemetery 'full of old people' who had somehow 'made a successful rise against Death – carried the place by assault – and built a city with their grave stones.' His audience was 'trying to look alive, but with very indifferent success.'[11] As his fiction also suggests, Dickens found both the city and its residents superannuated. In *Bleak House* we learn that the sixty-year-old Volumnia Dedlock, 'a poor relation' of the Dedlock family, has 'an extensive acquaintance at Bath among appalling old gentlemen with thin legs and nankeen trousers, and is of high standing in that dreary city' (Chapter 28). Samuel Pickwick takes the stagecoach to Bath in Chapter 35 of *Pickwick Papers* and is told on his arrival of the delights of a ball in the Assembly Rooms:

> 'This is a ball night … The ball nights in Ba-ath are moments snatched from Paradise, rendered bewitching by music, beauty, elegance, fashion, etiquette, and – and – above all, by the absence of trades-people, who are quite inconsistent with Paradise, and who have an amalgamation of themselves at the Guildhall every fortnight, which is, to say the least, remarkable.'

Despite such anticipatory praise from the Master of Ceremonies, Cyrus Bantam, Mr Pickwick is to find the Assembly Rooms rather less than paradisal (even though the despised trades-people are notable for their absence). Bantam is attired, with unbecoming youthfulness, in a wig, eye-glass, shirt-pin, cane and a bright blue coat 'with a white silk lining, black silk stockings and pumps'. He also reeks of scent. He presides over a packed Assembly:

> Dresses rustled, feathers waved, lights shone, and jewels sparkled. There was the music – not of the quadrille band, for it had not yet commenced; but the music of soft tiny footsteps, with now and then a clear merry laugh – low and gentle, but very pleasant to hear in a female voice, whether in Bath or elsewhere. Brilliant eyes, opened up with pleasurable expectation, gleamed from every side; and look where you would, some exquisite form glided gracefully through the throng, and was no sooner lost, than it was replaced by another, as dainty and bewitching.

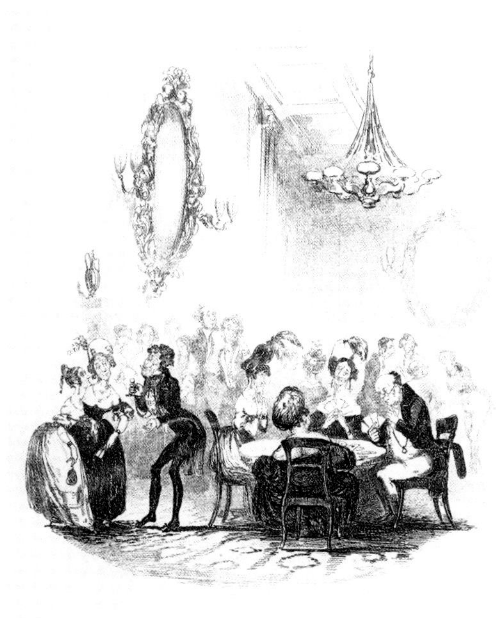

94 'The Card Room at Bath',
lithograph illustration by
Hablot Knight Browne (Phiz)
in *The Pickwick Papers* by
Charles Dickens, 1837.
Private collection

This sounds as if Bath in the late 1820s was still able to recapture the elegance and allure of its glory-days in the previous century. But the horrid truth gradually dawns (fig.94):

In the tea-room, and hovering round the card tables, were a vast number of queer old ladies and decrepid [*sic*] old gentlemen, discussing all the small talk and scandal of the day, with an evident relish and gusto which bespoke the intensity of the pleasure they derived from the occupation … Lounging near the doors, and in remote corners, were various knots of silly young men, displaying every variety of puppyism and stupidity … And lastly, seated on some of the back benches, where they had already taken up their positions for the evening, were divers unmarried ladies past their grand climacteric, who, not dancing because there were no partners for them, and not playing cards lest they should be put down as irretrievably single, were in the favourable situation of being able to abuse everybody without reflecting on themselves. In sort they could abuse everybody, because everybody was there.

Despite Bantam's protests that the '*élite* of Ba-ath' is parading through the Assembly Rooms, it is evident to Mr. Pickwick that it is not only the unmarried women who are 'past their grand climacteric.' So is the city.

Bath's pre-eminence as the queen of watering-places had started to decline in the early years of the nineteenth century when Cheltenham and Leamington began to assert themselves as fashionable rivals. It is indicative that, in the 1840s, it is to the spa at Leamington that Dickens's widowed Mr Dombey goes in search of a new wife. Bath's even more threatening competitors, the sea-side resorts and above all Brighton, were initially to flourish under the dual patronage of the Prince Regent and his circle and later of middle-class families seeking the kind of healthy amusements that were beyond Bath's increasingly fuddy-duddy capacity. The city's decline was not absolute, as the speculative late Regency terraces serpentining up its hills and the numerous early-Victorian, Italianate villas in its suburbs testify. Balls continued on Mondays and Thursdays at the Assembly Rooms until the end of the nineteenth century, but Bath lost its Master of Ceremonies in the 1860s. The great modern historian of Bath's architecture Walter Ison wrote in 1948:

> The popularity which had so suddenly raised Bath to pre-eminence among fashionable resorts, declined with equal rapidity towards 1840 … Plans of the city published around 1825 show fine streets and squares originally proposed to be built on sites now covered with a squalid chaos of buildings erected by later generations, who neither understood nor followed the fine principles of development so nobly observed by the builders of Georgian Bath.[12]

Property values had fallen so drastically because the city was increasingly looked on as old-fashioned and sedate and, more damningly, as a pleasant retreat for the retired. The waters were no longer taken as a temporary respite from rich food but to relieve the aching limbs of the aged and infirm, and visitor numbers had fallen sharply away. When Mr Pickwick is supposed to have visited it, Bath had around fifty thousand residents, but in the next twenty years its population only rose by a further four thousand. Its canals and the arrival of the railway in 1840 gave it a degree of industrial development but otherwise its established urban fabric was left largely unchanged by new architectural fashions. The many Victorians who had been taught by Ruskin to admire

Gothic Venice over Renaissance Florence, tended to despise its classical regularity. Its architectural eclipse is witnessed by the fact that not one of its buildings merited mention in James Fergusson's *History of the Modern Styles of Architecture* of 1862. With its white oolite stone terraces steadily blackened by domestic smoke, it was small wonder that Dickens felt moved to joke that he thought of the city as having been built out of gravestones.

The re-assessment of Bath's architectural charms began in the 1870s when the leading principles of the Gothic Revival were being questioned, and the certainties of 'High Victorian' culture were slowly being sapped by a new generation of readers and writers. This was also the period when the city corporation tried successfully to revive the fortunes of the spa. It was, moreover, around 1870 that an interest in the city was stimulated by a renewed response to the novels of Frances Burney and Jane Austen. Murray's *Hand-Book for Travellers in Wiltshire, Dorsetshire and Somersetshire* of 1869 summarises these literary associations, much in the manner of a modern guidebook (though with a rather greater sense of punctilio):

> The pen of the novelist has invested Bath with a vivid, though fictitious interest. The readers of Miss Burney's 'Evelina' will remember the scenes laid in the Pump Room and its vicinity, while Miss Austen has peopled the city with interesting remains for the lovers of her exquisite fictions. It was in Pulteney Street that Catherine Morland lodged with her friends, the Allens; General Tilney and his son and daughter occupying apartments in Milsom Street. It was at the Lower Rooms her first introduction to Henry Tilney took place. The pompous Sir Walter Elliot and his daughter had a house in Camden Place – their grand friends, 'the Dowager Viscountess Dalrymple and the Honble. Miss Carteret' in Lance Place; 'none of your Queen Square houses for us.' On the walk by Belmont from Union Street to Camden Place the eclaircissement, between Anne Elliot and Captain Wentworth took place; her humble friend Mrs. Smith lived in 'Westgate Buildings,' to which 'Lady Russell's carriage took her as near as it could.'

This is possibly the first time that Jane Austen's name had been so pointedly evoked in relation to what we might now call 'cultural tourism.'

The Regency architecture of Brighton might equally have not been to the taste of the early- and mid-Victorians, but the bracing air, the vast expanse of the sea-front, the whimsy, and the sheer convenience of its situation distinctly were. The Prince Regent launched Brighton's fortunes, but the advent of the railway maintained them. Where Bath declined into what was seen as dismal respectability, Brighton's salty tang and fresh air seems to have stirred Victorian visitors into affectionate responses and multiple return trips. Sedate nineteenth-century Bath had to face the rivalry of other inland spas in Britain, and later had to contend against the raffish sophistication of the German and Bohemian spas; Brighton always had the sea and its passionate *aficionados*. Many Victorians happily dubbed it 'Doctor Brighton,' but for Thackeray it was also London-super-Mare. Here he is expatiating on its delights in Chapter 9 of *The Newcomes* in 1853:

> In Steyne Gardens, Brighton, the lodging-houses are amongst the most frequented in that city of lodging-houses. These mansions have bow-windows in front, bulging out with gentle prominences, and ornamented with neat verandahs, from which you can behold the tide of human kind as it flows up and down the Steyne, and that blue ocean over which Britannia is said to rule, stretching brightly away eastward and westward. The chain-pier as everybody knows, runs intrepidly into the sea, which sometimes, in fine weather, bathes its feet with laughing wavelets, and anon, on stormy days, dashes over its sides with roaring foam … You see the citizen with his family inveigled into the shallops of the mercenary native mariner, and fancy that the motion cannot be pleasant; and how the hirer of the boat, *otium et oppidi laudans rura sui*, haply sighs for ease, and prefers Richmond or Hampstead. You behold a hundred bathing-machines put to sea; and your naughty fancy depicts the beauties splashing under their white awnings … See the worn-out London roué pacing the pier, inhaling the sea air, and casting furtive glances under the bonnets of the pretty girls, who trot here before lessons! … It is the fashion to run down George IV, but what myriads of Londoners ought to thank him for inventing Brighton! One of the best of physicians our city has ever known, is kind, cheerful, merry Doctor Brighton.

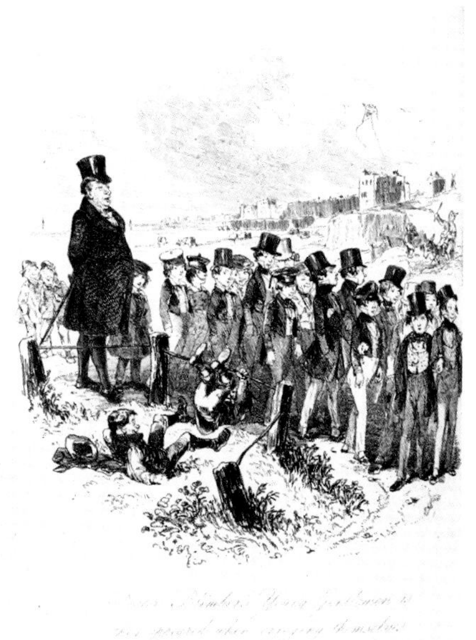

95 'Doctor Blimber's Young Gentlemen as
they appeared when enjoying
themselves', lithograph illustration by
Hablot Knight Browne (Phiz) in *Dombey
and Son* by Charles Dickens, 1848.
Private collection

One cannot imagine any Victorian expatiating with such enthusiasm about
Bath. This is Thackeray at his most engaged and at his most fulsome: a Londoner
observing his fellow Londoners at play; delighting in the whimsical sea-side
architecture; throwing in his quotation from Horace; indulging in 'naughty
fancies' while hinting at the odd sexual *frisson* on the part of his roué, and rejoicing
in the very vivacity and variety of the place. Thackeray might have named the
aristocratic roué of *Vanity Fair* the Marquis of Steyne, but here, with the Regent
long dead and his Pavilion sold to the corporation, Brighton's main thoroughfare
has become the preserve of sauntering middle-class Londoners.

It is to the healthful, but rather less joyful, Brighton that the ailing Paul
Dombey is sent in Chapter 8 of Dickens's *Dombey and Son* (1846-48). Mrs
Chick, Paul's aunt, insists of the efficacy of 'sea-air' (which she claims that she
and her own sons have been 'ordered … a great many times'). The boy is
consequently dispatched to Mrs Pipchin's house in 'a steep bye-street at
Brighton … where the soil was more than usually chalky, flinty, and sterile,
and the houses were more than usually brittle and thin.' Here Florence joins
him, while Mr Dombey, who comes down to visit once a week, lodges at the
Bedford Hotel (where Dickens himself often stayed). It is from Mrs Pipchin's
'brittle and thin' house that Florence wheels Paul down to the beach where

he will wax melancholic amongst the sea-shells, wondering what the wild waves are saying to him. At the age of six he is sent to Dr Blimber's expensive 'hot-house' of a school situated in 'a mighty fine house, fronting the sea.' This house has long been identified as the handsome, bow-fronted Chichester House, in Chichester Terrace, Kemp Town. Dickens tells us that Blimber and his boys go out for afternoon walks but he does not describe them. His illustrator, 'Phiz,' does, however, provide us with a particularly fine plate showing the party on the beach beyond Kemp Town (fig.95). It is a breezy day and a kite is whisked up in the air. All of Blimber's well-dressed boys sport caps or top hats, with Little Paul bringing up the rear next to the stiff, formally attired headmaster. The formality of the group contrasts with two smirking fisherman and a two hatless local boys kicking their legs in the air as if in mockery of the regimentation. In the background are the old Chain Pier, a child on a donkey and bathing machines. The plate delicately suggests the essential ambiguities of Brighton, where a degree of respectability contrasts with a culture of provocative informality. When the dying Paul leaves Brighton for the last time he remains haunted by Blimber's ticking clock and by the sound of the waves. At the very end of the novel, however, Dickens returns us to the sea-shore where we glimpse the white-haired Mr Dombey walking with his faithful daughter and his grandchildren.

The Brighton of *Dombey and Son*, like the Brighton of *The Newcomes*, is overwhelmingly the resort of the middle classes. Gone is the old, exclusive world fondly remembered by Mr Turveydrop in *Bleak House* who recalls the time when 'His Royal Highness the Prince Regent did me the honour to inquire, on my removing my hat as he drove out of the Pavilion at Brighton (that fine building), "Who is he? Who the Devil is he".' Turveydrop feels that civilisation has drooped since. 'A levelling age,' he tells us, 'is not favourable to Deportment. It develops vulgarity.' Brighton seems to have happily survived the demise of both the Regent and of Deportment, and tended to relish the consequent vulgarity. When the railway arrived from London in 1841 it has been estimated that more people visited the town in one weekend than in the whole of the previous year. Brighton's resident population stood at forty-six thousand in that same 1841, but it increased to sixty-five thousand ten years later. Having experimented with holidaying at the Royal Pavilion at the very beginning of her reign, Queen Victoria grew impatient with the fact that it was too hemmed in by the town, and was lacking in privacy. She abandoned it in 1843, stripped out many of its fittings, and finally sold it to the town's corporation in 1850 for £53,000 (an infinitely smaller sum than it had cost to build and decorate). The Queen does not appear to have been especially offended by the Pavilion's architecture, but relatively few of her subjects would have reflected Turveydrop's opinion that it was a 'fine building.' Haydn's *Dictionary of Dates* of 1853 disparagingly refers to its having 'a general resemblance of the kremlin at Moscow' and forty years later Murray's *Handbook for Travellers in Sussex* dismissed it as 'an example of faded splendour, incongruous taste, and jumble of styles.' In 1896 Augustus Hare described it as 'a foolish Chinese palace' and a 'ridiculous plaything.'[13] Even though the architecture of the residential streets, squares and terraces of Brighton and Hove was highly unlikely to win either the affection or the respect of a Victorian Goth, the stuccoed town continued to expand along the sea-front until well into the middle years of the nineteenth century. Adelaide Crescent in Hove, begun in the early 1830s, was not completed until 1850 while the neighbouring Palmeira Square, begun in the 1850s, was finished in the mid-1860s. In Kemp Town, parts of the huge Sussex Square was still being constructed in the 1840s, while Chichester Terrace (the supposed site of Blimber's school), started in 1835, was only completed twenty years later.[14]

What most impressively testifies to the extraordinary vitality of Brighton and Hove in the Victorian period is the architectural quality of its churches. These churches make aesthetic statements which seem at first to be quite at odds with the neighbouring stuccoed facades that typify the Regency town. Brighton's Victorian residents, who never wanted for style and 'theatre,' had religious tastes that were of the kind that were once described as 'advanced.' Away from the sea-front, and rising in the midst of grand squares and former slums alike, are some of the most significant nineteenth-century Gothic churches in Britain. The town's pious, and often decidedly Anglo-Catholic residents, could walk from the comfort of their snug villas, or their airy Classical drawing rooms, into an incense-laden vision of the revived Middle Ages. Despite the fact that Augustus Hare was prepared to dismiss the town in 1896 as 'absolutely devoid of beauty,' discriminating visitors, with an eye for the best in modern design, were drawn to a series of extraordinarily innovative, 'ritualistic' churches. Those who arrived from London by train (fig.96) could glimpse the vast brick bulk of St Bartholomew's (fig.97), constructed due to the munificence of the Revd. Arthur Wagner in 1872-74. The nave is higher than that of Westminster Abbey, but the wonders of the church are the furnishings installed in the closing years of the

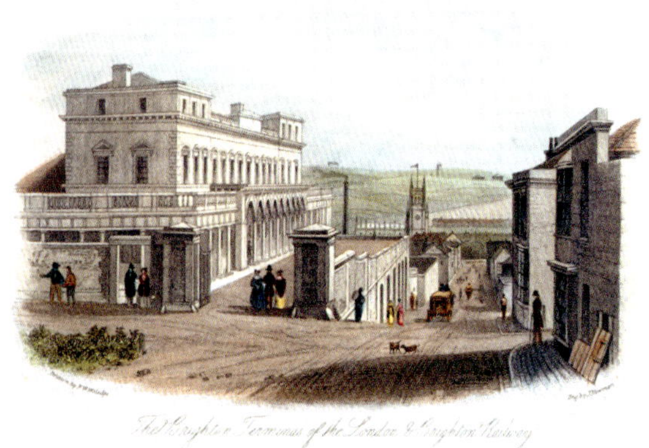

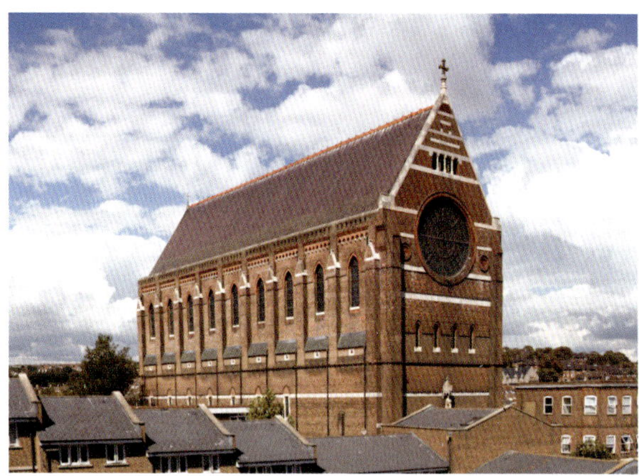

96 *The Brighton Terminus of the London & Brighton Railway, c1845, Colour lithograph of an engraving drawn by Frederick William Woledge and engraved by John Newman*

97 Exterior of St Bartholomew's Church, Brighton

nineteenth century: a great marble baldacchino, mosaics, brass and enamel altar rails and a silver-plated Lady Altar. St. Paul's in West Street was built 1846-48 by R. C. Carpenter and paid for by Arthur Wagner's father. It dramatically breaks away from the encroaching stucco, and its tower, added in 1873, with a lead-covered timber bell-stage, makes a significantly elegant mark on the town's sky-line. Inside, the church once boasted a painted altarpiece by the young Burne Jones and it still retains stained glass of 1849-53 by A. W. N. Pugin.[15] At All Saints, Hove, the architect, J. L. Pearson, gave the town a sumptuous cathedral-like parish church in the years 1889-91. Perhaps most intricate and complex of all Brighton's churches, however, is the red-brick St Michael and All Angels in Victoria Road (fig.98). The first part of the church was built 1855-61 by G. F. Bodley, but this was relegated to become a south aisle when the building was ambitiously extended in 1893-94 to the designs of William Burges. The church has choir stalls by Burges, a chancel roof decorated by William Morris, and a superb collection of stained glass designed by Edward Burne Jones, Ford Madox Brown and Philip Webb and executed by Morris & Company in the 1860s.[16]

BEYOND STUCCONIA

Brighton, a town which had grown rapidly in the late eighteenth century from extremely humble origins, had therefore, by the end of the following century, acquired a series of ecclesiastical monuments of international distinction. Each, in its distinct way, was a Victorian architectural statement that declared its independence from the Regency stucco environment from which it had grown. Although most visitors to Brighton seem not to have formed an active dislike of this stucco environment, Regency architecture was almost universally despised by informed Victorian critics. In a funeral oration for Sir George Gilbert Scott in 1878, Dean Stanley referred to the ecclesiastical architecture of the first third of the nineteenth century as 'the Dismal Period' and cited the drabness of Bloomsbury streets as an example of what he found most dismal in the domestic style of the same period. In his *House Architecture* of 1880 J. J. Stevenson referred, as did so many of his contemporaries, to 'the dreary uniformity of Gower Street' as if it were an accepted truism. In the same book, however, he was prepared to admit that white stucco had some small merit compared to the repetitive brick streets of the early 1800s:

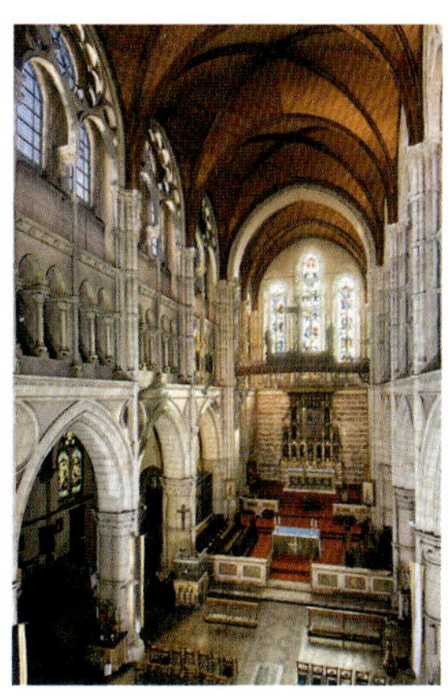

98 Interior of St Michael & All Angels' Church, Brighton

> The brightness of the new white buildings charmed every one; and if, in looking at examples of them (such as the terraces round the Regent's Park or on the cliffs of Brighton, which were among the first fruits of the movement), we can divest ourselves for the moment of our present ideas and forget that they are shams, we must admit that they exhibit something of the brightness, and even of the grandeur of Classic architecture. The builders, as usual, followed the fashion, and carried out the new style, in their rows of houses, in worse architecture and meaner design.[17]

This is not exactly a ringing endorsement. An attack on virtually every aspect of Regency architecture had been opened some forty years earlier by that proselytising Goth, A. W. N. Pugin. The frontispiece to the 1841 edition of Pugin's *Contrasts* (figs.99, 100) showed a series of modern buildings deemed worthy of ridicule by the 'Christian' architect. In a parody of a stucco façade, Pugin showed William Wikins's National Gallery, John Nash's All Souls, Langham Place and, as if in a niche, a saucer dome and lantern by Sir John Soane, with the architect's name on the cornice. A subsequent plate shows Nash's All Souls again, this time unflatteringly juxtaposed to the great mediaeval church of St Mary Redcliffe. Another shows the wretched interior of the Chapel Royal at Brighton, complete with a fat Bishop preaching, contrasted to a scene showing coped clergy celebrating High Mass at St George's Chapel, Windsor. Yet another depicts 'The Professor's [Soane's] Own House' looking awkwardly attenuated when compared to the rich wooden façade of a mediaeval house in Rouen. For Pugin

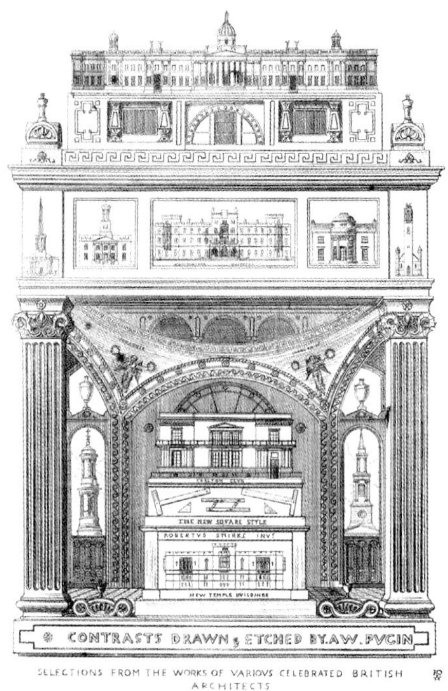

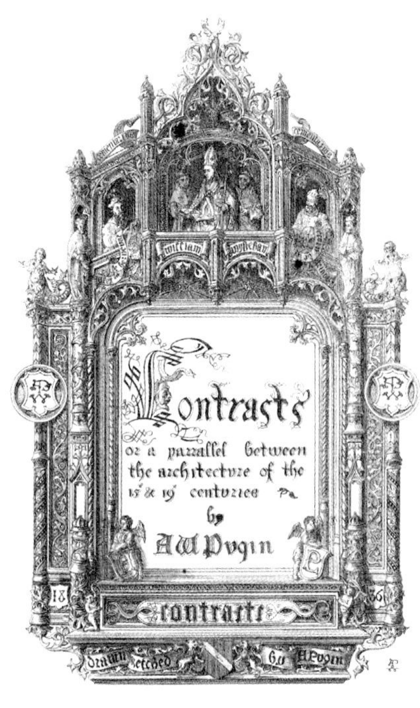

99 Frontispiece from
Contrasts by Augustus
Welby Northmore
Pugin, 1841.
Private collection

100 Titlepage from *Contrasts*
by Augustus Welby
Northmore Pugin, 1841.
Private collection

it was not just that modern architecture was aesthetically worthless, it was that modern prosperity was posing a threat to the whole built environment. To stress his point, the 1841 edition of *Contrasts* also included a plate parodying 'the practise of architecture in the 19th. Century on new and improved cheap principles.' It variously showed ready-made chimney pots and balustrades, advertisements for gothic cornices 'just pressed out from 6d. per yard,' and a puff for a book called 'Architecture Made Easy, or, Every Man his own Architect by which Gentlemen Amateurs may easily acquire every Information respecting Design and Practice.' In his *The True Principles of Pointed or Christian Architecture*, also of 1841, Pugin attacked not just the growing uniformity of modern English towns but the gimcrack quality of those who were imposing that uniformity of style:

> England is rapidly losing its venerable garb; all places are becoming alike; every good old gabled inn is turned into an ugly hotel with a stuccoed portico, and a vulgar coffee-room lined with staring paper, with imitation scagliola columns, composition glass frames, an obsequious cheat of a waiter, and twenty per cent added to the bill on the score of the modern

and elegant arrangements. Our good old St. Martin's, St. John's, St. Peter's, and St. Mary's streets, are becoming Belle-vue Places, Adelaide Rows, Apollo Terraces, Regent Squares, and Royal Circuses. … Timbered fronts of curious and ingenious design are swept away before the resistless torrent of Roman-cement men, who buy their ornaments by the yard, and their capitals by the ton. Every linen-draper's shop apes to be something after the palace of the Caesars; the mock stone columns are fixed over a front of plate glass to exhibit the astonishing bargains; while low-ticketed goods are hung out over trophies of war.

To illustrate his point Pugin added a wonderfully exaggerated illustration of 'Albert House,' an 'Emporium of Fashion' in front of whose new plate-glass windows ladies admire the latest industrially-produced fabrics.

In the 1840s Pugin readily recognised the inter-relationship between mass production and the kind of speculative building that he saw as scarring most English towns. Other later critics returned to the attack on the most prominent classical architects of the first forty years of the nineteenth century. John Nash, the Prince Regent's most favoured *protégé*, came in for the most venomous criticism. James Fergusson, for example, recognised in 1862 that Nash was particularly to blame for the low state of 'Street and Domestic architecture' which was characterised by 'a few columns stuck here and there, or rich window dressings and rustications,' and, worse, 'aided by the fatal facility of stucco.' Thus Nash had managed to 'get over an immense amount of space with a very slight expenditure of thought.' If Nash was essentially 'thoughtless,' by contrast, Sir John Soane strikes Fergusson as too eccentrically cerebral:

Soane affected an originality of form and decoration, which, not being based on any well-understood constructive principle, or any recognised form of beauty, has led to no result, and to us now appears little less than ridiculous … It probably may have been that he was crotchety and devoid of good sound taste; but it is a strong argument in the hands of the enemies of progress to find such a man succeeding when copying, and failing when he attempts originality.[18]

Despite the fact that John Nash's architecture was never quite forgiven for being thoughtlessly theatrical, his buildings gradually found admirers in the early years of the twentieth century, especially amongst the fashionable coterie who began to favour the Regency style over what were deemed to be the ugly aberrations of the mid-Victorians. It took far longer for Soane's work to be properly appreciated. His great interiors for the Bank of England were destroyed when the Bank was reconstructed in the 1920s, but they were lovingly recorded in a series of photographs published in 1930. Thereafter, Soane very gradually reclaimed his place amongst the greatest of English architects. It was not, however, until well after the Second World War that what Fergusson regarded as his 'failures,' his 'attempts' at 'originality,' came to be seen not as wilful eccentricities but as marks of genius.[19]

ROMANTICS AND POST-ROMANTICS

Had he not died at Missolonghi in April 1824, and had he not succumbed to any other mortal, or sexually transmitted, disease, the once notorious Byron might well have survived to the age of sixty-three and soberly witnessed the opening of the Great Exhibition in 1851. This was a speculation which may well have troubled many Victorians. Max Beerbohm drew a sketch of the elderly Byron as he might have appeared with a red face and mutton-chop whiskers. This is a Byron who would have proved a match for the fictional Lord Dundreary and the all too real, and irascible, Lord Lucan on the benches of the House of Lords. It was an idle speculation for Byron, like most of the other notable poets of the opening years of the nineteenth century, was famous for having been cut off in his prime. Only the giant figure of Wordsworth, the comparatively diminished Southey and Leigh Hunt, and the marginalised Clare had survived into the Victorian era. Keats had died in 1821, Shelley in 1822, Scott and Crabbe in 1832, Coleridge in 1834. Yet, to Victorian anthologists, they were all, with Tennyson and the Brownings, 'Poets of the Nineteenth Century.' In his study of the rising stars in the Victorian literary firmament, *A New Spirit of the Age* (1844), R.H. Horne included an essay on Wordsworth and Hunt, poets he referred to as the 'two laurelled veterans,' because the two men seemed to him to represent a 'highly important connecting link between past and present periods.' For Horne they were also men whose enterprise had stood the test of time. Having been 'wounded' by their first critics, they had survived to be 'finally victorious experiencers of popular changes of mind during many years.'[20]

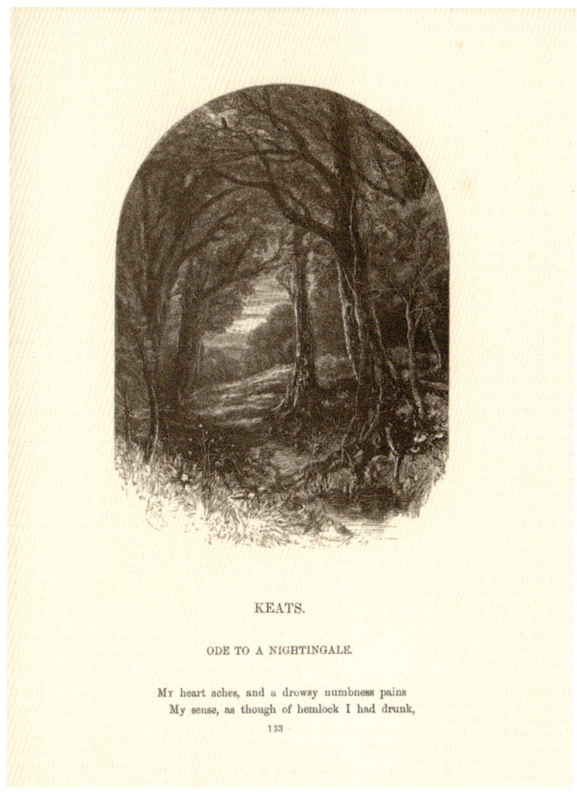

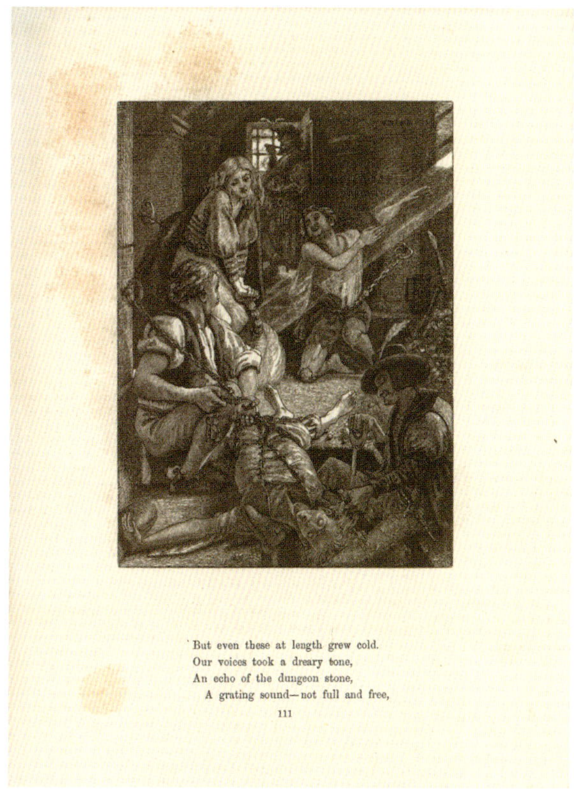

Robert Aris Willmott's anthology, *The Poets of the Nineteenth Century*, which first appeared in 1856, went into at least three editions by 1858 (figs.101, 102). Willmott's collection of verse covers a 'long nineteenth century,' albeit from a mid-century perspective. It opens with five once well-known poems by James Beattie (b. 1735) and ends with one by the now even more neglected 'Owen Meredith' (Edward Robert Bulwer Lytton, First Earl Lytton, b. 1831). Willmott's other poets include Charlotte Smith, Erasmus Darwin, Anna Letitia Barbauld, Joanna Baillie, Felicia Hemans, Reginald Heber, Winthrop Mackworth Praed, John Keble, Bryan Waller Proctor and Mary Howitt, all of whose verse is probably now exclusively appreciated by an informed elite amongst readers. Willmott's volume was not intended to appeal to an elite but to a mass audience. Its attraction lay not simply in its comprehensive range but in its one hundred engraved illustrations. The anthologist and his publisher,

101 Engraved illustration for John Keats's 'Ode to a Nightingale' in Willmott's *The Poets of the Nineteenth Century*, 1856, Wood engraving on paper, 12.3 x 19 cm. Private collection

102 Ford Madox Brown, engraved illustration for Lord Byron's *Prisoner of Chillon* in Willmott's *The Poets of the Nineteenth Century*, 1856, Wood engraving on paper, 12.3 x 19 cm. Private collection

George Routledge, had managed to secure the services of some of the finest artists of the day and, to reproduce their designs, he employed as engravers the celebrated Dalziel brothers. The artists included Arthur Hughes, John Everett Millais, Ford Madox Brown, John Tenniel and Edward Henry Corbould. Hughes illustrated William Hayley's poem 'The Vision of Serena'; Millais, Byron's 'The Dream' and Coleridge's 'Love'; Brown, Byron's 'Prisoner of Chillon'; Tenniel, Thomas Percy's ballad 'The Friar of Orders Gray,' an extract from Scott's 'Marmion,' Mary Russell Mitford's 'Rienzi and his Daughter,' and Sheridan Knowles's 'The Appeal and the Reproof'; and Courbould, Henry Hart Milman's 'The Hebrew Wedding' and Charles Mackay's 'Youth and Sorrow.' One of the illustrations to Wordsworth was provided by the noted landscape artist, Myles Birket Foster, and the five pictures of rural scenes that accompany the extracts from Tennyson's 'The May Queen' were drawn by one of the engravers, Thomas Dalziel. What is notable about the volume, both in terms of its selected texts and its illustrations, is the sense that the poems assembled are representative examples of the variety of nineteenth-century poetry. There is, moreover, a proper sense of continuity rather than of the common, but nonetheless artificial, modern distinction between 'Romantic' and 'Victorian' poetry.

Willmott is emphatic both about the justice of the prominent place he allots to women writers and about the line of poetic development evident in his chosen historical period:

> The volume embraces a period of about eighty-five years, for the first canto of [Beattie's] the Minstrel appeared in 1771; Beattie survived Cowper only three years; while Percy, exchanging the friendship of Goldsmith for that of Scott, lived into the eleventh year of this century. The dates of these poets might seem to exclude them from our calendar; but, in truth, the fancy of the present age was largely inspired and moulded by the past; and the sentiment of the Minstrel, the naturalness of [Cowper's] the Task, and the simplicity of [Percy's] the Reliques, very strikingly reappear in Campbell, Wordsworth, and Scott. Nor has the embellished landscape of [Erasmus] Darwin been without imitators.[21]

Willmott was to go on to produce further illustrated anthologies of historic English poetry for the popular market, but his enterprise in *The Poets of the*

Nineteenth Century did not stand alone. In 1846, for example, Samuel Carter Hall published *The Book of Gems: Modern Poets and Artists of Great Britain*, a volume which opens with examples of the work of Wordsworth, Byron, Southey, Moore, Shelley, Coleridge and Keats and concludes with Samuel Rogers, Letitia Landon, Adelaide Procter, Mary Howitt and Tennyson. The modern artists whose work illustrates the poems include Edwin Landseer (who provided a striking canine portrait to accompany Byron's epitaph to his dog), David Cox, Daniel Maclise, William Collins, Clarkson Stanfield and Turner (who illustrated Southey's 'Sunrise'). Hall's *Book of Gems* was in turn modelled on the publisher Edward Moxon's famous and, in their time, highly esteemed editions of Samuel Rogers's *Italy* and the *Poems*, volumes for which Turner provided many of the engraved vignettes. It was one of the issues of *Italy* which had so inspired the young John Ruskin and which he described in the first chapter of *Praeterita* as giving 'the entire direction to my life's energies.' In 1857 Edward Moxon was to produce what is perhaps the most impressive of all the many illustrated volumes of poetry produced in the nineteenth century, the *Poems, by Alfred Tennyson* which included pictures by established artists, such as Stanfield, Mulready and J. C. Horsley, and far more innovatively the striking illustrations by Millais, Holman Hunt and Rossetti.

These juxtapositions of modern poetry and modern art clearly found receptive audiences in the mid-nineteenth century. They also suggest to twenty-first-century readers the significant degree to which Victorian readers regarded both Wordsworth (b. 1770) and Turner (b. 1775) not only as their contemporaries, but also as artists who immediately informed mid-century culture. The built environment inherited from the early 1800s may well have struck observers of 1850 as unbecoming and as decidedly old-fashioned, but the same was evidently not true of the poetry and the painting of the late eighteenth and early nineteenth centuries. The architecture looked false and flimsy; the literature and art, by contrast, were solid and resonant. What does seem to have shifted was the way in which artists' private lives and their morals were received by public opinion. Victorian artists were allowed their eccentricities, but it was generally assumed that they led moral lives, at least in public. 'Middle-class morality' was frequently deployed as an aesthetic yardstick. When that yardstick was applied to the writers of the first third of the century, and above all to Byron and his circle, their moral fibre was all too often found wanting and their works deemed liable to corrupt impressionable

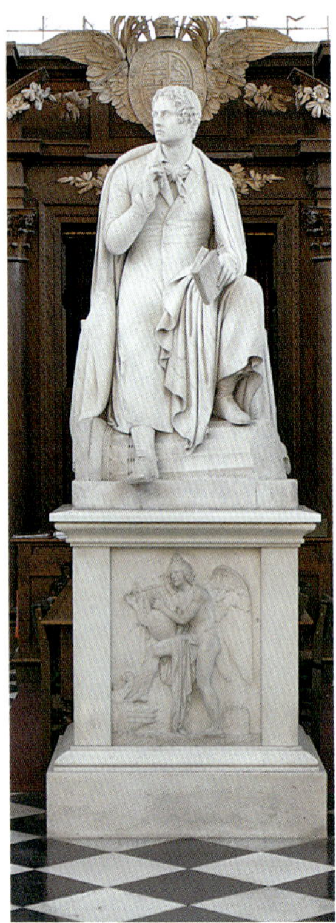

103 Bertel Thorwaldsen,
Statue of Lord Byron,
1834, Trinity College,
Cambridge

minds. Not only was the poet's embalmed body refused burial in Westminster Abbey when it was repatriated from Missolonghi, even Bertel Thorwaldsen's elegant statue (fig.103), commissioned by his admirers, had famously been refused a home in Poet's Corner in 1834. The issue of Byron's 'questionable morality' loomed large on both occasions, as it did again when the statue was declined by the Chapel authorities at Trinity College, Cambridge only to finally find a home in the College's Wren Library in 1845.

We are given a real sense of a cultural divide between what we now call 'Romantic' artists and a 'Victorian' perception of them in Dickens's *Bleak House*. Dickens had, from the beginning of his career, enjoyed the support and the companionship of many of the older generation of writers and painters who had survived into his time. His visits to Bath in the 1840s were responses to the pressing invitations of Walter Savage Landor. He was also acquainted with Turner, and owned a copy of *The Fighting Téméraire*, painted by his friend Clarkson Stanfield. Though, like virtually every other of their contemporaries, Dickens seems to have found the painter deeply eccentric, Turner seems to have been an acceptable enough companion on the boat trip down to Greenwich for a supper to celebrate the completion of *Martin Chuzzlewit* (on which occasion Turner sported 'a huge red belcher-handkerchief,' which he declined to remove despite the fact that it was a scorchingly hot day).[22] *Bleak House* of 1851–52 is however replete with characters based on what one might call 'Romantic survivors.' It is just possible that Grandfather Smallweed's unfortunate habit of slipping down in his chair, and having to be manhandled back into a sitting position, was modelled on Samuel Rogers's similar affliction. It is far more certain that the irascible Lawrence Boythorn was based on the character of another older acquaintance of Dickens's: Walter Savage Landor. As John Forster remarks, 'no objection was made' to that particular association, but Dickens's profound unease with the character of Leigh Hunt appears to have been of a very different stamp. The fact that the exploitative and indolent Harold Skimpole was directly modelled on Hunt was evident even to its most blinkered first readers and led, as Forster says, 'to much remark.' The ostensibly charming Skimpole had been assigned 'a part in the plot which no fascinating foibles or gaieties of speech could redeem from contempt.' Forster's apology on Dickens's behalf seems less than eloquent:

It is … very certain that the intention of Dickens was not at first, or at any time, an unkind one. He erred from thoughtlessness only. What led him to the subject at all, he has himself stated. Hunt's philosophy of moneyed obligations, always, though loudly, half jocosely proclaimed, and his ostentatious wilfulness in the humouring of that or any other theme on which he cared for the time to expatiate, had so often seemed to Dickens to be whimsical and attractive, that, wanting an 'airy quality' for the man he invented, this of Hunt occurred to him; and 'partly for that reason, and partly, he has since often grieved to think, for the pleasure it afforded to find a delightful manner reproducing itself under his hand, he yielded to the temptation of too often making the character speak like his old friend.'

Forster was, in part, quoting Dickens's exact words to him and to another mutual friend, Bryan Procter, both of whom knew Hunt well. It seems, however, that the one person who failed to recognise the resemblance was Hunt himself.[23] Though Dickens was later to claim that he had taken Skimpole's diary-writing from his knowledge of Benjamin Robert Haydon, a great deal of the airy duplicity in Skimpole's character derives from Leigh Hunt's personal *apologias*, his *Autobiography* which appeared in 1850 and his *Table Talk* of the following year. Dickens was at no point implying that Hunt was in any way guilty of any deep moral failing – he was manifestly un-Byronic by temperament – but that his manner, both personal and poetic, lacked the requisite earnestness. Other contemporaries were convinced that Hunt had wasted the talent he had manifested at the beginning of his career and that his *Autobiography* had exposed his essential lack of moral fibre. Take, for example, the opinion expressed by the literary-minded Edinburgh surgeon, and regular contributor to *Blackwood's Magazine*, David Macbeth Moir, in a lecture given to the Edinburgh Philosophical Institution in 1851:

It cannot be said that Leigh Hunt has quite fulfilled the promise of his early genius. Instead of concentrating his powers, and setting himself indefatigably to the rearing of some great and glorious edifice, combining the poet's invention with the artist's skill, he has contented himself with here a honeysuckle cottage, and there a woodbined grotto. He shunned the solemn and severe, and took to the light and familiar; and has at all times, and on all subjects, been most uncertain and

> capricious, alike in selection and in handling … this infirmity of purpose
> has been his drawback and his bane.[24]

Although he was probably unaware of Moir's censures, it is likely that Dickens would have accepted them as received opinion in the 1850s. He was certainly acquainted with R.H. Horne's generous comments in the *New Spirit of the Age* in 1844, for Horne's essay contrasting Wordsworth and Hunt concluded a volume that had opened with a striking essay on Dickens himself. Horne, who knows his Keats and who was well aware of Hunt's friendship for the younger poet, fancifully describes Hunt's hedonistic side thus:

> He has drunken deep from 'the beaker full of the warm south,' and
> loves to sit in the sun, indolently turning and shaping a fancy 'light as
> air,' or – and here he has never had justice done to him – in brooding
> deeply over the welfare, the struggles, and hope of humanity. Traces of
> this high companionship and these pleasant dispositions are to be found
> like lavender between the leaves of his books …[25]

This then is a benevolent Skimpole, toying with delights but somehow incapable of earnestness. Dickens may also have known the far more ambiguous opening to Macaulay's blistering review of Hunt's edition of the dramatic works of the Restoration playwrights. Macaulay's long review of January 1841 was republished in his collection of essays, the 1846 edition of which we know Dickens owned. It consistently reiterates the view that most of the drama in Hunt's edition was not only deeply salacious but that it ought never to have been reprinted. Nevertheless, Macaulay seems to have found Hunt a rather appropriate editor:

> We have a kindness for Mr. Leigh Hunt. We form our judgment of him,
> indeed, only from events of universal notoriety, from his own works,
> and from the works of other writers, who have generally abused him in
> the most rancorous manner. But, unless we are greatly mistaken, he is a
> very clever, a very honest, and a very good-natured man. We can clearly
> discern, together with many merits, many faults both in his writings and
> in his conduct. But we really think that there is hardly a man living
> whose merits have been so grudgingly allowed, and whose faults have
> been so cruelly expiated.[26]

What, one wonders, was Macaulay really implying? Does he really believe that the world had unjustly maligned Hunt? Or is he suggesting that Hunt shared not only a deeply anti-Puritan morality with the Restoration playwrights he had edited but, more damningly, that his own writings echoed what Macaulay felt was the central truth about Wycherley's *The Plain Dealer*, that they were all 'equally immoral and equally well written.'

If earnestness was the redemptive virtue required by Victorian critics, only Wordsworth seems to have passed the moral test imposed on the poets of the early century. When the great man died in April 1850 he was accorded what was still a rare thing for writers: an obituary in *The Times*. Here was a poet in whose 'legacy of song … we have nothing to regret':

> There is so much in the character, as well as the works of William Wordsworth, to deserve hearty admiration, that we may indulge in the language most grateful to our feelings without overstepping the decent limits of propriety and plain sincerity. We would point out, in the first place, one of the great excellencies of the departed worthy. His life was as pure and spotless as his song. It is rendering a great service to humanity when a man exalted by intellectual capacities above his fellow-men holds out to them in his own person the example of a blameless life.[27]

This 'blameless life' was conducive to a poetry which had 'purified and elevated, not soiled and abased, humanity.' Neither the poetry nor the example set by the man had 'corrupted or enervated our youth.' Wordsworth, *The Times* seems to be implying, was neither a dissolute Byron nor an atheistic Shelley. As his poem 'The Lost Leader' suggests, Robert Browning might have taken offence at the obituarist's insistence that Wordsworth did not truck 'the inspirations of his genius for mere sums of money' and that he 'might not have a single star or riband to hang up against the wall of his rustic cottage,' but otherwise this adulatory tribute seems to typify a Victorian norm. R.H. Horne, for example, does not seem to have been alone in characterising Wordsworth in prophetic terms as 'a great Christian moralist and teacher … sacerdotal both in gravity and purity; he is majestic and self-possessed.'[28]

In 1851 David Moir, an astute early admirer of *The Prelude*, sees Wordsworth's poetry as marking a new epoch and the man himself as a moral regenerator of English literature:

> Approximating to the Holy Scriptures themselves, his writings have a
> simplicity of thought, and a singleness of purpose, which we vainly look
> for elsewhere; and after perusing a fashionable clever trumpery work of
> the day, redolent of the scented vices and quibbling artifices of society, we
> turn to the pictures and moralisings of Wordsworth, like the 'captive long
> in city pent' to the green woods and blue skies, to the waterfalls and to the
> mountains, to the scenes of primitive bliss and patriarchal simplicity.[29]

A similar allusion to Holy Writ was made in 1862 by Thomas Arnold junior,
a writer who, thanks to his eminent parentage, had been intimately acquainted
with Wordsworth and his poetry from his youth up. Arnold, the Catholic
convert, finds Wordsworth deficient only in one thing: he is ethical caviare to
the general. Here he is expatiating on *The Wanderer*:

> The beautiful ideal of human perfection here presented to us differs
> from that which we find in the pages of the New Testament, perhaps
> only in this, that it implies an *intellectual* activity and culture possible
> only to the few, and must therefore for ever be unattainable by those
> unequal imperfectly balanced characters who constitute, nevertheless,
> the chief portion of mankind. To such characters Christianity alone
> opens out the means of reaching the highest grade of perfection
> compatible with their nature.[30]

Although Thomas's alienated brother, Matthew Arnold, admired Wordsworth's
poetry quite as much, it is scarcely surprising that he should have taken a far
less scriptural view of a poet than his older brother. Matthew's personal
religious indefinition is evident in his response to those 'fervent
Wordsworthians' who regarded the master's poetry as precious 'because his
philosophy is sound.' In the preface to the selection of Wordsworth's verse he
published in 1879, the younger Arnold was prepared to argue that 'poetry is at
bottom a criticism of life,' but he directs readers away from an extrapolated
morality and back to a close reading of the verse itself:

> The Wordsworthians are apt to praise him for the wrong things, and lay
> far too much stress upon what they call his philosophy. His poetry is
> the reality, his philosophy – so far, at least, as it may put on the form and

habit of 'a scientific system of thought', and the more that it puts them on – is the illusion … But however true the doctrine may be, it has … none of the characters of *poetic* truth, the kind of truth which we require from a poet, and in which Wordsworth is really strong … On the whole … not only is Wordsworth eminent by reason of the goodness of his best work, but he is eminent also by reason of the great body of good work which he has left to us.[31]

Matthew Arnold has shifted the moral ground, detaching the virtues of the poetry, which he is prepared to call 'good,' from the virtuous life of the poet. At the end of his introduction Arnold returns to family tradition before attempting to present a wider case for Wordsworth's literary significance to a far wider body of disciples:

> It is not for nothing that one has been brought up in the veneration of a man so truly worthy of homage; that one has seen him and heard him, lived in his neighbourhood, and been familiar with his country. No Wordsworthian has a tenderer affection for this pure and sage master than I, or is less really offended by his defects. But Wordsworth is something more than the pure and sage master of a small band of devoted followers … He is one of the very chief glories of English Poetry; and by nothing is England so glorious as by her poetry.[32]

Thomas Arnold had seen Wordsworth not simply as the culmination of a literary tradition that he had traced back to Chaucer but as a great moral teacher who spoke clearly to the modern age. For Matthew Arnold he was but the latest star in the literary firmament, but he glowed with a fire that far outshone his contemporaries and his Victorian successors.

In his essays on the 'Romantic' poets published in the 1870s and 80s Matthew Arnold continued to distinguish what are presented as his considered critical opinions from the mid-century aphorisms of his more censorious brother. Both saw Byron as a revolutionary, but for Thomas this was something that both attracted and repulsed. Byron had a 'turbulent, haughty, passionate, imperial soul' which, in *Childe Harold*, was 'the secret of its charm.' But the older Byron, in self-imposed exile, is exposed as a very distasteful figure ('so bright and powerful a spirit, degraded by the indulgence of pride and passion

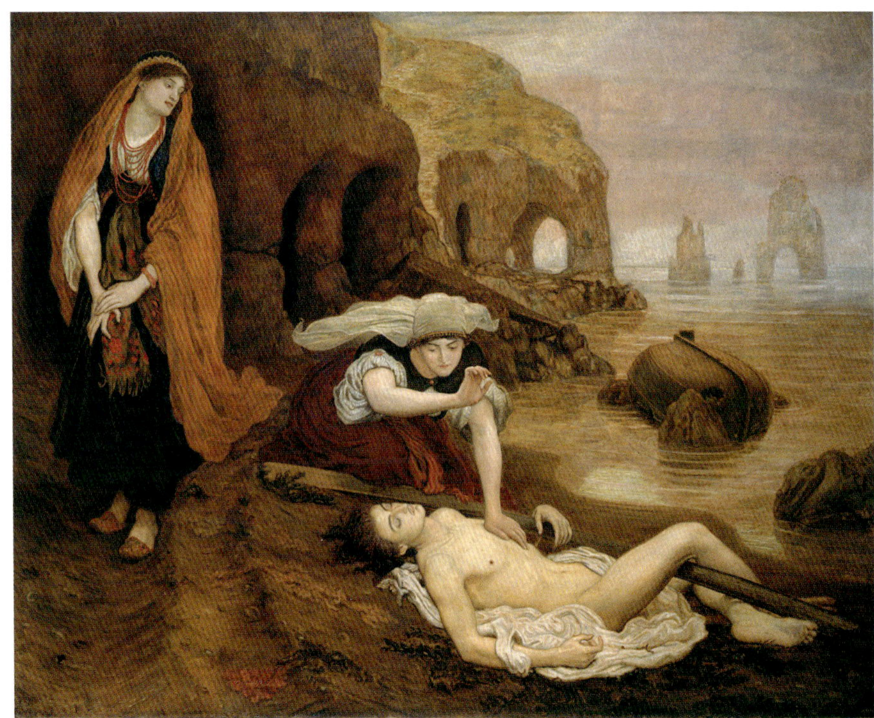

104 Ford Madox Brown, *Don Juan and Haidee*, 1873, Oil on canvas, 171 x 213cm. Birmingham Museums and Art Gallery

to a state of such deep moral defilement') while his *Don Juan* reveals not only 'the readiness, fullness and variety' of the poet's mind, but also 'the unbounded audacity of his temper, and his contempt for all ordinary restraints.' (fig. 104)[33] This then is the notoriously scandalous Byron, the poet whose private papers had been posthumously incinerated by John Murray in order to protect the public from their supposed indecency. Matthew Arnold took more a reasoned line in his introduction to a selection from Byron's poetry in 1881. His Byron is presented as having been provoked by precisely the kind of narrow social morality that Arnold himself had attacked in *Culture and Anarchy* (1869). Now, in the 1880s the poet has a renewed cultural relevance:

Byron found our nation, after its long and victorious struggle with revolutionary France, fixed in a system of established facts and dominant ideas which revolted him. The mental bondage of the most powerful part of our nation, of its strong middle-class, to a narrow and false system of this kind, is what we call British Philistinism. That bondage is unbroken to this hour, but in Byron's time it was even far more deep and dark than it is now. Byron was an aristocrat, and it is not difficult for an aristocrat to look upon the prejudices and habits of the British Philistine with scepticism and disdain.[34]

Rather than condemn Byron's moral stance, Arnold seems cautiously to endorse it in the face of what he identifies as an impending social cataclysm. Indeed, he sees Byron as some kind of hero for the new age, a prophetic voice echoing into the socially troubled 1880s. Gone is his brother's moral distaste, and gone too is the social and ethical confidence of which it was based. The old order is changing, and it is Byron who is ushering in the new:

His own aristocratic class, whose cynical make-believe drove him to fury; the great middle-class, on whose impregnable Philistinism he shattered himself to pieces – how have either of these felt Byron's vital influence! As the inevitable break-up of the old order comes, as the English middle- class slowly awakens from its intellectual sleep of two centuries, as our actual present world, to which this sleep has condemned us, shows itself more clearly – our world of an aristocracy materialised and null, a middle-class purblind and hideous, a lower class crude and brutal – we shall turn our eyes again, and to more purpose, upon this passionate and dauntless soldier of a forlorn hope, who, ignorant of the future and unconsoled by its promises, nevertheless waged against the conservation of the old impossible world so fiery battle; waged it till he fell – waged it with such splendid and imperishable excellence of sincerity and strength.[35]

Arnold was well aware that this was not the kind of thing that he was prepared to say about Wordsworth. Wordsworth had an insight into the 'permanent sources of joy and consolation for mankind' that Byron singularly lacked. In Byron's case, Arnold stresses not a source of consolation but of disconcertion; not of spiritual nourishment but of social provocation. Nevertheless, it is primarily to these two nineteenth-century poets that he assumes that future generations of Britons will look back with pride:

> When the year 1900 is turned, and our nation comes to recount her
> poetic glories in the century which has then just ended the first names
> with her will be these.

As with so many of his other theories, History was to prove Matthew Arnold
wrong.

For many mid- and late-Victorians the one name they most readily and
happily recalled amongst those of the 'Romantic' poets was that of Keats.
Arnold himself had made Keats the subject of one of his sharpest critical essays
in 1878, an essay in which he disputed the wisdom of publishing the poet's
love letters to Fanny Brawne ('we have the tone, or rather the entire want of
tone, the abandonment of all reticence and all dignity … It is the sort of
love-letter of a surgeon's apprentice which one might hear read out in a breach
of promise case, or in the Divorce Court'). This kind of debunking did not
mar the genuine appreciation of Keats's poetic achievement that is evident in
the essay, but it did go against the grain. Once they had rediscovered him in
the late 1840s, the Victorians took Keats, and virtually everything that pertained
to his short life, to their hearts. David Moir in 1851 was one of the first critics
to recognise the peculiar quality of his genius. He is particularly taken with
both the late narrative poems and the Odes ('all so pregnant with deep
thought, so picturesque in their limning, and so suggestive'). He sums up:

> In his earlier pieces Keats was too extramundane – too fond of the
> visionary. His fancy and feeling rioted in a sort of sun-coloured
> cloudland, where all was gorgeous and glowing, rose-tinctured or
> thunderous; but ever most indistinct, and often incomprehensible, save
> when regarded as dream-like imaginings – the morning reveries of a
> young enthusiast. His genius, however, was gradually coming under the
> control of judgment; his powers of conception and of expression were
> alike maturing; and his heart was day by day expanding to the genial
> influences of healthy simple nature … Altogether, whether we regard
> his short fevered life, or the quality of his genius, John Keats was
> assuredly one of the most remarkable men in the range of our poetical
> literature; nor while taste and sensibility remain in the world, can ever
> his prediction of his own fate be verified, when he dictated his epitaph
> as that of one 'whose name was written in water.'[36]

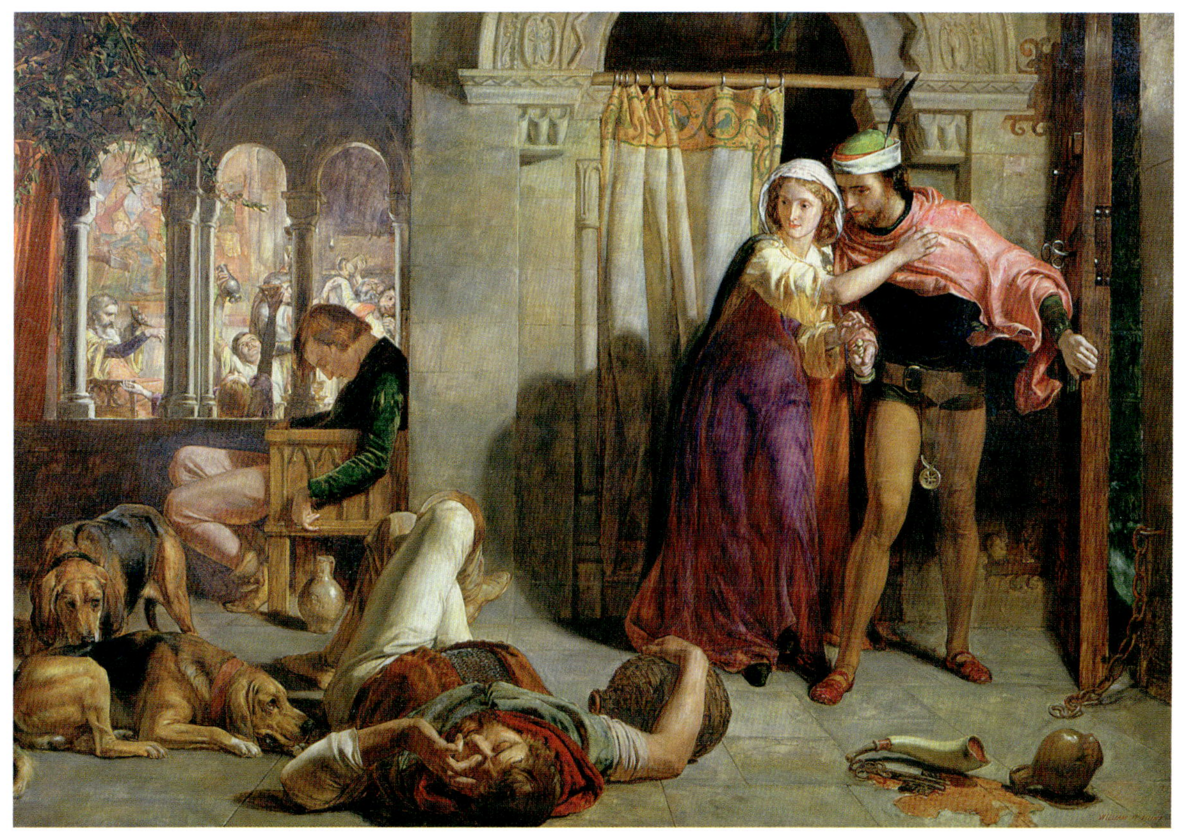

105   William Holman Hunt, *The Flight of Madeline and Porphyro during the Drunkenness Attending the Revelry*, 1848, Oil on canvas, 77.4 x 113cm. Guildhall Art Gallery, City of London

Although Keats's poems had appeared, with those of Shelley and Coleridge, in an edition published by Galignani in Paris in 1829, and *The Poetical Works of John Keats* had been issued in a paperback volume in 1840, it was not until the publication in 1848 of Richard Monckton Milnes's two-volume *Life, Letters and Literary Remains of John Keats* that the poet's reputation became firmly established. The volume, which published the greatest of Keats's letters for the first time, was re-issued in 1854 and amplified in 1869 (when a new collected edition of the poems also appeared). Coincidental with the first edition of Monckton Milnes's biography was the discovery, and adulation, of Keats's work by the Pre-Raphaelite Brotherhood. He was second only to Shakespeare as a source of subject matter for the young painters and no other nineteenth-century poet was to attract so much

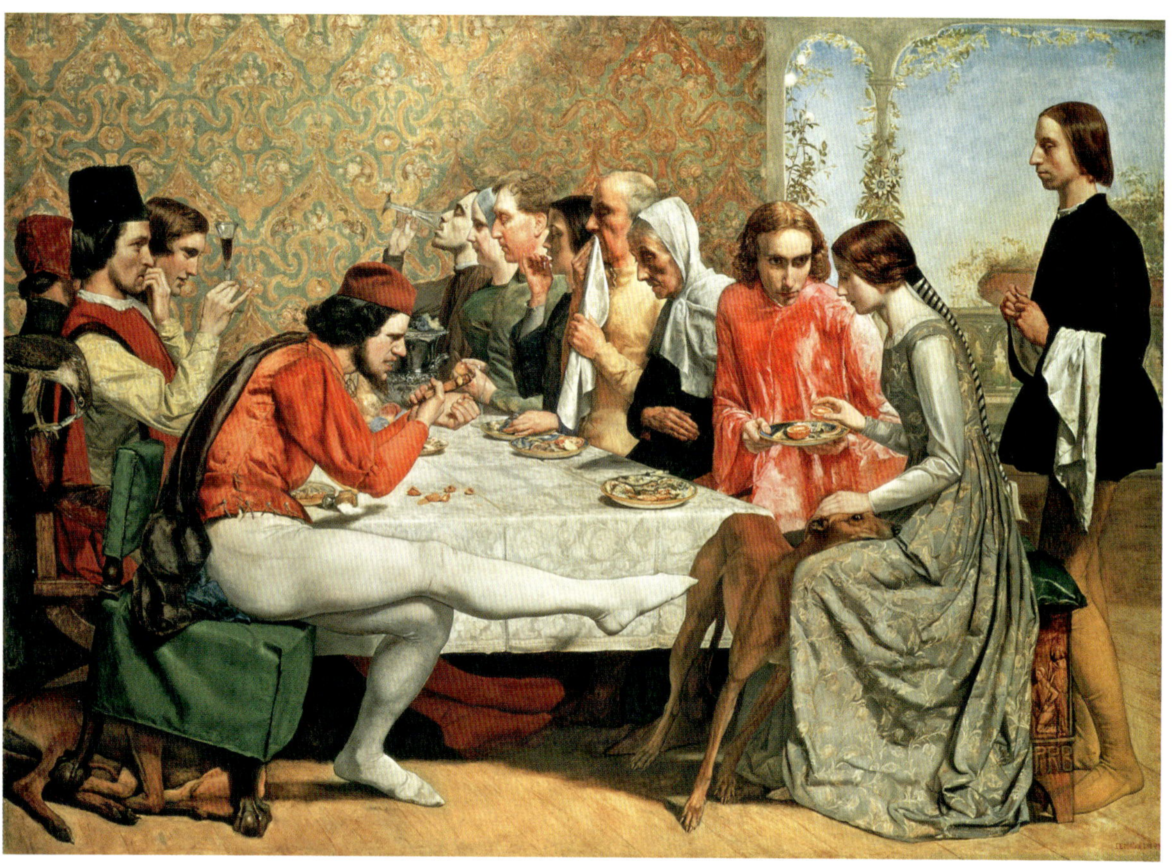

106 John Everett Millais, *Isabella*, 1848, Oil on canvas, 109.9x 142 cm. Walker Art Gallery, National Museums Liverpool

painterly attention. Holman Hunt exhibited his *The Flight of Madeline and Porphyro during the Drunkenness Attending the Revelry* (fig.105) at the Royal Academy in 1848.[37] He claimed to find the subject exemplary of 'the sacredness of honest responsible love and the weakness of proud intemperance.' In the same year Rossetti had produced a drawing based on *La Belle Dame Sans Merci* (a later watercolour of the same title appears to have no particular relation to Keats).[38] When Millais exhibited his *Isabella* (fig.106) at the Academy in 1849 it was accompanied by quotations from stanzas 1 and 21 of Keats's poem; Holman Hunt did a parallel drawing of *Lorenzo at his desk in the Warehouse* in 1848-50 (Louvre). Millais returned to a Keatsian subject with the first version of his *The Eve of St.*

Agnes in 1850, repainting the figure of Madeline undressing in a moonlit chamber in 1862-63. When Millais had begun his *Isabella* in 1848 he was a virtually unknown painter and Keats a relatively neglected poet; by the time the picture was acquired by the Walker Art Gallery in 1884, both the poet's and the painter's reputations were virtually unassailable.

The reassessment, or rather the redisicovery, of William Blake's work was quite another matter. It was not until the publication of Alexander Gilchrist's *Life and Works of William Blake. 'Pictor Ignotus'* in 1863 and William Michael Rossetti's pioneer edition of the *Poetical Works* in 1874 that Blake's paintings, engravings and verse became familiar to an audience beyond the tiny coterie that had kept his memory green.[39] Gilchrist's subtitle said it all: Blake had heretofore been an unknown. An early convert to his genius, Algernon Charles Swinburne worked on Blake's own editions of his works in the British Museum collection in order to complete his *William Blake: A Critical Essay* (1868), but even he had to battle against Gabriel Rossetti's contention that it was best to leave the Prophetic Books undiscussed. Unsurprisingly, no examples of Blake's art had been shown at the Manchester Art Treasures exhibition in 1857, and even when Edward T. Cook published his *A Popular Handbook to the Tate Gallery: 'National Gallery of British Art'* in 1898 not one picture by Blake was available either for discussion or for public display. The National Gallery had, however, been presented with the watercolour, *Epitome of Harvey's "Meditations among the Tombs"* in 1878; it purchased its first painting by Blake (*The Spiritual Form of Pitt guiding Behemoth*) in 1882; a third (*The Procession from Calvary*) was presented by Francis Turner Palgrave, whose *Golden Treasury* had not contained any of Blake's poems, in 1884. All of these pictures were transferred to the Tate in the years following the Great War when an active policy of acquiring his work had been undertaken. This followed the spirited advocacy of W.B. Yeats and Arthur Symons in the early years of the new century which had finally persuaded a wider public of the propriety of proclaiming Blake a major poet, a minor prophet, and a draughtsman of genius. Blake, the great outsider, was thus like, but unlike, Caravaggio and Vermeer, effectively a rediscovery of the twentieth century.

'Miss Austen' and the Janeites

Though never as neglected or ignored as Blake, Jane Austen's inexorable rise to fame in the latter half of the nineteenth century may surprise those who suppose that her fiction had been consistently appreciated. In her short lifetime, and in the years immediately following her death, her work was quietly respected and read by some of the grandest in the land (including the Regent, the dedicatee of *Emma*). Thereafter she was relegated to the status of a polite lady novelist who had described old-fashioned upper-class society in a predominantly rural England, a society untouched by the political and industrial changes which so marked the reigns of George IV and William IV. The last of Austen's novels to be published, *Northanger Abbey* and *Persuasion*, had appeared in 1818, the year after her death, but it was only in 1831 that the enterprising publisher, Bentley, re-issued her fiction as part of his 'Standard Novels Series.' In this collection her novels shared shelf-space with the work of a host of half-forgotten writers of the kind deemed to have a modest rather than a fashionable appeal. Bentley, who had acquired the copyright to 'Miss Austen's' fiction, did not issue his five-volume set of her novels until 1833. To give the volumes distinction, this edition contained illustrations (fig.107). It was through Bentley's collected edition, which was steadily reprinted in up-dated type-faces and bindings well into the late 1870s, that Victorian readers became familiar with Austen's work. An indication of her mixed appeal to readers can be gauged from the fact that, though George Eliot, Elizabeth Gaskell and Anthony Trollope were by their own admissions appreciative readers, neither Dickens nor Thackeray owned editions of her novels at the time of their deaths in 1863 and 1870 respectively.[40] No biography appeared until 1870 when her nephew, James Edward Austen-Leigh, published his *Memoir of Jane Austen*. When this slim *Memoir* was reprinted as an additional volume uniform with the rest of Bentley's collection, the unpublished *Lady Susan* and *The Watsons* were added in order to plump it out. The fact that the *Memoir* had been called for at all is testimony to the slow realisation among Victorian readers that there was something singular about Austen's work and that it could no longer be considered a slightly unfashionable curiosity. Austen-Leigh himself claimed that the novelist's immediate family had never assumed 'that the world would take so strong and abiding an interest in her works as to claim her name as public property.'[41]

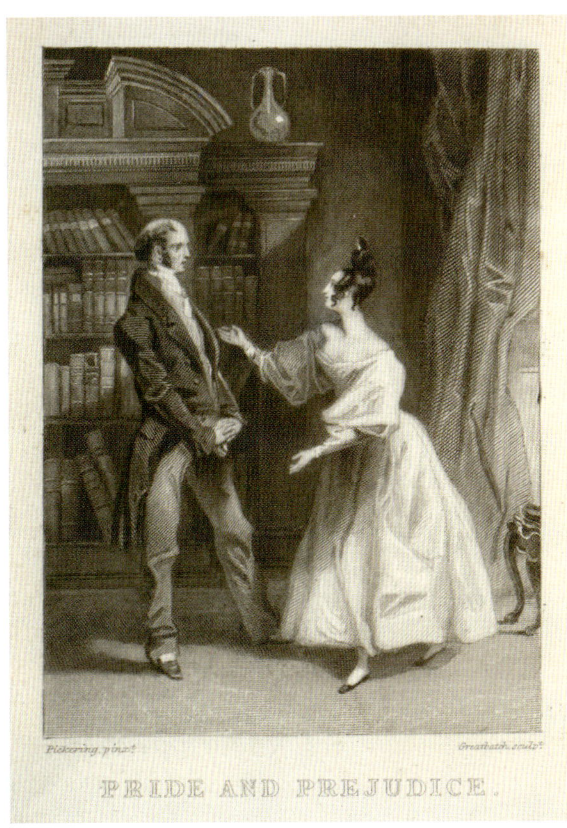

107 Plate from *Pride and Prejudice* in Bentley's edition of *The Works of Jane Austen*, 1833. The British Library

The reasons behind the shift in Austen's literary fortunes were, however, radically different from those that had determined the Victorian reassessment of the reputations of the poets who had been her contemporaries. Keats's posthumous acclaim as a major writer can be ascribed to the fact that his late narrative poems held an appeal for Victorian readers and painters alike, thanks to their acute evocations of objects, colours and moods and their distinctive appeal to the senses; his odes and lyrics were, on the other hand, ideally suited, both in terms of size and subject matter, to the requirements of anthologists. Byron, whose morals had so shocked the more prudish, had proved to be hugely influential in defining a new, slightly dangerous kind of Romantic hero, the brooding Brontëan hero as much as the dynamic, mould-breaking Carlylean one. To Matthew Arnold, Byron could also be redefined as the herald of a far more significant cultural redefinition: that of anti-bourgeois politics in the closing years of the nineteenth century. The revival of interest in Jane Austen's novels fitted neither a Keatsian nor a Byronic pattern. Her fiction evoked neither the lost enchantments of the Middle Ages nor modern *angst*, and her narrative method was neither lyrical nor politically charged. Educated readers started praising her work in the late 1860s for its delicate accounts of human relationships, and a steadily expanding body of readers took up the cause in the 1870s and 80s. The nineteenth-century term 'Janeite' was coined to describe readers who adulated her work almost in reaction against the established styles, fashions and morals of their own day. By the end of the century she was acclaimed not simply as a great writer, but as a great *woman* writer. Jane Austen had never attempted to reflect the raffish morals and extravagance of the Prince Regent's circle in her novels. Instead, she described what she knew best: established upper class life in the rectories, manor houses and mansions of provincial England. Despite obvious continuities in aristocratic and upper-middle class social life, as reflected, say, in Trollope's novels, Jane Austen's England was manifestly not the England of the second half of Queen Victoria's reign.

Nevertheless, Austen's work was often underrated, even belittled, by mid-century critics, most of whom regarded Scott as the undoubted genius amongst the novelists of her time. Thomas Arnold junior found her novels less obviously humorous than eighteenth-century fiction, but exhibiting 'a more delicate skill in the appreciation of shades of character, and greater purity and simplicity of language.'[42] In 1853 William Spalding gave his student readers the spare information that 'Miss Austen's scenes of every-day society had much merit for their cheerful reality, and their freedom from false sensibility.'[43] Thus, Austen had her bland sentence; Scott, by contrast, was granted two paragraphs. In his lectures on *British Novelists and their Styles* given in Edinburgh in 1858, David Masson, Professor of English at University College, London, finds space in his lecture on Scott to include Jane Austen amongst a body of 'lady novelists.' These 'lady novelists' strike Masson as a peculiarly British phenomenon:

> Reasons for it might be found in the state of British society in that period, as affected by the general condition of Europe, and as leading to a somewhat new adjustment of the various kinds of intellectual occupation between the sexes – men let us say (and this is statistically

the fact) transferring themselves to other kinds of literature, including metrical Poetry, and retaining the ascendancy there; while women took possession of the Novel. Be the causes of the fact, however, what they may, the fact itself is interesting. If the Novel or Prose Fiction was the first fortress in the territory of literature which the women seized – nay, if they seized it all the more easily because the men, being absent elsewhere, had left it weakly garrisoned – it cannot be denied, at all events, that they manned it well … May there not be still farther room in the realm of intellectual activity for the genius of women; may they not yet be in *all* the garrisons?[44]

Flattering as this comment might be to those that Masson categorises as 'strong minded women' it doesn't tell us anything about Jane Austen. She is named beside Ann Radcliffe and Maria Edgeworth, but that is as far as Masson's analysis goes. A fellow Scot, Joseph Angus, who was also connected to University College, London, grants her a passing reference as the mistress of 'the novel of common life,' but otherwise refers his readers to those critics, such as Macaulay, who obviously admired her work more than he was prepared to do.[45] Angus's reference to Macaulay's once celebrated short paean to Jane Austen, in the midst of his essay on Frances Burney, was yet another reminder of the extent to which Austen's work was steadily compared to that of Burney and Edgeworth rather than to that of male novelists. At the end of his essay of 1843 Macaulay also indentifies the new feminine preserve, one which having rejected the world of 'romance' and colonised that of the novel has purified fiction of any taint of indelicacy:

> Most of the popular novels which preceded Evelina were such as no lady would have written and many of them were such as no lady could without confusion own that she had read. The very name of novel was held in horror among religious people. In decent families, which did not profess extraordinary sanctity, there was a strong feeling against all such works … This feeling, on the part of the grave and reflecting, increased the evil from which it had sprung. The novelist having little character to lose, and having few readers among serious people, took without scruple liberties which in our generation seem almost incredible.[46]

Burney and Austen can then be seen as social benefactors who have contributed to the triumph of 'middle-class morality.' Some forty years later, the idea of a distinctively 'feminine' fiction was taken up by Margaret Oliphant, a successful women novelist herself, in her *The Literary History of England in the End of the Eighteenth and Beginning of the Nineteenth Century*. Oliphant dedicates an entire chapter of her study to women writers, but her chosen novelists are Austen, Edgeworth and Susan Ferrier (Burney, surprisingly enough, is ignored). Oliphant too explores the question as to why English readers had become so taken by fiction which described 'matters of such ordinary import.' She goes on, however, to discuss the much larger question of the place of women in the literary tradition:

> As we mark the growth and rise of the new flood of noble poetry at the meeting-point of the two centuries, we should be negligent of one of the first duties of a historian if we did not note likewise the sudden development of purely feminine genius at the same great era. Female writers have never been wanting. In the dimmest ages there has always been one here and there adding a mild, often a feeble, soprano to the deeper tenor of the concert. How is it that these have never risen to the higher notes and led the strain, as the feminine voice does in music, we need not inquire. Women are very heavily weighted for any race, but it can scarcely be that circumstances account for an inferiority so continual. But the opening of an entirely feminine strain of the highest character and importance – a branch of art worthy and noble, and in no way inferior, yet quite characteristically feminine, must, we think, be dated here in the works of these three ladies … The three sister novelists who came to light in the beginning of the nineteenth century were, in their own way, as remarkable and individual as Scott or Fielding, and opened up for women after them a new and characteristic path in literature.[47]

Oliphant is clearly aware of the extent to which the example of Austen has opened the path to her own acceptability as a respected woman writer. Austen, she knows, was no self-conscious pioneer and no proto-feminist, but she has been instrumental both in enhancing women's perspectives and in changing readers' expectations. Where writers of the early century had seen Austen merely as a singularly gifted woman writer among other women writers, Oliphant tries to ascertain what made her particularly distinctive. At the same time, she attempts to determine why Austen has such *rapport* with readers in the 1880s:

> What she has left us is perhaps more perfect workmanship in all than the work of any of her contemporaries. The change of manners is great since her day, though it is not so very far off. When we think of the comparatively small incomes with which she endows her rich men, and all that they seem to be able to do with their money, the difference makes us sigh: but in other points of view there are perhaps improvements to be recorded … Actual existence … as she sketches it, and all the amusing and delightful human creatures whom she introduces, in the warmth of natural life and humour, are more worth than the finest sentiments or the most skilful machinery: and in these points Miss Austen has no superior, and very few that can be called her peers.[48]

In the 1880s, with the income from great estates plummeting amid an agricultural crisis, it might strike us as odd that Oliphant deems Mr Bingley's 'four or five thousand a year,' and Mr Darcy's reputed ten thousand, relatively paltry sums. Nevertheless, as she also seems to be indicating, Austen's narrow world excluded the kind of characters who figured so prominently in her own time and who typified new wealth and all its attendant vulgarity: the vastly rich industrialists and financiers; the *nouveaux riches* who had invested in former aristocratic estates, and the American heiresses whose money had rescued many an old family from economic disaster.

When he lectured to the Contemporary Club of Philadelphia in January 1905, Henry James, who knew a good deal about the power and influence of new money, pondered the question of Jane Austen's 'material purpose … in what seemingly proves to be saleable, form.' In her lifetime, he seems to imply, Austen was uninterested either in popularity or posterity. By 1900, however, her very appeal lay in an unconscious charm which so contrasted to the noisy emotionalism and the palpability of design in so much nineteenth-century art. The 'Janeites,' who tended to refer to their idol as 'dear, our dear, everybody's dear, Jane,' have, he believes, tended to escape into her work while failing to recognise the artful subtlety of her achievement:

The key to Jane Austen's fortune with posterity has been in part the extraordinary grace of her facility, in fact of her unconsciousness: as if, at the most, for difficulty, for embarrassment, she sometimes, over her work basket, her tapestry flowers, in the spare, cool drawing- room of other days, fell a-musing, lapsed too metaphorically, as one may say, into wool-gathering, and her dropped stitches, of these pardonable, of these precious moments, were afterwards picked up as little touches of human truth, little glimpses of steady vision, little master-strokes of imagination.[49]

Austen's art concealed art, but the act of concealment was unconscious. Nevertheless, the manner in which James expresses himself here plays into the hands of the late-century 'publishers, editors, illustrators, [and] producers of the pleasant twaddle of magazines' who had exploited what was, by the turn of the century, the commercial potential of her work.

The Jane Austen evoked by Henry James, a woman embroidering in the cool country drawing-rooms of yesteryear, was precisely the comfortable, old-fashioned, prim Jane that readers craved to admire. This was the Jane Austen who so appealed to the illustrator Hugh Thomson and his publishers Macmillans. Thomson, who had made his name with pictures of ladies in sedan chairs and port-quaffing gentlemen as illustrations to nostalgic texts with titles such as *Days with Sir Roger de Coverley* (1886) and *Coaching Days and Coaching Ways* (1888), turned his attentions to 'decorating' Austen's novels in the 1890s. *Pride and Prejudice* appeared in 1894, *Sense and Sensibility* and *Emma* in 1896, *Mansfield Park, Northanger Abbey* and *Persuasion* in 1897. Such was the success of these editions that they seem to have contributed to the establishment of the enduring myth of 'Jane Austen's England.' This idyll offered an alternative to modern life as potent as that the parallel myth of 'Merrie England.' Instead of the familiar world of smokestacks and railways, neo-Gothic town halls and eminently stuffy Royal Academicians, Darwinian science and City accountants, 'Jane Austen's England' was clean, precise, ordered, elegant and exclusively populated by leisured ladies and gentlemen. As painters like Simeon Solomon, John Pettie, William Quiller Orchardson and George Dunlop Leslie had popularly demonstrated, girls in high-waisted Empire fashions looked more becoming, and danced minuets more winsomely, than Victorian girls encumbered by crinolines and bustles. By the 1880s paintings of Regency courtship seem to have had a peculiar currency in an art market that had grown

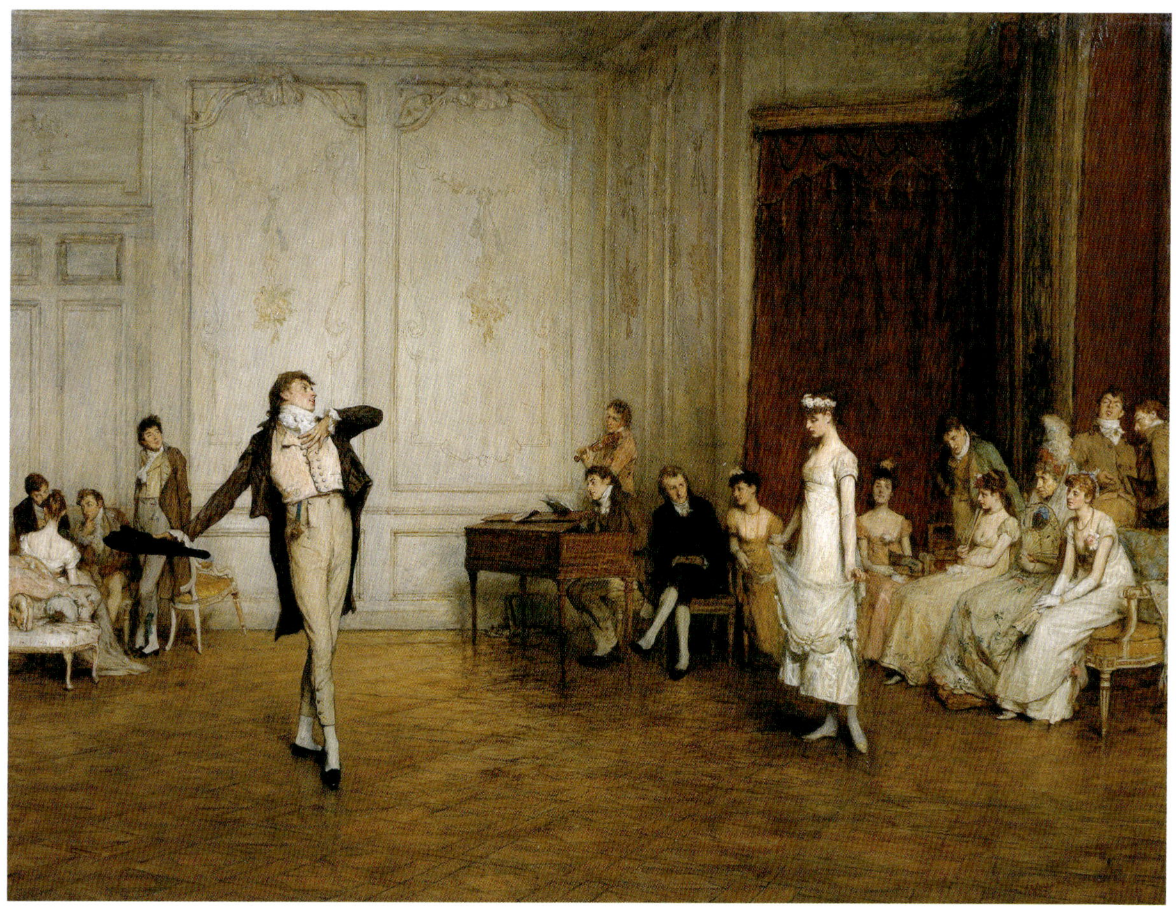

108 William Quiller Orchardson, *Her First Dance*, 1884, Oil on canvas, 101.6 x 138.4cm. Tate, London

restless with the allusive fussiness of the 'Queen Anne Style.' When Sir Henry Tate bought Orchardson's *Her First Dance* (fig.108) in 1884 he acquired a slightly absurd representation of a young man in pantaloons and pumps flamboyantly paying court to a timid girl in a simple Regency ball gown. 'The picture,' Walter Armstrong wrote when it was first exhibited, 'reads like a page from Miss Austen, whose delicate literary workmanship is represented by the delightful colour and airy, silvery tone of Orchardson's painting.'[50] This was the kind of 'history painting' that offered an escape not into the thrills and horrors of the distant past but into a semi-domestic idyll that was only just beyond the days of modern recall.

'Twas Sixty Years Since

When Thackeray published *Vanity Fair* between 1847 and 1848 the engraved illustrations he himself provided to his text made no attempt to show his characters in period costume. Not to have shown Becky Sharpe dressed in Regency fashions seems to have left both Thackeray and his first readers undismayed. Despite the fact that Thackeray the novelist had been so scrupulous in getting period detail right in his text, a parallel attention to visual detail does not seem to have prompted Thackeray the illustrator to delve into old fashion magazines in order to clothe his characters appropriately. By 1847 Regency and 'Empire' costume must have seemed amusingly quaint and unbecoming to readers. One only has to recall Mr. Turveydrop's padding and stays to sense that, in the 1850s, the fashions of the past often seemed absurd and affected. The fact that Thackeray's Becky, with her slightly billowing skirts, looks more like a woman of the 1840s than one of the 1810s probably reassured readers that this was a text for their own times and that its comedy was both immediate and pertinent. Period costume was, after all, considered to be the preserve of historical painters, not of modern novelists. Though none of Dickens's non-historical novels is precisely dated, the illustrations to those, such as *David Copperfield* or *Bleak House* – both of which appear to be set in the 1820s – also show characters in the dress-styles of the late 1840s and 50s. A reference to the fashions of twenty years before, and a precise visual location in a specific period, was probably deemed likely to defamiliarise them. Indeed *Pickwick Papers*, which is very specifically 'posthumous,' seems to make a point of the happy absurdity of Samuel Pickwick's slightly old-fashioned 'tights and gaiters.'

When Millais painted his hugely popular *The Black Brunswicker* in 1859–60 (fig. 109) he too seems to have avoided too precise a representation of a ball-gown of 1815. The anxious woman in the painting (modelled on Dickens's daughter, Kate) is wearing a superb white satin dress, but again the full skirt, the low waist-line and the long sleeves suggest the 1840s rather than the classically-inspired lines of the late-Napoleonic era. Indeed, the preliminary sketches for the painting, reproduced in J. G. Millais's *Life and Letters of Sir John Everett Millais*, show Kate Dickens in an even fuller dress. The subject of Millais's painting is, however, precisely dated to a specific historical moment. It represents the last meeting of two lovers on the eve of Waterloo. We are also led to presume that the death's head on the Brunswicker's historically accurate helmet indicates

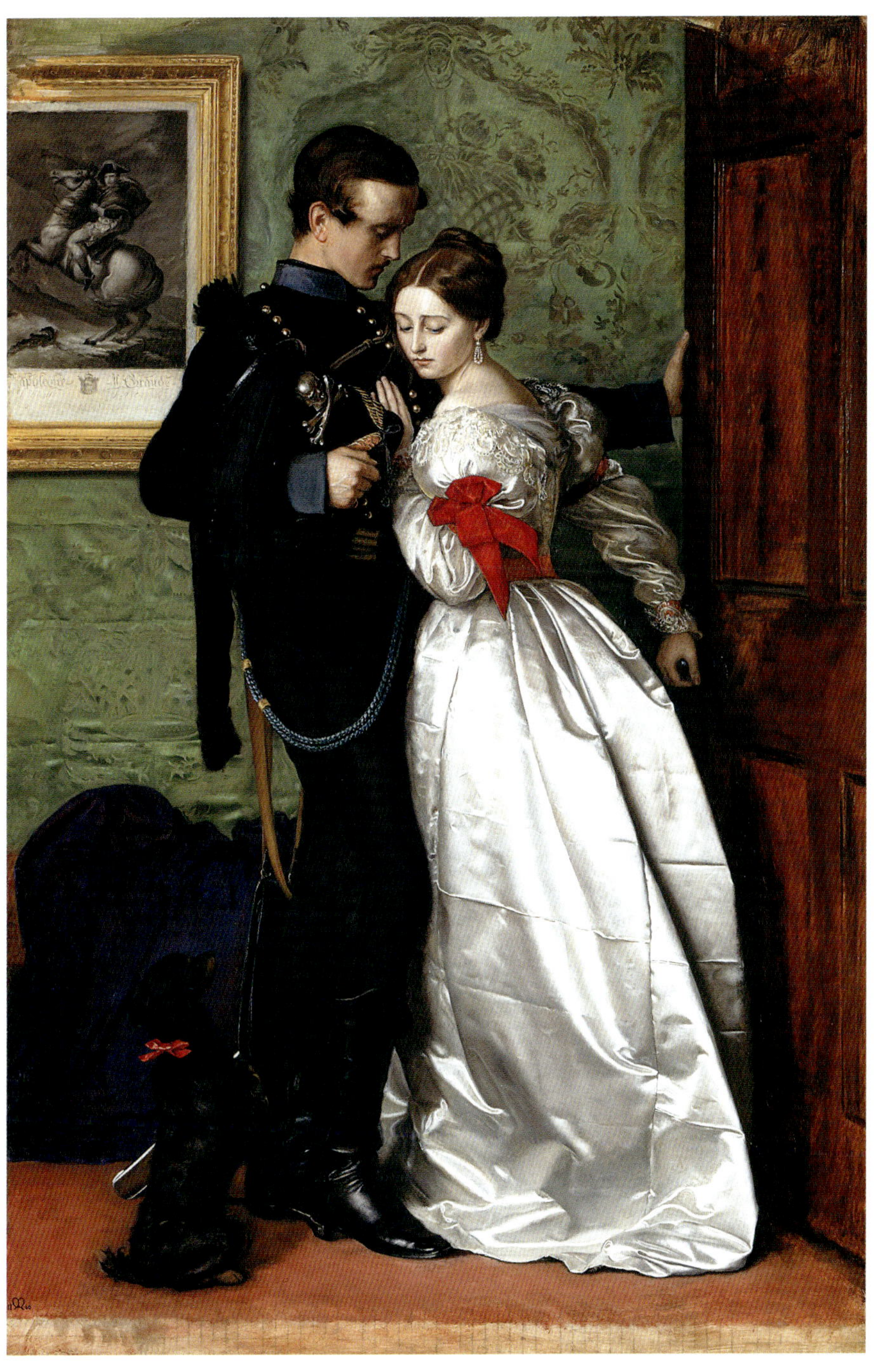

109 John Everett Millais, *The Black Brunswicker*, 1860, Oil on canvas, 99 x 66cm. Lady Lever Art Gallery, National Museums Liverpool

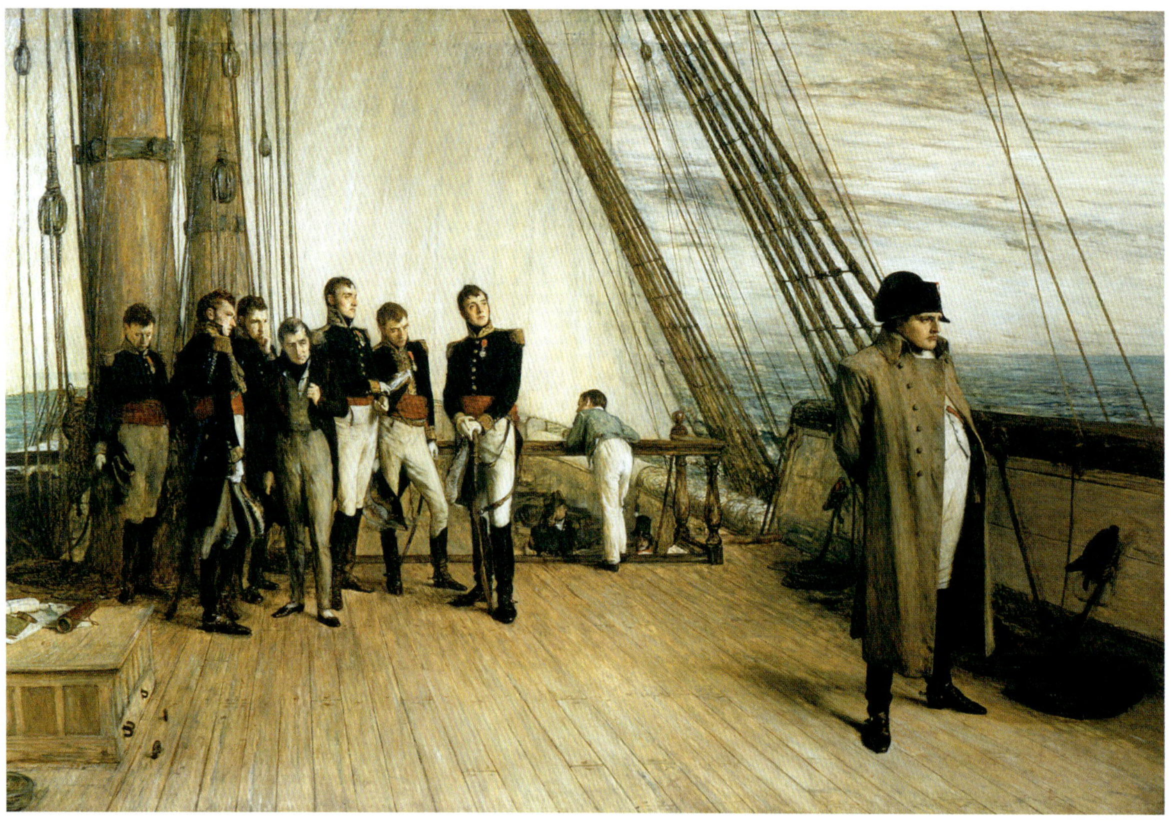

110 William Quiller Orchardson, *Napoleon on Board the H. M. S. Bellerophon*, 1880, Oil on canvas, 165.1 x 248.9cm. Tate, London

that he will fall amid the decimation of his regiment in the battle. The painting evokes the atmosphere at the abrupt end of the celebrated ball held in Brussels by the Duchess of Richmond, a ball described by Thackeray in *Vanity Fair*. The Brunswicker's departure is urgent, but his lover is shown holding him back, clutching the door-handle to delay his exit. Memories of Waterloo, and an acute awareness of the virtually unprecedented slaughter of soldiers on the battlefield, give the picture its poignancy, but it is also informed by other battles and other wars. An engraving of David's *Napoleon Crossing the Alps* on the wall behind the figures gives them a particular context, but it also reminds us that Napoleon's campaigns stretched back at least fifteen years. Despite the suggestion that the couple have just left the Duchess's ball, Millais and his first audiences would also have recognised that other officers, in other uniforms, had recently left lovers behind in order to fight in the Crimea and in India. Hence, one assumes, the acclaim accorded to the picture at the Royal Academy in 1860 and the steady popularity of later engraved versions of it.[51]

It is an illuminating aspect of the cultural changes wrought by the whirligig of time that, when Orchardson painted his *Her First Dance* in 1884, it was not the author of *Vanity Fair* whose spirit was evoked but that of the newly rediscovered Jane Austen. Compared to the way Thackeray had described them in the mid-1840s, the first thirty years of the nineteenth century were looked at from a very different perspective in the last thirty years of the century. Orchardson may well have been aware of the shift in perspective when he painted his famous picture *Napoleon on Board H.M.S. Bellerophon* in 1880 (fig. 110). It shows Napoleon defeated but Napoleon defiant, turning away from the receding coastline of France to face the empty Atlantic and the distant speck of land where he will spend his last exile. When Thackeray wrote *Vanity Fair*, through which novel the very name of Napoleon runs as a *leitmotiv*, the Duke of Wellington was still alive and with him, vivid memories of the long war against France. With Wellington's death in 1852 crucial links to an heroic past were severed. Younger veterans of his campaigns survived him of course, but the eighty-three year old, who had lived long enough to witness the ceremonial opening of the Great Exhibition, linked Victorians directly to the military triumphs of their immediate past. It was with a conscious sense of history that Queen Victoria had Franz Xaver Winterhalter paint the aged Duke presenting his infant godson, Prince Arthur, with a casket on the child's birthday (*The First of May, 1851*, see fig. 92). Behind the royal party and the uniformed godfather, Winterhalter shows the Crystal Palace. By 1880, however, the age of the Napoleonic Wars was fading as living history, and even the age of Thackeray tended to strike a new generation as stuffy and old-fashioned.

As Thackeray's *Vanity Fair*, Millais's *The Black Brunswicker* and Orchardson's *Napoleon on Board H. M. S. Bellerophon* suggest, Victorian men and women were haunted by memories of Napoleon and the French War. The War against Revolutionary and Imperial France represented the great prelude to their own era, and helped to determine their view both of heroism and of national success. However unpopular he remained in the eyes of the general public, Napoleon appears to have held a particular fascination for self-made men. As we know from the museums endowed by them, three great Victorian connoisseurs seem to have shared a fascination with the person of the Emperor, and all three assembled

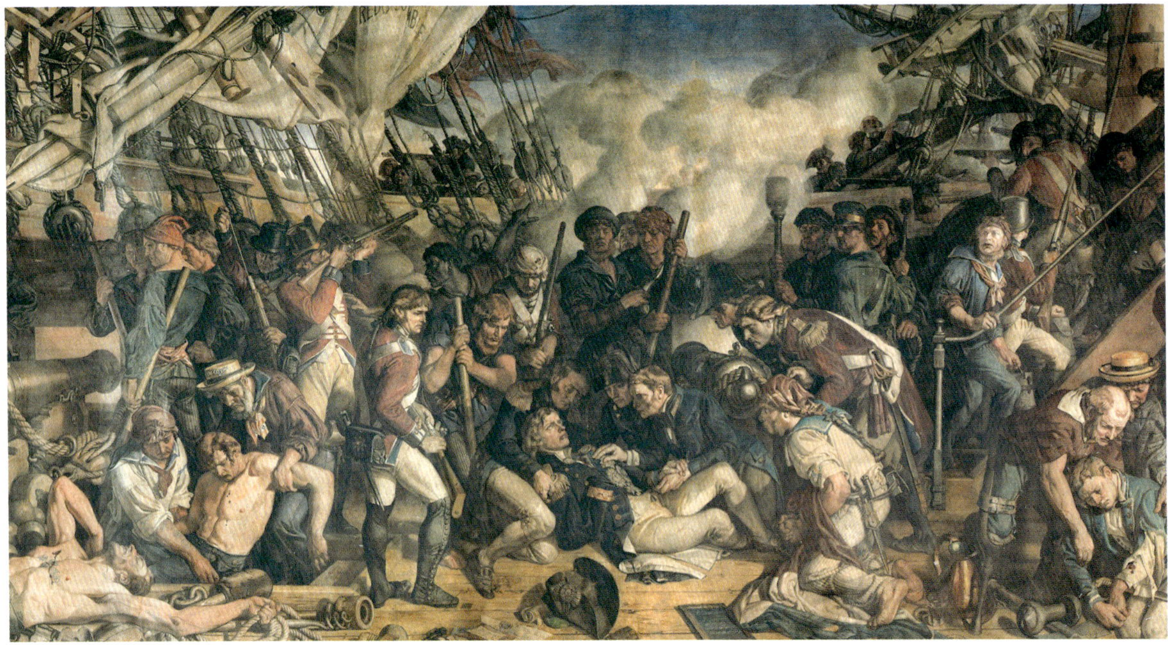

111 Daniel Maclise, *The Death of Nelson Supported by Captain Hardy on the Victory at the Battle of Trafalgar* (detail), 1866, Water glass painting, 368.3 x 1422.4 cm. Palace of Westminster Collection

collections of memorabilia; Sir Richard Wallace and John Bowes were both the rich, but illegitimate, sons of aristocratic fathers; the third, the first Lord Leverhulme, was an enterprising and philanthropic industrialist. A far larger, more sceptical, and overtly patriotic section of the population preferred to celebrate the victors rather than the defeated Bonaparte. The battles of Trafalgar and Waterloo were to provide Great Britain with more street and public-house names than any previous victories. Daniel Maclise's two great murals of *The Death of Nelson* (1859–65, fig. 111) and *The Meeting of Wellington and Blücher* (1859–61, figs 115, 116), both showing climactic moments of naval and military triumph amid scenes of carnage, were painted on opposing walls of the Royal Gallery in the Palace of Westminster. They remain there, in their gloomy splendour, at the beginning of the Sovereign's processional route through Parliament as markers of how the Victorian nation defined its ideas of glory and of sacrifice.

Queen Victoria's reign would prove, for the most part, to be remarkable for the absence of a pan-European war. Britain's semi-disastrous military involvement in the Crimean Campaign had been in alliance with the old enemy,

France, and only the suppression of the Indian Mutiny had rendered colonial wars a matter of active public concern. The years preceding 1815 were, however, consistently portrayed as being of vivid national interest, with the battles of Trafalgar and Waterloo as its great pivots. In an important way the Napoleonic Wars had emerged as a 'people's' war. In 1816 the Duke of Wellington had commissioned Sir David Wilkie to paint his *Chelsea Pensioners reading the Waterloo Despatch* (see fig. 114), and the Duke hung the finished painting in the Piccadilly Drawing Room at Apsley House on the same wall as John Burnet's *The Greenwich Pensioners commemorating Trafalgar* of 1818. The Duke was thus celebrating not simply his own part in the Wars, but the roles of the ordinary sailors and soldiers who had brought about the final victory. This was in the full knowledge that his own former soldiers might themselves be reduced to the honourable status of dependents of a grateful state. In 1875, exactly sixty years after the battle, Herbert von Herkomer's *The Last Muster* (fig. 112) showed a group of superannuated pensioners in the chapel of the Chelsea Hospital. We know that this group must have included veterans of Waterloo for, in the same year, Thomas Hardy visited the Hospital and talked to several survivors, including one John Bentley who vividly recalled sleeping in the rain on the eve and being able to perceive nothing in the smoke and haze except 'anything that shined.'[52]

Although Thackeray makes a long comic point about George IV's having 'heard so much of the war … and worn such a prodigious quantity of marshal's uniforms … that he actually fancied he had been present in some campaigns,' he also gives over a good deal of the last lecture in *The Four Georges* series to an account of the homely heroism of that 'man of the people,' Admiral Cuthbert Collingwood. Collingwood, who had taken over command at Trafalgar following Nelson's demise, had been promoted because of merit, not thanks to his connections. For Thackeray, Collingwood is the simple, unpretentious and upright man of action who somehow embodies the best qualities of the Englishman. His letters revealed him to be as attached to his family and his native soil as he is attentive to his duty as a sailor:

> There are no words to tell what the heart feels in reading the simple phrases of such a hero. Here is victory and courage, but love sublimer and superior. Here is a Christian soldier spending the night before battle in watching and preparing for the succeeding day, thinking of his dearest home and sending many blessings forth to Sarah, 'lest he should never bless her more.'

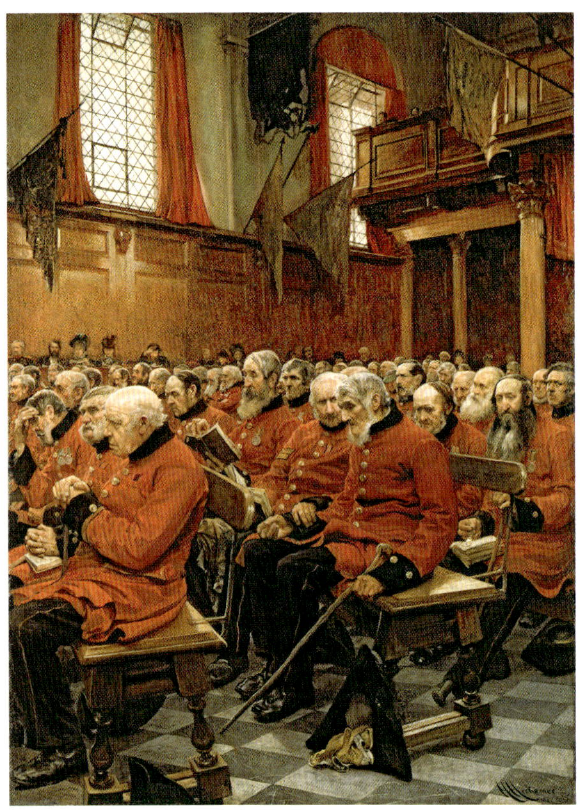

112 Herbert von Herkomer,
    The Last Muster, 1875,
    Oil on canvas,
    214.5 x 159 cm.
    Lady Lever Art Gallery,
    National Museums
    Liverpool

And who would not say Amen to his supplication? It was a benediction
to his country – the prayer of that intrepid loving heart.[53]

Memories of the sea-battles of Collingwood and Nelson, the campaigns of
Wellington, and of the defence of Britain from the threat of invasion were the
stuff of both legend and anecdote. Most writers of Thackeray's generation had
grown up with such military narratives as the matter of every-day discourse.
Thackeray himself always recalled glimpsing the figure of Napoleon at St
Helena in 1817 on his boyhood voyage to England from his birthplace at
Calcutta. 'That is he,' said his Indian servant, 'that is Bonaparte! He eats three
sheep every day, and all the little children he can lay hands on!'[54] Thackeray
was also delighted to have witnessed the ceremonial reburial of Napoleon
at Les Invalides in 1840 (an event described in 'The Second Funeral of

Napoleon'). Later in the century, another novelist, Thomas Hardy, would not only fondly imagine some family connection with Nelson's Captain Hardy, he would dwell on his grandmother's stories of the Wars and the threat of an invasion of the southern counties of England.[55] For Thackeray, Napoleon was part ogre, part figure of pretension. For Hardy, he was part threat, part unwitting tool of the Immortal Forces which he described as 'Dynasts.' For both writers, however, Napoleon seemed to define what was most enthralling about the history of Europe in the opening years of the nineteenth century.

Sir Walter Scott, whose much respected *Life of Napoleon Buonaparte* had appeared in 1827, was crucial to Victorian definitions of history and culture not simply because of his fascination with the Emperor. It was Scott who, in the sub-title to *Waverley* (*'Tis Sixty Years Since*), had defined what was to prove a crucial dimension in Victorian fiction. Scott's 'sixty years' allowed the present to come to terms with recent history because they covered the space of two generations. Living memory was thus properly conditioned by the passage of time. Private recall could also be supplemented by a multiplicity of public records. Those Victorian historical novels that deal with the period of the Revolutionary and Napoleonic wars were to make particular play with the sixty-year time-gap. George Eliot's *Adam Bede*, for example, is set exactly sixty years before its date of publication (1859): we are given the precise date – 'the eighteenth day of June, in the year of our Lord 1799' – on the first page of the opening of the narrative. Although the novel is far from military in its central concerns, we are well aware that Arthur Donnithorne is 'Captain Donnithorne' in the Loamshire Militia and that it will be his military duties that call him away from Hayslope to Windsor. Eliot also consistently plays with snippets of historical information interwoven with more domestic concerns. Mrs Poyser's perspective on larger events is, for example, represented in Chapter 33 by the fact that she finds the news that 'Bony' has returned from Egypt, and that the French have been repulsed in Italy, secondary to village affairs. Readers are, however, acutely aware of the degree to which military affairs are shaping private narratives. When Hetty makes her arduous trek to Windsor to look for Arthur, she discovers that he has moved with his regiment to an Ireland still restless in the aftermath of the '98 Rebellion. Although Arthur's joyful return to Hayslope in Chapter 44 is marked by his rushing out of doors and greeting 'every one who spoke to him, as if there had been news of a fresh Nelson victory,' his joy is rapidly replaced by devastation when he becomes fully aware of his part in Hetty's tragedy. Towards the end of the novel, when social stability has returned to Hayslope, Eliot herself addresses readers in order to remind them of the effects of the passage of time between the 'then' of the narrative and the 'now' of her first readers. As with her comments in *Middlemarch* on Henry Fielding having more time to muse than she does, Eliot speaks in *Adam Bede* of the demise of leisure:

> Leisure is gone – gone where the spinning-wheels are gone, and the pack-horses, and the slow wagons, and the pedlars, who brought bargains to the door on sunny afternoons. Ingenious philosophers tell you perhaps, that the great work of the steam-engine is to create leisure for mankind. Do not believe them: it only creates a vacuum for eager thought to rush in. Even idleness is eager now – eager for amusement: prone to excursion-trains, art-museums, periodical literature and exciting novels: prone even to scientific theorising, and cursory peeps through microscopes … Fine old Leisure! Do not be severe upon him, and judge him by our modern standard: he never went to Exeter Hall, or heard a popular preacher, or read *Tracts for the Times* or *Sartor Resartus*. (Chapter 42)

Eliot then suggests to readers of 1859 that her retrospect requires them to temporarily set aside modern manners and modern ways of thinking. Her account is of a pre-railway age, before time seemed to speed up with the steam locomotives and before England became uneasy with itself. She refers in particular to the new Victorian earnestness stimulated by the missionary provocations of Evangelical preachers at Exeter Hall, by Oxford Tractarians and by the noisy insistence of Thomas Carlyle that England look to its modern condition.

In the concluding chapters of *Adam Bede* Eliot forgets the Napoleonic wars in order to concentrate on the particular and private webs woven by her fictional characters. In Elizabeth Gaskell's *Sylvia's Lovers* (1863), however, the ramifications of the War are inextricably interwoven with the destinies of all her characters. None escapes its consequences. Her novel is set in the fictional sea-port of 'Monkshaven', a thinly disguised Whitby, and it begins just as specifically as *Adam Bede* with a day and a date: 'One hot day, early in October of the year 1796.' This is the time, Gaskell informs us, when the inroads of the naval press-gangs were violently disrupting the lives of mariners and their families in coastal ports. Her narrator is quite explicit in offering readers a condemnation of this brutal means of manning the wartime Navy:

> Now all this tyranny (for I can use no other word) is marvellous to us; we cannot imagine how it is that a nation submitted to it for so long, even under any warlike enthusiasm, any panics of invasion, any amount of loyal subservience to the governing powers. When we read of the military being called in to assist the civil power in backing up the press-gang, of parties of soldiers patrolling the streets, and sentries with screwed bayonets placed at every door while the press-gang entered and searched each hole and corner of the dwelling; when we hear of churches being surrounded during divine service by troops, while the press-gang stood ready at the door to seize men as they came out from attending public worship, and take these instances as merely types of what was constantly going on in different forms, we do not wonder at Lord Mayors, and other civic authorities in large towns, complaining that a stop was put to business by the danger which the tradesmen and their servants incurred in leaving their houses and going into the streets, infested by press-gangs. (Chapter 1)

Gaskell's mid-Victorian complaint was evidently one that was resonant in a peaceful England that remained inordinately proud of its navy, but which had abandoned the practise of enforced conscription. An emotive scene of a seaman being snatched by the press-gang as he leaves his wedding was painted in 1858 by Alexander Johnston (fig. 113). The press-gang, both Gaskell and Johnston are implying, was a challenge to natural liberties and represented a 'tyranny' worthy of a German Princeling or a Russian Czar, not of the land of the Bill of Rights and Habeas Corpus. Gaskell's words would have read rather differently in 1916 but by then, with the Great War at its most bloody, public attitudes to what constituted patriotism had shifted.

Gaskell's attitude to the State and to the conduct of the French Revolutionary Wars proves to be far more radical than George Eliot's. In the course of *Sylvia's Lovers*, Sylvia Robson's family circle is torn apart, her lover is taken by the press-gang, her father is hanged for his violent resistance to naval seizures of returning sailors, and her deceitful husband leaves her in shame and joins the marines. When the vicar of Monkshaven fudges a sermon preached in memory of local men killed in the press-gang raid, Gaskell offers readers another wry commentary of the differences between 'then' and the perceptions of 'now':

> In looking back to the last century, it appears curious to see how little our ancestors had the power of putting two things together, and perceiving either the discord or harmony thus produced. Is it because we are farther off from those times, and have, consequently, a greater range of vision? Will our descendants have a wonder about us, such as we have about the inconsistency of our forefathers, or a surprise at our blindness that we do not perceive that, holding such and such opinions, our course of action must be so and so, or that the logical consequence of particular opinions must be convictions which at present we hold in abhorrence? It seems puzzling to look back on men such as our vicar, who almost held the doctrine that the King could do no wrong, yet were ever ready to talk of the glorious Revolution, and to abuse the Stuarts for having entertained the same doctrine, and tried to put it into practice. But such discrepancies ran through good men's lives in those days. It is well for us that we live at the present time, when everybody is logical and consistent. (Chapter 6)

Gaskell's irony is patent here, for she knows, as with her passionately stated case against conscription, that another generation may judge affairs differently. It is because of anomalies, not all of which are ideological, and because of personal convictions, not all of which are logical, that the novel veers inexorably into tragedy. Even here, though, the personal tragedies of the characters are directly linked to the progress of the War. When the deceit of Sylvia's unloved husband, Philip Hepburn, is exposed, he disappears, 'driven forth like Cain,' and enlists in the marines. It is during his military service at the siege of Acre in 1799 that he is disfigured by an explosion and, broken and unrecognisable, he finally returns to the Monkshaven that he had left in disgrace. On a public level, Philip is a victim of war and resembles many another crippled veteran. Privately, however, he has brought suffering on himself as an act of atonement for pursuing misguided convictions and using dishonest means to attain the Sylvia he had yearned for.

Hardy's *The Trumpet-Major* of 1880 strikes a far more subdued tragic note, but it, like Gaskell's novel, deals not with the interaction of the officer class with the local gentry, but with provincial working people indirectly caught up in the disruptions of a long drawn-out campaign. It opens not with a specific date, but with a brief evocation of Wessex at war:

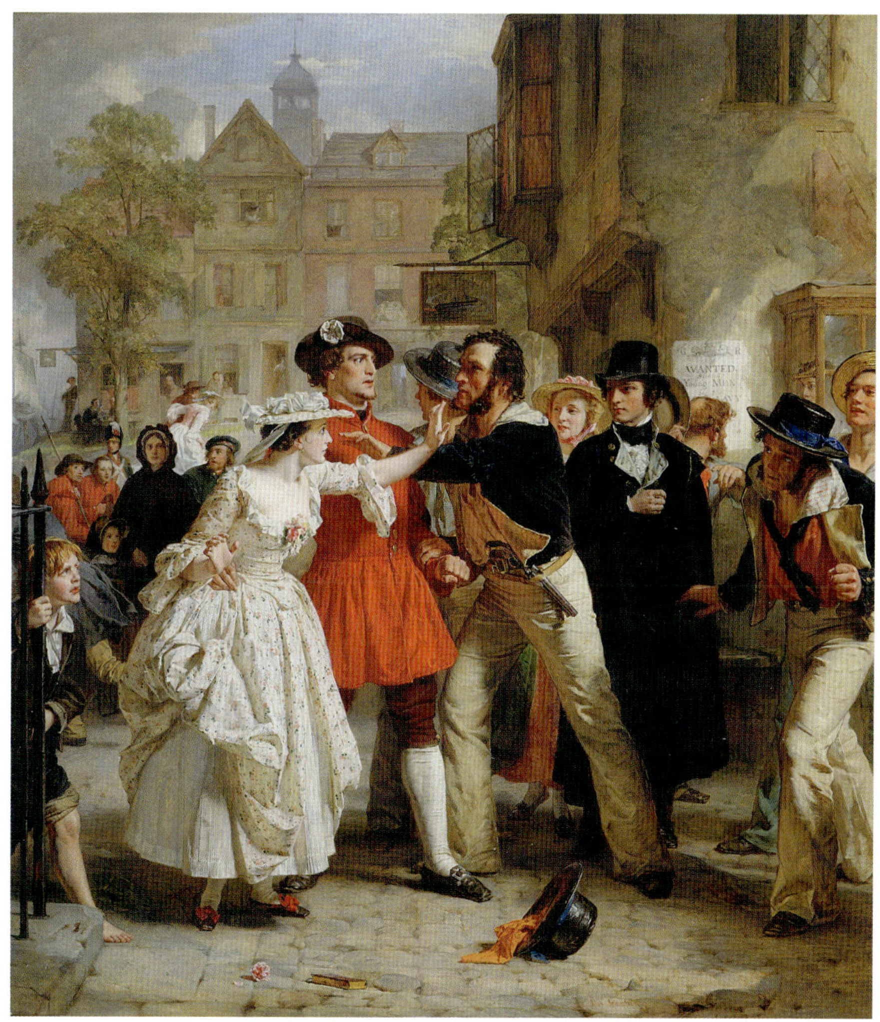

113 Alexander Johnson, *The Press Gang*, 1858, Oil on canvas, 138.4 x 123.2cm. Ferens Art Gallery, Hull Museums

In the days of high-waisted and muslin-gowned women, when the vast amount of soldiering going on in the country was a cause of much trembling to the sex, there lived in a village near the Wessex coast two ladies of good report, though unfortunately of limited means.

In 1880 this opening would have readily reminded readers of Jane Austen. It would also have told them that Hardy had the distinctive costumes of the early

1800s clearly in his mind. He describes Anne Garland as wearing a white handkerchief covering her neck, 'and a cap on her head with a pink ribbon round it, tied in a bow at the front.' What readers soon grasp, however, is that what Austen might have meant by 'limited means' does not apply to Hardy's characters. In *The Trumpet-Major* we have moved very distinctly down the social scale and into a rural Wessex 'where there is what is called no society' and where there is a manifest 'levelling of distinctions … at some sacrifice of gentility.' Anne Garland and her mother live not in a Manor House but in part of a Mill House. In order to emphasise what social class we are talking about, Hardy gives their neighbour, the miller Mr. Loveday, a mock ancestry which relates him to 'a vast body of Gothic ladies and gentlemen of the rank known as ceorls or villeins, full of importance to the country at large, and ramifying throughout the unwritten history of England.' This then is decidedly not 'Jane Austen's England,' of militia officers, gentry balls and grand houses, but the Wessex of middling country folk that was already familiar to Hardy's readers. It is a Wessex seen in an historical perspective, and a region that, thanks to the threat of invasion, is no longer left to its own devices. Having told us, with a delightful ambiguity, that the 'soldiering' of the times engenders female 'trembling,' Hardy suddenly introduces the reality of the military presence. In the first chapter two troopers appear 'armed and accoutred throughout' with 'the burnished chains, buckles and plates of their trappings' shining in the sunlight. The troopers are the vanguard of a cavalry regiment, the York Hussars, who will encamp near Overcombe Mill in order to secure the Wessex coastline from 'the arch enemy of mankind', Bonaparte.

Hardy's story interweaves the military with the domestic with its emphasis on the destinies of ordinary men and women. One of the miller's two sons is taken by the press-gang into the Royal Navy; the other is the Trumpet-Major of the title (a 'trumpet-major' is the chief regimental trumpeter). When characters are present at 'historical' moments, whether major or minor, they are always merely passive bystanders or, at most, incidental to an event beyond their immediate control. Mrs Garland is overjoyed to have seen George III and Queen Charlotte *en route* to Weymouth, while the miller's son, Bob Lovejoy, finds himself serving as a pressed man under Nelson on *HMS Victory*. As Anne Garland watches Nelson's flagship sink over the horizon her thoughts are centred on Bob, but Hardy's brief, lyrical description reminds readers that the ship has a grander destiny to fulfil than merely to separate lovers:

The courses of the *Victory* were absorbed into the main, then her topsails went, and then her top-gallants. She was now no more than a dead fly's wing on a sheet of spider's web; and even this fragment diminished. Anne could hardly bear to see the end, and yet she resolved not to flinch. The admiral's flag sank behind the watery line, and in a minute the very truck of the last topmast stole away. The *Victory* was gone. (Chapter 34)

As she leaves the headland, sobbing as she goes, Anne unexpectedly encounters King George taking a constitutional. The King, being in a particularly gracious and attentive mood, enquires the reason for her distressed emotional state. On being informed by Anne, he asks for her lover's name and insists that he will not forget it. On the way home, a now buoyed-up Anne speculates as to Bob's chances of royal promotion, but then a typically flat Hardyan reality intrudes into her dreams: 'she was not a girl who indulged in extravagant fancies long, and before she reached home she thought that the King had probably forgotten her by that time and her troubles, and her lover's name.' We later learn that Bob, who has survived the battle at Trafalgar, was one of the sailors who carried the dying Nelson to the cockpit, and who later boarded a French battleship as she struck her flag. He also forms part of Nelson's great funeral procession in London, serves in other campaigns, and is finally promoted to the rank of lieutenant (though we are led to assume that his promotion is due more to Captain Hardy's intervention than to George III's uncertain recall). In the end it is Bob, a worthy sailor but an unfaithful lover, who wins Anne. His far more stolid brother, John, is shipped to the Peninsula with his regiment, going off 'to blow his trumpet till silenced for ever on one of the bloody battle-fields of Spain.' There the novel ends. Throughout his narrative, however, Hardy had shown himself anxious to remind readers of the bloody reality of war as it shaped the lives and deaths of multitudes of common soldiers and sailors. In Chapter 12 of *The Trumpet-Major*, written some five years after the novelist had encountered Waterloo veterans at the Chelsea Hospital, Hardy moves from an account of the brightly uniformed troops reviewed by the King at Weymouth to a reflection on their likely future. The troops are drawn up on the downs overlooking the town:

They still spread their grassy surface to the sun as on that beautiful morning not, historically speaking, so very long ago, but the King and his fifteen thousand armed men, the horses, the bands of music, the princesses, the cream-coloured teams – the gorgeous centre-piece, in short, to which the downs were but the mere mount or margin – how entirely have they all passed and gone! – lying scattered about the world as military and other dust, some at Talavera, Albuera, Salamanca, Vittoria, Toulouse, and Waterloo; some in home churchyards; and a few small handfuls in royal vaults.

This is far more than a reflection on Death as the Great Leveller. The downs, which Hardy knew well, are the eternal hills, but the King, his family, and his fifteen thousand men, officers, trumpeters and cannon-fodder alike, are ephemeral. Their dust is either scattered to the winds or interred, with only the Royal Family having the privilege of a vault and the likelihood of being remembered beyond another generation. The Weymouth review, Hardy reminds his readers of 1880, was 'not … so very long ago,' but it is part of history, nonetheless. The last battle he names, Waterloo, was, in the year his novel was published, already 'sixty-five years since'.

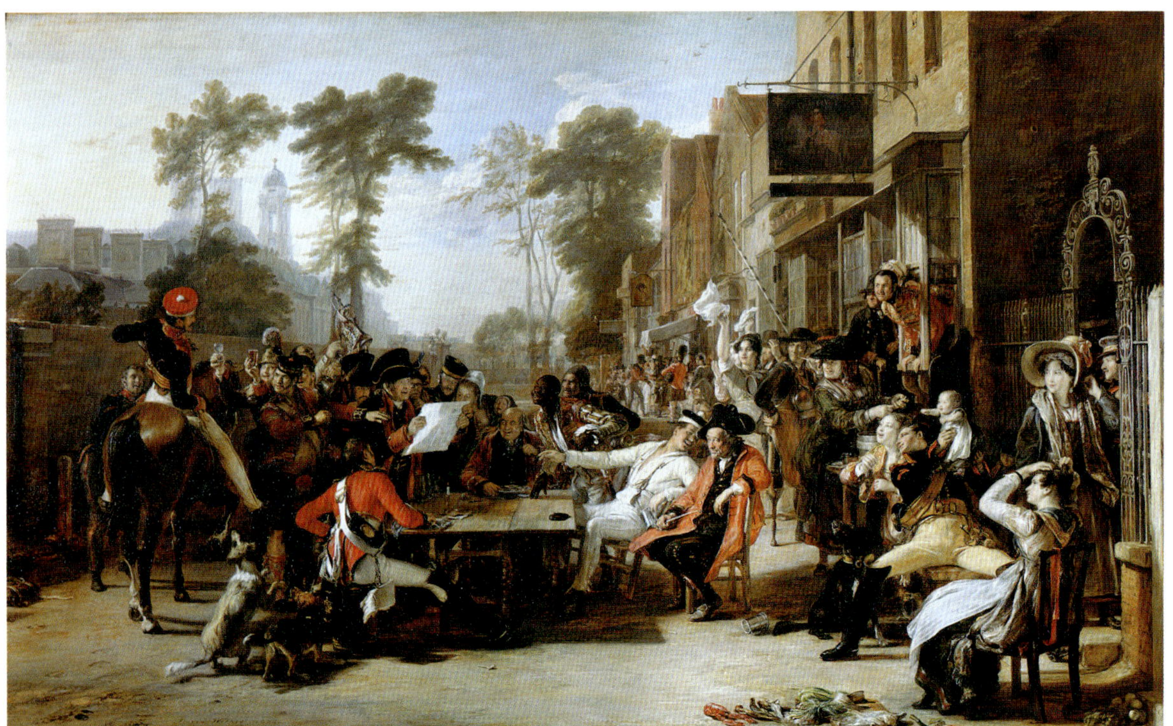

114   David Wilkie, *Chelsea Pensioners Reading the Waterloo Despatch*, 1816, Oil on canvas, 97x158 cm. Apsley House, The Wellington Museum, London

CODA

When, towards the end of his long life, Hardy divided up his literary manuscripts in order to present them to eminent libraries in the English-speaking world, he donated his most famous, *Tess of the D'Urbervilles*, to the British Museum Library. He also gave the Library the other work he most wanted to be remembered by: his long Napoleonic epic, *The Dynasts*. Not surprisingly, the Fitzwilliam Museum in Cambridge, rather than any library at Oxford, received *Jude the Obscure*. Perhaps more unexpected, however, was the presentation of the manuscript of *The Trumpet-Major* to the Royal Library at Windsor. Despite the fact that 'King Jarge' is somewhat wryly characterised in his novel, Hardy clearly felt that his novel had found a proper home. Just as the acceptance by the University of Cambridge of the manuscript of *Jude* might be seen as offering an *amende honorable* to Jude Fawley, so cruelly rejected by Christminster, so the receipt of *The Trumpet-Major* manuscript by the Royal Library may have struck its author, Thomas Hardy, OM, as justifying him in the eyes of his King as the proud descendant of Wessex 'ceorls and villeins.' His work had been found worthy of a niche, not just in the literary history of his nation but in an auspicious place on the library shelves of George III's great-great-grandson.

When Hardy spoke of 'the levelling of distinctions' and of the 'unwritten history of England' in *The Trumpet-Major* he knew that he was giving voice to common enough late-Victorian sentiments. He had been born in 1840, the son of a Dorsetshire jobbing builder; Hubert von Herkomer, the painter of *The Last Muster*, was born nine years later, the son of a Bavarian wood-carver and joiner who had emigrated to Southampton in 1857. Although Hardy was to decline the offer of a knighthood, he became a member of the new Order of Merit in 1910. Herkomer had, in his turn, been elevated to noble rank by Kaiser Wilhelm in 1899 (hence the 'von' in his name). Both Hardy and Herkomer were first-generation 'Victorians,' as distinct from the 'Georgians' who dominated the first great phase of Victorian culture. They were also both 'self made,' men of humble origin who had risen through their own talents. Both had found fame and respect through the practise of a socially responsive art, an art that had represented the sufferings and the endurance of the poor.

Both Hardy and Herkomer knew that by the late 1870s the composition of society was beginning to change. Most working men had been given the vote under the terms of the Second Reform Act in 1867, and the uncertain political future looked increasingly dependent not simply on the good will of the newly

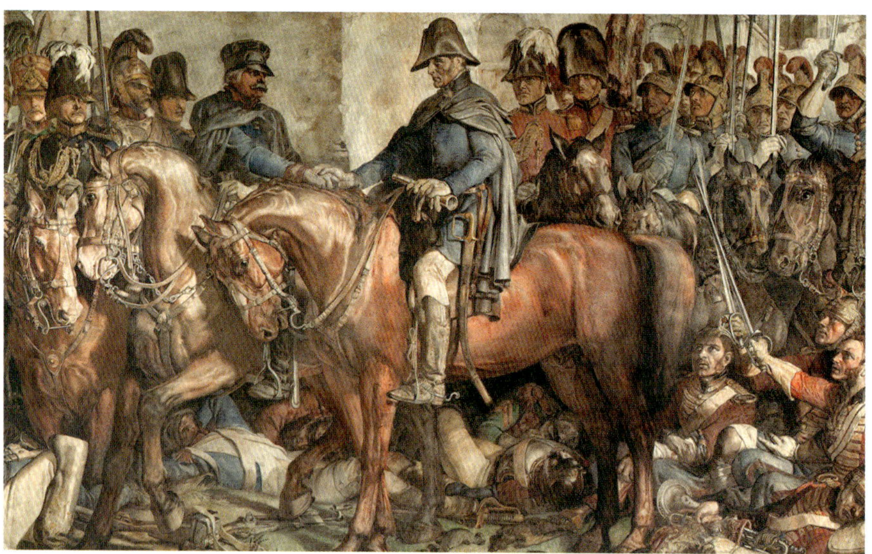

enfranchised, but also on their acquiescence to the political process. To many it seemed as if the first glimmerings of the dawn of the 'age of the common man' had manifested themselves. Hardy's *The Trumpet-Major* had given voice to ordinary sailors and soldiers as representatives of the anonymous thousands whose dust was 'scattered about the world' as a consequence of the nineteenth century's European and Colonial wars. The sacrifice of the lives of ordinary rankers was seen as being at least as instrumental in attaining victory in battle as the strategies of generals. In his murals in the Palace of Westminster, Maclise had shown a stricken Nelson and a victorious Wellington surrounded by the dead, dying and wounded servicemen who had contributed to their costly triumphs. Mindful of this, and immediately after his most successful campaigns, the Duke of Wellington had commissioned pictures of military and naval pensioners celebrating the victories wrought by their successors (fig. 114). Some sixty years later Herkomer painted those successors celebrating nothing but their survival into old age. Significantly, in his painting of the Chelsea pensioners in their chapel (fig. 112) no officer is present.

By the time Hardy presented the manuscript of *The Trumpet-Major* to the Royal Library in 1911 another European war was looming. The Great War saw battles in which the slaughter would have appalled even the most hardened and profligate Victorian general. Very few public memorials were erected to the common soldiers and sailors of Wellington's armies and Nelson's navy. Dead

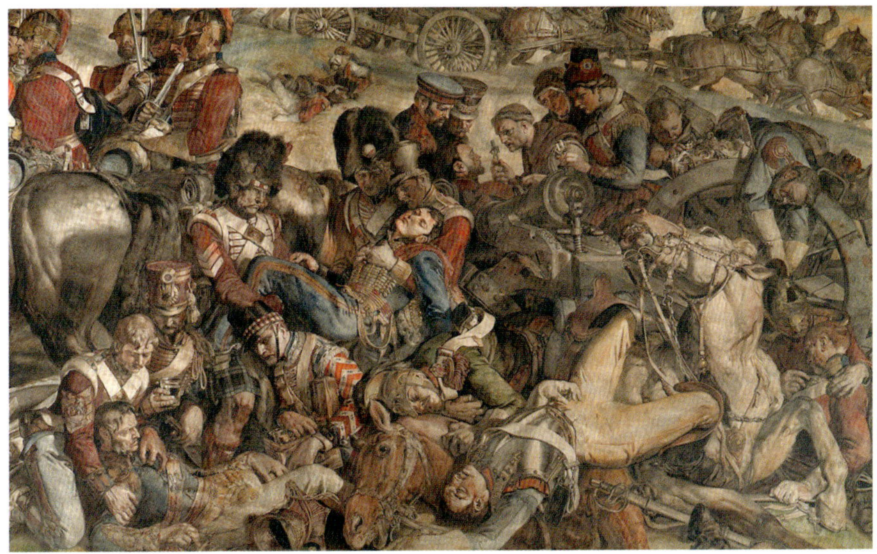

115, 116 Daniel Maclise,
*The Meeting of Wellington
and Blucher after the Battle
of Waterloo* (details), 1861,
Water glass painting,
368.3 x 1391.9cm.
Palace of Westminster
Collection

sailors found watery graves, and the bodies of ordinary soldiers were buried *en masse* in pits with their fallen enemies. During the First World War public sentiment had changed and the civil and military authorities responded accordingly. All of those who died in the First World War were named on public memorials and, where the bodies of soldiers were identified and interred, given individual headstones. These headstones, engraved in a uniform style and with a simple, uniform dignity, were set up in military cemeteries close to the battlefields where they had died. There was now to be no distinction in death between officers and other ranks (figs. 115, 116). When the 'unknown warrior' was buried in Westminster Abbey it was considered perfectly proper that he should honourably rest among the kings and statesmen.

The ordinary survivors of the great battles of the early nineteenth century seem to have been figures of interest only to their kinsmen and to historically curious novelists and painters. Orlando Figes ascribes the shift in a wider public responsiveness to the impact of the Crimean War. The heroism, as much as the suffering, of ordinary soldiers in that War he argues 'brought about a sea change in Britain's attitudes towards its fighting men … before the war the idea of military honour was defined by aristocracy … but the common soldier was ignored.'[56] Figes ascribes this shift in part to the 'recasting' of rank-and-file soldiers 'as saintly figures, martyrs of a holy cause' by Evangelical Christians.[57]

Nevertheless, there seems to have been no consideration in either 1865 or 1875 of an *official* commemoration of the fiftieth and sixtieth anniversaries of Waterloo and of the ordinary soldiers who died in the battle. By 1885 hardly any veteran of the Napoleonic wars was likely to have been capable of summoning up the energy, or the spirit, to respond to any kind of ceremony. The sacrifices of the First World War changed everything. Although scarcely a 'People's War,' the 'people' as a whole were, of necessity, involved on an unprecedented scale. The 'people,' both the fallen and the bereaved, now required public memorials that fostered both public and private memory. Since 1919 anniversaries have been scrupulously observed. Also since 1919, no great state ceremony commemorating the battles of the First and the Second World Wars would be considered dignified without the presence of the Sovereign or a senior member of the Royal Family. Given the longevity of surviving servicemen and women in the twentieth- and twenty-first centuries, anniversaries stretch out, if not quite to the crack of doom, at least to ninety years. Living history lives far longer than ever before. That 'living history' which, in the nineteenth century, would probably have been considered merely curious, became in the twentieth a vital constituent in how the present perceived and understood the immediate past.

As those who witnessed it, fought in it, and wrote about it, 'the Great War for Civilisation' had very little to do with heroism. To many it also suggested that the old ways in which history had been written about and pictorially represented were no longer either useful or valid. The art of biography was to be turned on its head by Lytton Strachey in his *Eminent Victorians* in 1918, just as the arts of sculpture and painting were taken in new directions. Even the way in which soldiers were represented was revolutionised in the war memorials created by Charles Sargeant Jagger and by Stanley Spencer in his chapel at Burghclere. In the years following the Great War even architecture, which had had a long and fruitful flirtation with the 'vernacular,' became determined to shake off all reference to the past, as if such reference tainted the required, and often imported, chastity of the 'modern.' History itself became suspect, either because it suggested a nostalgia for a lost order or because it seemed to limit the freedom of a post-war world to express itself. The past had to be shrugged off.

The 'levelling of distinctions' had, however, been part of a long drawn-out process. The captains and the kings may not have abruptly departed, but when they were represented it was generally in the company of less elevated men and women. History may well have become less 'colourful,' but by the dawn of the twentieth century it was both more 'popular' and democratic. Sir Walter Scott had shown the nineteenth century that history was best observed through the eyes of neutral participants who are caught up in the political process rather than being instrumental in it. In his *History of England* Macaulay had made use of extensive 'local colour,' providing a social and economic context in which his historical narrative evolves. For Froude, the real heroes of history were the unsung individualists who worked out their own destinies and thereby shaped the destiny of society at large. Even Carlyle, who emphatically believed in heroism, recognised that modern heroes were as likely to be humbly born men of letters as they were kings and emperors. For many artists and writers of the nineteenth century, political history seemed drabber after the Glorious Revolution. The lives of British monarchs were probably deemed to be less compelling than those of their predecessors because, after 1689, constitutional restraints limited not simply the 'Divine Right' of kings, but also restricted their personal and financial whims. Both power and patronage drained away from the Court, initially to a cultured aristocracy and steadily to a prosperous and educated bourgeoisie. The great reforms of the 1820s and 30s brought home the realisation not only that political influence now extended far beyond the old aristocracy but also that British society was essentially plural and no longer obedient to a single confession. Victorian England was obliged to accept the co-existence of once utterly opposed values and beliefs. 'Colourful' was a difficult word to apply to most nineteenth-century Parliamentary debates, however heated they were, but, to most of Queen Victoria's subjects, if 'colour' meant Civil War, it was better to be drab. As George Eliot noted in *Adam Bede* 'old Leisure' had been superseded by young earnestness, but that earnestness was conditioned by the kind of religious and political debate that, however contentious it became, was unlikely to topple over into revolution. The great social advances of Victoria's reign were not really susceptible to the kind of pictorial representation that had traditionally appealed to the historical painter. Unlike her 'Wicked Uncles,' the happily married Queen appeared to embody precisely the modest, domestic virtues that set her apart from her more 'colourful' ancestors, whether ancient or modern. The second Mrs. Markham reminded her children of Queen Victoria's domesticated virtues:

> She is possessed of those qualities and characteristics which especially endear her to English hearts and homes. She is a religious and singularly domestic woman; and as she herself enjoyed a careful education, under a most devoted and excellent mother, she has, amidst all the duties and seductions of her high position, fulfilled her duties as a tender and wise mother in the most admirable manner. This is perhaps the chiefest cause of the hold which Queen Victoria has on the hearts of her people. Her example in this respect is invaluable, and the blessing of it will remain to countless generations.[58]

This is Victoria for the Victorians. She is the mother of the nation, supreme, but temperate, both in the state and by the hearthside. Unlike Mary Tudor, this is no narrow-minded bigot; unlike the first Elizabeth this is no bad-tempered, painted tyrant, and, perforce, unlike the second Mary and her sister Anne, here is a woman willing and able to dedicate herself to her family and to family values and thereby to redefine the very nature of modern royalty. Thackeray ended his lecture on King George IV with what might be considered a loyal sigh of relief at the accession of an 'honourable and pure' woman. 'I am sure,' he told his audience, 'the future painter of our manners will pay a willing allegiance to that good life, and be loyal to the memory of that unsullied virtue.' We just about get the hint that Thackeray's sigh served to hide the merest suggestion of a yawn.

   Mary Howitt ended her *Mrs Markham's History of England* with Victoria bereaved. Nevertheless, she saw Victoria's kingdom as confident in its dynastic future thanks both to the Queen's fertility and to her educated instinct for good parenting. In the 1860s the 'Widow of Windsor' might well have thought of herself as meriting the privilege of an intensely secluded mourning such as any other rich widow might have sought. But such indulgence was unbecoming in a head of state much as the behaviour of her eldest son seemed set to revisit the sins of the queen's 'wicked uncles.' In some quarters this double royal indulgence was to provoke republican rumbles of dissent and questions about the public role of the monarch. As events were to prove, however, neither Victoria the wife nor Victoria the widow rocked the constitution. Nor did the virtual eclipse of Court life, and of what was left of Court patronage, do much to sap what was assumed in suburban homes to be British political culture. Retrospectively it could be argued that the character and bearing of the Queen had in fact been integral to the somewhat colourless security of mid-nineteenth-century Britain. Even in her drab widowhood, she helped define both middle-class aspirations to respectability and a universal devotion to domesticity. Victoria's private life was in many ways instrumental in establishing commonplace, domestic virtues as central to the self-definition of nineteenth-century Britain. The Queen was no longer above things, she was part of the dense social fabric. Her private life can also be seen as a constituent in the long process of social 'levelling,' for the Queen, like the majority of her subjects, habitually eschewed ostentation, was a faithful wife, and consistently honoured hearth and home.

The 'levelling' was, however, even more indebted to a far greater historical process. The 'old order' of flamboyant, tyrannical kings and of aristocrats, who could be caricatured either as class-oppressors or as indolent wastrels, was now effectively over. The three old 'estates of the realm' had been superseded by a far more complex class system which could itself be caricatured either as Disraeli's 'Two Nations' or as Matthew Arnold's 'Barbarians,' 'Philistines,' and the uncultured, indeterminate 'masses.' The 'old order' had changed, and it continued to change, but the 'new' order to which it yielded was generally acknowleged to be uncertain and ill-defined. The nineteenth century as a whole was marked by unprecedented economic, scientific and technological development and Victorian society could be interpreted, as Macaulay explained to his contemporaries, as the culmination of the underlying dynamic of English history: progressive change.[59] This history 'of a constant change in the institutions of a great society' presented a series of challenges to the modern world. It also stimulated historians, poets, novelists and painters to attempt to explain or at least to mediate these challenges. However drab, ugly and commonplace industrialized England seemed to Macaulay's contemporaries, Macaulay himself would have been amongst the first to warn them of the dangers of attempting to escape into the past. The past was there to tutor the present, not to dazzle it. As the century advanced, artists, writers and their audiences seem to have sensed that even the most 'colourful' of historical periods somehow needed to be de-heroised and domesticated.

Historical painting did not die in the nineteenth century, but, like the historical novel and the writing of historical narratives, it steadily adapted itself to representing the quotidian rather than the exceptional, the exemplary rather than the extraordinary. As a general rule, after *c*.1870, when period subjects were required, they showed men and women dancing, courting and lounging rather than plotting, praying and fighting. After 1900, painters tended to eschew period scenes and period costume unless the men and women they represented were awkwardly and self-consciously cavorting in fancy dress. The most awkward of fancy dresses was by then the Victorian, for the 'Victorians' were themselves rapidly becoming past history. Even the earnestness that the Victoria's subjects had so esteemed was deemed to be either suspect or ridiculous. Used pejoratively, the term 'Victorian' came to suggest a corseted, hypocritical, stuffy, and irretrievably ugly culture. The politics and the poetry, the art and the architecture, the histories and the habits of the middle years of the nineteenth century were increasingly deemed to represent a moral threat to progressive modern styles and to evolutionary manners. In the immediate aftermath of the First World War any flirtatious or nostalgic respect for the 1850s and 60s aroused the puritanical wrath of Roger Fry: in 1919 he wrote,

> It is evident … that we have just arrived at the point where our ignorance of life in the Victorian period is such as to allow the incurable optimism of memory to build a quite peculiar little earthly paradise out of the boredoms, the snobberies, the cruel repressions, the mean calculations and the rapacious speculations of the mid–nineteenth century.[60]

It would take at least another sixty years to fully shake off the prejudice.

NOTES

INTRODUCTION

1   For Wallis's *Chatterton* see Robin Hamlyn's extensive note in *The Pre-Raphaelites*, London 1984, pp.142–44. See also Tristram Hunt and Victoria Whitfield, *Art Treasures in Manchester: 150 Years On*, Manchester Art Gallery 2007, pp.29–30.

2   For the location see Hamlyn, *The Pre-Raphaelites*, pp.142–43.

3   George Eliot, *Impressions of Theophrastus Such* (1879). Reprinted as Vol. XII of the Warwick Edition of the works of George Eliot, Edinburgh & London 1910, p.26.

4   *Theophrastus Such*, p.28.

5   T. B. Macaulay, 'Sir James Mackintosh' (*Edinburgh Review*, July 1835). *Critical and Historical Essays*. 3 volumes, London 1854, vol.2 p.226.

6   'History' (May 1828). Reprinted in *The Miscellaneous Writings of Lord Macaulay*, 2 vols., London 1860, vol.1 pp.242, 277.

CHAPTER 1

1   For Bulwer-Lytton, his debts to historians and his understanding of Sir Walter Scott's *Waverley* novels see Andrew Sanders, *The Victorian Historical Novel 1840–1880*, London 1978.

2   *Handbook for Northamptonshire and Rutland*, 2nd ed. London 1901. G.H. Chettle, *Kirby Hall, Northamptonshire*, HMSO, London 1947.

3   Quoted by Oliver Fairclough in his *The Grand Old Mansion: The Holtes and their Successors at Aston Hall 1618–1864*, Birmingham Museums & Art Gallery 1984, pp.108–9.

4   Fairclough, *The Grand Old Mansion*, p.107.

5   Fairclough, *The Grand Old Mansion*, pp.114–20.

6   For this painting, the house's architecture and the often disparate costume details see Roy Strong, *And When Did You Last see Your Father? The Victorian Painter and British History*, London 1978, pp.90–3. See also ed. Mark Bills and Vivien Knight, *William Powell Frith: Painting the Victorian Age*, New Haven and London 2006, pp.8–9.

7   Bills and Knight, *William Powell Frith*, p.91.

8   Nash's illustrations are still commonly used to show Tudor buildings in use. They were republished in octavo form in an edition by Charles Holme in 1906 with an introduction by the architect C. Harrison Townsend.

9   For Charlecote see Alice Fairfax-Lucy, *Charlecote and the Lucys: The Chronicle of an English Family*, London 1958. See also the National Trust's guidebook to the house (1996)

10   P.F. Robinson, *Designs for Ornamental Villas*, London 1827. See particularly designs 11 and 12.

11   For these houses and their social context see Mark Girouard, *The Victorian Country House* (Revised and Enlarged edition), New Haven & London 1976. For Salvin and Harlaxton Hall see also Jill Allibone, *Anthony Salvin: Pioneer of the Gothic Revival*, Cambridge 1988.

12   A. Welby Pugin, *The True Principles of Pointed or Christian Architecture: set forth in Two Lectures Delivered at St. Marie's Oscott*, London 1841, pp.61–62. Ironically, Pugin had begun his career in the mid-1820s with designs for 'Gothic' furniture for Windsor Castle which owed a good deal to the 'corrupted design and decayed taste' of Elizabethan England. He later repudiated this work. See Rosemary Hill, *God's Architect: Pugin and Building of Romantic Britain*, London 2007, pp.74–75.

13   Charles L. Eastlake, *Hints on Household Taste*, 2nd ed., London 1869, pp.30–31.

14   Washington Irving, *Sketch Book* (1819, 1820), London 1838, p.201. *Bracebridge Hall*, 2 vols., London 1822, vol.1, pp.18–19.

15   Henry Vizetelly, *Christmas With the Poets*, London 1851. For this illustrated volume see Ruari McLean, *Victorian Book Design and Colour Printing*, 2nd ed., London 1972, pp.170–71.

16   Many commentators on *Bleak House* have assumed that Dickens based Chesney Wold on Rockingham Castle in Northamptonshire. Rockingham was owned by Dickens's friends, the Watsons, and it does indeed boast a long gallery (if not one of the proportions shown in another of Phiz's illustrations to the novel). There is no Ghost's Walk at Rockingham, and it looks nothing like the grand house shown in the Frontispiece to *Bleak House*. It would seem to be rather a backhanded comment on the Watsons' hospitality to assume that Dickens directly based Chesney Wold on Rockingham.

17   Charles Dickens, *A Child's History of England* (1851–53), Universal Edition, London 1914, Chapter 32, p.227.

18   Dickens, *A Child's History of England*, p. 246.

19   Delaroche's *Derniers moments de la Reine Elisabeth, 1603* was engraved in 1844. See Stephen Bann and Linda Whiteley, *Painting and History: Delaroche and Lady Jane Grey*, London 2010, pp.70–71.

20   Quoted by Lytton Strachey in his *Queen Victoria*, London 1921, p.44.

21   *The Times*, 10 November 1841.

22   See Richard Ormond, *Daniel Maclise*, London 1972, p.116.

23   See ed. Maurice Bond, *Works of Art in the House of Lords*, Her Majesty's Stationery Office, London 1980, p.14.

24   Bond, *Works of Art in the House of Lords*, pp. 66–74.

25   J. Mavor, *The Young Man's Companion, or Youth's Instructor*, New Edition, Improved, London 1824, pp.394, 398.

26   Elizabeth Penrose, *A History of England … by Mrs Markham* (1823), London 1875, p.260.

27   John Cassell's *Illustrated History of England*. Volume 2, 'From the Reign of Edward IV to the death of Queen Elizabeth', London 1858, p.568. Cassell's *History* went through at least 7 editions.

28 Lady Georgiana Fullerton, *Constance Sherwood: An Auto biography of the Sixteenth Century*, 3 vols., 1865, vol.1, p.215.

29 Fullerton, *Constance Sherwood*, vol.3, pp.34–35.

30 Jane Austen, *The History of England* reprinted in ed. Margaret Anne Doody and Douglas Murray, *Catherine and Other Writings*, Oxford 1993, pp.139–42.

31 Sir Walter Scott, *Kenilworth: A Romance*, 3 vols., Edinburgh 1821, vol.2, Chapter 8, p.219.

32 Roy Strong, *And when did you last see your father? The Victorian Painter and British History*, pp.161–63.

33 These and other nineteenth-century paintings of Mary are discussed in Helen Smailes and Duncan Thomson's *The Queen's Image* (National Galleries of Scotland) 1987.

34 Quoted in John Guille Millais, *The Life and Letters of Sir John Everett Millais*, 2 vols., London 1899, vol.2, p18.

35 For Millais and Literature see the essay by Andrew Sanders in ed. Debra N. Mancoff, *John Everett Millais: Beyond the Pre-Raphaelite Brotherhood*, New Haven & London 2001, pp.69–94.

36 The picture is imaginatively discussed by Alison Smith in eds. Jason Rosenfeld and Alison Smith, *Millais*, London 2007, p.158.

37 J. A. Froude, 'England's Forgotten Worthies' reprinted in *Short Studies on Great Subjects* (4 vols., London 1867–83), Everyman Edition, London 1964, pp.34–35. Much of James Anthony Froude's anti-catholicism was based on his religious definition of himself against his brother, a close associate of John Henry Newman and a passionate advocate of Tractarian reform.

38 Froude, 'England's Forgotten Worthies', p.44.

39 Froude, 'England's Forgotten Worthies', p.40.

40 J. A. Froude, *History of England from the Fall of Wolsey to the Defeat of the Spanish Armada* (12 vols., 1856–64), New Impression, London 1907, vol.10, p.501; vol.11, pp.473, 479, 493, 531.

41 Froude, *History of England*, vol.8, pp.1–2.

42 'Froude's *History of England*,' *North British Review* 51 (November 1856). Reprinted in Kingsley's *Plays and Puritans and Other Historical Essays* (1873), New Edition, London 1889, pp.221–22.

43 For the genesis of the novel see Frances Kingsley, *Charles Kingsley: His Letters and Memories of his Life* (1876), 2 vols., London 1894, vol.1, p.313.

44 Frances Kingsley, *Charles Kingsley*, p.330.

45 Hallam Tennyson, *Alfred Lord Tennyson: A Memoir*, 2 vols., London 1897, vol.2, p.251.

46 Hallam Tennyson, *Alfred Lord Tennyson*, vol.2, p.234.

47 Hallam Tennyson, *Alfred Lord Tennyson*, vol. 2, p.173, pp.176–81. Tennyson's reading apparently included works by Fuller, Burnet, Strype, and Lingard. His only sixteenth-century sources were Holinshed and Camden.

48 Hallam Tennyson, *Alfred Lord Tennyson*, vol.2, pp.180–82.

49 S. Schoenbaum, *Shakespeare's Lives*, Oxford 1970, pp.366–68.

50 Schoenbaum, *Shakespeare's Lives*, pp.374–80.

51 Thomas Carlyle, *On Heroes, Hero-Worship and the Heroic in History* (1841), Everyman Edition, London 1956, pp.344–45.

52 Charles Knight, *William Shakspere: A Biography* in *The Imperial Shakspere*, 2 vols., London n.d. [*post* 1873], vol.2, p.106. Schoenbaum somewhat ambiguously sums up Knight's biographical enterprise as 'a curious monument in the landscape of Shakespearean scholarship – in some ways still remarkable, in others mysteriously of another culture; like Stonehenge, gaped at by uncomprehending tourists on Salisbury plain', *Shakespeare's Lives*, p.396.

53 For the various representations of Shakespeare in painting see Jane Martineau *et al.*, *Shakespeare in Art* (Dulwich Picture Gallery), London 2003, in particular John Christian's 'Shakespeare in Victorian Art,' pp.217–45.

54 For Wallis's painting see the detailed entry by Jane Martineau in *Shakespeare in Art*, pp.76–77.

55 In his 'Buildings of England' volume on Warwickshire Nikolaus Pevsner wrote of Stratford's architecture in 1966: 'To appreciate Stratford-upon-Avon one has to make the gigantic effort of forgetting Shakespeare and the pilgrims and the trippers – over 250,00 of them a year visiting the Birth Place.'

56 Quoted by Richard Foulkes in his *The Shakespeare Tercentenary of 1864* (Society for Theatre Research), London 1984, p.4.

57 Foulkes, *The Shakespeare Tercentenary*, pp.11–38.

58 Foulkes, *The Shakespeare Tercentenary*, pp.41–45.

59 See Marian J. Pringle, *The Theatres of Stratford-upon-Avon 1875–1992* (Stratford-upon-Avon Studies 5), 1994.

60 For Devey see Jill Allibone, *George Devey, Architect 1820–1886*, Cambridge 1991.

61 For these houses see Andrew Saint, *Richard Norman Shaw*, New Haven & London 1976.

CHAPTER 2

1 For these two pictures see Stephen Bann and Linda Whiteley, *Painting History: Delaroche and Lady Jane Grey* (National Gallery), London 2010, pp.21, 112–15.

2 For the Wallace pictures see Stephen Duffy, *Paul Delaroche 1797–1856: Paintings in the Wallace Collection*, London 1997. For *Marie-Antoinette before the Tribunal* see Bann and Whiteley, *Painting History*, pp.122–23.

3 Bann and Whiteley, *Painting History*, p.17.

4 Bann and Whiteley, *Painting History*, p.110.

5 Bann and Whiteley, *Painting History*, p.74.

6 Augustus J. C. Hare, *Walks in London*, 7th ed., 2 vols., 1901, vol.2, p.172.

7   For the Banqueting House as Chapel Royal see the illustration in *London Interiors, with their Costumes and Ceremonies*, London 1841.

8   For Jones's and Webb's designs see John Summerson, *Architecture in Britain 1530–1830*, 5th ed., Harmondsworth 1969, pp.78–79. See also John Harris and Gordon Higgott, *Inigo Jones: Complete Architectural Drawings*, Royal Academy of Arts, London 1990, pp.108–23.

9   Hare, *Walks in London*, p.166.

10   Peter Cunningham, *Hand-Book of London. Past and Present*, New Edition, Corrected and Enlarged, London 1850, p.549.

11   Henry Bohn, *The Pictorial Handbook of London: Comprising its Antiquities, Architecture, Trade, Social, Literary and Scientific Institution, Exhibitions, Galleries of Art; together with the Principal Suburbs and the most Attractive Localities*, London 1854, pp.176–77.

12   James Fergusson, *History of the Modern Styles of Architecture*, London 1862, p.259.

13   Fergusson, *History of the Modern Styles of Architecture*, p.260. 'Pulvination' is a cushion-like swelling in the decorative stonework.

14   Fergusson, *History of the Modern Styles of Architecture*, p.263.

15   For the Commission and the decoration of the Lords Chamber see Michael Bond, *Works of Art in the House of Lords*, Her Majesty's Stationery Office, London 1980, pp.22–30, 84–91.

16   This point is usefully made in Bond, *Works of Art in the House of Lords*, p.92.

17   Bond, *Works of Art in the House of Lords*, p. 92. See also William Vaughan, '"God Help the Minister who Meddles in Art": History Painting in the New Palace of Westminster' in *The Houses of Parliament: History, Art, Architecture*, London 2000, p. 232.

18   For the Public Worship Regulation Act and for King's trial, see Owen Chadwick, *The Victorian Church*, Part 2, London 1970, pp.348–49, 353–54.

19   Quoted by C.P.S. Clarke in his *The Oxford Movement and After*, London 1933, p. 148.

20   See Sheridan Gilley, *Newman and his Age*, London 1990, p.23. So personally did Newman take Law's *A Serious Call to a Devout and Holy Life* that he rebuked Hurrell Froude for calling it a 'clever' book: 'it seemed to me as if you had said the Day of Judgement will be a pretty sight.' Quoted by R. W. Church in his *The Oxford Movement 1833–1845* (1891), London 1932, p. 29.

21   For *The Christian Year* see Chadwick, *The Victorian Church*, Part 1, London 1966, pp.66–68.

22   For Whittingham and Pickering see Ruari MacLean, *Victorian Book Design and Colour Printing*, 2nd ed., 1972, pp.5–20. For Pickering, see also Geoffrey Keynes, *William Pickering, Publisher: A Memoir and a Check-List of his Publications*, London 1969.

23   Ed. Robert Aris Willmott, *English Sacred Poetry of the Sixteenth, Seventeenth, Eighteenth and Nineteenth Centuries*, London 1861.

24   For Dyce's *George Herbert at Bemerton* see ed. Jennifer Melville, *William Dyce and the Pre-Raphaelite Vision*, Aberdeen Art Gallery 2006, pp.182–83. See also Marcia Pointon, *William Dyce 1806–1864: A Critical Biography*, Oxford 1979, pp.130–32, 175–76.

25   Quoted in Melville, *William Dyce and the Pre-Raphaelite Vision*, p.64.

26   For Neale and the Ecclesiologists, see James F. White, *The Cambridge Movement: The Ecclesiologists and the Gothic Revival*, Cambridge 1979. For Neale, see A. G. Lough, *The Influence of John Mason Neale*, London 1962. Neale had lived briefly in Shepperton, Middlesex, where his boyhood guardian was vicar.

27   J. M. Neale, *Shepperton Manor*, London 1845, p.56. The 'Quinquarticular controversy' concerned the condemnation of the teaching of Arminius outlined by the strict Calvinist theologians at the Synod of Dort.

28   Neale, *Shepperton Manor*, p.231.

29   For Egg's painting see Edward Morris and Frank Milner, *'And When Did You Last See Your Father?'*, Walker Art Gallery, Liverpool 1992, p.47.

30   Morris and Milner, *'And When Did You Last See Your Father?'*, pp.56–57.

31   For the tableau and for the popular uses of the scene in cartoons, films and plays see Morris and Milner, *'And When Did You Last See Your Father?'*, pp.110–27.

32   For this picture see Morris and Milner, *'And When Did You Last See Your Father?'*, pp.86–87. For a good analysis of its themes see also Roy Strong, *And When Did You Last See Your Father?: The Victorian Painter and British History*, London 1978, pp.136–38.

33   M. H. Spielmann, *Millais and his Works*, Edinburgh and London 1898, pp.93–94.

34   For the possible connection between Millais and *I Puritani* see Morris and Milner, *'And When Did You Last See Your Father?'*, p. 66. See also Jason Rosenfeld and Alison Smith, *Millais*, London 2008, pp.96–97.

35   For this, see Geoffrey Keynes, *William Pickering, Publisher*, p.31.

36   *The Diary of Lady Willoughby*, London 1844, pp.160–61.

37   See eds. Christine and Jacqueline Riding, *The Houses of Parliament: History, Art, Architecture*, London 2000, p.268.

38 For these sculptures, see Benedict Read, *Victorian Sculpture*, New Haven and London 1982, pp.112–13, 237.

39 Elfrida Manning, *Marble and Bronze: The Art and Life of Hamo Thorneycroft*, London and New Jersey 1982, p.129.

40 For Thorneycroft's 'Cromwell', see Elfrida Manning, *Marble and Bronze*, pp.128–31. For the statue in its context see Read, *Victorian Sculpture*, and Malcolm Hay and Jacqueline Riding, *Art in Parliament: The Permanent Collection of the House of Commons*, London 1996, p.45.

41 For Brown's *Cromwell*, see Ford M. Hueffer, *Ford Madox Brown, A Record of his Life and Work*, London 1896, pp.290–92. See also Teresa Newman and Ray Watkinson, *Ford Madox Brown and the Pre-Raphaelite Circle*, London 1991, p.77.

42 Ford. M. Hueffer, *Ford Madox Brown, A Record of his Life*, p.94.

43 Thomas Carlyle, *Oliver Cromwell's Letters and Speeches: With Elucidations*, 3 vols., London 1846, vol.1, pp.90–91.

44 J[ohn] Mavor, *The Young Man's Companion, or Youth's Instructor*, New Edition, London 1824, pp.402–3.

45 Carlyle, *On Heroes, Hero-Worship and the Heroic in History*, Everyman Edition, London 1956, pp.430–31, 440.

46 Carlyle, *Oliver Cromwell's Letters and Speeches*, vol.1 pp.12,18–19.

47 For these paintings see Ford M. Hueffer, *Ford Madox Brown, A Record of his Life*, pp.311–15.

48 In his *Praeterita* Ruskin records visiting a Waldensian chapel in Turin which contained a Sunday congregation of 24 'of whom fifteen or sixteen were grey-haired women.' Book 3, Ch.1.

49 Thomas Arnold, *Chaucer to Wordsworth. A Short History of English Literature, from the Earliest Times to the Present Day*, London 1862, pp.188–89.

50 Thomas Babington Macaulay, *Critical and Historical Essays Contributed to the Edinburgh Review*. 8th ed., 3 vols., London 1854, vol.1, pp.30–31.

51 Macaulay, *Critical and Historical Essays*, vol.1, p.46.

52 Macaulay, *Critical and Historical Essays*, vol.1, pp.60–61.

53 For the paintings in the Upper Waiting Hall, see Malcolm Hay and Jacqueline Riding, *Art in Parliament*, pp.94–95.

CHAPTER 3

1 Thomas Babington Macaulay, *The History of England from the Accession of James the Second*, London 1864, vol.1, chapter 2, pp.80–81.

2 Elizabeth Penrose, *Mrs Markham's A History of England, from the First Invasion of the Romans Down to the Present Time … For the Use of Young Persons*, London 1875, p.350.

3 Charles Dickens, *A Child's History of England* (1851–54), London 1914, pp.296–97.

4 Dickens, *A Child's History*, p.298.

5 Elizabeth Penrose, *Mrs Markham's A History of England*, pp.357, 360–61.

6 Dickens, *A Child's History*, p.303.

7 For the bibliographical background to the publication of Evelyn's and Pepys's Diaries, see ed. John Bowle, *The Diary of John Evelyn*, Oxford 1983, p. xxi; and eds. Robert Latham and William Matthews, *The Diary of Samuel Pepys*, vol.1, London 1970, pp.lxxvii–lxxix.

8 Quoted by Latham, *Diary of Samuel Pepys*, vol.1, p. lxxxii.

9 For Frith see eds. Mark Bills and Vivien Knight, *William Powell Frith: Painting the Victorian Age*, New Haven and London 2006.

10 The impact of Poole's canvas can be recognised in the extraordinarily lame wood engraving of 'The Enthusiast Denouncing London' in vol. 3 of John Cassell's *Illustrated History of England* (1859), p.433.

11 For the publishing history of *Old Saint Pauls* see S.M. Ellis, *William Harrison Ainsworth and his Friends*, 2 vols., London and New York 1911, vol.2, pp.365–66.

12 Ellis, *William Harrison Ainsworth*, vol.1, pp.424–25, 432.

13 For the construction of the new St Paul's see James W.P. Campbell and Robert Bowles, 'The Construction of the New Cathedral' in eds. Derek Keene, Arthur Burns and Andrew Saint, *St. Paul's: The Cathedral Church of London 604–2004*, New Haven and London 2004, pp.207–19.

14 Benjamin Ferrey, *Recollections of A. W. N. Pugin and his Father Augustus Pugin* (1861), reprinted London 1978, pp.333–34.

15 Ferrey, *Recollections of A. W. N. Pugin*, p.151.

16 James Fergusson, *History of the Modern Styles of Architecture*, London 1862, pp.267, 269, 271, 272–73.

17 John Forster, *The Life of Charles Dickens* (1872–74), ed. J.W.T. Ley, London 1928, p.11.

18 Augustus J. C. Hare, *Walks in London* (7th ed. revised), 2 vols., London 1901, vol1, p.109.

19 John Timbs, *Curiosities of London: Exhibiting the Most Rare and Remarkable Objects of Interest in the Metropolis; with Nearly Fifty Years' Personal Recollections*, London 1855, p.96.

20 Quoted by Nikolaus Pevsner in his *Some Architectural Writers of the Nineteenth Century*, Oxford 1972, p.78.

21 For Cockerell's lectures see David Watkin, *The Life and Work of C. R. Cockerell*, London 1974, pp.121–22.

22 George Godwin, *The Churches of London*, 2 vols., London 1839. vol.2, pp.8–9.

23 For the various decorative schemes at St. Paul's see Teresa Sladen, 'Embellishment and Decoration, 1690–1900' in *St. Paul's: The Cathedral Church of London 604–2004*, pp.233–56.

24   The story is repeated by, amongst others, James Fergusson (though he very properly dismisses it). See Fergusson, *History of the Modern Styles of Architecture*, pp.268–69.

25   Elizabeth Penrose, *Mrs Markham's A History of England*, pp.363, 368.

26   Macaulay, *The History of England*, vol.1, p.82.

27   Macaulay, *The History of England*, vol.1, p.93.

28   For the Commons Corridor see Malcolm Hay and Jacqueline Riding, *Art in Parliament: The Permanent Collection of the House of Commons*, London 1996, pp.86–89.

29   Macaulay, *The History of England*, vol.2, p.239.

30   *Handbook for Travellers in Wiltshire, Dorsetshire and Somersetshire*, new ed., London 1869, p.176.

31   *Handbook for Travellers in Wiltshire etc.*, pp.190–92.

32   *Handbook for Travellers in Wiltshire etc.*, pp.356–57.

33   Macaulay, *The History of England*, vol.1, p.294.

34   Macaulay, *The History of England*, vol.1, pp.213–14.

35   Charles Dickens, *A Child's History of England*, pp.311, 317–18.

36   For Carton's name and for the association with the Claret portrait of Jeffreys see Andrew Sanders, *The Companion to A Tale of Two Cities* (Dickens Companions Series), London 1998, pp.70–71.

37   For the 'Occasional Services' see Francis Proctor and Walter Howard Frere, *A New History of the Book of Common Prayer, with a Rationale of its Offices* (1901), London 1914, pp.644–47.

38   2 March 1831. Reprinted in *The Works of Lord Macaulay: Speeches, Poems and Miscellaneous Writings*, Albany Edition, London 1898, p.434.

39   Dickens, *A Child's History of England*, p.324.

40   James Thorne, *Handbook to the Environs of London, Alphabetically Arranged*, 2 vols., London 1876, vol.1, p.303.

41   See Simon Thurley, *Hampton Court: A Social and Architectural History*, New Haven and London 2003, p.318.

42   For Jesse, see Thurley, *Hampton Court*, pp.294–96.

43   Edward Jesse, *A Summer's Day at Hampton Court*, 4th ed., revised and enlarged, London 1841, p.65.

44   Bohn's *Pictorial Handbook of London*, London 1855, p.211.

45   Thorne, *Handbook to the Environs of London*, pp.303–4.

46   James Fergusson, *History of the Modern Styles of Architecture*, p.279.

47   Sir George Gilbert Scott, *Personal and Professional Recollections*, London 1879, p.375.

48   For the influence of Hampton Court on later English architecture see Thurley, *Hampton Court*, pp.308–9.

49   For 2 Palace Green, see Gordon N. Ray, *Thackeray: The Age of Wisdom: 1847–1863*, London 1958, pp.391–93. See also Lewis Melville, *The Thackeray Country*, London 1905, pp.160–63.

50   Alicia Bayne in her *Memorials of the Thackeray Family* (privately printed 1879) quoted in ed. Philip Collins, *Thackeray: Interviews and Recollections*, 2 vols., London 1983, vol.1, pp.86–87. Bayne's ascriptions are speculative, but may well be Thackeray's own. Daniel Mytens died before 1648 and although François De Troy painted members of the exiled Stuart family in France it is perhaps strange that he should have been accredited with a portrait of the Queen who occupied the throne that they claimed and celebrating a treaty that removed them from France.

51   Quoted by Melville, *The Thackeray Country*, p.162.

52   George Colman the younger's *Heir-at-Law* (1808) had included the line: 'Lord help you! Tell 'em Queen Anne's dead.'

53   Anne Thackeray Ritchie in her introduction to *Esmond* in the Centenary Biographical edition of Thackeray's works, London 1911.

54   George Brimley, 'Esmond' in *The Spectator*, 5 November 1852. Reprinted in *Essays by the Late George Brimley MA*, London 1860, pp.255–56.

55   W. H. Davenport Adams, *Good Queen Anne; or, Men and Manners, Life and Letters in England's Augustan Age*, 2 vols., London 1886, vol.1, p.xi.

56   Adams, *Good Queen Anne*, vol.1, pp.xxii–iii.

57   Adams, *Good Queen Anne*, vol.1, pp.53, 231.

58   Adams, *Good Queen Anne*, vol.1, p.229.

59   Charles Dickens, *Our Mutual Friend*, Book 2, Chapter 1.

60   Earl Stanhope, *History of England Comprising The Reign of Queen Anne Until the Peace of Utrecht 1701–1713*, London 1870, p.171.

61   Fergusson, *History of the Modern Styles of Architecture*, p.284.

62   Fergusson, *History of the Modern Styles of Architecture*, p.283.

63   For the most thorough and observant analysis of 'Queen Anne' see Mark Girouard, *Sweetness and Light: The 'Queen Anne' Movement 1860–1900*, Oxford 1977.

64   Quoted by Girouard, *Sweetness and Light*, p.xviii.

65   Sir George Gilbert Scott, *Personal and Professional Recollections*, p.375.

66   For G. G. Scott junior and 'Queen Anne' see Gavin Stamp, *An Architect of Promise: George Gilbert Scott Junior (1839– 1897) and the Late Gothic Revival*, Donnington 2002, chapter 6.

67   E. R. Robson, *School Architecture, being Practical Remarks on the Planning, Designing, Building and Furnishing of School-Houses*, London 1877, p.6.

68   Quoted by Girouard in his fourth chapter on educational buildings, 'The Architecture of Light,' Girouard, *Sweetness and Light*, p.64.

69   Robert W. Edis, *Decoration and Furniture of Town Houses*, London 1881, pp.14–15.

CHAPTER 4

1   For *The Minuet* see Jason Rosenfeld and Alison Smith, *Millais*, London 2008, pp.176–77. See also John Guille Millais, *The Life and Letters of Sir John Everett Millais*, 2 vols., London 1899, vol.1, p.392.

2   For the royal minuet, see ed. Jonathan Marsden, *Victoria and Albert: Art and Love*, London 2010, p.232.

3   Quoted by Walter Armstrong in his *Sir John E. Millais, Bart., Royal Academician. His Life and Work*, The Art Annual, London 1886, pp.25–26.

4   Armstrong, *Sir John E. Millais, Bart.*, pp.19–20.

5   Elizabeth Penrose ('Mrs. Markham'), *A History of England … For the Use of Young Persons*, London 1875, pp.396–97.

6   'Mrs. Markham', *A History of England*, p.401.

7   W. M. Thackeray, 'George the First', *The Four Georges* (1860), London 1861, pp.33, 35–37.

8   Quoted by Gordon N. Ray in his *Thackeray: The Age of Wisdom*, London 1958, p.253.

9   Ray, *Thackeray: The Age of Wisdom*, p.265

10 Ray, *Thackeray: The Age of Wisdom*, p.267.

11 *The Four Georges*, pp.26–28.

12 *The Four Georges*, pp.38–39.

13 *The Four Georges*, pp.52–55.

14 Ray, *Thackeray: The Age of Wisdom*, pp.141–42.

15 W. M. Thackeray, *The English Humourists of the Eighteenth Century*, London 1853, pp.53–54.

16 Thackeray, *The English Humourists*, pp.32–34, 40.

17 William Spalding, *The History of English Literature: With an Outline of the Origin and Growth of the English Language … For the Use of Schools and of Private Students*, Edinburgh 1853, p.321.

18 Thomas Arnold, *Chaucer to Wordsworth: A Short History of English Literature, from the Earliest Times to the Present Day*, London (1862), pp.316–17.

19 W.H. Davenport Adams, *Good Queen Anne*, London 1886, p.60.

20 T. B. Macaulay, 'The Life and Writings of Addison' (*Edinburgh Review*, July 1843). Reprinted in *Critical and Historical Essays*, 3 vols., London 1854, vol.3, pp.428–29.

21 Macaulay, *Critical and Historical Essays*, vol.3, p.479.

22 Thackeray, *The English Humourists*, p.81.

23 Thackeray, *The English Humourists*, pp.95–96.

24 Thackeray, *The English Humourists*, pp.102–3.

25 Thackeray, *The English Humourists*, p.185.

26 Joseph Angus, *The Handbook of English Literature*, London c.1860, p.203. The scene of *The Personification of Thames and English Rivers*, based on Windsor Forest, was painted in the Upper Waiting Hall at Westminster by Edward Armitage. The sixth poet was Scott.

27 Spalding, *The History of English Literature*, p.315.

28 Thackeray, *The English Humourists*, p.217.

29 For a thorough discussion of aspects of Pope's reputation in the nineteenth century see Francis O'Gorman 'The "High Priest of an Age of Prose and Reason"? Alexander Pope and the Victorians' in eds. Francis O'Gorman and Katherine Turner, *The Victorians and the Eighteenth Century: Reassessing the Tradition*, Aldershot 2004, pp.76–97.

30 Leslie Stephen, *Hours in a Library*, 3 vols., New Edition, London 1899, vol.1, p.94.

31 Stephen, *Hours in a Library*, p.131.

32 For Leslie Stephen on Pope see Noel Annan, *Leslie Stephen: The Godless Victorian*, London 1984, pp.222–23, 408 note.

33 Quoted by Christopher Hogwood in his *Handel*, London 1984, p.266.

34 For Handel and his posthumous reputation see Hogwood, *Handel*.

35 Hogwood, *Handel*, p.243. The 1791 concert was attended by Haydn who professed himself greatly moved. The event was also considered so important that it occasioned the postponement of Warren Hastings' trial in the nearby Westminster Hall.

36 John Parry, *Royal Music Festival*, London 1834, pp.9–10.

37 Quoted by Patrick Beaver in his *The Crystal Palace, 1851–1936: A Portrait of Victorian Enterprise*, London 1970, p.40.

38 Quoted by Hogwood, *Handel*, p.256.

39 Hogwood, *Handel*, p.256. See also Gordon S. Haight, *George Eliot: A Biography*, Oxford 1968, p.287.

40 Quoted by Robert Bernard Martin in his *With Friends Possessed: A Life of Edward Fitzgerald*, London 1985, pp.122–23.

41 Hogwood, *Handel*, p.208.

42 G.A. Sala, 'William Hogarth: Painter, Engraver and Philosopher' (9), *Cornhill Magazine*, October 1860, p.439.

43 See Marsden, *Victoria and Albert*, pp.230–31.

44 James Hogg, *The Jacobite Relics of Scotland*, Edinburgh 1819, p.x.

45 M.H. Spielmann, *Millais and his Works*, London 1898, p.103.

46 Eyre Crowe, *With Thackeray in America*, London 1893, p.49.

47 *The Letters and Private Papers of William Makepeace Thackeray*, ed. Gordon N. Ray, 4 vols., London 1946, vol.3, p.588 (March 1856).

48 *The Letters and Private Papers of William Makepeace Thackeray*, pp.592–93 (March 1856).

49 For contemporary American protests about *The Virginians* see Ray, *Thackeray: The Age of Wisdom*, pp.384–85.

50 For the heads on Temple Bar see Andrew Sanders, *The Companion to A Tale of Two Cities*, London 1988, p.55.

51 For the 'Dolly Varden' fashion see C. Willett-Cunnington and Phillis Cunnington, *Handbook of English Costume in the Nineteenth Century*, London (1959), 3rd ed. 1970, pp.493–94, 510.

52 See Edwina Ehrman 'Frith and Fashion' in eds. Mark Bills and Vivien Knight, *William Powell Frith: Painting the Victorian Age*, New Haven and London 2006, pp.116–17.

53 Bills and Knight, *William Powell Frith*, pp.47–53.

54 For the restricted access to the Soane Museum see Richard D. Altick, *The Shows of London*, Cambridge, Mass, and London 1978, p.417.

55 For Hogarth in the National Gallery see Jonathan Conlin, *The Nation's Mantelpiece: A History of the National Gallery*, London 2006, pp.216, 219–20, 291.

56 Conlin, *The Nation's Mantelpiece*, p.216.

57 Conlin, *The Nation's Mantelpiece*, p.219. Edward T. Cook, *A Popular Handbook to the National Gallery*, London 1888, p.435. Ruskin's quotation is from the *Edinburgh Lectures of Architecture and Painting* of 1854.

58 Cook, *A Popular Handbook to the National Gallery*, pp.425–26.

59 Thackeray, *The English Humourists*, pp.228–29.

60 G.A. Sala 'William Hogarth: Painter, Engraver and Philosopher', *Cornhill Magazine*, October 1860, p.454. Over the nine months that Sala published these essays the *Cornhill* also published Thackeray's *Four Georges*, Trollope's *Framley Parsonage*, and Ruskin's *Unto this Last*.

61 Sala, 'Hogarth' (4), *Cornhill Magazine*, April 1860, p.568.

62 *The Letters and Private Papers of William Makepeace Thackeray*, vol.1, p.412.

63 Review of Fielding's *Works* (September 1840). Reprinted in ed. Claude Rawson, *Henry Fielding* (Penguin Critical Anthology), Harmondsworth 1973, p.263.

64 Letter of May 1853. Quoted by Rawson, *Henry Fielding*, pp.282–83.

65 Leslie Stephen, *History of English Thought in the Eighteenth Century*, 2nd ed., 2 vols., London 1881, vol.2, p.380.

66 Margaret Oliphant, *The Literary History of England in the End of the Eighteenth and Beginning of the Nineteenth Century*, 3 vols., London 1882, vol.3, p.204.

67 Quoted by Rawson, *Henry Fielding*, p.302.

68 T. B. Macaulay, 'Horace Walpole' (October 1833) in *Critical and Historical Essays*, 3 vols., London 1854, vol.2, p.109. Walpole, letter to John Pinkerton, 26 June 1785. Quoted by Rawson, *Henry Fielding*, p.184.

69 Quoted by Rawson, *Henry Fielding*, p.173–74.

70 Macaulay, 'Samuel Johnson' (September 1831), *Essays*, vol.1, pp.374–76.

71 Macaulay, 'Samuel Johnson', *Essays*, vol.1, p.407.

72 *The Miscellaneous Writings of Lord Macaulay*, 2 vols., London 1860, vol.2, p.303.

73 For 'Dr Johnson at the Mitre' see Virginia Surtees, *Dante Gabriel Rossetti 1828–1882: The Paintings and Drawings: A Catalogue Raisonné*, 2 vols., Oxford 1971, vol.1, p.74; vol.2, illustration 183.

74 Thackeray, *English Humourists*, pp.320–21.

75 Thomas Carlyle, *On Heroes, Hero-Worship and the Heroic in History* (1840), Everyman Edition, London 1956, p.383.

76 Carlyle, *On Heroes*, pp.405–6.

77 Carlyle, *On Heroes*, p.407.

78 For a sound discussion of Johnson's reputation in the nineteenth century see Katherine Turner, 'The "Link of transition": Samuel Johnson and the Victorians' in eds. O'Gorman and Turner, *The Victorians and the Eighteenth Century*, pp.119–43.

CHAPTER 5

1 20 November 1855. *The Letters and Private Papers of W.M. Thackeray*, ed. Gordon N. Ray, 4 vols., London 1946–47, vol.3, pp.501–2.

2 John Forster in *The Examiner*, 4 February 1838. Reprinted in ed. George Rowell, *Victorian Dramatic Criticism*, London 1871, pp.64, 66.

3 Elizabeth Penrose, *Mrs Markham's A History of England*, London 1872, p.461.

4 *Mrs Markham's History of England, with Continuation by Mary Howitt*, London 1878, p.502.

5 *The Times*, 15 July 1830.

6 Peter Cunningham, *Hand-book of London: Past and Present*. New Edition, London 1850, p.86.

7 Thackeray, *The Four Georges*, London 1861, pp.225–26.

8 *The Four Georges*, pp.168–69, 187.

9 For this story see *The Letters of Charles Dickens* (Pilgrim Edition), vol.2 1840–1841, Oxford 1969, p.36, note 1.

10 *Letters of Charles Dickens*, vol.11, Oxford 1999, p.310.

11 *Letters of Charles Dickens*, vol.12, Oxford 2002, p.292.

12 Walter Ison, *The Georgian Buildings of Bath from 1700–1830*, London 1948, p.44.

13 Joseph Haydn, *Dictionary of Dates and Universal Reference*, 6th ed., London 1853, p.98. *Murray's Handbook for Travellers in Sussex*, 5th ed., London 1893, p.37. Augustus J.C Hare, *Sussex*, 2nd ed., London 1896, p.142.

14 For Brighton's development, see Nicholas Antram and Richard Morrice, *Brighton and Hove* (Pevsner Architectural Guides), New Haven and London, 2008.

15 For these churches see Anthony Wagner and Antony Dale, *The Wagners of Brighton*, London and Chichester, 1983.

16 See Antram and Morrice, *Brighton and Hove*, pp.48–51, 52–54, 55–57, 98–99. See also D. Robert Elleray, *The Victorian Churches of Sussex*, London and Chichester 1981.

17 J. J. Stevenson, *House Architecture*, 2 vols., London 1880, vol.1, pp.341, 346.

18 James Fergusson, *History of the Modern Styles of Architecture*, London 1862, p.302.

19 H. Rooksby Steel and F.R. Yerbury, *The Old Bank of England, London*, London 1930. See also Chapter 18 of Gillian Darley's *John Soane: An Accidental Romantic*, New Haven and London 1999.

20 R.H. Horne, *The New Spirit of the Age*, 2 vols., London 1844, vol.1, p.307.

21 Robert Aris Willmott, *The Poets of the Nineteenth Century*, 3rd ed., London 1858, p.v.

22 John Forster, *The Life of Charles Dickens* (1872–74), ed. J.W.T. Ley, London 1928, p.328.

23 *Life of Charles Dickens*, pp.549–50.

24 D.M. Moir, *Sketches of the Poetical Literature of the Past Half Century*, Edinburgh and London 1851, Lecture V, p.213.

25 Horne, *New Spirit of the Age*, vol.1, pp.318–19.

26 T.B. Macaulay, *Critical and Historical Essays*, 3 vols., London 1854, vol.3, p.147.

27 Reprinted in eds. Ian Brunskill and Andrew Sanders, *Great Victorian Lives: An Era in Obituaries*, London 2007, p.6.

28 Horne, *New Spirit of the Age*, vol.2, p.313.

29 D.M. Moir, *Sketches of the Poetical Literature*, Lecture II, pp.80–81.

30 Thomas Arnold, *Chaucer to Wordsworth. A Short History of English Literature*, London 1862, p.403.

31 'Wordsworth' reprinted in ed. F.W. Bateson, *Essays on English Literature*, London 1965, pp.100–1, 106.

32 'Wordsworth' in Bateson, *Essays on English Literature*, p.107.

33 Thomas Arnold, *Chaucer to Wordsworth*. pp.406–7.

34 Matthew Arnold, 'Byron' in Bateson, *Essays on English Literature*, p.179.

35 'Byron' in Bateson, *Essays on English Literature*, pp.182–83.

36 Moir, *Sketches of the Poetical Literature*, Lecture V, pp.220–21.

37 For this and other early Pre-Raphaelite paintings from Keats see *The Pre-Raphaelites*, London 1984, pp.57–58 *et seq.*

38 For these pictures see Virginia Surtees, *Dante Gabriel Rossetti 1828–1882: The Paintings and Drawings: A Catalogue Raisonné*, Oxford 1971, pp.7 and 39.

39 For Blake's posthumous reputation in the Victorian period see G. E. Bentley Jr, *Blake Books*, Oxford 1977, pp.24–30.

40 See ed. J.H. Stonehouse, *Catalogue of the Library of Charles Dickens from Gadshill … Catalogue of the Library of W. M. Thackeray*, London 1935. Dickens did, however, possess certain volumes of Bentley's Standard Novels in the 1840s, see the Inventory of his books drawn up in 1844 and reprinted as an appendix to *The Letters of Charles Dickens* (Pilgrim Edition), vol.4. Oxford 1977, p.716.

41 J.E. Austen-Leigh, *A Memoir of Jane Austen*, London 1987, p.207.

42 Thomas Arnold, *Chaucer to Wordsworth*, pp.422–23.

43 William Spalding, *The History of English Literature … For the Use of Schools and of Private Students*, Edinburgh 1853, p.383.

44 David Masson, *British Novelists and their Styles: Being a Critical Sketch of the History of British Prose Fiction*, Cambridge 1859, pp.179–80.

45 Joseph Angus, *The Handbook of English Literature*, London [1865], pp.618–19.

46 Macaulay, *Critical and Historical Essays*, vol.3, pp.424–25.

47 Margaret Oliphant, *The Literary History of England in the End of the Eighteenth and Beginning of the Nineteenth Century*, 3 vols., London 1882, vol.3, pp.206–7.

48 Oliphant, *The Literary History of England*, pp.236–37.

49 Henry James, 'The Lesson of Balzac' reprinted in ed. Leon Edel, *The House of Fiction*, London 1957, p.63.

50 For Orchardson's painting see Edward T. Cook, *A Popular Handbook to the Tate Gallery*, London 1898, pp.146–47.

51 For *The Black Brunswicker* see J. G. Millais, *The Life and Letters of Sir John Everett Millais*, 2 vols., London 1899, vol. 1, pp.350ff. For the engravings see M.H. Spielmann, *Millais and His Works*, Edinburgh and London 1898, p.179.

52 'Florence Emily Hardy', *The Early Life of Thomas Hardy 1840–1891*, London 1928, pp.139–41.

53 Thackeray, *The Four Georges*, p.218.

54 Gordon N. Ray, *Thackeray: The Uses of Adversity*, London 1955, p.66.

55 'Florence Emily Hardy', *The Early Life of Thomas Hardy*, pp.6, 282.

56 Orlando Figes, *Crimea: The Last Crusade*, London 2010, p.468.

57 Figes, *Crimea*, p.474.

58 *Mrs Markham's History of England, with Continuation by Mary Howitt*, pp.534–35.

59 'Sir James Mackintosh', *Critical and Historical Essays*, 3 vols., London 1854, vol.2, p.226.

60 Roger Fry, 'The Ottoman and the Whatnot', *Vision and Design*, London 1920, p.40.